APOLLO THEATRE, Manchester

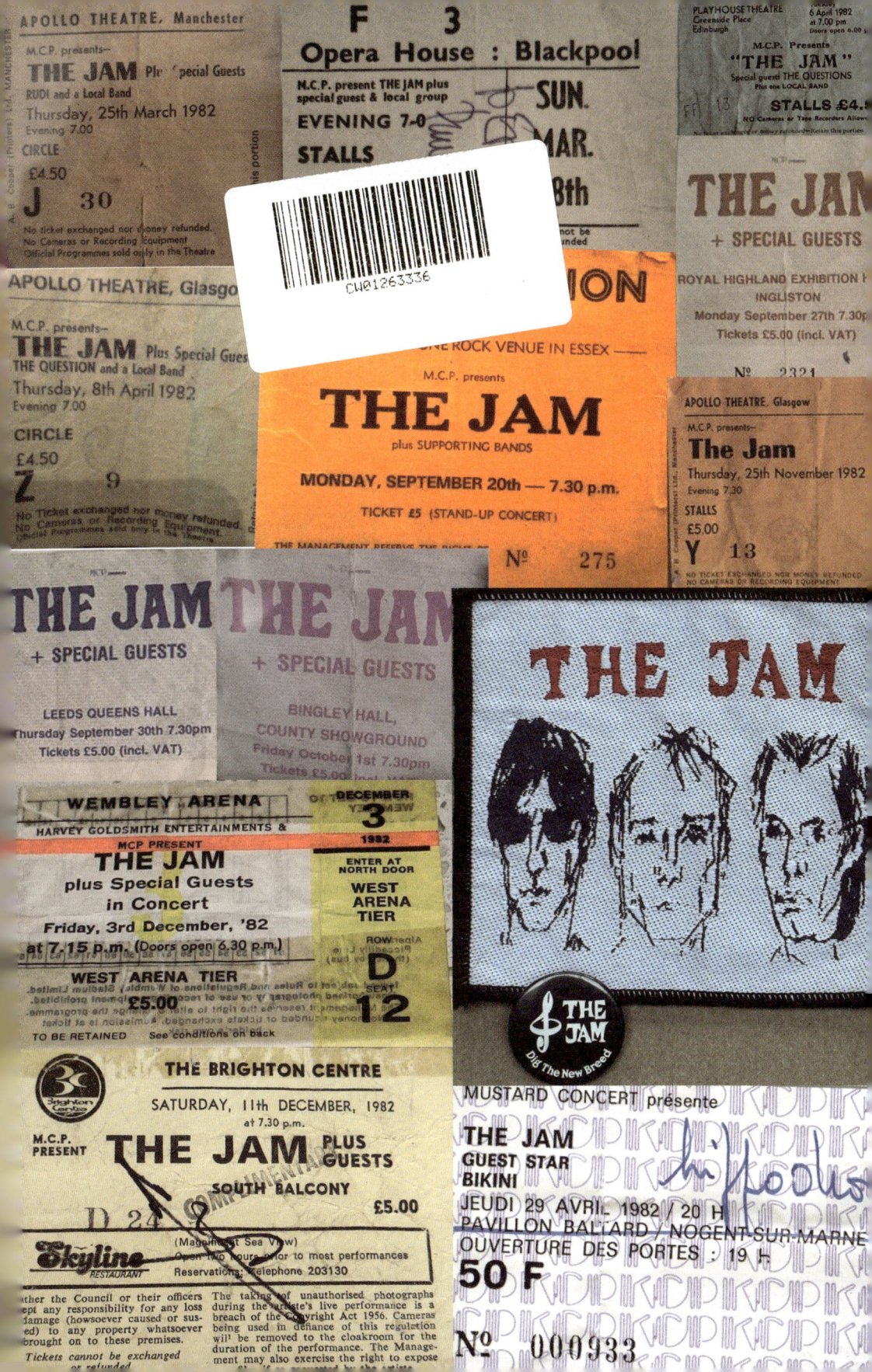

M.C.P. presents
THE JAM Plus Special Guests
RUDI and a Local Band
Thursday, 25th March 1982
Evening 7.00
CIRCLE
£4.50
J 30

No ticket exchanged nor money refunded.
No Cameras or Recording Equipment
Official Programmes sold only in the Theatre

F 3
Opera House : Blackpool

M.C.P. present THE JAM plus
special guest & local group
EVENING 7-0
STALLS
SUN.
MAR.
28th

PLAYHOUSE THEATRE, Edinburgh
Greenside Place
6 April 1982 at 7.00 p.m.
Doors open 6.00
M.C.P. Presents
"THE JAM"
Special guests: THE QUESTIONS
Plus one LOCAL BAND
STALLS £4.50
NO Cameras or Tape Recorders Allowed
FF 13

THE JAM
+ SPECIAL GUESTS
ROYAL HIGHLAND EXHIBITION H
INGLISTON
Monday September 27th 7.30p
Tickets £5.00 (incl. VAT)
No 2321

APOLLO THEATRE, Glasgow

M.C.P. presents—
THE JAM Plus Special Guests
THE QUESTION and a Local Band
Thursday, 8th April 1982
Evening 7.00
CIRCLE
£4.50
Z 9

M.C.P. presents
THE JAM
plus SUPPORTING BANDS
ONE ROCK VENUE IN ESSEX
MONDAY, SEPTEMBER 20th — 7.30 p.m.
TICKET £5 (STAND-UP CONCERT)
No 275

APOLLO THEATRE, Glasgow
M.C.P. presents—
The Jam
Thursday, 25th November 1982
Evening 7.30
STALLS
£5.00
Y 13

THE JAM
+ SPECIAL GUESTS
LEEDS QUEENS HALL
Thursday September 30th 7.30pm
Tickets £5.00 (incl. VAT)

THE JAM
+ SPECIAL GUESTS
BINGLEY HALL,
COUNTY SHOWGROUND
Friday October 1st 7.30pm
Tickets £5.00

WEMBLEY ARENA
HARVEY GOLDSMITH ENTERTAINMENTS &
MCP PRESENT
THE JAM
plus Special Guests
in Concert
Friday, 3rd December, '82
at 7.15 p.m. (Doors open 6.30 p.m.)
WEST ARENA TIER
£5.00

DECEMBER 3 1982
ENTER AT NORTH DOOR
WEST ARENA TIER
ROW D SEAT 12

THE BRIGHTON CENTRE
SATURDAY, 11th DECEMBER, 1982
at 7.30 p.m.
M.C.P. PRESENT
THE JAM PLUS GUESTS
SOUTH BALCONY
£5.00
D 24
Skyline Restaurant

MUSTARD CONCERT présente
THE JAM
GUEST STAR
BIKINI
JEUDI 29 AVRIL 1982 / 20 H
PAVILLON BALTARD - NOGENT-SUR-MARNE
OUVERTURE DES PORTES : 19 H
50 F
N° 000933

THE JAM
Dig The New Breed

SOLID BOND IN YOUR HEART
A PEOPLE'S HISTORY OF THE JAM

MALCOLM WYATT

First published in Great Britain 2025 by Spenwood Books Ltd
1 Totnes Road, Manchester, M21 8XF, United Kingdom

Copyright © Malcolm Wyatt 2025

The right of Malcolm Wyatt to be identified as author of this work
has been asserted in accordance with Sections 77 & 78 of
the Copyright, Design and Patents Act 1988.

All rights reserved. No part of this book may be reproduced in any form or by
any electronical or mechanical means, including information storage or retrieval
systems, without permission in writing from the publisher, except by a reviewer who
may quote brief passages.

A CIP record for this book is available from the British Library.

ISBN 978-1-915858-24-5

Hardback printed and bound in the Czech Republic by Akcent Media

Design by Bruce Graham, The Night Owl

All image copyrights as captioned

spenwoodbooks.com

SOLID BOND
IN YOUR HEART:
A PEOPLE'S HISTORY
OF THE JAM

Malcolm Wyatt

Spenwood Books
Manchester, UK

SOLID BOND IN YOUR HEART

I loved The Jam, from the first sighting on the cover of the NME *through to hearing the 'In The City' single in O'Neill's front room and then hearing 'David Watts' one summer's day out in O'Neill's back yard.*

Mickey Bradley, The Undertones

It's in my DNA, just like The Beatles are. It was the perfect time for me. I was 12 or 13 when they split up. Amazing. I love 'em.

Mathew Priest, Dodgy

1st November 1978, a 14-year-old me went to my first ever gig, at the Liverpool Empire with the older kids from our council estate street. My real world and the life I've gone on to live began that night. Whatever righteous power Paul Weller struck me like lightning with, it's still what I'm feeding off creatively all these years later.

Ian Prowse, Pele / Amsterdam

The Jam were still quite punky when I saw them but weren't really a punk band anymore. They were seen as a Mod band by then. That's the interesting thing for me – a punk band dressed in Mod suits. They had the intensity and angst of punk.

John Robb, The Membranes

Oh God, yeah. I mean, The Jam – what a sound!

Stephen Jones, Babybird

People often describe The Jam's performance as pure energy, which I would have to agree with 100%. You can't touch energy and you certainly can't re-create it if it's not there in the beginning. My memories of the band were likened to an amphetamine-fuelled speedball for the time they were on stage, then a Valium crash once they left! I remember feeling bewildered and slightly lost the weeks after the band split and little did I know what lay ahead, good and bad. I can honestly say I don't think any other band has come close to creating that type of phenomenon and loyal following. Let alone the quality of songs that sang our lives, as you'll see in this wonderful tribute in print to The Jam.

Russ Hastings, From The Jam

FOREWORD

I am very happy to be writing a little something for this book. I'm happy that our band still means so much to people, after all these years!

Our legacy is in the music and the music still stands up. I love that time, being so young, my life taking off in many directions. It feels like an eternity away now and yet, at times, so close that I can still feel the energy that was created at the shows. Pure, visceral, youthful energy ingrained in my heart… for all time… forever.

Thanks to all that were a part of it.

PAUL WELLER '24

INTRODUCTION

WASN'T IT SUCH A FINE TIME?

I never caught The Jam live. There, I said it. They did two July nights in 1981 at Guildford Civic, two miles from my childhood home, but a fortnight earlier I shelled out for The Undertones there – my first big gig – and a 13-year-old paper-boy's wages didn't go far. I dithered, missed out, and the next time this dynamic trio from neighbouring Woking (where my own family roots went back to Victorian times) returned it was too late. News of the split broke on my 15th birthday (thanks, Paul) and I had bugger all chance of scoring a ticket, that Civic Hall send-off seen by many as the real finale (the follow-up down the road in Brighton all too emotional). Yep, the bitterest pill was mine to take.

I've seen Paul, Bruce and Rick many times since, and five decades beyond the first live accounts in this book, they still have that stellar pull on this perennial teenager. It's been an absolute joy catching all three live, following Paul's continually creative path and catching the others on stage and in person as well as interviewing them several times (and for the record, Paul's right up there with his Beatles namesake and a certain Noddy Holder on my 'must interview' list). And the beauty of what unfolds over the next 400-plus pages makes up to some degree for missing out first time around, this impressive, often insightful, always entertaining collection of anecdotes, stories and memories bringing it all back, as is the case when I play those wondrous LPs and singles all these years on, the songs just as fresh today and as pertinent.

My personal Jam odyssey harks back to hearing Capital Radio's Nicky Horne play 'The Modern World' just after my tenth birthday. And I recently rediscovered correspondence with Bruce from my mid-eighties *Captain's Log* fanzine years (during his solo act days), first catching him live in 1984 and seeing From The Jam regularly since 2007 (at that point with Rick and Bruce involved, meeting both backstage), most recently in July 2024 in an intimate setting, Bruce on fine form alongside long-time bandmate/close friend Russell Hastings and co. in East Lancs. And as with Paul live and on record, I still get shivers at key moments.

Our contributors here – there are more than 500 accounts – offer differing perspectives on key dates from 1973 onwards, but what comes across time and again is exactly what I hoped for – that innate love for the band and sense of loyalty to the Jam family. It was always about more than music – those artistic, cultural and political aspects and the fashion were integral – but wouldn't have counted for much without that over-riding strength of the songs and musicianship and sense that this was a band that truly cared for its fans, as so many of these tales reveal.

Hopefully the finished product goes some way towards honouring that legacy.

This was definitely a labour of love, and moving 300-plus miles from Lancashire to Cornwall at a key stage didn't help my accompanying stress levels. Add to that an eleventh-hour dilemma, having collated more great material than one volume could withstand. But the publisher then suggested a winning solution that paves the way for my follow-up, already on its way to fruition.

Many have written about The Jam in book form, and I've enjoyed a great deal of those from Paolo Hewitt's *A Beat Concerto* onwards. And we have stories a-plenty here that are seeing the light of day for the first time, proving beyond doubt the long-term draw of this iconic outfit, 50 years after their first character-building forays on the South-East live circuit.

Recent conversations with Paul's Maybury neighbour Steve 'Tufty' Carver and my ex-workmate Alan 'Buzza' Burrows brought up something we're collectively afflicted by, a penchant for trotting out Jam lyrics in everyday situations, not least politics-related. I certainly recall more Weller lyrics word for word than any of the poets I learned about at school. Those words remain with me, as do those memorable bass, guitar and drum licks. As recording artists, The Jam spanned barely five and a half years, but filled that time remarkably, so many of their six studio albums and 18 hit singles (four reaching No.1 when that mattered, three going in at the top, following Slade's lead) among my favourite ever records. There will never be another Jam. But what a time to be alive, eh?

Malcolm Wyatt
Redruth, Cornwall
November 2024

1 SEPTEMBER 1955
Bruce Douglas Foxton is born in Woking in Surrey, the family settling on Albert Drive, Sheerwater.

6 DECEMBER 1955
Paul Richard Buckler, later known as Rick, is born in Woking, five minutes before his twin, Peter. They live on Church Street, Woking.

I WAS THERE: RICK BUCKLER
There used be a main road that ran right the way through Woking, called Church Street, and I was at the Goldsworth Road end. And if you carried on up Church Street, you'd end up with Stanley Road cutting across it.

25 MAY 1958
John William Weller, soon renamed Paul, is born in Woking, his parents John and Ann then moving from Walton Terrace to nearby Stanley Road.

SHEERWATER COUNTY SECONDARY SCHOOL
1972, WOKING, UK
Paul Weller and pal Steve Brookes practise covers and original material in the school music room during lunchbreaks, with their microphones plugged into a record player and attracting a mostly female audience.

THE ALBION
1972, WOKING, UK
Paul and Steve put on a lunchtime performance in the pub, near Woking railway station, covering Donovan's 'Colours', to rapturous applause.

BALL AND WICKET
31 DECEMBER 1972, UPPER HALE, UK
Paul and Steve play a two-hour New Year's Eve set, the landlord cutting their four-hour booking in half.

Steve leaves Sheerwater to start at a Sussex boarding school. Neil Harris joins Paul on drums and Dave Waller on rhythm guitar, with Paul playing a McCartney-style

Hofner violin bass. The fledgling four-piece is named 'The Jam' and the early set includes a few Beatles numbers.

I WAS THERE: NICKY WELLER, PAUL'S SISTER

I remember him having his Beatles records in his clothes drawers and his shirts in a little neat pile on the floor – that was his pride and joy.

I WAS THERE: STEVE CARVER

Paul was in my brother Pete's year at Sheerwater School. Bruce was in my year, but not on my radar. I think Rick was in between. My first encounter with The Jam was at a talent show at Sheerwater Social Club. I was drafted in to take photos of another band, including a few mates. I wouldn't cross paths with The Jam again for a couple more years.

OLD WOKING COMMUNITY CENTRE
12 MAY 1973, WOKING, UK

MY FAMILY WERE THERE: ABIGAIL CHRISTINA

My sister played in a talent competition in Woking, and Paul Weller was competing. She was playing piano. He won and went on to be famous. She was playing a duet with our dad. It was put on by Freddie Pring. She came second to The Jam. Small world! Later, I worked in the bank and used to see Bruce Foxton.

Neil Harris, less enthusiastic about the band's progress, leaves and is replaced on drums by Paul Buckler. The new drummer soon becomes 'Rick'.

I WAS THERE: STEVE CARVER

Neil 'Bomber' Harris lived next door but one. I was aware he was a drummer. I think he gave up The Jam gig to concentrate on 'proper' military type drums. I'd see him load his kit in the car in a smart red marching band uniform. I lost touch but later he was in a Showaddywaddy-type rock 'n' roll band. A few years back someone told me he was in the hospice across the road from where I live now. Sadly, I didn't get to say goodbye. I turned up one day late for his funeral. Nice guy. Bless him.

I WAS THERE: RICK BUCKLER

We'd only really just started, never did any shows. When I got offered the chance to join Paul and Steve and play at the Youth Club, I jumped at it. It was Paul and Steve Brookes to start with, and they asked me to join on drums, one of the first shows at Sheerwater Youth Club. It was a matter of, 'There's a stack of Chuck Berry records there. Learn those!' It was a music I wasn't that familiar with, being around 16 or 17.

The revised quartet rehearse in Paul's bedroom, playing sixties covers and originals, working towards first gigs at Sheerwater Youth Club, a pub in Egham and at Chobham Youth Club. In time, more self-penned love songs are added.

I WAS THERE: RICK BUCKLER

Anybody interested in music or playing an instrument hung around in the music rooms at lunchtime. I knew Steve and Paul because of that. It was more of a duet, although Steve and Paul wanted to make it into more of a band, have a full-time drummer. If anything, Steve was the proper musician. Still is. A really good guitarist.

I pretty much taught myself by listening to records but did have an older guy who was very good, very much into the big band thing, taking me to see Buddy Rich play. He was really good in showing me a few fundamentals. The rest I picked up as I went along. I wish I'd taken proper lessons, but with any instrument you have to discover it, whichever way round you do it.

MICHAEL'S
JANUARY 1974, WOKING, UK

Dave Waller leaves and the band gain an upstairs residency at Michael's, despite being under age. The Jam now consists of Steve Brookes (guitar, vocals), Paul Weller (bass, vocals) and Rick Buckler (drums).

I WAS THERE: STEVE BROOKES

When we started playing, we were just a three-piece – two guitars and drums, so had to make quite a good noise between us.

I WAS THERE: RICK BUCKLER

There's no place to hide. We learned that quite early. We were struggling to be a four-piece, so really felt we had to work hard, that alone justified what the band were about. I think that's why we were so powerful on stage – everybody pulling their weight and filling all those gaps with interesting things. We were big fans of cutting out the rubbish. If we thought it was getting boring or irrelevant, we'd drop it straight away – cut straight to the chase.

PARKSIDE CLUB
26 MAY 1974, NEW HAW, UK

I WAS THERE: DARRON ROBINSON

I grew up in Surrey Towers, Addlestone, the ninth floor of a tower block, but when I was seven, we got a three-bedroom council house in New Haw, a couple of miles outside Woking, and at the end of street was a working men's club. Monday to Fridays it was full of drunk men, but on Saturday nights it was brilliant, like a Butlin's holiday camp. There'd be a live band, all the mums and kids went down, we absolutely loved it. You'd get your bottle of pop and packet of crisps, the stage in a corner. We'd pull up all the chairs, ten to 15 of us, watch the band. That's where my love of music started, seeing the joy it brought ordinary hard-working people on Saturday nights up and dancing.

I was fascinated by these men putting drum kits together, plugging things in, and remember four bands – Crystal Glass, Rainbow (not *the* Rainbow!), our favourites July, and The Jam. They played there four times in '74 and we were there each time. July were Teddy Boys playing rock 'n' roll, and we'd get up and dance. The lead singer stood out. They'd do a cover of 'Wipe Out' where he'd jump on the dancefloor with his drapes and beetle crushers and join his girlfriend, in petticoats and bobby sox, and they'd do this jive routine. Rainbow were our next favourites… but we didn't much care for The Jam.

I remember them as a four-piece. They were a lot younger, weren't as slick as these wedding bands. Paul Weller looked like my uncle, a bit of a wrong 'un! The big thing for us boys watching – it was mostly boys – was the drums. We were fascinated by drummers, our gauge to how good a band was how many drums they had. These bands had seven toms, cymbals, all that, while poor old Rick was just…

One night the mums had a rare weekend trip to Jersey. That was the night The Jam first played. Just dads and kids. Steve Brookes' style was more rock 'n' roll blues, but there's a great difference between a songwriter and song creator/maker. It's about adding that magic, taking it out of the ordinary, like Paul does. That charm. I hate to say it, but it's that X-factor. It's the same with Costello, Strummer, it's that innovation.

All those bands were playing the same kind of songs, rock 'n' roll. My old man knew John Weller, as he was a builder. In those days working men in Surrey, if you weren't at a factory or services like a milkman, postman or had a trade, you were on the building, and everybody knew everybody.

I was unaware of their rise to the point they were on *Top Of The Pops*. But the first time on telly, the word around the street in Parkside was, 'You won't believe it, that bloody lot…'. My next-door neighbour, Mark Redman, from a big Irish family that ran the Parkside club, was one of Bruce's close friends. I often saw Bruce coming round to Mark's. We'd have been 13 or 14, I remember him pulling up in his pink Jaguar, us kids singing, 'Oi Mister! Eatin' trifles!' He'd give us two fingers and drive off. They were always around, and my old man had a caravanette and would often be the chauffeur for the free tickets Bruce handed out when he drank down the Parkside club, lunchtime sessions. He'd say, 'I beat that berk again at pool,' then suddenly, 'You won't believe this, they're on the bloody telly!'

With Bruce Foxton, on second guitar, now permanent after an earlier stand-in shift (having previously been with prog band Zita), Paul switches to guitar and Bruce to bass, the band increasingly busy on the working men's club and pub circuit, including dates at The Albion and Woking's Liberal, Working Men's and Conservative Clubs.

BUNTER'S NIGHTCLUB
5 OCTOBER 1974, GUILDFORD, UK

A show is cancelled – the band having set up and nipped home – after the first of two IRA bombs are detonated uptown at The Horse & Groom pub. They return the following night to collect their gear.

I WAS THERE: RICK BUCKLER

We didn't actually get to play the gig. The bombs went off, and everything got closed down. Our first non-gig! We set up the equipment, went home to Woking and had tea, because we weren't going to be on until really late. Then we got a phone call saying we can't come back – they'd literally shut the whole of Guildford down. We were a good seven or eight miles away, but yeah, it was a devastating blast.

THE GREYHOUND
27 OCTOBER 1974, FULHAM, LONDON, UK

I WAS THERE: STEVE BROOKES

(The Jam support Thin Lizzy at The Greyhound, Fulham.) They were a proper sort of live band. I wasn't really a Thin Lizzy fan, but they were pretty impressive. We had a lot of fun back in the day when we were doing it. We were young fellas just doing what we loved. I had a warm-hearted recollection of it all.

WOKING FC
23 MAY 1975, WOKING, UK

Paul, Rick, Steve and Bruce play a 'Rock & Roll Evening' supported by the Norman Hale Trio. They also play Sheerwater Community Centre, Woking's Working Men's Club and Michael's nightclub that week, continuing to build a strong following.

I WAS THERE: PAOLO HEWITT

My good amico Enzo Esposito had been hanging out with Paul, the pair of them driving round Woking on Paul's scooter. Both were musicians. Paul played in a band called The Jam, Enzo was in an outfit called Squire. They paid me a visit at the shop.

It was 1975, the year of the soul boy, of David Bowie's *Young Americans* album, of flared trousers, platform shoes and tank tops. Paul stood in front of me in a green parka, black Sta-Prest trousers, white socks, button-down shirt and loafer shoes. He looked so backdated it was startling, a man truly out of time.

Paul nodded at me, didn't say a word the whole time he and Enzo were there. But the meet did mean that if he saw me around Woking he would pull over on his scooter and have a brief chat. 'You're Enzo's mate, aintcha? (Yes.) You seen Enzo? (Yes.) Is he okay? (Yes.) How's his band Squire doing? (Not so well. They are still playing bad Status Quo covers.) OK then, see ya.'

Of course, I knew about Paul's band, The Jam, but it was impossible to see them play. Although they had a residency at a local club called Michael's, the band performed upstairs, in the members-only section. Us young leaves of Woking were not allowed in. However, thanks to a very loud Australian girl tourist that Vic Falsetta, another Italian amico of mine, and I met in the Wheatsheaf pub one night, we managed to gain entry.

At the time, The Jam were a five-piece, playing a lot of R&B covers, Smokey Robinson especially, and I remember thinking how very slick, how very professional they were. A year later, their name, which I actively hated, was suddenly on everyone's lips. EMI Records were showing some interest. The buzz in Woking was palpable. Were there actual stars in our midst, in Woking? Impossible. The buzz died down and the long hot summer of 1976 kicked in.

In July 1975, Steve Brookes quits.

I WAS THERE: STEVE BROOKES

It was only like four years of my life. Last week, playing somewhere in Camberley, they billed me as co-founder of The Jam. I said, 'Look, before we go any further, I get people sometimes turning up thinking they're going to see this bloke with spiky hair, black and white shoes, doing Mod covers … that ain't me! That's something that happened 50 years ago. I've made the joke that the good thing about being a 'never was' is that no one can ever call you a 'has been'!

An argument over money sees Bruce Foxton and Rick Buckler quit, Paul Weller continuing with various other players until John Weller smooths things over.

Photo by David Coombs

Steve Brookes 'had a lot of fun back in the day'

CIVIC HALL
21 OCTOBER 1975, GUILDFORD, UK

Paul Weller sees Dr Feelgood in action. Suitably impressed by Wilko Johnson, the guitarist's influence is soon heard on the band's demos.

I WAS THERE: STEVE CARVER

Me and Paul did talk about that Feelgood gig. We were both there, separately, late 1975.

BOB POTTER'S STUDIO
DECEMBER 1975, MYTCHETT, UK

The Jam, now an established trio, record 'Uptight', 'Takin' My Love', 'Left, Right And Centre', 'Again', 'When I Needed You' and 'Please Don't Treat Me Bad'.

I WAS THERE: RICK BUCKLER

Most songs written in the early days were love songs, our influences coming from being a covers band. We thought that was okay, but it really wasn't enough. When we encountered what was going on in London's pub rock scene, saw all these other bands, that sort of broadened our horizons. It was becoming boring, doing the same thing over and over, but we had the foresight to say we wanted to go and play the London scene.

THE GREYHOUND
8 MARCH 1976, FULHAM, LONDON, UK

A fly-posting trip to London ends with John Weller crashing his car. Rick Buckler fractures an ankle but performs with the band the next evening against doctor's orders.

I WAS THERE: BRUCE FOXTON

It was unique to have Paul's dad manage us, and John was a nice guy, and looking back he gave up a lot of his time to try and turn our career, from getting us gigs in working men's clubs onwards, to beg, borrow or steal equipment, and everything. We really couldn't have done it without him.

I WAS THERE: JON D BROMBERG

My first gig was The Greyhound in 1976. I went with my older brother, who knew Rick. The raw energy was amazing, Paul sweating buckets and with really amazing vocals. My second gig was a promotional one for *In The City* at the 100 Club on Oxford Street. They had me hooked on this amazingly tight sound. They were just raw talent. I saw a couple more gigs in 1977, at The Marquee and a youth club in Woking. In 1978 I saw them a few times. 1979 was a busy year with loads of gigs, the best being a *Setting Sons* promotional gig at the Rainbow. We went in the stage door as my mum's mate was stage manager Lambert Pluck. We were introduced to the band, but Paul was being an arse so it was disappointing. That was the infamous gig where fans ripped up rows of seat and passed them down to the stage.

Me and my mate had to leave our front row and move back and to the side, in front of the speakers. My hearing's never been the same since.

I went to many gigs during the eighties, including the Rainbow again, Milton Keynes Bowl, Brighton and more. I finally got to talk to Paul in the nineties. He had just been given a new Mini with a union flag roof and was filling it up for the first time at a Texaco garage on the Edgware Road. He told me he was given it to promote the car. I told him I'd been following him since the Greyhound in '76. His answer was typically Paul: 'Then you must be fucking old.'

HOPE & ANCHOR
8 MAY 1976, ISLINGTON, LONDON, UK

The Jam's first performance at the Hope and Anchor.

PRINCESS OF WALES
AUGUST 1976, MAYBURY, WOKING, UK

I WAS THERE: STEVE CARVER

I met Paul for the first time down the pub, introduced myself as his neighbour. We started talking, and he asked if I'd seen the Sex Pistols. I told him I was 'following' them in the music press. That pic of them 'beating up their audience'. Paul had already seen them. He told me he was going to the 100 Club 'next Tuesday', invited me along. That's the first time I met Dave Waller and Tony Pilott – both RIP. We became a gang. The first – and only – punks in Woking. 50p to get in.

Steve Carver (right) with good friend and old neighbour Paul Weller

ROCK ON RECORD STALL
16 OCTOBER 1976, SOHO MARKET, LONDON, UK

The Jam play 'In The City' as part of an outdoor lunchtime set to an audience that includes The Clash, Melody Maker *writer Caroline Coon,* Sounds' *John Ingham and* Sniffin' Glue's *Mark Perry, leading to music press coverage.*

I WAS THERE: RICK BUCKLER

It was something that brought everything together – that attitude of not needing big record companies and this mega-arena rock attitude. That was very strong. People starting fanzines, saying they could do all this themselves – create our own audiences, make our own magazines. There was that ethos, which was fabulous.

I WAS THERE: STEVE CARVER

We started drinking in the pub around the corner – the Cambridge. We'd meet the *Sniffin' Glue* gang there – Mark Perry, Shane MacGowan and so on. On the day of the 'busk', Joe Strummer turned up. The plan was to play Soho Market then move on to Carnaby Street. The Lord John shop. But the second one never happened.

QUEENSWAY HALL
21 OCTOBER 1976, DUNSTABLE, UK

The Jam open for the Sex Pistols. A support gig with The Vibrators at the 100 Club then leads to promoter Ron Watts offering them several gigs.

UPSTAIRS AT RONNIE SCOTT'S
23 NOVEMBER 1976, SOHO, LONDON, UK

The Jam's incendiary performance is reviewed by Shane McGowan for punk fanzine **Bondage**.

TUMBLEDOWN DICK
24 DECEMBER 1976, FARNBOROUGH, UK

I WAS THERE: STEVE CARVER

The landlord pulled the plug after three numbers, 'cos no one was dancing. Obviously, the punters wanted Slade, Mud and The Rubettes. On the way home, Paul declared, 'That is the last time we play any of those kind of gigs.' The assault on London started in earnest in January 1977. The rest, as they say…

100 CLUB
11 JANUARY 1977, LONDON, UK

John Tobler calls the band 'exceedingly promising' in an **NME** *review.*

THE GREYHOUND
25 FEBRUARY 1977, FULHAM, LONDON, UK

I WAS THERE: IAN BURBEDGE, AGE 11

I was living in the Hammersmith area of London. I didn't realise how lucky I was with all the venues within half an hour's walk, places such as The Greyhound, The Red Cow, The Nashville, and of course Hammersmith Odeon. I went to them all. I got into music at a very young age, having an older brother who has always been a big rock fan. He lit my 'listening and appreciating music' fuse, and although our tastes differ, I've been to a lot of gigs with him as well as lots with various mates.

1977 was a revolutionary time for music. Whilst I liked the Pistols and The Clash, I wasn't into the look of the punk thing. Bondage trousers and spiky hair wasn't for me. Then I read in *Melody Maker* about these three fellas in suits.

A mate I played football with had an older brother who knew someone who would let us in at The Greyhound, and on 25th February aged eleven (I turned 12 that April) I fell in love ('with any guitar and any bass drum') with The Jam, blown away by the music, the look and the sound. I didn't fully understand what all the words meant but I understood the excitement they gave the crowd. I couldn't wait to see them again.

I couldn't see all the gigs they did in the area. I couldn't have too many late nights and I couldn't find the excuses to tell my mum I was going to stay out late. But a couple of weeks later my mate, his brother and me were at The Red Cow (2 or 9 March). How he managed to blag us in I don't know, but he was a blessing. And a month later – 19 April – we were at The Nashville by West Kensington station, 'as long as we didn't drink, we were alright.' I had no interest in that at all. I just wanted to see the band.

A month later, there was my first Jam gig on 'foreign' soil – at the Rainbow, Finsbury Park (9 May), at the time the second biggest venue in London after Hammersmith Odeon. And even in a bigger venue they were still as exciting, their energy making a big venue seem like a pub.

The first album I bought with my own money from my paper round was *In The City*, alongside The Clash, when it came out in May, from Our Price on Kensington's Church Street. My feet didn't touch the ground in my bid to get that on my record player as soon as I got home. I drove my Mum mad as I kept playing it. Brilliant.

RED COW
2 MARCH 1977, HAMMERSMITH, LONDON, UK

I WAS THERE: PAUL GULBRANDSEN

I was 16 and went to school in Hammersmith. I was starting to get interested in punk through listening to John Peel and a friend at school told me about a punk band that was doing a one-month residency at a pub close to the school, called The Red Cow.

I asked my friend what the band was called. He said The Jam. I'd never heard of them and to be honest the name didn't sound very punky, but it was free to get in, so we agreed to give it a go. It was my first ever gig and I wasn't sure we'd get in, being underage, but the door staff didn't seem too bothered.

Pretty soon, the boys hit the stage, and what a performance they put on. They were dressed in sharp sixties suits and pointed shoes, the songs were short and fast, and the sound was loud! I realised later that The Jam weren't actually a punk band at all, but the energy they put into their live performance was definitely punk-like.

They played every Wednesday that month – I went to all their shows at The Red Cow, and I can honestly say it changed my life. I never saw them again, as those shows at that small venue were so magical. I didn't think seeing them at a larger venue would be quite the same.

RED COW
9 MARCH 1977, HAMMERSMITH, LONDON, UK

I WAS THERE: MICK TALBOT

I saw them before the first single came out, in very early '77. They did a month's residency at a pub in Hammersmith, The Red Cow. My friend Clive went the first week and we went to the second and went there twice or three times. That second week, there was a queue around the block. I think they'd already been signed, but nothing had come out. They had badges, one with 'In The City' on it. And we just knew that was a song in the set, but I don't think that came out until later. I think they played that twice. They didn't have very many of their own tunes in there. What was good about it was that they played a lot of songs I knew, some of which I played in our bands. And as much as it was that nihilistic sort of punk sound, they were still playing 'In The Midnight Hour' and 'Sweet Soul Music', or whatever, in a way I imagined The Who would, that sort of power trio way. 'Slow Down'? I think that was in the set, and one track from the first Who album, 'Much Too Much'. I had the first two (Who) albums, knew that and just thought, 'I wonder how many other people know this?' They could have played 'My Generation' or 'Substitute', but that was quite subtle really.

When I first clapped eyes on The Jam, I just thought, 'This is the junior Feelgoods really,' in a visual way. I think Wilko (Johnson) had just left Dr Feelgood, my favourite live band at the time, but I thought, 'This is the new lot. This is the next step on.'

I WAS THERE: STEVE CARVER

The gig that changed everything was The Red Cow, Hammersmith, just down the road from the Hammy Odeon. The Jam played four times there in one month, every Wednesday. The first gig attracted the usual 20-plus punters. By the final night fans were queuing down the road. Purely word of mouth – a 'punk band' that could actually play their instruments. Fire and skill. It was mental. Blood, sweat and tears, pushing and shoving, lager and pogoing. The Jam would finish with 'Batman', the doors would open, fans and steam escaping out into the night air. Myself and my brother, Pete, and Paul's sister, Nicky, picking up enough cash off the floor to buy everyone a pint. There was a late-night cafe on the road home. We would stop to eat there. I recall they sold spotted dick and custard. At midnight. Funny what you remember. It was obvious that this was a real turning point. There was definitely something in the air.

SOLID BOND IN YOUR HEART

I WAS THERE: JEFF SHADBOLT, THE PURPLE HEARTS

Bob Manton, the lead singer of The Purple Hearts, introduced me to The Jam. We were still at school and decided to go up and see them at The Red Cow, a tiny little pub in Hammersmith. They had a sort of residency there. We went on the bus straight from school in our school uniforms, all the way over from Romford in Essex. We got there and they had just finished. We didn't know that it was their soundcheck they had just finished. We sat down thinking, 'Well, perhaps they'll come back on.' Bruce Foxton came over and sat next to us and he was chatting away to us. He said, 'I thought you were a couple of Mods.' We said 'we are, we are!' We really had no clue. Grant Fleming was there, Chip and Hillary were there, quite well-known Mods at the time, and then The Jam came on to play and they totally blew us away. Imagine a steamroller of sound. It was unbelievable.

We went on to see them a couple of times at the Nashville in Kensington High Street, and then at the 100 Club and then at the Rainbow on May 9, 1977. This was a big festival, with The Jam, The Clash, loads of bands. I had to choose. Did I buy a £2.50 ticket to the gig or did I buy my sister a birthday present…? It was a great gig and I don't think my sister has spoken to me since! (Only joking!)

And then when I was a little bit older, when I was in The Purple Hearts, there was a clothes shop in Romford called Mintz & Davis. I was always in and out of there, trying to blag some clothes. One day I was in my mum's garage, where I used to live working on an old scooter and she said, 'Oh Jeff, there's someone on the phone for you,' and I went 'who is it?' She came back and she said 'it's Paul' so I said 'what? Paul from Mintz?' and she went back and asked and she came back and said, 'No, it's Paul from The Jam.'

I spoke to Paul on the phone and he said he really liked the band. 'Why don't you come and see me up at my office and we'll have a chat?' I think the office was at One Hyde Park Place at the time. He was quite shy. He told us about when he came to see us down The Marquee and he couldn't get to see us because he was getting mobbed. I swapped some singles with him and he gave me a pair of his Jam bowling shoes.

We'd see them on stage almost every weekend. We'd turn up at the gigs and if we couldn't get hold of John Weller we'd get hold of Paul's sister, Nicky, and she'd let us in the back door and we'd watch the soundchecks and stuff. They were just unbelievable times. I don't think anybody who hasn't gone through it would really understand what it was like.

As The Purple Hearts, we did four or five dates on their last but one tour. We did Woking Sheerwater Youth Club with him, we did Norwich, we did Brighton,

Crawley. All the time we'd been going to see The Jam and, all of a sudden, there we were in the studio, with Paul Weller producing our album. It was uncanny. It was great going from seeing a band and admiring a band and, all of a sudden, you're on tour with them. John Weller made sure that the sound guys looked after us.

Paul did a bit of piano and a bit of backing vocals on one of the songs we recorded with him. We were after a certain bass sound and he disappeared and came back with a white Epiphone bass and said 'use this'. I had this bass in my hand and I was thinking, 'Oh my God, I'm using the bass that Bruce used on 'Start!'.'

ROCHESTER CASTLE
24 MARCH 1977, STOKE NEWINGTON, LONDON, UK

The start of a five-week residency at the Rochester Castle, Stoke Newington.

I WAS THERE: STEPHEN HUNT

It was 50p to get in. I went back the week after and I've been a fan ever since! I saw them load of times over those fantastic years.

PARIS PUNK FESTIVAL, PALAIS DE GLACE
28 MARCH 1977, PARIS, FRANCE

The Jam share a bill with The Police, Generation X and The Electric Chairs.

THE NASHVILLE
5 APRIL 1977, LONDON, UK

The Jam start a Tuesday night residency.

ROUNDHOUSE
17 APRIL 1977, CHALK FARM, LONDON, UK

I WAS THERE: DYLAN WHITE, AGE 19

In the summer of 1976, I'd already seen Dr Feelgood twice, I was into Eddie and the Hot Rods, and progressive long-haired rock was starting to bore me. That autumn, 'Anarchy In The UK' was out and the grenade had gone off. I got the punk ticket and the set of friends I had who were into Genesis, Barclay James Harvest, etc. didn't, so there was a parting of the ways. We'd been on holiday together. We'd been to Guernsey for a week, got drunk, we'd been to Torquay for a couple of holidays, and they had another holiday coming up – it must have been the following year, in '77 – and I said, 'I don't want to go.' I didn't want to hang around with them anymore. (We're friends again now; we've grown up a bit.) I remember seeing a photo of them on that holiday in '77. They all had flares on. They all looked the same. I thought, 'No, not me.'

So, 1976 was the year of change. I'd now embraced my short hair, drainpipe trousers, and the world of punk. Sunday afternoons at the Roundhouse was a big gig. Three bands, starting at half past five. I'd seen loads of long-haired bands there, like UFO, Stray. John Curd, the famous London promoter who was Straight Music, embraced punk and Straight Music put all the punk bands on. He was an absolute character: 'Shoehorn 'em in.' I'd seen The Damned there.

Dylan White went to the Roundhouse to see the Stranglers headline & got The Jam third on the bill

I was a massive, massive Stranglers fan. I first went to see them in '76. Very quickly they flew and before we knew it, they were headlining at the Roundhouse. The middle band was Cherry Vanilla, and the first band on was The Jam.

They came out with the shoes on, with the Rickenbacker guitars, and it was '1-2-3-4!' Like a tornado they blasted through the first album. It was absolutely amazing. I was of an age to know that they'd nicked all this from The Who, which Paul Weller would readily admit. He's even said that the first album was a copy of The Who. They had The Who's look, with the suits, and The Who's instruments. There were no flashing lights. It was just the suits, the guitars and '1-2-3-4!' – bang! It was fast. And that was the thing about punk.

Paul didn't say much apart from '1-2-3-4!' He's not a stage entertainer talker. He lets the music do the talking. Bruce Foxton was an integral part. He was doing the backing vocals and he was doing the jumps. They jumped when they played. It was exciting. Before we knew it, they were doing the Rainbow and everything else. Then the first album came out and the rest is history. I never saw them again. I don't know why.

I WAS THERE: STEVE CARVER

The Jam was a bit of a 'soft' name (literally) in 1977. It could have got lost amongst

The Stranglers, The Damned, The Clash, Sex Pistols… Too late to change now though – they had pedigree and hundreds of gigs behind them. Then there were the (Burton) suits. No rips, razor blades or safety pins in sight. I asked Paul if maybe they looked a 'bit old fashioned'. But here's the genius. The Jam stood out and apart from the crowd. Instantly different and recognisable, easy for the new breed of fans to copy. School uniform chic, and girls in dad's shirts plus stockings and suspenders. Perfect.

BBC MAIDA VALE STUDIOS
26 APRIL 1977, LONDON, UK

The Jam cancel a Dingwalls show to record their first John Peel session, featuring 'In The City', 'Art School', 'Changed My Address' and 'The Modern World'.

HOPE & ANCHOR
28 APRIL 1977, ISLINGTON, LONDON, UK

I WAS THERE: JON ABNETT, AGE 14

I was into punk from early '77 and remember that summer – the Queen's Silver Jubilee – being a really hot one. I first heard 'In The City' on John Peel's show. As with most songs, you only catch the music and the chorus or song title in the lyrics. As soon as I heard it, I knew I had to find out more about this 'new' band on the scene. Then the single was released, followed by the album of the same title.

I first saw them at the Hope & Anchor in Islington, North London, the night before the album was released. I used to hang about with some punks from Strood, older than me but they took me under their wing. We travelled to London by train, and they all took the piss because I was the only one who paid for the train ticket! They got me in through a toilet window at the back of the building. I stayed at the back while they were at the front. They were a cool bunch, not into any dope or glue sniffing, it was more fashion and the music. There were probably around 150 punters in attendance.

It was a pretty scary experience, I'd only been to London Zoo prior to that. I was so young and out of my comfort zone. Nobody believed me, I told Mum I was at a sleepover. It was school the next day, but nobody there was really into The Jam and they were not that well known at the time. My schoolmates were into Thin Lizzy… as I was until I started hearing punk. It was 75p to get in. Not that I paid, of course.

The argument was always that they weren't a punk band. They just broke through on the London circuit at the time the punk explosion was happening. Yes, they played songs with three chords, one more than the Pistols and one less than The Clash! They played R&B at a faster pace and played it well, in a rough and ready state, albeit very loudly.

'IN THE CITY' RELEASED
29 APRIL 1977

The Jam's debut single brushes the Top 40, spending one week at No.40.

ERIC'S
30 APRIL 1977, LIVERPOOL, UK

I WAS THERE: JOHN THOMPSON

It's the spring of 1977 and I'm lucky enough to be a regular visitor to Eric's club in Mathew Street, Liverpool. Looking back, I don't know whether to smile or cry. Smile, because of the amazing bands I saw – The Jam, The Clash, The Damned and Wayne/Jayne County and the Electric Chairs. Or cry, because of the bands I could have seen but didn't – the Ramones, Blondie, The Stranglers. But I'll always have the night The Jam played Eric's.

Memories are of frenzy. Frenzy on the dance floor as punks pogo and go generally demented. Frenzy on the stage as the band play their songs at breakneck speed.

It was the week The Jam's debut single, 'In The City', was released so most of the 200 or so members of the audience would not have been familiar with the band's material – they just knew they were witnessing, experiencing, something new, something very exciting, something their older brothers and sisters would have known little about. Can I say the gig changed my life? No, it just was my life. Another day, another band. Surely everyone in every generation had nights like this. Well, possibly not as it turns out. We had no way of knowing we were in just the right place at just the right time to enjoy the wild, trailblazing early days of era-defining music. Lucky us.

JOHN PEEL SESSION
2 MAY 1977

The band's debut John Peel session broadcast is premiered on BBC Radio 1.

NME COVER STARS
7 MAY 1977

The Jam are on the cover of the New Musical Express.

A PEOPLE'S HISTORY OF THE JAM

I WAS THERE: PAOLO HEWITT

Like Paul, I was an avid *NME* reader, so I knew all about the developing punk scene in London. I didn't realise that The Jam had now dropped their soulful prettiness and were now purveyors of punk-energized R&B, however – until the month when everyone suddenly realised that something serious was going on with The Jam. The next issue of the *NME* arrived in Woking as usual on a Thursday afternoon. Paul Weller, Bruce Foxton and Rick Buckler were on the cover. I'd been reading the *NME* since I was 14 and I was mightily impressed. It meant this band was being taken very seriously. I read the interview three times and was left puzzled and bemused by Weller's comments on politics (pro Tory) and the Royal Family (pro the Queen).

That night I turned on *Top Of The Pops* and there they were performing the song in question, 'In The City'. I bought the record the very next morning, played it several times in the afternoon, and in the evening went to meet friends, at the Cotteridge pub in Woking. By chance, I was early. I walked in, went up to the bar, glanced round and froze. Who should be sitting behind me at an empty table, on his own, chewing his nails, smoking furiously, wearing a black Harrington and bright red cords, with a scowl the size of Woking across his face? Immediately I turned back to the bar, hoping Paul Weller hadn't seen me.

This was the thinking. If I said hello and sat with him, he might think I was only doing so because he had been on TV the night before. Didn't want that. I was into punk, and admiring pop stars was strictly off the agenda. But if I didn't say hello, he might think I saw him as a dreaded pop star. Didn't want that either. (Punk's rules and regulations certainly introduced a lot of complexities into seventies teenage life.)

As I weighed up my options, Paul unexpectedly came to the bar and solved my problem.

'You're Enzo's mate, aintcha?'

Weller was waiting on friends as well. We sat down at the table, spoke for a few minutes before people began arriving. The conversation as I recall it was about *NME* writers, a breed I was obsessed with at the time.

'You've met Tony Parsons? Fucking hell.'

'Yeah, he and Julie Burchill took me down to Twickenham to meet Townshend.'

'You've met Julie Burchill? Fucking hell. And they took you to meet Pete Townshend?'

'Yeah.'

Paul took a drag on his ciggie, nodded his head calmly. He was already nonchalant, worldly wise. To me, it felt as if he lived in a galaxy it would take me a lifetime to reach.

'What about Charles Shaar Murray? Nick Kent?' I asked.

'Nah, haven't met them, although Tony Parsons told me there was a lot of office politics going on, between the punk writers and the others.'

For me, this was glamour. Paul Weller, privy to *NME* office politics, hanging out with writers I read avidly every week. Amazing. Paul was a massive *NME* reader as well, but he kept quiet on the subject. He often kept a lot of his enthusiasms under wraps – no doubt a lesson learnt from his poker-playing father. Never show your cards early; always keep them tight to your chest.

Friends arrived, and on that boisterous teenage night all of us drank to excess. A couple of memories stick. I recall Paul trying to light the back of the jacket of the bar owner every time the old man wobbled by. I also clearly remember him ripping the cords he had on, from the bottom up, leaving his legs showing.

PLAYHOUSE THEATRE
7 MAY 1977, EDINBURGH, UK

The Jam, along with Buzzcocks and The Slits, support The Clash on the **White Riot** *tour. They only manage three dates in total – at Manchester's Electric Circus the day after and then London's Rainbow Theatre, before walking out on the tour, accusing the headliners of denying them a proper soundcheck.*

RAINBOW THEATRE
9 MAY 1977, FINSBURY PARK, LONDON, UK

I WAS THERE: GRAHAM JONES, HAIRCUT 100

Like some London kids into the punk scene, I think I first came across The Jam in fanzines. I'd been into punk since hearing 'Anarchy In The UK'. A 'different kid' brought it into school and seeing a real copy was an exciting and special moment. Before that I was into other rock music, like The Sweet, Slade and T. Rex.

'In The City' was the first Jam single I bought. I loved the guitar sounds and pick scrapes, and Paul's aggressive and grown-up vocal style. I wasn't sure about Bruce's haircut... or the suits! But I did get some Jam shoes later from Shelly's in Carnaby Street. I knew Paul liked a good pair of shoes!

The first and only time I saw them was on a bill with The Clash at the Rainbow Theatre, Finsbury Park, along with The Prefects, The Subway Sect, and Buzzcocks. I went with my schoolmates by bus and was picked up by my dad in his Ford Escort estate company car. That show was so exciting and scary at the same time. There was heavy dub on the sound system, courtesy of Don Letts, and all these punk rockers from all over town who descended on the venue. It was electrifying, especially when The Clash came on, fans ripping up front-row seats. The Jam went on just before.

I always loved the feedback sounds and pick-up selector tricks on the early singles. I was never a Jam fan as such, but as long as they made singles with the sound I liked, I'd buy them… and I bought a few. As a guitarist, Paul's had an effect on me… mainly from those early singles.

Haircut One Hundred and Boys Wonder guitarist Graham Jones with treasured Jam vinyl

If I listen to any Jam track, it's most often 'Smithers-Jones', the B-side version (the other's not so good). Quite an emotional song, and I didn't know Bruce sang it until years later!

'When You're Young', 'Going Underground', 'All Around The World', 'The Eton Rifles', 'Strange Town', 'The Dreams Of Children' and 'Town Called Malice' are also favourites, and would have been on my Walkman later. The Englishness of the vocal delivery and subject matter always resonates. And I'll always be thankful The Jam existed and had a massive musical influence on the British scene, and that they spread that worldwide.

I WAS THERE: ALAN BUTCHER

The Clash and The Jam were both powerful live bands. Paul Weller joked with Mick Jones of The Clash about The Who being more powerful than The Kinks. And with the Buzzcocks having their fanbase in Manchester, this made the night very special. I've not seen Weller better than this live onstage, as if he really had a point to prove. The Jam had improved so much since those early days, when they were compared to pub rock bands. The aggression in their songs was so exciting to witness.

TOP OF THE POPS
19 MAY 1977, LONDON, UK

The Jam appear on Top Of The Pops *performing 'In The City'.*

I WAS WATCHING: BRIAN YOUNG

I picked up 'In The City' when it was released, watching The Jam make history as the first of the new bands to make it on to BBC flagship show *Top Of The Pops*. (Admittedly, The Hot Rods had been on late in '76 and the Damned were on *Supersonic* that February.) In those matching suits, they looked kinda straitlaced but it was obvious from the first chord that these were very angry young men indeed – a short, sharp, shock of pure adrenalin. Frontman Weller attacked his Rickenbacker guitar furiously, glowering into the camera and barking out the words to 'In The City'. Bassist Bruce Foxton, who still needed a haircut, was equally animated, his fluid bass playing providing the muscle behind the main riff. Drummer Rick Buckler held it down at the back with a series of beefy and commanding drum rolls and flurries. They leapt into the air at every opportunity too… I was impressed!

IN THE CITY RELEASED
20 MAY 1977

The Jam's debut LP, produced by Vic Coppersmith-Heaven and Chris Parry and recorded at Polydor's Stratford Place studio, London W1, is released. It reaches No.20 in the UK album charts.

BARBARELLA'S
7 JUNE 1977, BIRMINGHAM, UK

The Jam commence their first headlining national tour.

CORN EXCHANGE
10 JUNE 1977, CAMBRIDGE, UK

I WAS THERE: DEBSEY WYKES, DOLLY MIXTURE

I first saw The Jam on *Top Of The Pops* as I, along with most of the young population, watched it every week. But I took more notice of them when we went to see them play live at the Corn Exchange. I remember being struck by their sharp-suited appearance and by how serious they were. My friend Hester (Smith) and I were a little less serious, dressed up as Marilyn Monroe. Hester was blonde and I wore a blonde wig, and we wore fifties dresses, blue eye shadow and black flicked eyeliner.

It was mainly memorable for hearing them play 'In The City' which we'd heard on the telly. So that was exciting! We didn't form our band until the following

February, so were just school kids going to every gig that we could. As for buying records, I would mainly listen to other people's records, particularly my friend Rachel (Bor)'s older brother's.

To go to London was always the dream. It seemed to be where everything happened. There wasn't really a scene in Cambridge, and it got really boring living there. There wasn't anything cool about coming from Cambridge then. No one was interested in Pink Floyd (who'd gone to school there, Syd Barrett having grown up in the same road Rachel and I lived on), and even though the wonderful Robyn Hitchcock was quite successful, his band felt like a bit of a different generation.

Debsey Wykes with Dolly Mixture, who saw and then supported The Jam

SEABURN HALL
17 JUNE 1977, SUNDERLAND, UK

I WAS THERE: MICHAEL LINSLEY
I recall Paul briefly stopping playing due to pint glasses being thrown, and all the spitting.

I WAS THERE: PETER SMITH
Think of late '70s punk rock, and an image of safety pins, spitting, pogoing, and fast furious rebellious rock. In reality, that scene was a pretty broad church drawing from a wide range of influences. The Jam burst onto the scene in 1977, blending Mod sharp suits with attitude, arrogance and great catchy pop songs. Influenced by soul, R&B, The Who and Small Faces, you could tell lead singer/guitarist Paul Weller was a big fan of Steve Marriott and Pete Townshend.

I attended a few early Jam concerts in the North-East, first at Seaburn Hall and then at Newcastle Mayfair (1st July and 18th November 1977). These were pretty wild affairs, with Weller and the guys having to dodge a hail of glasses (real glass in those days) and waves of spit. The Seaburn Hall gig was particularly ferocious, a group of skinheads ('We hate punks!') looking for trouble, with several scuffles.

SOLID BOND IN YOUR HEART

The set in those days drew from the first album and early singles, a nifty cover of the *Batman* theme closing the show. They were a breath of fresh air, and it was evident even at those early gigs that this was a band that stood above the rest and would ultimately transcend the punk movement.

CIVIC HALL
18 JUNE 1977, POPLAR, LONDON, UK

I WAS THERE: DAVID FROST, AGE 15

I was at Poplar Civic. I also made it to Hammersmith Odeon, with Q-Tips as support maybe, with Paul Young their lead singer, and another London show supported by The Piranhas, at the Marquee, billed as John's Boys.

ELECTRIC CIRCUS
19 JUNE 1977, MANCHESTER, UK

The band are captured on film for the first time by Granada TV, with two of five recorded tracks ('In The City' and 'All Around The World') later broadcast on the Tony Wilson-fronted programme So It Goes.

CLUB LAFAYETTE
22 JUNE 1977, WOLVERHAMPTON, UK

I WAS THERE: DON POWELL, SLADE

I went to see The Jam very early on in their career at a small club in Wolverhampton, and I was very impressed. Club Lafayette was only a smallish place, but it was a great gig. I'd heard about this band, and we were both on the same label (Polydor). That's why I went, and I was well impressed.

The Lafayette was more like a village hall. We rehearsed there a few times when we first got together with Nod (Holder) and Jim (Lea), when we were with the Astra agency in Wolverhampton. They took over that hall, turned it into a late-night gig with a couple of bars. We called it The Laf. Y'know,

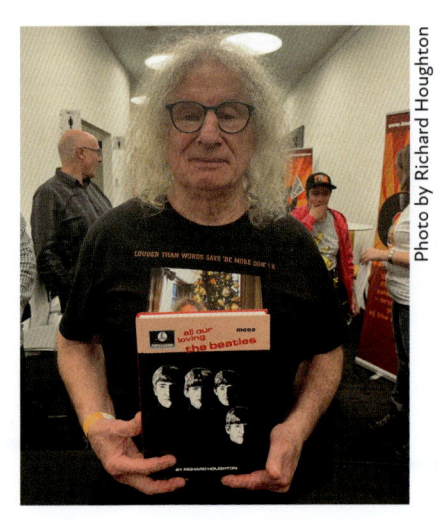

Don Powell and Paul Weller share that Beatles bond

Photo by Richard Houghton

'See you at the Laf, later!' A decent place. It's all gone now – when I go back to Wolverhampton, remembering all those places where we started, it's strange. I mean, where do young bands start today?

But The Jam, yeah, Polydor knew what to do to get them straight to No.1.

They learned that from us, from 1973. Our manager at the time, Chas Chandler, plus Polydor's John Fruin and the promotions guys, made sure it all worked out, the records were in the shops, and we got radio airplay, to try and do The Beatles' thing – getting to No.1 on the first day of release (a feat The Beatles managed just once, with 'Get Back' in 1969, yet Slade and The Jam managed three times each). So their knowledge helped The Jam as well. I'm sure there were still quite a few of them there from when we were having our success.

POLYTECHNIC
23 JUNE 1977, HUDDERSFIELD, UK

I WAS THERE: NICHOLAS BINNS

I remember both Huddersfield gigs being in the main hall of the Polytechnic, in June and again in November 1977. Other times I saw them were at St George's Hall in Bradford, the Exhibition Centre in Leeds, Bingley Hall, Stafford, and Wembley Arena on the farewell tour.

BRUNEL ROOMS
24 JUNE 1977, SWINDON, UK

I WAS THERE: NICK KEEN

It was early autumn 1976 when I first caught the short blitzkrieg anthems of New York delinquents the Ramones on John Peel's late-night radio show. Their self-titled debut LP was released that spring to little fanfare. As the sun set on that long hot summer, I couldn't quite believe what was pouring out of my little Triton transistor radio. Still in my teens, I'd already seen the Faces, The Kinks, Dr Feelgood and Graham Parker (playing his barnstorming *Howlin' Wind* album till my record player blew a fuse). And it wasn't just funked-up British R&B pulling my young heartstrings. I dug the psychedelic soul of The Temptations, witnessed the wacky Can, even French jazz violinist Stephane Grappelli. In my early teens I hung out with mates at football and church youth clubs, where we'd hear and read about how great it was to have experienced the swinging sixties, having to make do as suedeheads dancing to glam and stomping to Slade, which wasn't too bad.

The Ramones grabbed my attention. They were yankee rebels, and that autumn

SOLID BOND IN YOUR HEART

Peel started throwing more of this punk stuff on the show and the *NME* liberally peppered its front pages with punk as it screamed into the country's consciousness. Before too long it was all I listened to. We went to as many gigs as possible, living and breathing punk. The Clash, The Damned, Generation X; we couldn't believe our luck that we were now dedicated followers of a movement. The blank generation was sweeping the nation. We knew we had to be involved, stumbling out of clubs like four peas in a pod, ears ringing and clothes dripping in sweat, all for the love of punk.

Sartorial 65 author Nick Keen caught The Jam in Swindon in '77

The punchy Village Bowl in Bournemouth and shoebox-size Affair Ballroom, Swindon were havens for young punks. Many bands followed the same circuit up and down the country. I think the bulk were signed to the Cowbell agency, so you were pretty much guaranteed to see at least two or three impressionable bands per week. And we loved to get up close. I saw so many great bands at the Affair – The Clash, Buzzcocks, Slits, Rich Kids, The Members, and XTC several times. The list goes on.

Fanzines, postal orders, badges, 45s, queues and bouncers became an integral part of our lives while still holding down a full-time job. Some of it's a blur, but many anarchic moments shone brightly through the mayhem: Hell's Angels kicking off at a Stranglers' gig, The Clash riot at the Winter Gardens, punks with safety pins pierced in bloody cheeks at early Boys' gigs, Richard Hell wiping saliva from his hair.

Several bands stood head and shoulders above the rest. In particular, the Buzzcocks and The Clash. And I had a soft spot for XTC. But it was The Jam I fed into immediately during their first nationwide tour in the spring of 1977, their first UK tour, just as the *In The City* album and single were released. I went to the Bournemouth date (15 June), then Swindon nine days later at the Brunel Rooms, an amazing place, always packed. The Ramones also played there, and Friday night – my favourite - was funk night, when it was heaving.

The Jam had an incredibly powerful sound system, far superior to anybody else, and knew how to use it. Rick's drums and Bruce's bass steamed like the Mallard, but it was Paul's Rickenbacker guitar sound that was the true marvel. He'd shred it, run the plectrum up the strings and swing his arm like a windmill constantly whilst feedback poured out the speaker. It was both rhythm and lead. At the Brunel Rooms, I was literally stood against a speaker on my own watching him, barely two feet away during the complete performance. You could feel perspiration, hunger and passion pour from every pore. I couldn't take my eyes off him. As far as I was concerned, he was The Jam. He looked cool, sang with an English accent, and his stage presence was magnetic.

I was a short-haired punk wearing a Fred Perry or mohair sweater, but still loyally held on to my ropey old Parka. The Jam's second album in less than six months, *This Is the Modern World*, reflected how I felt. I identified with Paul through song, sound and style. The illustrations on the inner sleeve designed by Conny Jude summed it up perfectly. The year zero bands were absorbed into the establishment before they knew what was happening.

By 1979, the Reading Festival, *All Mod Cons* and *The Jam Pact* tour, we'd had enough. Punk had imploded and the Mod revival took hold. The punk camaraderie now resembled a school playground. Still a punk at heart, I witnessed many a Clash gig and excitedly grabbed all those eclectic double and triple album releases, but I never saw The Jam live again, although I avidly collected all those ground-breaking singles and albums on the week of release.

Beyond 1982, I felt The Style Council were a beautifully defined concept, and Paul's solo career still to this day enthrals me. I'm still in love with the guy.

TOWN HALL
27 JUNE 1977, BATTERSEA, LONDON, UK

I WAS THERE: RAY GANGE, *RUDE BOY*

I was fortunate enough that one of the many days I went to see the chaps at Rock On happened to be the day The Jam did their thing at Soho Market. Not that I was an instant fan or anything like that. All through the first two years of punk, I was working in record shops, so had copies of the *In The City* album and single on release, so I was well aware of them. I first heard The Jam either from working at Harlequin, Old Compton Street, or on John Peel. I don't precisely remember the first time.

Also, the Roxy, Red Cow and Nashville Rooms were all regular haunts, so I saw them a couple of times at some of those venues… though don't ask which ones – those days are all a bit hazy! But the Battersea Town Hall show was so intense and incendiary that I doubt anyone there would have forgotten it. The energy at that was as punk as any other bands on the scene at that time.

SOLID BOND IN YOUR HEART

The Pistols and The Clash were the apex, but I don't remember anyone questioning or deriding any of the bands for being from out of town. Not sure it was ever thought about. I guess the Burton suits thing fuelled it a little, and maybe as the Mod revival grew, but I'd moved to LA by then so was oblivious to that. When it came to comparisons to Dr Feelgood, The Who, and all that, The Clash were certainly guilty of that (magpie approach), but again until the music press brought up such discussions, I doubt any of the punk hoi polloi paid much attention, especially as we all pretended we didn't listen to anything but punk!

I'm not sure I'd have classed myself as a fan from the second album on, but again that was probably just due to being preoccupied with making *Rude Boy* and then moving to California, where The Jam weren't really on the radar until a small Mod revival that happened for a while in LA.

I WAS THERE: JAMES ARLOW

They played Battersea Town Hall early in their career. A young punk girl at this show was wearing a see-through top. That was quite mind blowing! The Jam had so much energy and passion. I thought the show was all over until my then girlfriend pointed out that they hadn't played 'Batman'. She was more familiar with them and knew they finished with it back then. Later on, I saw them at the 100 Club. Again, so much passion and energy.

CAT'S WHISKERS
29 JUNE 1977, YORK, UK

I WAS THERE: GARRY HORNBY

It was the second time I'd seen them. The first time was supporting The Stranglers at Leeds Poly in April that year, their name misspelled as The Jamm. I saw them again in '77 at Leeds Poly, the New Hearts supporting, who went on to be Secret Affair. Local heroes Cyanide supported The Jam in York and got the audience, myself included, pogoing. Cyanide later signed for Pye but could never recapture their live sound on vinyl, releasing one album and three singles.

There was a lot of electric energy and a buzz around the place in those early new wave days. I recalled in my diary that The Jam were really tight. You knew they were going places. They did two encores – 'Art School' and 'In The City', which they played twice. At one point, Paul Weller took his thin black tie off and threw it off the stage. I was at the front and caught it. I went backstage after and handed it back to him.

TOP RANK
5 JULY 1977, PLYMOUTH, UK

I WAS THERE: STEVEN TALLAMY, AGE 15

I had just turned 15 and had bought the first single by The Jam. I recall liking the track but not being as bowled over as by the first Damned single or as utterly transfixed as by 'Anarchy'. I was at home when our family radio was tuned to the local Plymouth station. Suddenly the DJ announced that 'a new, young group – The Jam' would shortly be interviewed by him. The interview was quick, superficial and slightly cringeworthy (due to the DJ, not the guys) but at the end they announced a competition. The person that called in with the best question would get to attend the concert that night and receive a signed copy of their debut album. I called a couple of times, got through and asked them where the inspiration came for the logo and the 'bathroom wall' background on the single. I think I won principally as I appeared to be the only caller who had any idea who the band actually were!

I turned up at the gig that night, the band signed the LP and gave it to me. Paul wrote 'To Steve. Best Wishes' which I now think of as admirably polite during the white heat of punk. I saw them play the gig and was converted. (Miraculously, the album survived the gig with only one small crease on the sleeve.)

Five years later, as a rabid fan, I was lucky enough to get tickets for the Bingley Hall, Birmingham concert, the third-to-last gig on their final tour. It was an almost religious experience as we all said goodbye to them and, in some senses, our youth.

Weller had released six albums, changed the perception of what music could mean to a generation and then broke up his band at the peak of their commercial powers. He was 24.

'ALL AROUND THE WORLD' RELEASED
15 JULY 1977

The Jam's second single reaches No.13 in the UK charts.

COUNTERPOINT RECORDS
15 JULY 1977, CRYSTAL PALACE, LONDON, UK

I WAS THERE: TONY FLETCHER

At the record shop that summer 1977 day, I found myself clutching a copy of 'All Around The World' by The Jam, the punk group I really disliked. They were wearing black suits and white shirts, like they were office boys or something. Didn't they realise that kids of today hated uniforms? Then again, their ties were loose at the collar like most of us wore them at Tenison's, and they each had these distinctive black-and-white shoes that made them look… different. And they were standing in front of a bright orange background, with their logo spray-painted behind them, all three staring at the camera with an expression that seemed equal parts pride and contempt. I turned the single sleeve over. Now one of them was in a pink button-down shirt, just like the one I'd refused to wear as a hand-me-down from my brother, and he was holding over his right shoulder a black-and-white chequered jacket, in exactly the same pattern I'd also refused to wear on a duffel coat my mum had bought me as a little kid. How could they possibly think this stuff was fashionable?

The camera had zoomed in on their faces here on the back, and it only made their expressions harder to read. (The one in the middle, who I figured must be the singer, was wearing dark, square shades. Because you couldn't see his eyes, his face was a totally blank canvas.) They looked like yobs – like punks – but they were so well dressed that you could hardly place them in the same camp as the Sex Pistols. I couldn't make them out.

And then, at the bottom of the back cover, there were three words, one under each band member: 'Direction Reaction Creation'. This reminded me of The Who's second single, 'Anyway Anyhow Anywhere'. And there was something else, too: a credit for their hairdresser. No band, no rock star, no pop singer ever credited their hairdresser on the back of a single sleeve. Not unless they wanted people to think they were poofs. And I knew, instinctively, The Jam were not poofs. But there it was: 'Hair: Schumi.' And for a scruffy 13-year-old like me whose straight blond hair defied all attempts to shape it or style it, I had to admit: their haircuts were ace. They were short, and they were sharp. I needed no more convincing. I bought the single sleeve.

ERIC'S
16 JULY 1977, LIVERPOOL, UK

I WAS THERE: RAY HICKS, AGE 15

I saw The Jam five times live before they split. I went to every gig on my own. None of my mates were into them back then. I'll never forget those days. From the first time in Eric's to Liverpool's Empire Theatre in November 1978, then Mountford Hall in May 1979, Deeside Leisure Centre in North Wales at the end of that November, then the Royal Court Theatre back in Liverpool, 27 April 1981, and a Deeside Leisure Centre return in 1982, it was a blast.

I was in complete shock when I heard they were splitting. I walked round in a daze for weeks, not quite believing it. I had a bit of a fall-out with Weller at the time and didn't understand why he broke up 'the best fucking band in the world'. I couldn't get into The Style Council, although I liked a few of their singles. I got back into Weller when he went solo, seeing him a few times. Then From The Jam arrived… bang! I was back in the old days – all those songs I hadn't heard live for so long. I've now seen From The Jam more times than the original band – catching them for an eighth time in March 2024 at the Tivoli in Brisbane, having emigrated to Australia in 2009. As for The Jam… my fave band ever!

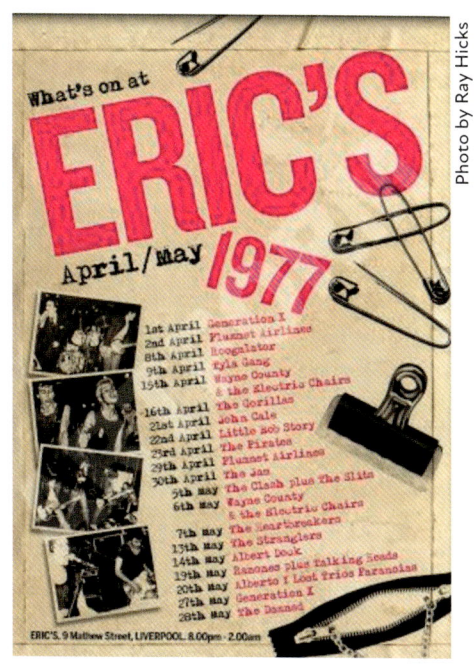

Ray Hicks saw The Jam at Eric's in Liverpool

BBC MAIDA VALE STUDIOS
19 JULY 1977, LONDON, UK

The Jam record a second John Peel session, featuring 'All Around The World', 'London Girl', 'Bricks and Mortar' and 'Carnaby Street'.

TOP OF THE POPS
21 JULY 1977, LONDON, UK

The Jam are on Britain's premier TV music show, performing 'All Around The World', a new entry in the UK charts that week at No.30.

CIVIC HALL
22 JULY 1977, MIDDLETON, MANCHESTER, UK

I WAS THERE: MARK LEWIS, AGE 10

I went with my uncle and all I remember is that it was the biggest crowd I'd seen since school assembly!

HAMMERSMITH ODEON
24 JULY 1977, LONDON, UK

I WAS THERE: RICHARD MUDD

For a number of years, The Jam were my life really. From 1977 through to 1982, I saw them maybe 15 or so times. I'm from Hertfordshire, born and raised in Potters Bar, going to school in North London, where they played quite a few venues.

I have two boys in their twenties now, and because I remain very much into Mod I still bump into people on the Northern Soul scene and through *The ModCast*, co-run by Eddie Piller, and often think how lucky we were in those times. I was there when they played their first big London gig, at Hammersmith Odeon, when they just had downstairs open. That year they were mostly playing pubs and places like that. I don't think it was a sell-out. They were promoting the *Modern World* album. And from there I carried on seeing them.

At first, their home ground in London was the Rainbow Theatre, Finsbury Park. I saw them there on a number of occasions, joining them on stage a few times. I also got backstage a few times and met them. No pictures, but there was around a half-hour chat with Paul Weller, chewing the fat, having a good old chinwag. He was lovely, a really nice guy, and said, 'You're the bloke who keeps coming on stage!' But he left me a gig pass for the next show.

I was a lot younger, fitter and more agile then. I got up there, had a little dance and was then dragged off. But they were so good to the fans that you went straight back up! They were very reasonable, and I had the pleasure of meeting John Weller too. He was an absolute gentleman. They looked after the fans, always had time for us, signed autographs, and John was like a second father to a lot of fans. They made time for you, chatted to you, allowed photographs and that.

I WAS THERE: ALAN BUTCHER

The Jam, The Saints and The Boys at Hammersmith Odeon – three of the best new wave bands together in the punk explosion of 1977. The Jam looked backwards to The Who and Mods of the sixties for influence and fashion, but forward through the songwriting of Paul Weller, who led from the front with an aggression that matched any other band at the time.

The Saints were an Australian garage band who had a bit of a cult hit with a single called 'Stranded', while The Boys were among the finest musicians of the age, influenced by the New York Dolls, Flaming Groovies and the Ramones as well as The Beatles and sixties power pop bands. The audience were in for a treat, as The Jam were easily one of the most exciting bands around. A power trio, excellent live.

I WAS THERE: STUART CUSHING

As a 14-year-old soul boy that went to the Royalty in Southgate three times a week, discovering The Jam in 1977 was a real change in my music style of choice (soul music remains my first love). My first gig was at Hammersmith in 1977 and from then on, the affinity I felt to The Jam just grew and grew. I was still at school and many were 2 Tone fans at the time but I and several mates just loved our new found leaders – Paul, Rick and Bruce.

Stuart Cushing was a soul boy until he discovered The Jam

I did the usual: got the Parka, Jam shoes, Ben Shermans and Fred Perrys and lived and breathed what they did. It was quite strange really, because my love for soul and disco lived on and I attended those events too.

I remember coming out of the Michael Sobell Centre after one gig and it had snowed. It was freezing, especially as we were covered in sweat. It was so cold that I got a kebab at Finsbury Park and the grease dripped down my Parka and froze on the surface.

I went to many gigs and followed the boys in everything they did or said. It's funny, it wasn't just the Paul Weller show then. All the band were equal to us. Everything they wrote seemed to relate to my life at the time and I still listen to them now and think 'do you know, they were right?'

I remember going to the last five gigs at Wembley and feeling like it was the end of my 19-year-old life. Why, oh, why were they doing this to me? I must admit I never got into The Style Council or, to a smaller degree, Paul's solo work. I just felt I had been dumped!

JOHN PEEL SHOW
25 JULY 1977

The band's second John Peel session gets it first airing on late-night BBC Radio 1.

PATCHWAY
31 JULY 1977, BRISTOL, UK

I WAS THERE: PAUL GAMMON

There wasn't much in the way of excitement in the charts for a 12-year-old in 1977. All our glam rock favourites had long gone from *Top Of The Pops*. But still

I liked to tape the chart show on Radio 1 on our little cassette recorder, through a cheap microphone in front of a cheap medium wave radio. It's difficult now to imagine how distorted, tinny and – well – cheap these lowest of low fidelity recordings were. And to be honest, they made most records sound pretty rubbish.

But then one Sunday in the summer of 1977, Tom Browne played three songs in quick succession that were so angry and snarly and aggressive. They sounded incredible and sublimely perfect through the cheap, tinny distortion of my cassette player. It was so exciting, I honestly remember my heart rate speeding up as I played it back, turning it up to full distortion and playing it over and over again.

'Pretty Vacant' at No.8, 'Something Better Change' up at No.15, and 'All Around The World' up at No.20, were the songs, and what really grabbed me about those records, apart from the pure energy and aggression, were all the slogans they were shouting out. It was like a movement or a revolution going on. 'We're pretty vacant, and we don't care!' 'Change! Change! Change!' 'Youth explosion!' I found that really exciting. Everything changed in my world right there and then. In fact, nothing's ever been quite the same since.

SECOND PUNK FESTIVAL
5 & 6 AUGUST 1977, MONT-DE-MARSAN, FRANCE

The Jam fly over with The Clash, The Damned and The Stranglers to play a punk festival. A post-soundcheck drinking session ends with police cautions and a change in the running order leads to John Weller stopping the band from playing, alleging a breach of contract.

MARC
24 AUGUST 1977, MANCHESTER, UK

I WAS WATCHING: JOHN WINSTANLEY

I first became aware of The Jam at Balshaw's High School, Leyland, Lancashire, amid a gathering of us third years not long after I started there. We huddled together listening to a portable transistor radio during lunch breaks outside the sixth form block. Us into music discussed what we liked, who we thought were 'peach', who we found 'not credible', and who we'd seen on TV shows like *Top Of The Pops* on Thursday evenings. The more serious of us stayed up late to catch 'whispering' Bob Harris or the attractively savvy Annie Nightingale on *The Old Grey Whistle Test*, raving about who they'd seen the following day.

The Jam had been on *Top Of The Pops* in May and July '77, performing 'In The

City' and 'All Around the World'. I hadn't seen these appearances, but the appeal to me was how others described them. They dressed in black suits and wore white shirts and black ties – the same as our school uniform (albeit our ties were black with a silver stripe). A Mod-looking trio who were clean shaven and had hair styles to match that retro look was the consensus. But this band were also associated with punk, and I struggled to reconcile that. From what we'd heard or seen in a magazine John 'Deano' Dean showed me one day, punks didn't dress in suits, and most had bright rainbow-coloured spikey hair.

John Winstanley raises a glass to memories of The Jam's appearance on Marc Bolan's show

I first saw The Jam on the first Marc Bolan TV show, broadcast by Granada TV and recorded in Manchester, 25 miles south-east from our house in Euxton. They were introduced by Marc as 'the biggest and best so far this week… an amazing group called JAM!' All through the song, I was enthralled. Looking back at that footage, it still reminds me of the sheer energy, grit and determination in the eyes of all of them, especially Paul – he fucking meant every word while slashing at his guitar, making it sound like an assault rifle firing out his wake-up call to find 'the new'.

When Paul shouts, 'Looking for you!' I felt he was calling to me. I was hit between the ears from that moment. The thumping bass, pounding drums and crashing cymbals sounded like an explosion in a glass factory. Paul sliced up his strings and Bruce Foxton jerked his head while they both jumped up and down. Unlike *Top Of The Pops*, this was live. A few seconds before the end, Rick Buckler dropped his sticks. That sealed it for me, a budding self-taught drummer – I wanted that authenticity, from a live set which was just over two minutes long. That was enough to bind me to this day. The Jam were my band from then on.

'All Around The World' was my first Jam vinyl – a gift from Aunt Irene on a shopping trip to Birkenhead's indoor market. The record store had a punk section and posters of bands on the walls. The *In The City* album cover was in bright orange and in the singles underneath was a picture cover for the disc. My aunt bought this and the poster when I explained how I'd seen them on TV and thought they were brilliant. I suspect she felt at ease because of The Jam's smart dressed appearance compared to the Sex Pistols, Damned, Clash and Siouxsie and the Banshees posters.

Word got around school that I was a big fan, and girls started to cut out articles and pictures if they appeared in *Jackie* and *Oh Boy!* As I didn't have any money to spend on records, I relied on cassettes from my friends. Michael Robinson taped the first two albums on a C90. Deano gave me a copy of The Jam's June '78 BBC *In Concert* set, during which Paul introduced 'Billy Hunt' as the next single. Every TV appearance glued me to the screen, and I listened to John Peel, as we all did, to catch any new release.

100 CLUB
11 SEPTEMBER 1977, LONDON, UK

I WAS THERE: GARY WOOD

The shock of seeing the Sex Pistols swear on television only a few months earlier woke up and spurred on an entire generation. Music was exciting again, bands forming all over the country, kids going to gigs to see people their own age playing for them. We'd had enough of prog rock and bubblegum, manufactured pop. At this point, clued-up DJs were the only people playing punk rock and new wave.

To see The Jam explode onto your TV screen in May '77 without warning was a life-changing experience for millions like us! 'In The City' – a great title and great song... anthemic! The studio audience didn't seem to know what to make of The Jam. They played with such passion and power – Weller's Rickenbacker guitar sound at the front of the aural assault, Foxton playing tight with Buckler's insistent drumming. And the Mod two-piece black suits made them stand out from any of the other bands. What a look! What a sound!

I started buying the music papers again, the first time in five years, since the giddy heights of T-Rextasy. Now every week I scanned four papers and kept any clippings about The Jam I could find.

'All Around The World' did better on the charts than 'In The City', peaking at No.13. Word went round that The Jam were appearing on Marc Bolan's new show, *Marc*. Few people knew Bolan had been a Mod 'face' 15 years previously, which probably explained his championing them. Their performance was electric, the fact they were playing live adding to the excitement. I had to see them live and September's gig at London's 100 Club in Oxford Street would prove to be the one. I bought two tickets, then waited for the date.

It was a quiet Sunday afternoon in the West End as we neared the 100 Club and noticed a long queue snaking along the pavement. My adrenaline started pumping. There was an assortment of looks and styles from the kids present – punks and new wavers mostly. New wavers didn't have a regimented look, they were all dressed differently in regular clothes that they adapted one way or another. I made a stencil with the word 'JAM' on it and sprayed my t-shirt with red paint on the front. Years later I met somebody who said they saw me wear it.

The doors opened and we filed in, my heart beating faster as we descended the stairs into the basement club. I found a great spot to stand at the right of the stage but was moved by the bouncers, because a film crew needed to set up there. We moved to a few yards from the stage and got by a pillar. The place was packed now, the heat and expectation rising dramatically. A band called The New Hearts burst onto the stage and played a really good set of power pop tunes. They were obviously destined for greater things and would turn up again a year or so later as Secret Affair, climbing to greater heights.

The crowd expectation was palpable. Being my first gig, I'd never experienced anything like this. There was no room to move, the air hot with everybody sweating profusely, when suddenly there was movement behind us and The Jam were led through the crowd to the stage. The buzz of a live gig really came on strong, everyone pushing to get nearer the stage for a better look. It was a great feeling – a weird sort of unity, hundreds of people as one!

The Jam did their hellos and launched into a song. I couldn't tell you which – it was a blur from start to finish, as if electricity was coming off the stage, the crowd electrocuted. There was no room to move, most of us jumping up and down on the spot. Now I understood why punks did the 'pogo' at gigs. You couldn't do anything else. The punk next to me had a leather biker jacket on. By the end of the gig my arm had a burn mark all the way down.

They played a lot of their first album, their singles and a couple of B-sides, the set lasting less than 40 minutes. They raced through the numbers. All too soon it was over. It was obvious they were going places.

Second album *The Modern World* was a couple of months away, with the single of the same name. That album hinted more at sixties Mod imagery, its songs and sleeve drawings setting people thinking about modernism in a broader sense. We had no idea just how large Mod would become over the next couple of years. It grew steadily through 1978, kids wearing sixties suits (Jam Boys, some called them), the band still with a mixed following.

The release of *All Mod Cons* was the starting pistol for 1979's Mod revival. Other Mod bands were coming through, people everywhere defining themselves Mods. The Jam got bigger and bigger and better and better before splitting in late 1982. They did outstanding shows over those years, but I'm glad I caught them at the start.

SOLID BOND IN YOUR HEART

DAD'S DANCEHALL
23 SEPTEMBER 1977, MALMO, SWEDEN

The Jam play Malmo as part of a mini-tour taking in Sweden and The Netherlands. The first dates are targeted by local biker gang the Raggare, a date in Stockholm is subsequently cancelled and a night at the Paradiso, Amsterdam, is put back a day.

PARADISO
30 SEPTEMBER 1977, AMSTERDAM, NETHERLANDS

I WAS THERE: KORS EIJKELBOOM

I first saw The Jam at Paradiso, my second show there, the first being The Clash four days before, supported by Siouxsie and the Banshees. There's a couple of things I remember. First, the suits and two-tone shoes illuminated by white light only. Also, the way the stage was laid out: everything tightly arranged, not a flaw, to the last bit of cabling. Last, but not least: the onstage presence of John Weller before, which of course made us young brats go, 'Who's that old geezer?'

I cannot remember the songs they played. I guess I was too busy being impressed. A newspaper review of the time mentions a tight performance and good sound, features not to be taken for granted in those days. More often than not, things were messy and noisy mainly...

Eton Crop drummer Kors Eijkelboom with his copy of In The City

In general, it was mostly their energy and drive that appealed, as well as proper songs. Historically, there was the connection with the Mod and Who era. I was an ardent Who fan from the age of 12. With The Jam, we now had the aesthetics and the songs ('Batman'!) to ourselves as a generation. Mind you, from the Dutch point of view, this is mainly about entertainment – the bonding and politics of pop culture the way it exists in the UK largely lacking from a Netherlands perspective.

What was really important personally is this: the larger shows I saw prior to the punk era were all very impressive, but distant. The Who, but also the likes of Santana, Clapton, Zappa: great but unattainable. The smaller shows quite often were – amongst other things – a display of musical virtuosity; quite boring really. This started to change with shows I saw by Dr Feelgood and The Fabulous Poodles, then radically changed with The Jam, The Clash, Ramones, The Boys, Buzzcocks, and so on. Now it was 'up close and personal', literally as well as metaphorically.

I was never a big radio listener, but guess there was a buzz among friends about the new wave of exciting bands. And I liked the *NME*, rushing to Athenaeum News Centre in central Amsterdam every week to hopefully be the first to get the latest edition. Then, if there was mention of a new Jam single, on to Get Records in Utrechtsestraat to see if they had it. Usually, it didn't arrive in the shop until much later, and in Holland only in specialised record stores like Get Records, not the mainstream ones.

I still own all the seven-inch singles available here, as well as all the albums. The first LP was my favourite, but I liked them all… except maybe *The Gift*, which to my ears was a bit far-fetched. Weller was obviously ready to move on, that's for sure. Maybe I should give it another try one of these days…

WHISKY A GO GO
8 OCTOBER 1977, LOS ANGELES, CALIFORNIA

The Jam play the first of two nights at the Whisky, kicking off their first American mini-tour. They also play the Rathskeller (aka The Rat) in Boston and CBGBs in New York City. Two further San Francisco dates are pulled, along with planned European dates for later that month. On 16 October, Paul Weller appears on NBC TV's The Tomorrow Show *with Tom Snyder.*

'THE MODERN WORLD' RELEASED
28 OCTOBER 1977

The Jam's third single debuts in the UK chart at No.38, slipping out the next week but re-entering at No.36 on 15 November.

HUDDERSFIELD POLYTECHNIC
17 NOVEMBER 1977, HUDDERSFIELD, UK

The band open a 25-date UK tour.

THIS IS THE MODERN WORLD RELEASED
18 NOVEMBER 1977

The band's new album is released just six months after their first. It enters the UK album chart at No.22, slipping to No.37 the following week in its two-week run before dropping out of the charts amid somewhat lukewarm reviews.

I WAS THERE: MARK RAILSTON

Some people find themselves on a trip to India, some find themselves in God. I found my true self in a record, 'The Modern World', all two minutes 33 seconds of it, in 1977 in Whitley Bay. A young teenager trying to make sense of the world, making that difficult transition from boy to man, brought up in effect in a single home like lots of other kids, there were certain other family issues going on which left me adrift at times. In school I developed a bit of contempt for some of the teachers, due to the utter incompetence of the system around us.

That summer found me enthusiastically reading the music weeklies. The exploding punk movement seemed exotic and exciting. Individuals named Johnny Rotten, Sid Vicious, Rat Scabies… Bands with names like the Buzzcocks and The Vibrators… There seemed to be a cartoon element, but nonetheless it had an appeal. I'd already bought The Stranglers' debut album, to the derision of some mates who declared, 'Punk is shit. We could do better on pots and pans.' But looking at the album cover I thought, 'Bloody hell, they're old!' The drummer looked wizened, old enough to be my dad. Only the bassist seemed anywhere near my age… and he was 25.

Towards the end of that summer, I badly broke my leg playing football, dashing extremely faint hopes of being Newcastle United's next legendary centre-half, in the mould of Bobby Moncur. As a result, I was laid up at home, bored for long periods, way before X-Box, PlayStations and daytime TV. My mates came round one morning, said they were going into town and did I want any new records? I dug out my WH Smith birthday vouchers, asked them to buy three punk albums… and they had to include *This Is The Modern World*. I'd heard snatches of the single, which sounded great, I'd seen press ads for the new album, thinking it must be worth a listen. A few hours later they turned up with my gleaming new LPs.

'We couldn't get The Damned or The Clash, but we got The Jam album.' 'Great,' I replied. 'And what else?' 'Err, well… we got 10cc and Queen.' 'Fucking Queen and 10cc!' I thought, but not wanting to sound an utter twat, I said thanks, and 'Let's have a listen.' We lifted the lid of the record player, took

A PEOPLE'S HISTORY OF THE JAM

Queen's *News Of The World* out and with trepidation, gave it a spin. 'We Will Rock You', followed by 'We Are The Champions', kind of okay if you like that sort of thing. I didn't. As for the rest, it seemed to trail off into overblown turgid crap, typical of the time.

Next, we put on *Deceptive Bends* by 10cc. The cover featured a deep-sea diver with helmet, walking from the sea, on a jetty with a young woman in his arms. What the fuck was all that about? Now, 10cc may have made a good record at some point in their career, but this wasn't it.

Finally, The Jam. Wow, this looks a bit more edgy. A young band, more our older brothers' age, but more stylish. We turned to the back cover. 'Fuck, that looks cool,' my mate said. We pulled the sleeve out... 'Wow, it's got the lyrics and there's a drawing of a girl with her kit out!' Cue sniggers. I lifted the record from the sleeve, put it on the turntable, lowered the needle... the guitar exploded, throwing chords like hand grenades.

'This is the modern world! This is the modern world!' this angry voice shouted.

We looked at each other, eyes slightly wide in surprise, the remaining couple of minutes perfectly encapsulating exactly what I was feeling but was struggling so badly to articulate. Never mind a lightbulb above my head, it was more a mini-nuclear explosion in me bonce. My pulse quickened in time with each bar. This was my epiphany. If I'd been an ancient Greek I might have shouted 'eureka!' Being a Geordie lad, I opted for a more predictable 'fucking hell!' Here was this raging, young, gruff voice saying exactly what I thought, as if someone had been reading my mind. I had a feeling my life was never going to be the same again. I was right.

Next was 'London Traffic'. Okay but not as good as the first song. Then 'Standards'.

'Oh, we make the standards, and we make the rules, and if you don't abide by them, you must be a fool. We have the power to control the whole land, you never must question our motives or plans.'

That was it. I was hooked. Who exactly was this band, and which was P. Weller, credited with writing virtually the whole album? I soon found out. Over the next few years, like many devoted fans all over the country, I bought all the records, joined the fan club (No.537, if you please), scoured charity shops for Mod-style clothing, went to all the Tyneside gigs and followed the band on as many extra dates as my meagre pocket money/paper round could afford – like Glasgow, Carlisle and London. I sneaked into soundchecks and sent off for bootlegs and imports. So many great memories and experiences.

LEEDS UNIVERSITY
19 NOVEMBER 1977, LEEDS, UK

The Leeds gig is followed by a Golden Lion hotel stay, where Paul Weller is involved in a fight with a travelling Australian rugby team. Arrested and charged with a breach of the peace, he appears at Leeds Magistrates' Court the next morning where the case against him is dismissed.

I SAW IT ON TV: CRAIG EDWARDS

Weller got arrested after a gig in Leeds and it was on the local news. They finished the gig and got into the bar for a few beers and there were a load of Australian rugby players in there and they started taking the piss out of him and pushing him around and stuff. With Weller being a bit handy, because he learnt off his dad, he boxed one or two of them so there ended up being a bit of a fracas in the bar.

EMPIRE THEATRE
20 NOVEMBER 1977, LIVERPOOL, UK

I WAS THERE: LES GLOVER

By the age of 12, music had become my life and the casual radio listens had turned into an obsession. Using my Philips mono cassette recorder, wrapped in its faux leather case with a pocket for a little plastic microphone, I began to record my favourite songs from the weekly Sunday chart rundown – Alice Cooper, David Bowie, Sweet, Slade… I eventually became a fully-fledged rock fan and progressed to vinyl, buying all a paper round could afford. Then punk came along, and I was torn.

    I knew the musicianship wasn't as good, but the excitement and simplicity were both achievable and appealing, especially to someone who desperately wanted to play guitar. I'd seen a clip of The Jam live on a Northern news programme presented by Tony Wilson, and on Marc Bolan's TV show, and was so impressed I purchased a ticket for their next local gig at the Liverpool Empire.

    The Empire was an exciting place in the seventies. I'd already seen Queen, Be Bop Deluxe, Nazareth and a few other bands there, but this was to be my first 'new wave' gig, and boy, what a way to start. The support was The New Hearts, who good as they were, would not find success until a name change to Secret Affair a couple of years down the line.

    While waiting for a few changes by the co-ordinated road crew working the stage, like scruffy worker bees dwarfed in front of the enormous, spray-painted backdrop, I noticed Paul Weller's Rickenbacker guitar, 'I am nobody' scratched into the body, sat proudly in front of his Vox AC30 amps. When all the scurrying had died down, the wait was finally over.

The Jam hit the stage and took the crowd kicking and screaming by the scruff of the neck for the best part of an hour, ploughing through songs from debut album *In The City*, a bunch from current LP *This Is The Modern World*, and a few well-chosen soul numbers.

Weller's playing was aggressive, angular but beautifully structured and interesting, while Bruce Foxton's bass lines created tension, counter melodies and lots of

Les Glover had a chat with The Jam on the steps of the Empire

power. And the driving force was Rick Buckler, with his machine gun snare drum and hardly a break between numbers. Their coordinated black and white suits sharply contradicted the safety-pinned charity shop chic of the rest of the punk scene. The lighting was basic and so was the sound, but the songs and playing were honed to a rough perfection from several years of London social club shows, served up with a diet of old school R&B and Motown. We seemed to hold our collective breath until the very last note.

The Jam sailed through the rough seas of punk and surfed into the new wave on much calmer waters, tight, slick and for three young guys incredibly powerful, with great heartfelt songs full of social injustice and romantic sentiment. When the gig finished, we piled out of the neoclassical hall onto Lime Street and around the side of the Empire to the stage door, already ten deep with eager, excitable Jam fans. As more people gathered it seemed a lost cause to try and meet them, so I went back around to the front and sat on the steps to await our lift home… when out strolled Paul, followed by Bruce and Rick.

Paul sat beside me and asked if I was okay, I told him I was and how much I loved the show. I asked if he'd sign my ticket and poster and he agreed, encouraging Bruce and Rick to do the same, to which Bruce agreed but Rick refused, saying his hands were too cold. Paul snapped, 'Sign the lad's fucking stuff, you miserable twat!' He still refused, so that was that.

I asked why they were at the front instead of the stage door and Paul told me they were meeting his dad there, who'd gone for their van. Just as he finished telling me, John Weller pulled up, and with that they said their goodbyes and left.

I saw them a few more times in the next few years. They were always exciting, always full of energy, and song-wise the best was yet to come, releasing the seminal *All Mod Cons*, followed by the equally stunning *Setting Sons*. When they disbanded in December 1982 it really was the bitterest pill.

FRIARS
26 NOVEMBER 1977, AYLESBURY, UK

I WAS THERE: IAN BORSING, AGE 15
'All Around The World' had just been released. Me and a mate had to lie about our ages. Tickets were £1.75 plus £1 membership for Friars. I've still got Bruce's autograph on a bit of paper plate somewhere.

APOLLO THEATRE
30 NOVEMBER 1977, GLASGOW, UK

I WAS THERE: JIMMY SMITH, AGE 14
I remember the first time hearing them on Radio 1 – John Peel used to play new sounds, and I was hooked with that aggressive guitar, the sound and the lyrics, which even to this day are apt. Going into Glasgow with older lads to attend my first gig, from the minute I purchased my ticket it seemed an eternity, waiting on the date to come around, like a kid waiting on Christmas. Walking to the venue, the smell of hot dogs and onions, everyone buzzing to see 'the best fucking band in the world', as Paul's dad John introduced them. Even watching the support group was a joy. And when the first chords were struck, I was away in a Modern World.

I WAS THERE: NEIL MCLEAN
I'd been to see many groups at the Apollo and wondered how this three-piece band would look up on that massive stage and what sound they could generate. After the support groups – The Jolt and The New Hearts – warmed up the crowd, and after the usual new wave hits were played over the PA, these three young guys strolled onto the stage. I swear to God I could not believe the noise that came out of them. It was deafening! For a three-piece band it was unheard of, and it was 190mph too. They blasted through their whole set and I was hooked right there and then. They were tight as hell.

I WAS THERE: IAN MCDIARMID, AGE 15
I was in the fourth year at Stirling High School when I heard 'All Around The World', and I was hooked, first getting to see The Jam in November 1977 at the Apollo.

I met my wife, Caroline, through our love of the band. She wrote a letter to a newspaper about them, I replied, and we began writing to each other. Six months later we met, getting engaged two years later. Two years after that we married, celebrating our fortieth wedding anniversary in May 2024. The newspaper tried to arrange a meeting with the band when we went to Wembley in 1982. That fell through, but they gave us a personalised signed photo in compensation, which we still have.

Ian & Caroline McDiarmid met through their mutual love of The Jam

We saw them four nights in a row at one stage – twice each at Edinburgh Playhouse and Glasgow Apollo. Weller fell on his backside that first night in Edinburgh. I bought eight tickets, two for each night, and those were Caroline's first Jam gigs. Tickets were £4 each. Being a gentleman, I couldn't possibly take any money off her.

We visited my aunt in 1981 when she lived in Romford, Essex, and had a trip out to Woking. We made it to Balmoral Drive, having our photos taken there. We didn't have the bottle to chap the door of No.41. I was a member of The Jam Club, run by Paul's sister Nicky Weller. I still have my membership card, a couple of photocopied letters from the band and a book of matches sent as a piece of memorabilia. I can't imagine a box of matches being sent in the post nowadays.

I WAS THERE: JAMES MCCALLUM, AGE 15

The build up to this gig has stayed with me until this day. A month or so before the gig I had been reading one of the *NME* or *Melody Maker* (as I did religiously) and seen a picture of punks in London on their way to either a gig or on a march. One of the guys at the very front had a tweed jacket on with names of bands painted on it. I thought he looked so cool.

I knew my dad had a tweed jacket in his cupboard that I was sure he never wore… Two or three weeks before The Jam gig, I moved it to under the bed in my room to see if he noticed. No one said anything so a few days before the gig I painted it with all my favourite bands' names in white paint – Jam, Clash, Pistols, ATV, Damned, SLF, etc. I thought it looked so cool.

On the night of the gig, I sneaked out of the house (with the jacket rolled up;

I couldn't take the chance my mum or dad might see it) to the bus stop across the road. I put this jacket on in the bus shelter and when the bus came along, I jumped on. My friends had got on the bus a few stops before and were sitting at the back of the bus. On the way into town everyone was saying how great my jacket was. It was only when we were getting off the bus and I turned round that I realised the paint hadn't dried properly and there on the old leather seats were my bands' names painted in reverse. We all fell about laughing and I had to throw the jacket away. I couldn't take the chance of covering everyone in paint as I pogoed around. I was freezing.

The gig itself was amazing, and the atmosphere in the Apollo was electric, with everyone waiting in anticipation for the band to appear. At the same moment, everyone rushed to the front of the stage. Not *right* to the front, as the stage at the Apollo seemed so high you couldn't see anything if you were too close. The band were amazing and the raw energy and the noise were breathtaking. Paul Weller was an icon. After a few hours, we left the gig with our throats sore from singing, our ears ringing and us knackered with jumping around and feeling on top of the world. What an experience!

About a month later, my mum asked me and my sisters if anyone had seen Dad's 'good' tweed jacket… I just looked bemused and denied all knowledge of it.

CIVIC HALL
3 DECEMBER 1977, WOLVERHAMPTON, UK

I WAS THERE: KEITH CHAPMAN, AGE 15
My first proper gig. The ticket price was £1.60 in advance, £2 on the door; I know this as I still have the stub. I went with my friend Paul and his elder sister, a teacher at Wolverhampton Polytechnic. I'd just turned 15 and Paul was 14. We travelled to the Civic from my hometown of Leamington Spa.

The support was The New Hearts, singer Ian Page soon forming Secret Affair. I recall the audience were mainly punk rockers, as The Jam were considered part of that movement in 1977. It was the first time I'd really seen people dressed as punks. Leamington Spa had yet to really embrace the scene. There were certainly none at school. Paul and I stood near the back, all the punks at the front jumping up and down, which I later understood to be pogoing. I was familiar with the first album, as Paul had it. I also bought the single 'In The City', and I'm pretty sure 'This Is The Modern World' had just been released.

On the back of this gig I became a big Jam fan, despite being into heavy rock, going on to see them on each subsequent tour until December 1982's split.

I WAS THERE: ROB POLLARD, AGE 15

I was in school blazer and trousers, a white school shirt and my brother's black tie. All I remember is being stood right at the front and some six foot punk who was stood behind five foot me launching a gob and hitting Bruce full on the lapel just before the first number, nearly causing a riot.

TOP RANK
7 DECEMBER 1977, BRIGHTON, UK

I WAS THERE: ALAN BUTCHER

I hadn't seen Mods head from London to the seaside since I was a schoolboy on holiday in Margate. I was down the front with my mate Stuart and we loved it, the band going through their early set, including Who covers and their own 'In The City'. I saw the band a lot in those days, but this was memorable as it was just before the band got bigger… and bigger.

CROYDON GREYHOUND
11 DECEMBER 1977, CROYDON, LONDON, UK

I WAS THERE: JONATHAN BILLINGTON, AGE 16

My friend, Andrew, and I were both 15, listening to John Peel, watching Bill Grundy, and enjoying great tunes by The Clash, The Adverts, The Damned, Siouxsie… and The Jam! I bought 'In The City' after seeing them on Marc Bolan's show or *Top Of The Pops* in the summer of 1977. I was 16 that June.

Andrew started looking around at concerts we might go to, and we saw the *Five Live Stiffs* tour at Fairfield Halls, Croydon and thought, 'We like gigs!' Down the road was Croydon Greyhound, where on 11 December we decided we'd go and see The Jam on their *In The City* tour. The second album had been released by then. We were both still at school, and because punk rock was a thing, my mother made me a very nice potato sack thing to wear, unlikely as it sounds. She cut armholes and a neck hole in and said, 'Go upstairs and see your father.' He wasn't so well, resting in bed, but gave me a fiver and my mother took me to East Grinstead railway station, where I met Andrew and another fella called Colin. We got a return to East Croydon, walked down to the Greyhound and paid a pound to get in to see The Jam, possibly supported by The New Hearts. I have memories of Shane McGowan and The Nips also being there, although Andrew remembers that being at a Damned concert a few weeks later. I managed to buy two pints of Double Diamond.

I've never seen so many people pogoing, jumping up and down all at the same time, absolutely front to back, side to side, all having a fantastic time. Two years before I'd been to Streatham Odeon with my dad to see Jack Parnell and George Chisholm, a different world altogether! The Jam audience was mostly punks or hippies. I was probably wearing bellbottom jeans. It wasn't even new wave – it was still early enough to be full-on punk. We pogoed to complete and utter exhaustion until I had a stitch and was unable to move or walk. Do that on a pint of Double Diamond and you're going to throw up. I'm proud to say I'm the only punk I've ever seen throw up at a gig.

They played the *Batman* theme, 'In The City', 'This Is The Modern World', 'London Girl' (which I loved), and I've vague memories of 'Midnight Hour'. 'Modern World' stood out for me, and I remember them playing 'Life From A Window'.

I went to gigs at Croydon Greyhound in January, February and March 1978, and in April went to see Patti Smith at the Rainbow in Finsbury Park but managed to miss the Tube home. Getting myself and my 15-year-old girlfriend home from North London was a bit of a palaver and I was banned from going to concerts for the rest of the year. My dad was suffering from cancer and passed away that September.

I started going to gigs again in early 1979, with my second Jam concert at the Rainbow that December. I went to all three nights. This was the *All Mod Cons* tour, but they still did 'Batman' at the end, and 'London Girl' – we were sat near the back and I remember that little change of tempo or rhythm in the middle, my whole mind and body syncing with the music. I don't think I've felt a moment like that since. And they did 'Sounds From The Street'. After all that on a Sunday night, it was maths and geography the next morning, but by 1979 I'd left school and had my first job.

Later, we went to Cornwall Coliseum, near St Austell, staying in a bed and breakfast in Charlestown. We went to the gig, walked back to our B&B for the night and at about two in the morning the support band came back to the same digs. They were called Apocalypse and demanded sandwiches from the landlady there and then.

LANCASTER UNIVERSITY
14 DECEMBER 1977, LANCASTER, UK

I WAS THERE: KEVIN TOOTLE, AGE 17

The support band was China Street, I think, then Weller's dad introduced The Jam. I went with my friends Gibby and Gav. I went on to see them around a dozen times.

VICTORIA HALL
15 DECEMBER 1977, HANLEY, STOKE-ON-TRENT, UK

I WAS THERE: JOHN TIDESWELL

When I got my first guitar that Christmas, I'm wearing a Jam tie I bought at this concert. God knows what I've got on my head, but you get the drift of the band's influence on me. Also, there's a photograph of our fruitless attempt of a band picture from early '79. Again, you see the Mod influence with our Parkas and so on. Oh, for camera phones in those days.

The first time I heard about The Jam was in early 1977 in the music papers, *Sounds* or the *NME*. I was 19. It was difficult to hear new bands then, with only three TV channels and poor radio coverage. However, I had a mate who'd record John Peel's show direct from the microphone into a cassette recorder. He played 'In The City', and that got me going. Shortly after, I bought that single and then the debut album. I was soon totally immersed in the music and the image of the band on the iconic spray paint cover, and after seeing them on *Top Of The Pops* I decided I wanted the Mod look.

John Tideswell, plugged in, way back

A shopping trip to Birmingham later, I was £40 lighter (two weeks' wages in 1977) and had a set of new clothes, including a pair of Jam spats (albeit all black), button-down shirts, tie and straight trousers, a pretty radical look in those days.

I didn't pass my driving test until 1978 and getting to see bands out of town was difficult, so it was pleasing to see The Jam coming to the Victoria Hall in Hanley on the *Modern World* tour.

Tickets purchased, I invited a girl I knew to come along, and Janet's now been my wife for 35 years. (Yes, Janet and John!) I think we took the bus the short distance from my home to the venue, getting there as support band New Hearts were playing. They were okay and definitely looked the part, dressed in their suits.

During the interval I purchased that thin tie from a stall selling t-shirts, promptly putting it on. With the lights up I think the hall was about two thirds full, only a handful dressed like Mods. And when The Jam came on stage, it was electric! I went to the front of the stage and stood with a lad affectionately known locally as

'Martin the Bag'. He was a plump, bespectacled guy, about 17, a regular at gigs in those days. When the band started to play, he produced a large brown paper bag with eye holes cut into it, placed it over his head and pogoed through the whole set like a man possessed! The guy was a local legend.

The Jam were a young band playing fast, with plenty of energy, leaping about the stage. I remember making my way to the front with about 20 others, bouncing about enjoying the show. It was something to behold for a 19-year-old to witness, by far the best gig I'd seen, the standout songs 'Changed My Address' and 'Carnaby Street'. From that night on, my life changed, and I saw The Jam another three times.

I WAS THERE: PETER BOWERS

Sunday afternoons in 1977 were mainly spent at my cousin's house in Stoke, listening to punk records and playing football. At 18 going on 19, I was a few years older than Mark but he had a great collection of punk singles and a few punk LPs. It was here that I first heard the 'In The City' single. I was struck by the energy and tautness of the sound. Having heard sixties singles by The Who, courtesy of my elder brother Roy, I instantly made a sonic connection. This wasn't a nostalgia trip though – The Jam's music sounded urgent, modern and rooted in the present.

Mark also had the *In The City* LP, which we both dug but it was the follow up album, 'This Is The Modern World', which I really adored. I bought it the week it was released and listened to it incessantly, digging the songs, the great live photo on the back cover and scrutinising the inner sleeve with its words and colourful sketches. When I heard The Jam were playing the Victoria Hall, I bought a ticket well in advance. By the time of the gig, I was a student at Keele University and drove to the venue.

With the anticipation building, I took a place right near the front. The lights dimmed, John Weller strolled on to provide the introduction and the band appeared on stage wearing black and white sixties suits and with Paul and Bruce sporting red and white Rickenbacker guitars. The Jam launched into their set and I was immediately transfixed. The pogoing at the front meant being knocked around to various vantage points but the excitement was unrelenting. The songs I loved from the two LPs came alive, hammered out with energy and urgency. I was absorbed in every moment, every leap, every cymbal crash, every barked word, every slashing Rickenbacker chord. The set seemed to be over in no time. There was an encore – maybe two – before the lights went up and the gig was over.

Hardly able to catch a breath, I turned towards the side exit doors, along with the rest of the sweaty young punks and felt as if I'd returned from a different place.

Unexpected tingles rushed up and down my spine and my mind felt like it was glowing. Surges of excitement overwhelmed me as I walked towards the winter air outside. I had never experienced anything like it and drove back to Keele reliving the thrills I'd just witnessed. I hadn't the words to describe the emotions of the night so when friends asked how the gig had been, I just muttered 'yeah… really good' before taking myself away to sit down and try to make sense of it all.

It's been a long time since that night in December 1977. I must have attended hundreds of gigs over the years, including Jam gigs at various venues but the sheer excitement and joy of that night tops all of them.

The Victoria Hall is still there. It's been modernised a bit but whenever I'm passing, I'll often stop, drift away in thought and relive the late teenage thrills of seeing The Jam that night in December 1977.

HAMMERSMITH ODEON
18 DECEMBER 1977, LONDON, UK

I WAS THERE: RICHARD WESTNEY, AGE 15

I was just the right age for punk – I turned 15 in 1977. I was buying anything and everything as the first punk singles started to emerge. The Pistols, The Clash, The Stranglers, The Boomtown Rats, The Damned, Buzzcocks, The Adverts and The Jam. I can't remember when I first heard it, but I bought 'In The City' on single, then the album. I was more into The Stranglers and the Pistols, but I loved 'Away From The Numbers' because of the lyrics. I really related to them, that whole thing about being different and going your own way. Also, the band were from Woking, and I lived a few miles away, near Guildford.

I definitely liked 'All Around The World' more when that came out and then, only a few months later, *This Is The Modern World*. I think that was when The Jam really got to me. I know most people don't, but I loved that album and the direction they were going in. Me and a few mates decided to see them at Hammersmith Odeon in December 1977.

Unfortunately, I had the ritual of a pre-Christmas annual visit to family in Tunbridge Wells the same day and was panicking that I wasn't going to be allowed to go. Fortunately, I was able to persuade my mum to let me leave early and go from there. My uncle dropped me at the station and I caught the train into London, then the Tube to Hammersmith to meet up with my mates.

It was the first punk gig for all of us. We were terrified! I think we all thought we'd get beaten up. It was intense. I remember liking the support bands – The Jolt and The New Hearts, then a long wait for The Jam. When they came on it was like nothing I'd ever experienced, like being hit by a thunderbolt. Stark black and white stage, apart from a Union Jack, black and white suits, and the noise! The pace and energy never let up, song after song. I knew them all. I was hooked. That was probably the moment they became my favourite band.

L'ANCIENNE BELGIQUE
13 FEBRUARY 1978, BRUSSELS, BELGIUM

The Jam's first gig of the year is followed by three French shows and four London 'Blitz' shows in preparation for an upcoming second US tour.

THE MARQUEE
24 & 25 FEBRUARY 1978, LONDON, UK

I WAS THERE: ED SILVESTER

On a bitterly cold Saturday in those grey and austere days of February, our little group of Epping punks and new wavers set off excitedly on the usual 40-minute Tube journey to the mysterious West End. Central London was where all the so-called punk venues seemed to be. Legendary names such as the Roxy and the Vortex. This trip was going to be a bit different from our earlier outing to an infamous Sham 69 gig at the London School of Economics, a memorable event for all the wrong reasons. On this occasion we were to going to see another of the rising stars of new wave… The Jam.

The venue was the famous Marquee club on Wardour Street in London's Soho. Back in 1965, The Who held down a residency there, sealing both their place and the venue's in the Mod hall of fame. For all this, the Marquee was an intimate, atmospheric club that held a few hundred paying punters at most. That night was to be part of The Jam's *London Blitz* tour to promote new single, 'News Of The World'. What was it about these 'smart punks' that interested me so much? They certainly had the energy and manic sound typical of most punk bands of that time. But rather incongruously, these guys wore smart black

Ed Silvester and his brother John were at the Marquee Club in February 1978

suits and black and white shoes.

My brother John and I had been attending punk gigs in our torn and paint-splattered t-shirts, leather jackets and bondage trousers. Lately this rather derivative punk look had begun to feel a bit passé. Growing coverage of The Jam in the music press and on television served only to accelerate this process for us. After a quick visit to a charity shop for inspiration, and using the same punk DIY ethos, we mixed white Oxford weave button-down shirts with old black school blazers and adorned them with the obligatory punk pin badges. Now we looked the business.

By then, the rush of excitement I'd felt in early 1977 for the punk explosion was beginning to wear off. The Sex Pistols had gone to the United States, where they imploded, breaking up a few weeks earlier. It really did feel like the end of something special. Maybe The Jam were just the band to take this energetic new wave sound to exciting new places.

Their second album hadn't been well received by the music press and the band were being written off by many commentators. Although very different from their debut studio set, I and thousands of other like-minded kids loved it. More than 40 years later, I still believe the album stands the test of time. The final track was a cover of sixties soul classic 'In The Midnight Hour' by Wilson Pickett. Along with their retro suits, this was yet another sign to me of their modernist influences. In fact, The Jam reeked of Mod.

That February evening, we jumped off the Tube train at Oxford Circus, rushed up the escalators and hurried excitedly along Oxford Street before turning into Wardour Street. We arrived early and after a couple of liveners in The Ship, we queued with other eager teenage punters near the entrance. Tickets cost the regal sum of £1.50 each, bought the week before by my brother during his lunch hour as he also worked in the West End. Even allowing for inflation over the years, this was a steal compared to today's prices.

After what felt like an age, just past seven we were in. The atmosphere in the shady, dimly-lit club was thick with smoke and expectation. At a small bar on the left of the venue we nursed a solitary pre-show beer. None of us were exactly flush with cash.

It was apparent that other kids had made efforts to 'dress up' like The Jam, and it was easy to start chatting with complete strangers and feel part of an exclusive happening.

After a terrific warm-up set by Scottish punksters The Jolt, in snappy blue suits with dark lapels, expectation and excitement began to increase exponentially. Sometime after nine, The Jam crashed onto stage, dressed sharply in black three-button jackets and white trousers, a departure from their trademark black suits. On their feet were the standard issue, black-and-white Jam shoes. We worked our way to the front of stage, where we could feel the sweat of the band and the full energy of the swaying audience. The band smashed their way through the first two albums in a little over an hour before leaving the stage. After an enthusiastic encore they were gone. We were left breathless.

We could see the future. This band were going to be huge and, although few could have recognised it then, The Jam had just sown the seeds for a revival of mankind's greatest youth subculture.

Once home from the Marquee, the night's ticket was stuck on my bedroom wall. There it would stay for a number of years, silently marking the day my Mod journey of the next six or seven years began.

I WAS THERE: IAN BURBEDGE

Early 1978 was the last time I saw The Jam in a small venue, playing the Marquee. A mate got tickets via his brother, who worked nearby. I'd have loved to have gone to the later secret gigs, but I wasn't that close and was too young to know the older fans to be able to get in. I did get into a soundcheck at the Rainbow though. That was fantastic but being shy I kept to the back.

I also saw them on 29 November that year at the Empire Pool, Wembley, and as the band got bigger the gigs became fewer. But they still had that magic and excitement about them. There were fights at gigs occasionally, but I was clued up enough to keep out of the way.

'NEWS OF THE WORLD' RELEASED
3 MARCH 1978

The Jam's fourth single, 'News Of The World', spends five weeks on the UK charts, reaching No. 27. The promo video is shot on the roof of Battersea Power Station.

I WAS THERE: RUPERT TRACY

I was born in London but brought up in Southampton. We used to go to this youth club where there was this slightly older guy, Gerard, who was cooler than everybody else. He was the first one to wear bondage trousers, and brothel creepers. He was very personable. He brought 'Suspect Device' by Still Little Fingers' to the youth club, which I fell in love with, and he also brought the *In The City* and *The Modern World* albums. I thought *In The City* was a fucking masterpiece.

Punk was fun and shocking. It drove my mum fucking bananas, to begin with at least, but she used to dye my hair for me. The music grabbed me. It was the music I'd been waiting for all my life. It spoke to me in a way that Gary Glitter or Suzi Quatro or Mud never, ever did. And Paul looked so fucking cool. You ended up thinking, 'I want to be this guy.' Which was in contrast to what he was preaching, because the Mod ideal is to be individual and to think for yourself. But I had the most influential guy right in front of me. Why wouldn't I want to be like him?

These youth club days were towards the end of '77, beginning of '78, so I was down my local record shop. 'When's the next Jam record coming out?' And 'News Of The World' was the next single, and I was just completely hooked. It was the first Jam record I ever bought myself. I'd saved up for it. It completely took over my life. From that moment onwards, gone were all the ripped-up t-shirts, bondage trousers and home-made punk outfits. I just wanted to look like Paul Weller.

My mum bought me tickets to see them at Southampton Gaumont. I had a mate who was a bit older and my mum trusted him and said I could go if we went together. My whole life from then on was waiting for the next Jam release or the next Jam tour. And they never kept kids in the UK waiting too long, with two or three tours a year. And if you were prepared to go to London…

HARVEY BUBBLES GYMNASIUM
16 MARCH 1978, BRIDGEPORT, CONNECTICUT

The Jam begin a 24-date North American tour, mainly supporting rock band Blue Öyster Cult, but also the Ramones in Philadelphia. The New York Four Acres Club date is broadcast on local radio station WOUR 96.9FM.

THE COLONIAL TAVERN
21 & 22 MARCH 1978, TORONTO, CANADA

I WAS THERE: IVAR HAMILTON

A fan since day one, I've faithfully attended all but two of The Jam's shows in Toronto and all but one of Weller's solo shows, only missing his 2003 Palais Royale gig. The Style Council unfortunately never played Canada. I became a fan when I spent six weeks in the UK in the summer of 1977. A group of friends went to Reading Festival the first year punk and new wave acts played, alongside the old guard. I was introduced to a young woman named Jane who said, 'Call me 'Jam fan Jane'.' I was hooked from there on this cool woman, needed to discover the band and, 46 years on, I'm still avidly following all things Jam, solo and related acts.

I was fortunate enough not long after to get my dream job in the music department

SOLID BOND IN YOUR HEART

at CFNY, Toronto as import music director, as well as having on-air duties and running a video roadshow for the station. We were one of the first alternative and free-form radio stations in North America, where we didn't follow charts and could programme what we wanted. I took full advantage, ensuring we played all The Jam's records.

When they played Toronto in March 1978, people in the city were still feeling out punk and alternative music. The previous year saw the short-lived OCA (Ontario College of Art) host Talking Heads and local acts The Viletones, Teenage Head, the Diodes, and more. The Ramones also made a few appearances in the city, and The Dead Boys, Eddie and the Hot Rods, and The Vibrators played shows. But if you went to a punk show, chances were that you'd see the same 300 people.

The Colonial had been around since the late 1940s and was known for hosting jazz legends such as Billie Holiday, Oscar Peterson and later blues acts such as Bo Diddley and John Lee Hooker. But as the seventies wore on, they started booking rock acts. Rush played some of their earliest shows there, as did Rory Gallagher.

The Jam were one of the first big punk or alternative acts to play Toronto, followed three weeks later

Photos by Doug McClement

The Jam at Toronto's Colonial Tavern

by The Stranglers debuting at the Horseshoe Tavern. The Jam's two shows did not sell out, but the band played an explosive set, had great gear, and were as sharply dressed as you'd have expected.

One of the photos sound engineer Doug McClement took on the first night was later used in a book sold at The Jam exhibitions in London and Liverpool. One show was filmed but never released, and there's a bootleg of the first night. Suggestions that the band also played the El Mocambo on the same date are incorrect, although that venue was a 'go to' for most international acts due to notoriety gained as a result of the Rolling Stones playing there in 1977.

CBGBs
30 & 31 MARCH 1978, NEW YORK, NEW YORK

I WAS THERE: STEVEN SALEMI

Turn the 'way back' machine to the late 1970s. I'm a sophomore at Brown University in Providence, Rhode Island. My cousin Jack is living in New York City and calls me to say he has tickets for The Jam. I skip classes, hop on the train and head south. Jack picks me up and before heading to the concert in Lower Manhattan, we make about five stops, in as many boroughs of New York City, picking up (or dropping off) various mind-altering substances, partaking of at least some of them along the way. Arriving at the concert hall, on time, we feel no pain, absolutely stoked to see the best fucking band in the world. And The Jam do not disappoint. Pure energy and total Mod bliss from beginning to end. I remember Bruce jumping around and the sheer brilliance of the performance. One of the most memorable nights of my life, recalled fondly so many decades later.

THE OLD GREY WHISTLE TEST
23 MAY 1978, LONDON, UK

The first broadcast of The Jam performing 'In The Street Today', 'Billy Hunt' and "A' Bomb In Wardour Street'.

BBC TV IN CONCERT, PARIS THEATRE
1 JUNE 1978, LONDON, UK

The Jam perform ten songs for a show broadcast nine days later and also record a session for David 'Kid' Jensen on Radio 1.

KING GEORGE'S HALL
12 JUNE 1978, BLACKBURN, UK

A week-long UK mini-tour begins in Blackburn and ends six shows later at London's Lyceum Ballroom.

I WAS THERE: PAUL BROMLEY

My first of 57 Jam gigs was two and a half hours away from my County Durham roots in Blackburn. I first saw them on TV a year earlier, playing 'In The City', that debut single my first Jam purchase. And when you listen to the lyrics, it's about us – the youth of the day. Like we all said, Weller was the spokesman for under-25s.

I was a fan of The Who from a very young age, influenced by my cousin Mark, and just loved the energy of The Jam, who reminded me very much of The Who. About half a dozen of my friends started following them, but it was my cousin that drove me to and from that first gig, all the way from Billingham, near Middlesbrough... quite apt as his surname is Blackburn.

I loved the raw energy and how tight the band were musically, even at such a young age. The lyrics also impressed. The audience was made up of a mixture of punks and Mods, and the mosh pit was amazing and kind of overwhelming at my age.

Looking back, I think both *All Mod Cons* and *Setting Sons* were ground-breaking. Lyrically, every song had a meaning and was about what was happening in the world. And single-wise, 'Tube Station' has to be my favourite. I'm nearly 59 now and every time I go to London, I still do an obligatory Tube train coming out of the tunnel pic, posting it online with lines from the lyrics.

I WAS THERE: MALCOLM STAVES

The first punk singles I bought were 'Pretty Vacant' and 'Peaches', closely followed by 'In The City' by The Jam. The Pistols looked and sounded like street urchins. The Stranglers, dirty old men in raincoats. The Jam, with their sharp suits and youthful front man, stood out amongst the rows of spikey hair and leather safety pin chic. Young and defiant. They appeared fresh out of school with the tunes and the raw energy to excite a bored teenager feverishly seeking a purpose in life and a music of his own. I was hooked and eagerly anticipated seeing the band live. So when the gig was announced I couldn't wait to get my ticket and get down to King George's. I'd already seen a few punk bands there.

It was a warm night. I remember me and my skinny mates huddled in the

A PEOPLE'S HISTORY OF THE JAM

Ribblesdale pub opposite the venue, supping on foamy Thwaites bitter and speculating on what was about to unfold. Fast forward to The Jolt. What little I recall of them is they were half decent for an unknown support act, but not particularly memorable. We were all there to see the headliners.

The atmosphere in the hall was electric. The boys didn't disappoint. My recollection is they opened with 'Modern World' but I could be wrong. Whatever it was, the crowd erupted, spraying beer and hurling gob. I wasn't a fan of gobbing at gigs and certainly not on my new found idols. Weller was gnarly and full on thrashing his guitar. Rick and Bruce were motoring along. The songs were played much faster live than on record. What was really impressive is how tight they were for a 'punk' band. The sound in the hall wasn't the greatest but they knocked out all the early stuff with aplomb… 'In The City', 'Away From The Numbers', 'Non-Stop Dancing', 'News Of The World'. Hearing and seeing them live raw and in the flesh for the first time was a revelation. I came away buzzing and couldn't wait to see them again. They were the best of the new wave of bands on the circuit. Great songs. Great performance. I was a solid gold believer!

The next time was December 12th 1979. Expectations were a lot higher following the release of *Setting Sons*. Once again they were at a packed King George's, this time supported by The Vapors. By now The Jam were well established as the nation's favourite post punk outfit, a band on top of their game and Mr Weller having fully blossomed into the nation's brightest songsmith. I remember the set was action packed with hit after hit: 'Thick As Thieves', 'When You're Young', 'Strange Town', 'Eton Rifles', 'Tube Station', 'David Watts'. The stand out song on the night was 'Private Hell', and it's still a personal favourite almost 45 years on.

I've seen Paul Weller and From The Jam numerous times over the years. The Jam's music is just as compelling now as it was when I first heard it way back then. Any guitar and any bass drum!

Malcolm Staves was open-mouthed with awe at how great The Jam were

LYCEUM BALLROOM
18 JUNE 1978, LONDON, UK

I WAS THERE: RICHARD WESTNEY

A few months later, we saw them again at the Lyceum one Sunday night. I had an old light blue t-shirt I ripped up and put The Jam logo on with a marker pen. We met Paul Weller in the bar, and he signed it. Sadly, it's long gone now but I kept it for decades and never wore it again. That was closely followed by the first of many Guildford Civic Hall gigs on 30 July, a few weeks before 'David Watts'/ "A' Bomb In Wardour Street' came out as a single.

I WAS THERE: ROBIN QUARTERMAIN

I was hooked on The Who and their unique sounds. Fast forward a year, a group of school kids watching the Marc Bolan show after school, and wham bam! The Jam came out of that screen like a vision with 'All Around The World'. That was it, I was hooked. I got hold of 'In The City', and that proved life changing at the age of 15.

It wasn't until 1978 that I first saw them live, at the Lyceum, supported by Scottish Modsters The Jolt and the weirdest support band ever, Jab Jab. Another bonus for us was standing with Billy Idol and Tony James from Generation X. A fantastic night for a 16-year-old's first gig up in the smoke.

By the end of 1978, there was the *All Mod Cons* tour, and next was Wembley Arena, with a great line-up alongside Slade, Generation X and The Pirates, The Jam headlining on a night of running battles between the burgeoning Mods and skinheads, resulting in someone getting stabbed. It was back to school in the morning after that adventure.

Around then, *Quadrophenia* was being filmed and I just missed out on making it down to Brighton for the beach scenes. I was gutted. By early 1979, most Saturdays were spent down Carnaby Street looking at Parkas, Jam shoes and so on. I was also member 282 of The Jam Club, receiving newsletters and handwritten letters from the band. Most importantly, I had early notification of live gigs and access to tickets before anyone else (which is quite normal these days).

From 1979 through to the final gigs in 1982, there were some fantastic shows, like the Rainbow in North London, Hammersmith Palais, Alexandra Pavilion, and so on. There were the support bands too, and pre-band music educating us in Northern Soul, ska and Mod. For Wembley Arena on the final tour, I managed to secure three nights. I took my mates one night, my then girlfriend another night, and was on my own for the last time… then they were gone!

I saw Bruce, Rick and Paul in their separate guises over the next decades, then in 2006 Rick started going out as The Gift with Russ Hastings and Dave Moore. I booked them for an event I was doing and got offered the re-named From The Jam before anyone else, so in 2007 – with Bruce as well as Rick on board – they played my event and that led to me DJing on many of their tour dates in the coming couple of years. And my next was at the Royal Albert Hall in May 2010, after a tip-off to get seats for a certain night and three numbers, 99.9 per cent of those there having no idea it was on the cards.

Would I go if they reformed? Well, there's little to no chance of that happening, so let the memories be memories. Those teenage years were explosive and influential and are still part of my code now.

I WAS THERE: MARK ANDREWS

Potentially the first ever concert I would attend – The Jam at the Lyceum Ballroom in London, but it took some sorting out. First off, my friend Matt and I had school the next day, so we had to get both sets of parents to agree. Job done. Next my dad agreed to buy the tickets from the box office as he was working in London and I was panicking for days as I waited for him to come home with them. As always, he delivered. What to wear was the next problem. I finally went with a military-style shirt, tie and assorted badges to show my allegiance.

The day finally arrived and I had my tea at Matt's mum and dad's. We set off for London on a blistering hot day – excited, nervous and not at all sure what to expect. Outside Charing Cross Station, we bumped into a group of lads who were dressed to impress and they put us both to shame. They pointed out the venue and we both knew from that day on we would need to work harder on 'the look'. Once inside the venue we tried to work out where to stand for the first support band, Jab Jab. We were on the stairs.

For the second, The Jolt, I think we were in the middle and as we prepared for The Jam we had a good spot left of centre, closest to Paul. The rest of the gig is a blur – I started bouncing from the moment they hit the stage. Matt did not believe I would be able to keep it up for all the gig and he was right. It was loud, I was sweating and it passed in a flash. Time for a cliché but it really changed my life. We wandered wide-eyed outside with our ears ringing and there was my dad in his Ford Capri waiting to take us home, proper rock and roll.

POLYDOR STUDIOS
29 JUNE 1978, LONDON, UK

The Jam arrive to record demos for what will become **All Mod Cons.**

I WAS THERE: BRUCE FOXTON
All Mod Cons was a crucial turning point for us, and in terms of with the record company it was 'make or break' really. If they didn't rate that or the sales weren't very good, we'd have been out on our ear.

I WAS THERE: DEN DAVIS, OFFICIAL ARCHIVIST FOR THE JAM
There's a picture of me from the summer of '78, aged eleven, wearing my first Jam t-shirt. My brother was 16 and had got into going into Manchester with his mates, and the whole punk thing had taken off. He got into The Jam, and once *All Mod Cons* came out, I couldn't wait for him to go out as I'd be playing it to death in our bedroom in Stockport.

Den Davis with Paul & Nicky Weller, *About The Young Idea* exhibition, Liverpool, 2016

Den Davis with Bruce Foxton in The Jam days

CIVIC HALL
30 JULY 1978, GUILDFORD, UK

I WAS THERE: KEITH WELHAM
They were supported by Pinpoint and Squire.

I WAS THERE: MARTIN WATSON
We were at the bar while the support band played… and so were Paul, Bruce and Rick, getting a lager in before playing.

I WAS THERE: DAVID WEST, AGE 18
I was right at the front. My ears had just about stopped ringing when I started my first job with London Underground eight days later! After that concert, Sham

69's Jimmy Pursey came out to where we were all waiting for autographs and said, 'You're all friends of Paul Weller, aren't you?' before leading us all into their dressing room. I got autographs from each of them on my concert ticket, which I still have.

Later, I had conversations with Rick Buckler at a Rich Kids gig at the Civic Hall, Bruce Foxton in Guildford High Street, and memorably Paul Weller in Woolworth's in Victoria the day 'Down In The Tube Station At Midnight' entered the UK singles chart. He told me at midday it was entering the charts at No. 15. They came out at 1pm, so I know it was a Tuesday.

I'd been a fan since hearing 'In The City' in 1977. That Civic Hall show was the first time I saw them live, and that was my first single. I was with other members of my band, The Last Resort, namely Ian Smith and Jon Law, plus his sister Katy. I lived in Park Barn, Guildford, so went there on the bus. I saw them live again at Wembley Arena in 1982 after they announced the split. I was devastated.

I WAS THERE: MIKE O'SHEA

I grew up on a diet of Northern Soul. Me and my best mate Donkey (Dave) went to Wigan Casino the year before it closed. I was 15 and Donkey was 16, but I suppose we both looked older. One night I was at his house, in late '76 or early '77, chucking records on his record player, when he played a Jam single. I can't remember which, but immediately I fell in love with the sound. That was the start of everything 'The Jam', and eventually Paul Weller solo. I had 'The Jam – English Rose' tattooed on my right forearm. From that day I bought everything they did.

At the time, living in Newcastle-under-Lyme, I lived for music and would go anywhere in Stoke-on-Trent to watch bands, particularly of an indie nature. Neither of us were punks – we were more rude boys, dressing in Harrington jackets, tight jeans, t-shirts and trainers. I had my haircut like Bruce Foxton. I was massively into him, more than Weller.

Donkey and I would go anywhere to watch good music. We saw The Clash at least 12 times, Stiff Little Fingers more times than I remember, and loads of others. Two Jam gigs come to mind, though. In 1978, at the tender age of 17, I hitchhiked on my own all the way to Guildford, without a penny to my name and without a ticket, to see if I could get in on the guest list. I set off first thing in the morning (never, ever telling my parents what I was doing or where I was going), getting there early afternoon.

At the time there were two rear doors to Guildford Civic, one of which was packed with fans. I went and stood at the other, along with a handful of other hopeful fans,

SOLID BOND IN YOUR HEART

standing there for what seemed ages. Suddenly there was a noise from the other door, fans starting to cheer and the others I was standing with ran off. I stayed where I was. There was a bouncer on the door, a young black guy wearing a blue capped-sleeve t-shirt, very muscular. He asked what I was doing there – I told him I'd hitchhiked all the way from Stoke with no money or a ticket. I rolled my sleeve up and showed him my tattoo. He said I must be nuts, then walked off. I watched him come back around the corner a few minutes later, checking to see how many people were at the door, and he then beckoned Paul Weller to come over. I was absolutely gobsmacked.

The bouncer opened the door a little and Paul said 'show me your tattoo' which I promptly did. He invited me in. I walked behind him into a room and there was Rick Buckler tuning a drum, Bruce playing quietly in the corner, John Weller, and some roadies. Paul only spoke to me for a few minutes, giving me a small can of Harp lager and a sandwich. He gave me a ticket and told me I could go in and watch the soundcheck and to enjoy the gig that night. It was brilliant, and something I'll never forget. I hitchhiked back to Newcastle afterwards, arriving home around five the next morning.

I also recall when Donkey and I read that The Jam were to play the Rainbow Theatre. We sent off for and were surprised to get tickets for the gig. Again, we hitchhiked to London from Newcastle-under-Lyme, which was easy back then, setting off early doors and arriving mid-afternoon. I popped in to see distant family in Fulham and then headed over to Finsbury Park on the Tube. We were up in the gods, the only tickets we could afford, and watched skinheads kick off in the front stalls, fighting amongst themselves and smashing seats up. In the end Weller told them to pack it in or they'd walk off. Thankfully it all calmed down a bit.

They played a brilliant set, including quite a few tracks from *Setting Sons*, such as 'Thick As Thieves' and 'Private Hell', and my all-time favourite Jam track, 'When You're Young'. They closed with 'Tube Station', coming back for an encore. We sang along to everything, dancing on the spot as much as we could. After the gig it was still a bit tasty outside the Rainbow; we hung around half an hour or so, taking it in, then had to head to Hendon to try and hitch home.

In total, I think I saw The Jam 26 times, including Stoke, Deeside Leisure Centre, Loch Lomond, Carlisle, Stafford's Bingley Hall, Brighton, the Michael Sobell Sports Centre and Leicester's De Montfort Hall. I never got to see them abroad, sadly. I then saw The Style Council a dozen times and Weller as a solo artist I've seen stacks of times. I'm 62 now and own loads of Jam, Style Council and Weller records, playing them regularly. I look back and think of 17-year-old me hitching to Guildford without a penny and no ticket. It seems crazy, but it was a massive adventure, and I got to see the band I loved.

TOWN HALL
31 JULY 1978, TORQUAY, UK

Ahead of a headlining slot at Reading Festival and the release of their next single, the band set off on a Seaside Tour, taking in Guildford (more than 30 miles from the sea), Torquay, Plymouth, Bournemouth, and Swindon (nearly 50 miles from the sea).

FIESTA CLUB
1 AUGUST 1978, PLYMOUTH, UK

I WAS THERE: STEVE DOWNING, AGE 18

I saw them at Manchester Apollo, twice at Queen's Hall in Leeds and at Plymouth Fiesta, on their Reading Festival warm-up tour. I ran coaches to the Leeds gigs. Sheffield's Top Rank gigs sadly coincided with Sheffield United's home games, and the Blades came first so I only saw the back end of those shows. At the Plymouth gig, the stage was small. Afterwards, there was a meet and greet with the three of them. They were impressed we'd travelled 360 miles by train to see them, from South Yorkshire. It was a £35 return. Sadly, when they split, I couldn't get to any of the farewell tour dates.

REVOLVER
12 AUGUST 1978, BIRMINGHAM, UK

The Jam appear on ITV's short-lived Saturday late-night live music programme, fronted by Peter Cook, performing 'David Watts' and "A' Bomb In Wardour Street'.

'DAVID WATTS' RELEASED
18 AUGUST 1978

The band's fifth single, a double A-side with "A' Bomb In Wardour Street', reaches No. 25, spending eight weeks in the UK Top 40.

READING ROCK FESTIVAL
25 AUGUST 1978, READING, UK

I WAS THERE: PAOLO HEWITT

This Is The Modern World in no way built on the potential Paul had shown in the previous year. I recall going to see the band at Bracknell Sports Centre (2 December 1977) and it all felt a bit heavy going, a bit dour compared to previous shows I had seen. The tension that had infiltrated the band, due to poor record sales, was now showing on stage. Still, The Jam were given the Friday night headline slot at Reading Festival in August 1978, and at that show the band previewed some of their new album, *All Mod Cons*, songs such as 'Mr Clean' and 'Billy Hunt'. That's when I knew they were back on track.

I WAS THERE: PETER SMITH

The year punk finally arrived at this iconic festival, now officially the Reading Rock Festival, jazz dropped from the title and line-up, weekend tickets costing all of £8.95. Our old friend John Peel was compere, as always. A van load of us drove part of the way down from Newcastle on Thursday, going for a drink in Wetherby and sleeping on the racecourse.

Highlights for me were fellow Friday acts Penetration (I was a big fan, and it was great to see North-East punk heroes on that massive stage, despite a murky sound throughout) and Sham 69, plus Saturday's Status Quo and Patti Smith.

Friday's bill also included Dennis O'Brien, The Automatics and New Hearts (who later became Mods, changing their name to Secret Affair), while Radio Stars were good for a laugh and The Pirates rocked the place with no-nonsense rock 'n' roll (ace guitarist Mick Green being a big influence on Wilko Johnson), while the John Foxx version of Ultravox! played a moody, atmospheric electronic set.

The main event was Sham 69, Jimmy Pursey his usual cockney 'boy on the streets' self, with the anthems 'What Have We Got?', 'Borstal Breakout' and 'If The Kids Are United' impressing, the Sham Army out in force – all braces, No.2 cuts and DMs, ready to take on the hippies. We were right at the front but moved aside when the fights started. A bunch of skins climbed on stage, Pursey trying to call order, pleading with the crowd to stop fighting, to no avail. He was in tears, bedlam and violence around him, unable to do anything. It was the nature of a Sham gig at the time. He brought Steve Hillage on to show it was ok to mix with hippies, but that annoyed the skins more. It was a nasty, frightening experience marring an excellent performance.

Then came The Jam. They were great, Weller the edgy young mod getting in a strop at the poor sound, trashing his gear. A 30,000-crowd got behind them, singing along with the songs we knew and loved, particularly 'Down In The Tube Station At Midnight' and 'In The City'. They were sharp, sleek, punchy, and pure energy. The black-and-white of the suits, shirts and shoes contrasted well with the usual denim. It was fantastic, a revelation which blended punk with sixties Mod in the Modern World. Weller spat out the words with venom, anger and energy. A force to be reckoned with. Punk really had arrived at Reading.

A PEOPLE'S HISTORY OF THE JAM

I WAS THERE: STEVE PACKHAM

It was a blistering hot day. I'd been a fan since day one, but not managed to catch them live previously. Anticipation was high. Earlier, a succession of punk bands played, our band of teenage fans edging closer to the front until we reached the stage. There were no barriers and I touched Pauline Murray of Penetration's foot. Swoon! She gave me a look I saw as a 'come-on' but, in retrospect, was more 'get off my foot, you spotty virgin'! All was good until Sham 69 came on, hordes of skinheads appearing from nowhere, violently making their way to the front. It was a scary time and the security was non-existent. The skins dispersed after Sham, but we watched The Pirates' excellent set from further back just to be sure.

Then came the mighty Jam, the set almost entirely made up of numbers from the first two albums. A couple of new numbers were played though, and I recall being blown away by 'Down In The Tube Station At Midnight' after hearing it for the very first time. I read later that Paul Weller was irritated, maybe with the poor sound. But I didn't notice that at all. To me it was a dream come true. I just thought it part of an angry young man act!

Reading '78 was my inauguration to The Jam live, and six more outings followed. They remained a firm favourite and to me their consistency was matched by none.

I WAS THERE: JOHN WINSTANLEY, AGE 15

I arrived the night before to stay with best friend Robin Godwin, who lived in Cheltenham. Our mums agreed to allow us to go on a day-trip to the festival, on our own. I had no idea this had been set up and couldn't believe I'd see the band I'd been obsessed about for the last year. We went by train and walked from the station. Back then, this Jazz and Blues festival was on fields, with two stages. We didn't have tickets (£8.50 for the weekend, £3.50 per day). I bought a programme (70p) as it had a two-page spread on The Jam.

Having queued alongside the fencing on the right of the main site, we headed for the toilet, deciding to sit halfway back on the left of the sound tent. The weather was sunny and warm and stayed dry all day and night, Friday's bill getting underway with The Automatics (a kind of punk and new wave mishmash, comparable to the early Boomtown Rats), New Hearts (more like The Jam, dress-wise, but with a less threatening mid-sixties MOR set, singer Ian Page and guitarist David Cairns going on to form Secret Affair), Radio Stars (singer Andy Ellison crossing the stage via the rigging mid-set, whilst being pelted by cans) and Penetration (Pauline Murray the only female performer that day, bringing colour and charisma, despite the spraying of beer and spittle aimed at her).

SOLID BOND IN YOUR HEART

Sham 69 were the only band whose songs I knew. Their fans had a police escort from the train station. I recall the fencing at the right of the stage opening up and a flood of fans marching in. When 'Borstal Breakout' struck up, Rob and I went full pogo mode, fisting the air, shouting out the chorus loud as we could. That stirred up the crowd, a band that appealed to most of the kids I grew up with – uncomplicated, streetwise and anthemic.

Ultravox followed and I was impressed by how the stage was bathed in either deep red, green or blue as it got dark. They used synthesisers and made their guitars sound like nothing I'd heard before. I'd like to say how impressed I was with The Pirates, but I was impatient for their set to end as The Jam were next and we had a train to catch.

As they came on, a can was thrown at Weller, who dodged out of the way. He went straight to the microphone to declare why they were there. The stage was filled with white light that made them almost disappear in their pale grey suits. They played 17 songs, starting with 'In The City', the silver chrome dazzling as they ripped through the set, songs I knew every word to. I was elated and dazed by a realisation that I was actually there. I sang my lungs out but we had to leave halfway through to catch the last train to Cheltenham. As I reluctantly walked, I turned every few steps, 'Away From The Numbers' fading the further I got away from the numbers.

'DOWN IN THE TUBE STATION AT MIDNIGHT' RELEASED
13 OCTOBER 1978

The Jam's sixth single is released, going on to reach No.15 and spend six weeks in the UK Top 40, its cover shot photographed at Bond Street on the Central Line.

I WAS THERE: ADRIAN CORBETT

It always hits me, and it puts hairs on my neck up even talking about it, that line in 'Down in the Tube Station at Midnight': 'They took the keys, and she'll think it's me.' That's every man's fear, isn't it?

I WAS THERE: JACKIE DAVIES

I was 13 when I heard 'Down in the Tube Station'. I was hooked from then on. Sadly, I never saw them live. Not for the want of trying. I did meet Paul Weller at a Style Council gig though, and still have a huge jar of Jam badges. There must be at least 100. Great memories, great music and genius lyrics. I still listen to them, and always will.

EMPIRE THEATRE
1 NOVEMBER 1978, LIVERPOOL, UK

The 20-date Apocalypse *tour opens in Liverpool.*

I WAS THERE: BILL DAVIES

I saw them a few times, first at Liverpool Empire with Patrik Fitzgerald and US punk stars The Dickies supporting. They were always brilliant live. They were such accomplished musicians.

I WAS THERE: JOHN CONNOR

My first Jam concert was at Liverpool Empire, where we waited at the stage door to meet the band. A lad I was mates with (Alan Murphy) had his white shirt signed by the band. I wonder if he still has it? The concert was amazing. Weller split his pants jumping with the guitar and had to go off. They were showcasing *All Mod Cons* and the setlist was great. For the final encore they played "A' Bomb' and set off a pyro. Dust and plaster fell from the ceiling, covering the crowd. Hilarious. Great band, great concert. Pity they'll never reform.

I WAS THERE: IAN PROWSE, AGE 14

Say what you like 'cause I don't care
I know where I am and going to
It's somewhere I won't preview
Don't have to explain myself to you
I don't give two fucks about your review

A Wednesday night in Liverpool, November 1978. I was 14. Paul Weller walked on to the Empire stage, pencil thin, sharp black suit, black shirt, bright green tie, Jam shoes. He plugged in his bright red flashing Rickenbacker blade, slashed at it a few times and bellowed into the microphone: 'Seen you before, I know your sort, you think the world awaits your every breath.' That was that. All was changed utterly in that instant. It's never been unchanged. Whatever alchemy took place within my teenage self at that very moment, it hit hard, so deeply and with such force it's still the artistic fuel I'm running on 38 years later.

My first ever gig was The Jam and like your first match, when you emerge from the stand and see the green pitch for the first time, your first concert never leaves you. It's outside all your previous experiences. The noise, the lights, the massive PA (Muscle Music!), the theatre of it all.

But it wasn't just the Jam gigs that affected me so profoundly. (I attended another

SOLID BOND IN YOUR HEART

five Jam concerts, including the infamous blood bath that was the first Deeside Leisure Centre show.) It was the songs, and in particular Paul Weller's words. He was singing about me and my world. Working class, council estate kid, parochial, resentful, in awe of the nearby big city, but most of all, teenage. My overriding memory was how teenage they were. I don't recall any old people (and I mean over 23). It really was all about the kids.

This Is The Modern World was my first album, the lyrics at the top of this piece my Road to Damascus moment, listening

Ian Prowse experienced The Jam at the Liverpool Empire

to it on my terrible little cassette recorder. By the time he sings the expletives with such rage, such venom, I was a goner. If the Liverpool Empire gig made me want to be in a band, the songs themselves were like missives from the one who understood us, our leader.

I was too young and uncool to realise much of this era Jam was appropriated from The Clash. That all became irrelevant two days after the Empire gig, as they released *All Mod Cons*. A masterpiece. The backwards guitar coda to 'In The Crowd' can still reduce me to tears, 'Down In The Tube Station At Midnight' remains the bench mark for all lyric writers, 'Mr Clean' still does punk anger better than punk did, and it's the best song ever written by anybody about class war. They still copied The Clash, but this time brilliantly on "'A' Bomb In Wardour Street'. Weller also did the unthinkable and included acoustic love songs, 'English Rose' and 'Fly'. Good God, he knew our working-class angst was complicated by feelings for girls too!

He was 20. Bastard.

With the next LP they had a genuine hit with 'The Eton Rifles' and became massive. I kind of got off the bus then. I couldn't stand all the nerds getting into my band, but privately loved them as much as ever, buying every single thing they put out. I love that they will never get back together, love that he split them up when he did, at the very height of their fame and power. I love the righteousness of it all, his clear reasoning, brimming still with conviction. So brave. They were our Beatles. Thank God they never became our Rolling Stones.

I followed Paul intently through The Style Council's oft-wonderful output and got to meet him a few times via our A&R guy in the early nineties, when my band, Pele, got signed. He was just getting his solo thing going, playing us 'Sunflower' at deafening volume in Nomis studios. What a joy. I also got to play 'Mr Clean' with Foxton in the Cavern, rehearsing for a big Arena Jam tribute night. Unfortunately, that was a dispiriting encounter.

If it wasn't for the band, I doubt I'd have picked up the guitar. I definitely wouldn't sing like my life depends upon it. Thank you, The Jam.

DE MONTFORT HALL
2 NOVEMBER 1978, LEICESTER, UK

I WAS THERE: DICK JONES

The set mainly consisted of *All Mod Cons* tracks, but they did 'In The City' and 'Away From The Numbers', both of which I love. They also played the 'Batman Theme'. I recall blinding lights at the end of "A' Bomb In Wardour Street'. A truly great gig. The backdrop was a curtain with The Jam's logo on it. Very minimalistic compared to nowadays!

I WAS THERE: TIM FILOR

I'd only seen two bands prior to this – 10cc in 1975 and The Stranglers in 1977. The Jam came on framed by a painting of a big tower block. I'd heard nothing like it before. They blew me away, the stuff from *All Mod Cons* leaving me breathless. I hadn't purchased or heard the album prior to the gig but storming versions of 'To Be Someone' and 'Mr Clean' left a lasting impression.

Halfway back, people were leaping about in front of us. I just stood there, stunned by the power. Choice cuts from *The Modern World* and *In The City* followed, plus most of the recent singles, leading up to the final number, "A' Bomb in Wardour Street', the backdrop lit up as it crashed to the end. We screamed for more and got it, though I can't remember what the encore was.

The next day I went Christmas shopping with my mum and dad to Peterborough. I rushed into Boots and got the album. It was straight on my music centre when I got home. It didn't disappoint. The only track I don't like isn't listed on the back, but I know lots of Jam fans love it. Even Mike Read, the DJ, played it a lot. I won't harp on any further about 'English Rose' but recall a critic in one of the music rags reckoning that LP was Weller's rewrite of *Revolver*. I want to know what track he thought was the new 'Yellow Submarine'!

ALL MOD CONS RELEASED
3 NOVEMBER 1978

The Jam release their third long player, **All Mod Cons.** *It reaches No. 6 in the UK album charts, spending five weeks in the Top 40.*

I WAS THERE: JOHN BRAMWELL, I AM KLOOT

From that moment on, (Weller) shunned being part of the new wave or punk thing and was actually despised for that – there was quite a lot of anti-Jam sentiment, because they weren't fitting in with all this art-house London feel and the Soho set. He was an isolationist too. And that's important.

I WAS THERE: MATTEO SEDAZZARI, AUTHOR

My brother gave me two things – The Jam, and a love of the Italian national team. By the time of the 1978 World Cup, discovering a love for Juventus the year before, I got into all that. I still get that tingle when the Azzurri come on and the national anthem plays. As for The Jam, I discovered them by accident. I knew of them but didn't know too much about them. Playing *All Mod Cons* for the first time was probably my most spiritual, pivotal moment when it comes to music. There were two sets of Jam fans – older ones, my brother's age, four years older than me, and 'puppy' Mods like us, still at school, asking for permission to go to gigs, having to go with an older person. Because you were with that older gang, you could have a fag. You wanted to look old. It was rebellion, like the more hedonistic things later on such as acid house and raving. But that wasn't as intelligent as the Mod thing. It was more about living it up.

I WAS THERE: DAVE VAUGHAN

My earliest memory of discovering The Jam came via one of my closest pals. Paul was always ahead of everyone else at school when it came to discovering exciting new music. He said I had to go around to his house because he had a newly acquired LP that was fantastic. It was *All Mod Cons*, and it was better than fantastic. It was from another world. I was in awe of the noise coming out of his speakers. I was 14 and my life was, for a small part, forever changed. I wasn't

Dave Vaughan (here in his army issue Parka) was captured by Paul Weller's poetry

really aware of Paul Weller's influences so I had never heard a guitar sounding like his Rickenbacker did. Backed by the magnificent rhythm of Foxton and Buckler, every track blew me away.

But what really captured my imagination was the poetry of Paul Weller. English was my favourite subject at school. I loved everything about it, but his use of the language was beyond anything I'd read at that time. I saved up my pocket money and as soon as I could afford my own copy, I went to Liverpool and eagerly snapped one up. To this day, it is still my all-time favourite album.

In June 2023, I attended a weekend in Woking, celebrating Paul Weller's days in The Jam. There was a playthrough of the full album and the sleeve designer of *All Mod Cons*, Bill Smith, was present, providing his memories of the recording. I was transported back to my friend Paul's bedroom and my first listen to that magical vinyl. By the time the album finished playing, I was choking back tears of joy and euphoria. My lifetime love affair with The Jam neatly bookended. 45 years and counting.

HMV ENFIELD
NOVEMBER 1978, NORTH LONDON, UK

I WAS THERE: KEVIN ACOTT

I was never a Mod. Too awkward, too uncertain, too utterly lacking in cool or style, too scared of my own shadow. But I bloody loved The Jam. I remember thinking – and saying, and believing – in the late seventies, that Paul Weller was writing the songs I would write if I had whatever it was he had. The music – that first album and *All Mod Cons* particularly – made me feel alive, raw, real, certain, understood. And Weller sticking a Shelley quote on an album cover helped dig poetry – and politics – deep into the soil of the rest of my life.

When I say I wasn't a Mod, it wasn't through a lack of trying, particularly for those few months around the time of *All Mod Cons*. I bought a (terrible) Parka in Second Time Around. I tried to get my hair cut like Weller (ending up with something that made me look more like Buckler). I bunked off school and went down to the Royalty, Southgate to try and get a part (unsuccessfully) as an extra in *Quadrophenia*. I even sang 'Down In The Tube Station At Midnight' live on stage at The Pegasus, Stoke Newington, to what was almost certainly huge acclaim from adoring fans, though I don't really know – I was too drunk on rum and black and fantasies of the unattainable Linda turning up to be properly aware of my moment of glory.

There are those who would question whether Weller was a Mod, whether The Jam were really a Mod band. I don't know the answer. I suppose I'm still not sure what 'Mod' really means. I'm not sure how subversive, how modernist, how European, how expansive, how genuinely political it ever was, or is. I'm not sure it even matters. I do know it was – as a movement, as a series of moments – proud and pyrotechnic and glittering and embracing and good-looking and precious and exclusive and – sometimes – beautiful, and that it wrapped itself around some of the greatest black/white music ever made. And I know that, while I wasn't ever a Mod, however hard I tried, some of its pride and glitter spilt onto my ill-fitting two-tone suit, and some of it has stayed stuck to me, to my hands, in my heart.

Someone said the other day Weller was 'the man we all wanted to be', 'more of a man' than us. Maybe, yes. And, absolutely, no. I watch old clips and see why he enraptured us. I listen to the albums – particularly *All Mod Cons* – and see why I've spent half my adult life talking about him. And through it all, I recognise the part of me that still wants to be him (at least the 20-year-old him). Yet... so much written and spoken about him is fantasy, so much avoids the darkness in us all, so much is hagiography, relying on weird, cartoony panegyrics. I'd never have complained about being seen as The Voice of a Generation, I remember thinking, but I'm sure now it must have felt emasculating, crushing, bewildering.

I envied Weller, but he wasn't a bloody saint. And he was, often, to English kids of our age, a projection, a screen, a mirror, like all heroes. He was, like us, a single-minded, selfish twat at times, full of righteous and unrighteous rage. He was a bully. He was romantic and charming and clever and an occasional genius and I once watched him be hugely, unnecessarily kind to a mate at a gig. He's still utterly unlike me (apart from the selfish twattiness and the charm, obviously), and we'd probably hate each other if we met: I can only play the driven, sure-of-himself, working-class hard man convincingly for about a second. That might be the point. I wonder if, without his slow-burning, finely-crafted public brand, without his songs, without his fame, without his myth, Weller could only actually play the driven, working-class hard man himself for a few seconds...

I can't be sure where I bought *All Mod Cons*. Chances are it was HMV, Enfield, where one of the 242 girls I fancied-but-could-never-bring-myself-to-talk-to worked. I remember where I bought *In The City* – in Guernsey, of all places, Woolworth's, St Peter Port. I was never quite the same. It opened me up to Weller and our music, revealed to me the chinks of light shining through the cracks in adolescence walls, and it meant that by the time of *All Mod Cons*, I was primed and ready to dive in. Oddly, I never actually bought the second album. It somehow passed me. I really must listen to it again.

Wen my youngest first listened to each of The Jam albums, I remember her saying,

'I suppose I never heard them chronologically, you just showed me the individual songs you liked, not the full albums in order. I'm jealous, honestly, that I didn't grow up with this in the same way you did.' I felt hugely guilty for a moment: what kind of father am I? And I began, oddly, to envy both her distance from it all and the thrill of discovery.

Listening to *All Mod Cons* again now, there's a gentleness and an Englishness that I know offered a way out – still offers a way out – for those of us with both pride in and hatred of our country. And there's a harshness and a rage that offered us – still does – reassurance that we're not on our own. It makes it clear that those who came before – Ray Davies, The Who, The Beatles, Nick Drake, Jacques Brel, Marvin, Stevie, Curtis, Sly, whoever – had said as much about who we were now and who we could be as the punks of our generation did, the punks who never quite got The Jam or Weller, who saw '76 as some kind of Year Zero.

So, *All Mod Cons*. The fuck-you rage of 'Mr Clean'. The paranoia of '"A" Bomb'. The nothing-like-any-other-song-everness of 'Down In The Tube Station'. The hippy sweetness and romance of 'Fly' and 'English Rose'. It's unique and derivative, political and personal, experimental and conservative, radical and careful, very masculine and very feminine. It's Weller and it's me. And it's one of the greatest albums ever made.

CITY HALL
4 NOVEMBER 1978, NEWCASTLE-UPON-TYNE, UK

I WAS THERE: STEVEN SCOTT

I was 14 when I first heard The Jam. Music was a big thing at school and two camps were forming, one for rock and a new breakaway camp for punk, which I was part of. I enjoyed guitar-based rock so the raw guitar of The Jam was particularly appealing. My first single was 'News Of The World', quite a heavy song with a driving riff and nice guitar solo. Soon after came the launch of *All Mod Cons* and a UK tour. We bought tickets for Newcastle City Hall, and I'm sure the album came out just before.

We were in the third row, but soon as The Jam came on everyone rushed to the front and I ended up in front of Bruce Foxton. In all the times I've been to the City Hall it was only for The Jam where everybody rushed down there. It was scary – quite a crush but also exhilarating. I was amazed to find I wasn't alone in knowing every word of every song. It was fantastic to join a mass chant, fists pumping and heads frantically nodding! I'd been to a few gigs but this took things to a new level.

SOLID BOND IN YOUR HEART

After this, it was The Jam all the way. I bought all the singles and albums, along with a Parka and Jam shoes. I started a scrapbook, where my ticket stubs are stored, and went to all their City Hall gigs. They were all great. I remember a Q&A session Weller did for a music magazine where his answer to 'best venue' was Newcastle City Hall. I liked a lot of other bands, especially The Clash, The Stranglers and Ramones, but The Jam were different, and with Weller you felt part of a like-minded, youth movement.

My worst experience? Loch Lomond, where skinheads there for Bad Manners started throwing cans when us Jam fans ran to the front. I got hit on the head with a full can and spent the set in the medical tent getting my head stitched. I also lost my mate and ended up spending the night sleeping in a hedge in someone's back garden. Happy days!

The only local Jam gig I didn't go to was Whitley Bay Ice Rink in 1982. I thought they'd lost their values by playing such a large, cavernous venue which had no atmosphere or intimacy. I think Weller realised the game was up too, as they split soon after.

I WAS THERE: KEN DENT

My mate Davey was into punk from the beginning and introduced me to The Jam. I struggled with *In The City* and *The Modern World*. But when *All Mod Cons* was released, Davey said 'come and have a listen to this.'

I went to see the *All Mod Cons* tour. It was only the second time I'd ever been to the City Hall. My dad had died in September '74, when I was only young. Mum loved Slim Whitman and my nan wrote to somebody explaining what had happened to my dad, and so we ended up going to see Slim Whitman there. The second time I was there was to see The Jam. I was just absolutely blown away by it – the noise, the smoke, the colour. I was up in the balcony but came downstairs for the encore and we got quite near the front. They were playing 'Batman' and there was this greeny-coloured smoke going across the stage. It was amazing.

APOLLO THEATRE
5 NOVEMBER 1978, GLASGOW, UK

I WAS THERE: BRIAN GIBBARD

I was 16 or 17 and the new punk scene changed everything for us. There was a lot of hype in the papers about The Jam and I couldn't wait to get hold of 'In The City'. From then, I was at my local record shop on the day of release for every Jam record.

We lived in Coatbridge, just outside Glasgow, so had to get home by train. The main thing I remember was us singing 'Down In The Tube Station At Midnight' as loudly as we could at Glasgow station, which is underground. A fantastic time to be alive. I will never forget those days.

SCENE & HEARD RECORDS
10 NOVEMBER 1978, BARNSLEY, UK

I WAS THERE: CRAIG EDWARDS

I was 15 or 16. I'd watched *Top Of The Pops* and it was really crap, with stuff like Showaddywaddy, Mud and Queen. And then punk came along and me and my mate started listening to the Clash, The Sex Pistols and all them bands. And then there was this other band called The Jam. I first went to see them with my best mate, Tim Helsley. I was still at school. Tim's brother was at Leeds University and he got the tickets and he took us to the Refectory to see them. The New Hearts were support.

It was our first gig and we were buzzing, like two little kids in the best toy shop in the world. The gig was full of students and a few Mods, and we ended up upstairs on the balcony, where we stood on a table. It's the best Jam gig I ever saw. It was all their early stuff, 'In The City' and all that, and they had the Jam logo on the backdrop behind them. I bought a t-shirt, which I've still got, and a tie.

My two bibles at that time were the *NME* and *Sounds*, and they kept saying 'these are a Mod revival band'. I started dressing like them, buying a two-tone suit and a Parka. I went and bought a pair of black-and-white shoes from a shop in Leeds on a Saturday morning and the woman said, 'Oh, that's the first pair we've sold. We've only just put them out.' I felt like $1 million in my Parka and my black-and-white shoes. I got a Vespa and a Lambretta and all sorts and I joined a scooter club.

It was the *All Mod Cons* tour when they came to this little record shop in Barnsley. One of my friends was going out with one of the girls who worked there, so we got in before everybody turned up. They had massive piles of records they were hoping to sell. The band arrived in a minibus and the front of the shop outside was mobbed. There must have been 1,000 kids outside. When they opened the doors, this little shop was absolutely rammed. There were kids pinching albums, giving them to the band to sign and then getting them back. I cadged a 'Tube Station' badge off Gill Price, Weller's girlfriend. When everybody left after a couple of hours, it was just the band, John Weller, the staff and us. John Weller said to us, 'Alright lads, are you coming tonight?' Because they were playing in Sheffield that evening. And we said, 'Well, we would but we've got no tickets.' He said, 'I'll put you on the guest list.'

We did have tickets actually, so come the evening me and my mate were queuing up outside and we had a smug look on our faces – 'ha-ha-ha, we've got free entry' – and we went up to the desk and said to the girl on the desk 'we're on the guest list' but she looked through the list and we weren't on it! We said, 'Oh shit, we'll have to use our tickets,' and we just turned to walk away when John Weller came out of the side door. We grabbed him, brought him over to the desk and he said, 'Yes, these two lads are on the guest list' and we got through that way. Lo and behold, Weller was talking to some kids with Parkas on and we got talking to him again and we asked him about Barnsley and he said 'it was phenomenal'. My mate went outside and sold our tickets.

I went to see them at the Queens Hall in Leeds a couple of times. It was just like an underground car park, the sound was absolutely crap and the crowd looked really small inside the place. The Vapors came on and they were booed off because nobody was bothered about them. When The Piranhas were support and played 'Tom Hark', it just exploded with everybody singing and jumping up and down.

We got to see The Jam a few other times. Once was at Sheffield University, and I saw them at the Top Rank in Sheffield on the *Trans Global Express* tour, when they had the two guys on saxophone and trumpet. We'd gone with our girlfriends, but they stayed at the back while me and my mate went down the front. We were lapping everything up.

I was a Jam club member and used to get things every now and again through the post. But it was quite hit and miss. You'd get something one month and then you'd get nowt for two or three months. I've got quite a few photos that Polydor did and which they gave out. And a lad at school did some photos as ten-by-eights, but I could only afford two or three because he was charging 50p each for them.

When Weller split the band up, I just fucked him off straight away. I'm only just coming back round to listening to his music now. I've met Bruce a few times, including at the Alternative Music Festival in Skegness in 2022. I'm a bit of a bugger for getting backstage and we were watching Bruce through the one-way glass. He couldn't see us but 30 of us could see him having a piss against the minibus. He laughed when we told him.

Since throwing my old punk gear away to buy a two-tone suit, it's always been The Jam for me. Den Davis said that some of my old t-shirts are worth a couple of hundred quid apiece. I've still got my original t-shirt with 'This Is The Modern World' on the front. It won't fit our dog now.

CITY POLYTECHNIC
10 NOVEMBER 1978, SHEFFIELD, UK

I WAS THERE: STEVE WHITE

Having seen The Jam at Reading Festival in August, I was a firm advocate of booking the band for Sheffield City Polytechnic, where I was a student and a member of the entertainments committee. Fulfilling my wish, my by then favourite group were booked for Friday 10 November on their *Apocalypse* UK tour at the Phoenix Building. I was responsible for creating and distributing flyers and posters for music events for that academic year and the highlight was creating one for The Jam, in a term that also saw gigs by Japan, Generation X, Hi-Tension, and The Shirts.

On the day of the concert, I finished my studies in the library early and made my way to the Phoenix Building for the soundcheck. I then went to the bar and found myself stood next to Paul Weller. We sat down and had a good chat about the band, how they fitted into the punk scene, and the impending gig. Before he returned to the rest of the band, I remembered I had a copy of my flyer, and he readily signed it.

The concert was a sell-out and a great success, the audience dancing and singing along to numbers such as 'All Mod Cons', 'Down In The Tube Station At Midnight', 'David Watts', and 'In The City'. I even managed to find some 'spare' tickets to get some of the travelling Jam fans from London into that sold-out gig.

I went on to see them at Manchester Apollo and on several occasions at the Top Rank, Sheffield, as well as The Style Council and Paul Weller solo over the years. Many years later I found the autographed flyer and had it framed as a reminder of a truly special evening.

UNIVERSITY OF LEEDS
12 NOVEMBER 1978, LEEDS, UK

I WAS THERE: GRAHAM WALKER, AGE 16

This was the first time I saw The Jam live. The price of the ticket was £1.70, and support was from Patrik Fitzgerald and The Dickies. I hadn't heard the latter but they delivered an explosive set, 100mph American punk songs. Excellent, going down a storm with a crowd of people in suits, Parkas, pyjamas and other punk outfits. Being 16 I couldn't get beer, so just had to soak up the atmosphere. The lights went out and on came Paul's dad, John. He introduced the band and they kicked off with 'All Mod Cons' followed by 'Mr Clean'. We were off.

I couldn't believe I was there watching them, or how good they were. Halfway through, someone spat at Paul. He stopped and there was silence, then he shouted something along the lines of 'fucking wanker – get the bastard out!' A small group responded by dragging the culprit out before the concert resumed. I loved every minute and didn't want it to end. We then had to get back to Castleford. It's fair to say I didn't want to get up for work that Monday morning, but it was well worth it. I went on to see them many times after that.

APOLLO THEATRE
13 NOVEMBER 1978, MANCHESTER, UK

I WAS THERE: MIKE LEA, DEPARTMENT S

My older brother walked in with *In The City* in May 1977. I'd just turned 13 and was intrigued by a cover which looked nothing like any of his Kiss, Rush or Deep Purple albums. He asked if I wanted it. That was it! I stuck it on the family turntable and was blown away, not just by the intensity and anger but great melodic songs which stood out over any of the other bands at the time. I was getting more interested in punk but wasn't really into the safety pin thing. On first listen, I also remember loving 'Away From The Numbers', confirmation that The Jam weren't just a thrashy punk band but had great melody in their songs. I couldn't wait to hear more.

A few months later I remember going down to Sifters Records in Didsbury and looking through the racks. Under 'J' was *This Is The Modern World*. The fact I'd just discovered them and now learned they had a second album out was like Christmas had come early! I picked up the album, paid my hard-earned £2.50 and raced home to play it.

I saw The Jam 13 times between 1978 and 1982. My brother saw them on their first nationwide tour in November 1977 at Manchester Apollo. I was too young so wasn't allowed to go, but saw them the following November on the *Apocalypse* tour at the same venue. Dad dropped me off outside, picking me up after.

The Jam coming to Manchester was always a big event, and I'd follow them to their hotel. I bumped into them a few times. Then there was a quick dash to the Apollo in the afternoon, where they always let fans into the soundcheck. These became like mini-Jam gigs.

I WAS THERE: JANET BLAIR, AGE 22

I don't think I'd been a fan for long. Before that I was focused mostly on soul and Tamla Motown. I was a student at Manchester Poly and lived in Didsbury, so didn't have to travel far. I was a local girl anyway, from Hyde. I went to see them with a Poly friend. I don't think I felt afraid at all, but it was very easy to get pushed around in the audience if you weren't careful. My favourite song? 'In The City'. I was just getting into punk and felt that was very punky. I recall we tried, half-heartedly, to dress a bit punky, in black with a few safety pins. I think it was my younger brothers who introduced me to their music. I carried on watching punk bands for a while, so I guess they influenced that. I was disappointed when Paul announced the split but accepted it as inevitable. But I made it to the Jam exhibition in London, and it was great to go back in time.

I WAS THERE: IAN EDMUNDSON

With my friend Colin Berry, I went into Manchester and HMV on Market Street, where The Jam were signing copies of their new album, *All Mod Cons*. It was packed out, about as many there as were going to be at the Apollo later. Bruce was unwell, but I got Rick and Paul's signatures and a photo of Paul signing albums. Asked if he'd smile, he gave a sort of sour grimace. He wasn't very talkative with anyone – the signing thing something he could have done without. But that's a hell of a lot of albums sold on the day. They were probably tired out

Paul Weller at an *All Mod Cons* promo event at HMV, Manchester, November '78.

after travelling from Leeds the previous evening. There was no time to ask questions – a disorganised heaving scrum in front of them – so I got my LP signed and got out of the way.

We went to back to our car, near the Piccadilly Hotel. A young chap walked up to us who turned out to be Patrik Fitzgerald, support act on the tour. In exchange for a lift to the Apollo we got his signature. He couldn't get us through the stage door.

That night The Jam started with an opening salvo of new songs from *All Mod Cons*, with 'To Be Someone' and 'Billy Hunt' exhilarating, hitting us right between the eyes with a Rickenbacker attack from Mr W, Bruce having defected to a more anonymous Fender Precision bass. The pace relaxed slightly as they delved into the previous album with 'In the Street, Today' before new songs 'It's Too Bad' and 'Mr. Clean' got a good airing, the latter scrappy but dramatic.

SOLID BOND IN YOUR HEART

Photos by Ian Edmundson

Then came a run of older songs: 'Away From The Numbers', 'Sounds From the Street', 'I Need You (For Someone)', 'The Modern World' really raising the roof. 'The Place I Love' and 'Down In The Tube Station At Midnight' picked up the pace. Bruce's highly inventive bass really shone. When you hear Paul's initial demos without bass, you realise exactly what he brought to the band, turning the songs into tuuunes!

The band cantered towards the end with 'Tonight At Noon', 'News Of The World', 'Here Comes The Weekend' and the dramatic "'A' Bomb In Wardour Street", returning for two encores, 'Standards', 'The Combine' and 'David Watts' followed by 'In The City', 'Bricks And Mortar' and 'Batman Theme'. I snuck my camera in!

ODEON THEATRE
14 NOVEMBER 1978, BIRMINGHAM, UK

I WAS THERE: ROD GILES
I went with a couple of mates from college when I was doing my apprenticeship. We were on the balcony, and it was so bouncy I thought it was going to collapse!

I WAS THERE: JONATHAN ROSE
It all started for me in 1977 with my brother, two years older, playing *In The City* on an upright JVC reel-to-reel tape recorder, part of my dad's fancy Sony stereo system with KEF speakers in our front room. (Dad only listened to classical music). I was 14. Prior to The Jam, I listened to The Beatles, Simon and Garfunkel, Bowie, The Sweet, glam rock and *Top Of The Pops* hits, tuning in to Radio 1 and recording the charts every Sunday. I owned a few singles too – Sweet, The Jackson 5, even Abba. But that day the first song I heard belting out of the front room was 'Art School'. I wasn't welcomed in by my precocious brother but hearing that absolutely blew my mind.

I listened to the other big tunes, 'In The City' and then the incredible 'Away From The Numbers' crashing out. I had to know from my brother who this was.

From that moment I liked many of the punk/new wave bands I heard Kid Jensen and John Peel play – The Boomtown Rats, The Damned, The Clash, Buzzcocks, Skids, The Undertones, The Stranglers… This was my musical initiation, and it was like ground zero. I was exactly the right age, 15, and in a city that was violent and decaying, Weller's lyrics instantly connected.

When *All Mod Cons* came out I bought it immediately, playing it repeatedly. I couldn't believe it was the same band. Much more melodic and polished, the sound was immaculate and the songs crisp. I was glued to *Top Of The Pops*, ecstatic when 'David Watts' and 'Tube Station' were on. I had a school friend also into The Jam, and he got us front row tickets for the Birmingham Odeon.

Just me and him and a few girls in my year liked punk and new wave, and more specifically The Jam. Others were into Queen, Whitesnake, Black Sabbath, AC/DC, Led Zeppelin, Rainbow... My friend sent poems to Paul Weller and had a couple published in one of the fanzines. He left school in '79 while I stayed on for sixth form, but he'd always pop in when a Jam single was released or with news of the latest tour and dates.

That first gig at the Odeon was incredible. I was all in black – mohair jumper knitted by my mum and drainpipe jeans, DMs… Not really appropriate attire for the amount of jumping up and down that took place and the heat generated by a testosterone-fuelled crowd. I remember Weller saying he could see people being beaten up in their seats as they played ''A' Bomb'. The Odeon had Wolverhampton-based Hell's Angels bouncers that liked a scrap and liked preventing people running down the front. The gig was electric, the noise from these three-piece gods incredible. Drenched in sweat, my ears buzzing and ringing, I came out on a high. Utter excitement.

I saw them again at the Odeon on the *Setting Sons* tour. Weller wore a brown khaki tunic that buttoned all the way up, with a round-neck, looking the part as always, especially singing 'Little Boy Soldiers'. I remember someone filming one of those gigs, but I've never seen any footage.

I was at Bingley Hall, Birmingham for the *Sound Affects* tour. I remember queuing outside this hangar-like building to get relatively near the front, where it was an all standing audience (unlike the Odeon). I remember the stage lights flashing green for 'Pretty Green'. It was like being in a football crowd, with the audience of predominantly teenage boys like myself bouncing throughout, singing 'You'll Never Walk Alone' and chanting 'we want The Jam!' ahead of the encore.

The next Bingley Hall gig the following year was definitely filmed, and I went by train to Stafford's Bingley Hall with the same friend. By 1981 I was a student in Sheffield, seeing them at the Top Rank, catching the soundcheck. Weller didn't speak much between songs, simply letting that incredible music do the talking.

Nothing comes close to seeing The Jam as a teenager. The raw energy, sound, electricity, angst and excitement in the air was never bettered, not even by football (and that from a lifelong football fanatic). Random highlights: 'Tube Station' from the *All Mod Cons* tour, ''A' Bomb' for the craziness that ensued; 'Little Boy Soldiers' on the *Setting Sons* tour; 'Ghosts' and 'Pretty Green' from Bingley Hall; the live versions of 'Strange Town', 'When You're Young' and 'The Butterfly Collector'. When I look back now, I wonder why I didn't follow them around, getting trains to Coventry, Derby, Wolverhampton, Nottingham...

I WAS THERE: JACKIE MCGEOUGH LEES

My first time was at the Odeon in New Street, Birmingham, 1978, then Bingley Hall in 1979 and 1980. As for The Gift and From The Jam, I've lost count. Brilliant – no one comes close. My boys, aged 20 and 41, come with me these days. It doesn't get better than that.

I WAS THERE: KEVIN SMITH, AGE 16

I first got into The Jam in 1977. My friend, Neil, lived a few doors away and his older brother, Anthony, was always buying records and let us listen to anything he thought we'd like. For me it was listening to the radio and trying to tape any song you liked, or *Top Of The Pops* on Thursdays, so to have a chance to listen to a complete album was a great way to listen to new music. Anthony had both LPs from 1977 and I remember Neil telling me to come and listen to *This Is The Modern World*.

In June '78 I left school and that September started an apprenticeship at Rover Group. At last, with a weekly wage, I was now able to buy myself *NME*, *Sounds* or *Record Mirror* on a Thursday. In one edition I read about the new album, *All Mod Cons*, and saw an advert for a tour. In October, 'Down In The Tube Station At Midnight' was released, one of the greatest songs ever recorded. Anthony and Neil got me a ticket for Birmingham Odeon. A seated venue, as it also operated as a cinema, I was in the circle, and although looking down on the action, it was the start of a journey following Paul Weller and his music.

SPORTS HALL, UNIVERSITY OF KENT
23 NOVEMBER 1978, CANTERBURY, UK

I WAS THERE: CHRIS PRITCHETT

The Jam were one of the top three punk/new wave bands for me, Shawn, Ginger and Phil, our group of mates. I saw them in 1977 at Canterbury Odeon, then the following year at Kent Uni Sports Hall, the latter made more memorable as Paul Weller asked if I was 'alright mate' as we passed in the gents. It made my day. The gig was really good too.

I saw them again in late 1979, again at the Sports Hall, and you could tell they were mellowing into the more soulful stuff. There were a lot of kids in Parkas and

Mod gear. I loved all their albums up to *Sound Affects*, which I was a bit disappointed by. The Jam still sound great.

GUILDHALL
24 NOVEMBER 1978, PORTSMOUTH, UK

I WAS THERE: ANDREW GENT
My first gig, on the *All Mod Cons* tour, with The Dickies as support. It was The Vapors as support back at the Guildhall on the *Setting Sons* tour the following year. I wish I'd seen the last tour. I learned bass to their albums and singles.

I WAS THERE: ANDY STRICKLAND, THE LOFT
My mate Chris and I used to scan his older brother's *Melody Maker* for 'tour news', hoping every week to see a listing for a band we liked at the Guildhall – a short ferry hop from our Isle of Wight base. When we saw The Jam were playing, we sent off our postal order and stamped addressed envelope to the box office and then had the anxious wait. A few weeks later – bingo! – our envelope containing the little white tickets dropped through the letter box.

That Friday in the pub we triumphantly brandished our prized tickets, to the envy of the rest of our gang. An apprentice printer called Ray was in the pub that night, and he cast a professional eye over our treasure. 'I could easily print up half a dozen of those at work,' he said. 'Let me borrow one.' The deal was struck – we agreed to meet Ray in a week but were sceptical about him fulfilling his side of the deal. A week later, in the tap room at the pub, we crowded round as he produced a fat envelope with six pristine tickets and our slightly crumpled original. It was impossible to tell them apart. We were in – all of us.

That Friday November evening, we caught the ferry from Ryde Pier, went one stop on the train from the harbour and approached the Guildhall. A rumour was going around – they were checking for forged tickets. Had Ray been making a killing along the south coast? Such was the impact of this rumour that one of our party refused to go any further, turned on his heel and headed straight back to the harbour and home on the last ferry. Our sailing back to the Island would be the customary gig-goers 4am 'mail ferry' and a long walk home.

The gig? Oh, yes. We kept our heads down, picked the busiest door and breezed past the stewards. The Jam were amazing too. Ten years later, I recounted this story to Paul Weller in a bar in Brussels. He seemed impressed, and we chinked glasses. Cheers!

I WAS THERE: RUSSELL HASTINGS, FROM THE JAM

I was very much into music from oddly young – when I was four, I got my mum to buy 'Ob-La-Di, Ob-La-Da' from Timothy Whites in High Street, Bognor, when you were able to go in the booths and listen. And from five, six and seven I was recording *Top Of The Pops* on a little reel-to-reel recorder – pause,

From The Jam's Russell Hastings and Bruce Foxton in acoustic mode, with the original trio looking on.

play, record: Leo Sayer and all that. All of a sudden, a big rock fell out of the sky – *Never Mind The Bollocks* – and it changed my world. It put a stop to everything going on, one of the biggest political statements you could make without verbally saying anything.

My brother got me into the Pistols, The Stranglers and all that. I recall him coming home with *Never Mind The Bollocks* and *No More Heroes* coming out. It would have been 'In The City' I heard first by The Jam, seeing them on *Top Of The Pops*. I was also into John Peel. My brother got a Binatone for his birthday, one of those bedside clock radios. I had flu in '77 and was lying in bed listening to Peel. The lightning bolt for me came with *This Is The Modern World*, tracks like the title song and 'Life From A Window'…

I don't believe there's any such thing as a favourite or best album of anybody. It's all personal choice. People love to jump on a bandwagon, or criticise that album, but I listen to its delights and think it's a great album. 'I Need You', fantastic – one of the gems. If you've got three great songs on it, you've got a great LP. 'The Modern World', 'Here Comes The Weekend', 'Tonight At Noon'… all great tracks.

It was still the black and white suits then. The jury went out on their career around then, a lot of early *All Mod Cons* demos thrown out, (the label) saying, 'Unless you can fucking come up with something else…'. A lot of it was because Paul was with Gill, having troubles with his relationship, not wanting to be in the studio, wanting to go home. They were drinking a lot, and there were a lot of rows. They'd come up with a great idea, but Bruce and Rick would be left to work on it overnight while Paul was at

SOLID BOND IN YOUR HEART

home. They'd do so much, then Paul would lay a vocal on it.

Paul understood the working man, and could put that into lyrics you could relate to, and for somebody so young… all put together very close to where we rehearse now and where Bruce grew up, near Monument Way.

The Modern World album did it for me, then made me reflect on *In The City*. Later, Rick told me about that fight between Paul and Sid Vicious (which took place in October 1977). He was there. That's what the row was about – the Pistols nicked that 'Holidays In The Sun' riff from 'In The City'. He said they tried to squeeze in front of Paul, pull his legs out, and Vicious tried to walk past him. That's when he hit him with a bottle. All folklore, but I got it from the horse's mouth!

I first saw The Jam at Portsmouth Guildhall three weeks after the release of *All Mod Cons*. Listening to tracks like 'To Be Someone', I hadn't heard anything like that. It lit me up. Like my first drink, it changed the world for me. I can even smell the vinyl. I liked the 'Mr Clean' type songs but identified with all of it. That's why so many people loved it so much. I went the whole hog – It inspired me to read George Orwell, things like that. If it's good enough for Paul… He was a great schoolteacher, from a young age, switching you on like an older brother turns you on to something unbeknown to you.

I was 13 when I first saw them, surrounded by other twelve, 13 and 14-year-olds. I went with my brother, who'd only just got into going to gigs. It was the energy I remember most. If you only have one common denominator… the way the fans stormed on the stage, did what they did, then stormed off.

And what was magical was that you didn't see a picture of a band until you bought the *NME* or *Record Mirror*. There was no social media. You went to bed, put your head on the pillow and had this image. Then, next time you saw them, the hair was four or five inches longer, or shorter.

At Portsmouth Guildhall, when they did "'A' Bomb" they set off fucking pyrotechnics and nearly blew the place apart! All the crew knew it was coming, but it was a real explosion. I saw shockwaves from the front where they went off right the way down the venue, down the side of the walls. You wouldn't be able to get away with it now!

I remember them talking about the tour in America and all that on Radio 1, listening on medium wave through all the crackling. I don't think I've ever experienced anything of such a hit and a buzz. But it came and it went, and went back into a box. The event happened, there was no social media to report on it the next day. You didn't get to peep behind the magician's curtain.

Now I'm part of the magic show, whether it's down in New Zealand, Australia, wherever, seeing the painful part, the rabbit being put into the hat before it's pulled out. What I do for a living now sort of ruined that other side of it.

COLSTON HALL
26 NOVEMBER 1978, BRISTOL, UK

I WAS THERE: MATT BARKER, A BAND CALLED MALICE

Like most teenagers, I watched *Top Of The Pops* on Thursdays. Showaddywaddy, Gary Glitter, Gilbert O'Sullivan, The Rubettes… That seemed to be the norm, not particularly exciting for a young lad. It wasn't until I saw The Jam do 'All Around The World' that my eyes and ears pricked up.

The look, the aggression, the Rickenbackers, the music, the anger. This was the band I wanted to follow, saying things that meant something to me. Even though I had a middle-class situation, it was the idea that youth had a voice somehow, and we could express ourselves. My bedroom filled up with Jam posters, and I retraced the steps back to 'In The City', snapping that single up.

My mates were equally impressed. It was a subject we talked about a lot. Our clothing started to change. We wanted to imitate our heroes – Harrington jacket, two-tone suit, Fred Perry tops… It wasn't until '78 that I saw them live and it struck me that there were lots of people just like me and my mates following them. It was good in some ways that they touched so many people, but in another way we felt like sheep – everyone looking the same.

We had a band and copied their songs much as we were able, doing gigs in Bristol. We followed them through to '82. They were fantastic live events, full of aggression from the band, although I wasn't overly keen on the mosh pit, running into people and jumping about like an idiot was not my thing. When all the chairs got ripped up at the Rainbow in '79, that was pretty aggressive. I preferred to watch them play and recreate those songs I heard on vinyl.

The music got better and better. I loved the *Modern World* album despite its critics. They could do very little wrong in my eyes, the message through all the albums and singles was really strong and meaningful. Jumping forward to December '82 and one of the last gigs in London before they finished in Brighton was tough. It was confusing to see the band split – they still meant so much to us.

Memories live on though, and I now play in tribute act A Band Called Malice. We play all the songs and try to recreate the aggression of those gigs. It's fantastic to have people come up at the end and share memories, telling us how much we've taken them back to those years. The Jam period was a special time for me, a movement, a religion, a voice, and I know from our tribute gigs that many people feel the same. Despite only six years in the limelight, they left a lasting impression on so many. It was deeply emotional, a relationship. It's also one I still feel has relevance today in the lyrics and messages of the songs. They'll live on for some time yet.

GREAT BRITISH MUSIC FESTIVAL
29 NOVEMBER 1978, WEMBLEY, LONDON, UK

I WAS THERE: DON POWELL
That was a good gig. (Slade were sharing the bill, along with Generation X and The Pirates.) I was well impressed with The Jam again, and I could see how much they'd come on since that small club in Wolverhampton the year before. But I never got to speak to them. I don't really know what happened there! I believe there was a bit of trouble between Mods and skinheads, which was a shame. That reminded me of the early days with us and our skinhead following.

I WAS THERE: BRIAN YOUNG
I finally got the chance to see for myself what all the fuss was in relation to The Jam. The line-up was a real mish mash and Slade had attracted a large contingent of skinheads. Several scuffles broke out between the skins, punks and Mods and someone was stabbed. John Weller introduced the band, warning the audience to stop fighting or The Jam wouldn't play. Then The Jam came out and stormed through what was one of the angriest, most incendiary, live sets I'd ever seen. Paul Weller was almost seething with rage and Foxton and Buckler matched his furious pace beat for beat. To my surprise I recognised all the old songs and the new ones from *All Mod Cons* were every bit as impressive as my mate Dave, who'd been raving about the album, had insisted. 'Tube Station' in particular was much fiercer than on record and I made a mental note never to write The Jam off again.

LANCASTER UNIVERSITY
14 DECEMBER 1978, LANCASTER, UK

I WAS THERE: BARRY LUCAS, ENTS SEC
Another of the truly great bands thrown up by the punk revolution, like several others The Jam would have always broken through and established themselves as major stars. Punk just made it quicker and easier for them. They were touring extensively, and I had a date on the 1977 tour, which was a great show. I was talking to Paul Weller's dad, John, their manager, all afternoon and evening. He was a

tremendous guy. I don't know if he actually was from a market trader background, but he could easily have been a memorable character from *Only Fools And Horses* or *Minder*. He obviously wasn't sure how long this fame and accompanying fortune would last, but he was going to look after his lads and make it as profitable as possible for them. He was a diamond geezer, a terrific bloke, and we got on well.

In 1979 I noticed that the band were doing some dates. All were to be major venues and noticeably, for the first time, no university dates were in the schedule. I phoned their agent to request a date, only to be told, 'Sorry, the band are too big to play universities now. They wouldn't even consider a gig at Lancaster.' I asked him to phone John Weller and say, 'Barry Lucas at Lancaster University wants a date, he'll pay you cash on the night.' The agent rather snootily replied, 'I don't know what you're talking about. Waste of time. They won't play universities – too big. I'm not going to waste my time, it's too valuable.' But I was convinced I knew what would appeal to John Weller.

'Just make the call,' I insisted. I knew he would have to put the offer in front of the band's manager, because if he didn't and John was to find out, then he would most probably lose the band, and at that stage of their career that was not something he or his bosses would want to contemplate. About an hour later, instantaneous in music business terms, the agent called me back. 'I just don't understand it. We all agreed they wouldn't do any more colleges. They're too big. It would be a backward step and it could damage their careers… we had all agreed.'

'So what did he say?' I asked.

'He told me to ring you and fix the date. I just don't understand it…'. I remember smiling. I understood, and so would Del Boy.

The agent never forgave me for – in his eyes – making him look foolish. He tried for years to get his revenge, avoiding offering me bands. But by that time Lancaster was too important to need any agent's goodwill. Incidentally, after I left university, I opened a small rock music club, 350 capacity, but I mainly organised on behalf of promoters and good causes and city councils. One of these was on the Isle of Wight, just under the walls of Carisbrooke Castle. Headlining? Paul Weller.

THE MUSIC MACHINE
21 DECEMBER 1978, CAMDEN, LONDON, UK

I WAS THERE: TIM BOYLE, AGE 15
I was brought up on melodic, poppy sort of music by my mum and dad. The music that I found for myself was David Bowie. I remember getting *Diamond Dogs*

on cassette. My mate used to listen to Bowie all the time in his shed. I was 14 in 1977, so a bit too young to go to gigs and a bit too young to appreciate the different bands. I had my first gig experience in early 1978, when some of the teachers at my school organised a trip to Victoria Park in East London. The band that was headlining was The Clash. That was probably my first punky-type influence. The Clash sang with a bit of heart and a bit of energy, whereas some of the punk music was never that great because it wasn't that melodic.

Me and my mate then went along to try and get tickets to see The Clash, who were doing four nights at the Music Machine. It was sold out, but The Jam were playing. We had all heard of The Jam, but nobody was really jumping up and down about them because they were slightly different to the punk scene. But we phoned our mates and said, 'We can't get tickets to see The Clash. You fancy going to see The Jam?' The gig was in December so we got the tickets and we went along and the place was absolutely rammed.

I was 15 and it was such an experience. That was the *All Mod Cons* tour. My mate had *In The City* and *The Modern World* and we used to go round to his place and play the records.

When *All Mod Cons* came out, it was like a revelation. It was introducing Mod and I didn't know what Mod was, although I'd heard of Mods and rockers. On the album sleeve were all these references to scooters and Mod and the pictures and the art.

It was the whole package of this Jam thing. It was such a polished sound.

I remember 'Mr Clean' being introduced and Weller said 'this is about people who invested money in that film.' I didn't know what he was talking about, but as a song it was absolutely brilliant. I only found out recently that it was about the *Quadrophenia* film which came out in 1979. I remember him introducing 'Down In The Tube Station At Midnight', saying 'this is about some of our mates who got beaten up at Elephant and Castle'. This struck a chord because in the late seventies everything was tribal. You were in a pocket. You were in a community. You're with your friends, you're in your comfort zone and there were lots of different gangs, lots of different hostilities. If you went into a pub you weren't familiar with, you had to behave in a way that you didn't create any animosity between you and anyone else. Everyone had experienced getting beaten up. We weren't fighting people, but you don't run away. You defend yourself.

I WAS THERE: KEITH EGGLEDEN

I only got to see them once, somewhere in London. I recall Paul saying they almost cancelled because he had a sore throat prior, but that he had decided to tough it out as he didn't want to let anyone down. They stormed the place, sore throat or not! I got separated from my pals in the melee on the dancefloor that night, and whilst dancing I slipped over. Instead of helping me back up, a bunch of skinheads proceeded to give me a bit of a kicking whilst I tried to get back to my feet. I was battered and bruised but managed to eventually get away from the morons. It did spoil my night a bit, but I managed to have a great time!

I saw Paul once more, about 45 years later, in very different circumstances. My partner and me had tickets for the semi-final of *Strictly Come Dancing*, the year gymnast Louis Smith won it. Killing time in Westfield Shopping Centre, there was a bit of hubbub around us. I looked up and there was Paul Weller walking past with a couple of kids in tow!

I WAS THERE: RICHARD MUDD

The Music Machine (now KoKo) in Camden Town was a good venue, smaller than the Rainbow, with a standing area in front of the stage and a number of balconies where people could stand and see the band. To the right there was a VIP bar area and I got chatting to Shane MacGowan, who was in a band called The Nipple Erectors, or The Nips as they became. They supported The Jam on a number of occasions. The gig was another good one from the band.

I was with my pals outside after the gig when one produced a tour jacket with the Jam logo (the original one used for *In The City*) on it. I asked, 'Where the bloody hell did you get that from?' He'd nicked it from the VIP area. The jacket had the name 'Bear' written inside. 'Bear' was John Weller's nickname. I bought the jacket from my mate for £30, a fair amount of money in '79. The following year, under the guise of 'John's Boys', The Jam played The Marquee, most definitely a small venue for the band to be playing. I got prior notice because I knew The Chords, who were on the same label. A crowd of us made our way to Wardour Street but it was the worst kept secret I've ever known – Mods everywhere!

I wore my 'Bear' jacket, which gained me a bit of attention. As I approached the

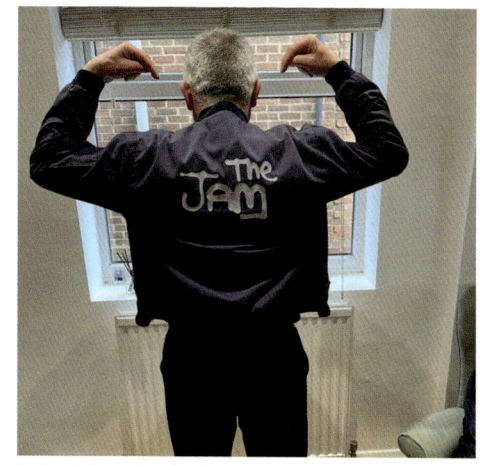

Richard Mudd with the jacket that might have been John Weller's

entrance, who should be standing outside but John Weller. He pointed directly at me and asked me to come to him. He wasn't particularly happy. 'Where did you get that from?' I stuttered, said I 'bought it from a bloke outside The Music Machine'. He said he had the jacket stolen from that gig. He looked at me and said, 'Go on, keep it.'

When John died some years later. I wrote to Nicky Weller, told her the story. I offered to return the jacket to the family. Unfortunately 'Bear', written in felt tip, had faded away. I sent the jacket to her via Black Barn Studios. Nicky thanked me but said it would have been too small for John, returning it. I know what I know, and that jacket was John Weller's. Tour jackets for road crews would always 'come up tight'.

The **NME** *dubs* **All Mod Cons** *the second-best LP of the year. The music paper's readers' poll, published early in January, sees The Jam voted the second-best group (behind The Clash), with* **All Mod Cons** *the top LP and 'Down In The Tube Station At Midnight' at No.4 in the singles poll. The latter also charts at No. 24 in John Peel's* **Festive Fifty** *on BBC Radio 1.*

UNIVERSITY OF READING
16 FEBRUARY 1979, READING, UK

I WAS THERE: DCJ, AGE 13
It's the only time I saw them, and I've never experienced anything more exciting, powerful or visceral. I was 13, lucky to get into a licensed premises, my older school friends looking the part in Mod gear. I just wore my grammar school jacket. Needs must! Beyond 15 or 16, I was never really interested in the whole Mod aesthetic. Jam conventions resembled scooter rallies and the like, and dreadful imitators like Secret Affair.

I see The Jam ideally as a post-punk phenomenon separate from all that, and I'm in a subsection of admirers looking back in mild disappointment that the group didn't follow a more experimental route sonically, hinted at by 'Funeral Pyre', the closing sections of 'Private Hell', 'The Eton Rifles', 'In The Crowd', 'Set The House Ablaze'… Weller and the group seemed to become more conservative musically. Their real peers should've been the likes of PiL. Which is not to say that Weller didn't write some beautiful songs late on. 'Carnation' comes to mind… and he's far more adventurous in old age, I'm always being told.

I WAS THERE: CATHIE STROVER
I was very much a West Coast pop girl – I liked The Eagles and gentle stuff. But in my first year at Reading University, I was hanging out and pogoing with a pseudo-punk

in the student discos who put me on to the Ramones and The Damned. I don't recall hearing The Jam much before year two, but I was in a common room with some art students who had a copy. Then my boyfriend bought the third album, *All Mod Cons*, and we got into that and *In The City*. *All Mod Cons* was the most amazing, powerful thing I'd ever heard. I went on to see The Jam four times. My second Jam gig was at the Rainbow, not long before it closed. It was such a beautiful venue, and they did 'Heatwave' at blistering speed for an encore. I don't think I've ever been happier than in that moment.

THE STAR CLUB
20 FEBRUARY 1979, HAMBURG, GERMANY
The Jam start an eight date European tour, taking in Germany, France and Belgium.

'STRANGE TOWN' RELEASED
9 MARCH 1979
The Jam's seventh single peaks at No.15 in the UK.

TOP OF THE POPS
15 MARCH 1979, LONDON UK
The Jam perform 'Strange Town' on **Top Of The Pops.**

KEN'S RECORDS
MARCH 1979, PUMP STREET, DERRY, UK

I WAS THERE: PAUL 'PJ' MCCARTNEY

'Strange Town' was the first Jam single I bought. I had some of the others that followed – 'The Eton Rifles', 'The Bitterest Pill', 'A Town Called Malice' and 'Beat Surrender'… yet never actually owned a studio album. I'm more a greatest hits fan. 'Strange Town' made connection with life in the North of Ireland at that point. We know this song describes a young vulnerable male alone in a big city, but I think what Paul Weller talks about here as well is the possibility of violence if the young lad turns the wrong corner:

You've got to move in a straight line
You've got to walk and talk in four-four time
You can't be weird in a strange town
You'll be betrayed by your accent and manners.

SOLID BOND IN YOUR HEART

In Derry at the time, it was so fragmented. I suppose Belfast too, areas divided in a sectarian way, so you were constantly wary of where you were going. If you were going to a strange place – one with which you weren't really familiar – there was always trepidation. I'd have been 14 or 15 in '79 and '80, and there was almost some plastic thing that went on, people saying, 'Oh, they're a retro band... they're Mod... they're sixties.' I didn't think that. I found the production on those records unreal. Still do. They sound amazing, when you hear the intros, the way the records were produced and arranged... Like The Clash, they were at the top of their game.

Problem was, it was that silly back then that, with The Jam having the Union flag and stuff like that, idiotic people would have made an issue of that. I'm quite sure if The Jam had come here at their peak, they'd have sold out the Ulster Hall three times over, and I know friends of mine were obsessional with them. When they broke up, as a 17-year-old I was totally bemused. I thought these guys could hack up sideways and have a No.1 song. They were peaking, selling out Wembley Arena several times over.

'Down In The Tube Station At Midnight' and 'That's Entertainment' transmit and consolidate that same heart-breaking sentiment as 'Strange Town'. I loved everything around then. Born in '65, I was buying records by around '73 – glam stuff, rubbish as well – and by '77, Darts and maybe Pickwick albums. But by '79 you had bands like The Specials coming through, the whole thing going widescreen. And while it was music that took influences from the past, that particular year was absolutely thrilling. The Jam, The Specials' debut LP, The Undertones' 'You Got My Number', Joy Division's 'Transmission'... All great.

REX DANFORTH THEATRE
10 APRIL 1979, TORONTO, CANADA

The band begin a nine-date North America tour, playing medium-sized theatres up to 3,000 capacity.

I WAS THERE: IVAR HAMILTON

A year after debuting at the Colonial, the band returned to play the Rex Danforth, a movie theatre before its short life as a concert venue, its capacity approximately 1,100. *All Mod Cons* had been released and radio station CFNY was all over that. You'd regularly hear 'To Be Someone', 'David Watts', 'English Rose', 'In The Crowd', "A' Bomb In Wardour Street' and 'Down In The Tube Station At Midnight'. This meant a much bigger, sell-out crowd that discovered the band through CFNY. It was magic! The opening act was the Dwight Twilley Band – an odd pairing with The Jam, but a treat for CFNY listeners, where Twilley's band also got regular airplay.

SHEFFIELD UNIVERSITY
4 & 5 MAY 1979, SHEFFIELD, UK

Another UK tour, initially badged as **The Jam 'Em In** *tour but renamed* **The Jam Pact** *tour, takes in 15 dates, all sold out weeks before, starting in Sheffield and ending on Paul Weller's 21st birthday at Portsmouth Guildhall.*

I WAS THERE: TRACY KING COOPER

I saw them live three times – in 1979 in Sheffield, then 1980 when I was 17 and in Leeds, where Paul Weller signed my t-shirt, when you could wait to see them at the end, and in 1982, for one of the last concerts at Wembley Arena. I was devastated when they split but have all the albums and singles and always went down Carnaby Street to get boating blazers and shoes. I still do, at 60. I love them, and I've continued to see Paul most years since.

I was into all punk and the Sex Pistols at that time, with 'In The City' a favourite. My all-time favourite is 'Thick As Thieves' from *Setting Sons*, but there are many more I love. They remain on my playlist to this day. I love it when Mr Weller does Jam songs live. He did 'Mr Clean' at The Octagon in 2021, and a few more.

CITY HALL
6 MAY 1979, NEWCASTLE-UPON-TYNE, UK

I WAS THERE: PETER SMITH

The Jam called at the City Hall three more times in 1979, in May then twice in December. Glorious occasions. Paul Weller was developing as a songwriter, the set changing all the time. My live favourites were 'David Watts', 'Billy Hunt', the wonderful 'Away From The Numbers', the singles, and 'Smithers-Jones', while 'Batman' still appeared now and then – always good fun.

The beautiful 'Butterfly Collector' was also part of the set by late 1979 and remains a favourite. Paul Weller was on fire at these gigs, spitting and snarling the vocals, Bruce Foxton bopping about alongside him, Rick Buckler smashing away at the back.

The programme for the spring tour has some smashing period adverts, inviting us to buy Jam shoes from Shelly's of London, which came in 'all colours', priced £12.99 plus £1 postage. You could also get Jam jackets in plain colours (£35) and Union Jack (£55) from Carnaby Cavern Ltd ('we supply The Jam, The Four Tops, so why not you?'), while a 'genuine American fishtail parka as worn in the '60s, US Army surplus, not new but in good condition' was 'only £12.50 from

ACME Clothing Co.' Wow! What a wardrobe. I wonder if I send my cheque off now if I can still buy these? They'd sure look great next time I go to a Who or Paul Weller concert.

I WAS THERE: DAVE PRATT

Me, Mike Tinkler, Steve Thompson and Derek Scott went to see The Jam at the City Hall, and were blown away. I'd bought their records since 1977, their most recent album *All Mod Cons* being probably my most played record. But it was the energy they produced live that made this band extra special. Tight as a duck's arse, performing catchy, powerful three-minute gems. They kicked off with 'Modern World', treating the audience to an absolutely stunning concert at full throttle throughout, Paul Weller running around the stage like a man possessed. By the time they split in 1982 I had seen them live at least 14 times, even travelling to Manchester on my own for two nights at the Apollo in 1980.

I WAS THERE: ANDREW CLARKE

Aged twelve in 1977, I got a cassette of *In The City* and played it to death, probably just to jump around to 'Batman'. But then I really got into the rest of the songs. 'Away From The Numbers' and 'I Got By In Time' are still two of my favourite Jam tracks.

 I loved *All Mod Cons* from the blast of the opening track. I was 14 and really got into the lyrics. I can visualise putting that album on and just playing it and playing it and playing it, and reading through the lyrics, the pictures, the schematic scooter. It was the most complete album I'd heard to date

 Setting Sons was another album with incredible songs like 'Thick As Thieves', 'Private Hell' and 'Burning Sky'. We were those 'Saturday's Kids', we went to the Lite a Bite, our girls worked those Saturday jobs and our parents smoked those Capstan non-filters. (Well, mine didn't but you know what I mean!) In the east end of Newcastle, where I grew up, they were bulldozing the old terraced flats. There was a constant trail of smoke as they burnt the old doors and window frames – it was our 'wasteland'. Kids we knew with no academic inclination went off to join the armed forces – they were the 'Little Boy Soldiers'.

 And as for Eton Rifles, I got it more than most. I was that dichotomy, at a private school but living in the urban sprawl. It felt like Weller lived around the corner. I'm sure that's how most Jam fans felt; he got us and we got him. He wrote about our everyday lives. He was so relatable.

 It still freaks me out to think that Weller had barely turned only 20 years old when he was writing these songs. Like many other Jam fans, I started to take on his politics, his references, his influences. I was introduced to George Orwell, CND, socialism, The Small Faces, The Action and The Yardbirds. I could see the Beatles influences – Lennon was still with us then. Some of us still are 'Thick As Thieves' 45 years on!

I had all the singles. I can remember going into town with a pal, Larry, and waiting outside HMV at nine o'clock to get 'Start!' and then us going back home on the bus, going to our respective houses and each playing both sides of the single to death.

Every Thursday night on the way home from school, I'd go to WH Smiths and religiously look through every copy of *Record Mirror*, *Sounds* and the *NME* and the girls' comics like *Jackie* and buy the ones that had anything about The Jam in them. My bedroom walls were a montage of newspaper cuttings.

City Hall in May 1979 was the first of 18 times I saw them. A Jam gig was an event. I used to sneak off school early, knowing the band would let you into soundchecks, taking pictures of them with an instamatic camera. The local ITV station, Tyne Tees, did a short documentary on them called 'Check It Out' on the *Sound Affects* tour. When they cut it together for the start of 'Pretty Green', there's me in Newcastle City Hall with my school uniform on. I'd nicked off school! In the same programme is Weller's famous 'it's like living in a goldfish bowl – like the kids up there' nodding to a window high up in the dressing room. That was three of my mates who were hanging around without tickets. The TV crew spotted them, asked them to go and bang on the windows and shout 'Paul!', which they did. The crew then let them into the gig!

Weller loves playing Newcastle and they'd always do two nights. I later saw two nights on the *Sound Affects* tour, two nights for *The Gift* and two nights at the Whitley Bay Ice Rink on the *Solid Bond* tour.

They hadn't toured in '81 so me and a pal, Tony, headed down to London on the overnight National Express bus and saw them at the Hammersmith Palais and the Michael Sobell Sports Centre in December. It cost like seven quid and took something like nine hours but we'd sleep on the bus, see the gigs and then come back.

Before the Michael Sobell Sports Centre gig, we were walking around outside. We were 16 and dressed like Paul Weller, with boating blazers, berets and Jam shoes. These three wacky-looking girls were walking towards us, sniggering at us, and we were thinking 'what's wrong with you?' We got into the show and watched the support band and out came these same girls that had taken the piss out of us a couple of hours earlier. It was Bananarama.

At Hammersmith we saw John Weller cutting across the back between the support bands. We went up to him and said, 'We've come all the way down from Newcastle. Any chance of meeting the band?' He said, 'I'm not going to point because everybody's looking but' – and he nodded – 'hang around on the balcony up there afterwards. Don't let them send you away and we'll see what we can do.' So we let the crowd go out and then we went to this balcony door. Half an hour after the show ended, out came the three of them. I stood and took a photo of Paul Weller from two feet away. I didn't think to give the camera to someone else and have them take a picture of me and him. I was too starstruck. I took the photos to Newcastle on the next tour and Bruce signed his and wanted to know where I'd taken it.

On the *Trans Global Express* tour, we returned to London (via train this time; we must have got our student grants) and saw them at Brixton Fair Deal and Alexandra Pavilion. They played 'Malice' and 'Precious' for the first time and I remember telling a pal later that it went something like 'the housewife clutches empty milk bottles to her chest and shops at the Co-op cos the prices are best'! Well, that's how I remembered it!

I saw the *Bucket and Spade* tour in Carlisle. We travelled across in the back of a battered old Transit, all our boating blazers hung up on the inside, and to Edinburgh and Glasgow on the *Gift* tour. I remember the build-up on the day, when The Jam were in town. There were these friendship groups you built up. I still see the same people at the Weller concerts now that I saw at the Jam concerts then.

When they did the *Solid Bond* tour, they played Whitley Bay for the first time. There was a lot of trouble at Jam gigs. People would trample down the seats trying to get to the front, and rows of seats would collapse and then everyone was on top of them. So I understand why they made the switch from the seated City Hall to the Ice Rink. But every year there'd been an album and then a tour, heavily promoting *Setting Sons* or *Sound Affects* or *The Gift*. But this was a retrospective greatest hits tour and perhaps they were playing this to unsuspecting audiences because they knew what was going to happen. They announced the split shortly after. It was a friend's dad who told me they were splitting up, and I thought 'what does he know about The Jam?' But he said, 'No, no, it's in the paper.' I couldn't believe it.

I got a ticket for the third night at Wembley, because the Wembley gigs were meant to be the final ones. I just remember feeling gutted that this was the last time I would ever see them ever. But the gigs had changed – it had become a bit like a football match, with the trouble. I can remember many a gig stopping because fights had broken out. And you had the people who were just there singing 'we are the Mods' and not really taking it in – they were like sheep.

When Weller brought the brass section in on the *Gift* album and doing songs like 'War' and 'Move On Up', you could see that soul influence that he carried on into The Style Council. Quitting at the very top is what has given them legendary status. I don't think them reforming would be a good idea, not even for a one-off, but I'd probably want to go.

I never saw The Style Council, they only played Newcastle once. But in 1991 I saw that the Paul Weller Movement were playing in Middlesbrough and me and my pal Larry jumped in the car and went down. I've seen Paul 64 times now, 18 with The Jam and 46 solo. His lyrics introduced me to politics and so, so much more. I know he hated being called the spokesman for a generation and all that, and he would play it down. But I think there's a whole generation of people, like me, who've got the belief system that they have because of The Jam. They weren't just a pop group. From 1979 to 1982 they were the most important band in England. In fact, they were a way of life!

UNIVERSITY OF SALFORD
8 MAY 1979, SALFORD, UK

I WAS THERE: MIKE LEA, DEPARTMENT S
On the *Jam Pact* tour in May 1979 at Salford Uni, Paul wasn't very happy with the sound. At the end he threw his Rickenbacker into his AC30 before storming off stage.

I was devastated when they split. However, looking back, by the time *The Gift* came out, along with 'Precious' and so on, there was a shift in direction that I wasn't so keen on. I bought the first singles and albums by The Style Council, and there are some great songs there, but like a lot of Jam fans I didn't really get it. But I got massively into The Vapors, who supported The Jam on the *Setting Sons* tour in 1979, and they became my favourite band.

I wasn't really into the political aspect, but I was turned on to other bands who had until then passed me by, like The Kinks. I made my dad buy one of their albums after hearing 'David Watts'. I also saw them live a couple of times. A great live band.

My younger brother had classical guitar lessons and taught me the rudiments of the bass, and I've always loved Bruce's style of playing. I went on to play in many bands and with Department S we supported The Jam in 1981. I listen to Paul Weller's solo stuff occasionally. There are very few British songwriters with the legacy he has and that drive to continue releasing new music. I've seen From

SOLID BOND IN YOUR HEART

Photos by Ian Edmundson

Salford University, 8 May 1979

The Jam a few times too, even with Rick in the band. Initially it was just great to hear those fantastic songs performed live again. And I like some of the Foxton and Hastings releases.

I've been listening to The Jam constantly for 40 years, and those songs sound as fresh to me now as when I was 16. My favourite LP is *Sound Affects*. As soon as that bassline to 'Pretty Green' (my mobile ringtone) kicks in, I'm back at the Apollo, enthralled by the spectacle of the best band in the fucking world!

I WAS THERE: IAN EDMUNDSON

This time they were supported by The Records, as fine a power pop band as you could get, promoting their ace album *Shades In Bed*. (I'd seen them on '78's *Be Stiff* tour in the same venue, playing a full set as Rachel Sweet – who they were meant to be backing – was unwell.) The Jam were promoting 'Strange Town'. *Setting Sons* was some way off and the set was not changed massively from the previous November. Not that we cared very much. Paul was still using Rickenbacker guitars, though I was intrigued to spot a custom-made Eccleshall Junior type guitar. Bruce was on Fender Precision throughout. Again, I snuck my camera in.

RAINBOW THEATRE
10 & 11 MAY 1979, FINSBURY PARK, LONDON, UK

I WAS THERE: TERRY DANIELS, AGE 14

My first gig. I was painfully dressed in a bright blue plastic jacket but my brother, two years older, insisted I attend. We were in the balcony, packed solid with hot, sweaty, teenage devotees. The lights dimmed, the announcement was made, and three men walked on to the stage. The euphoria was breathtaking. The first song was 'The Modern World', followed by 'Billy Hunt', the balcony bouncing up and down as hundreds of young Mods pogoed in front of their seats. Forget the safety regulations; this was a gig that would stay with me forever. The whole atmosphere took my breath away and from that instant I vowed to myself I wanted to be Paul Weller. I'm so privileged to have seen The Jam at their peak, and very grateful to have found their music at that stage. It's the most amazing gig I've ever experienced.

I WAS THERE: IAN CRABB

It started when I went to a friend's house one late afternoon for a game of Subbuteo. My parents made it clear I needed to be home on time. My friend's older brother arrived home with three albums – one by The Stranglers, another I can't remember, and *In The City*. The first two were played and I wasn't overly impressed.

I said I needed to be home, or else! But the brother was determined for me to listen to the final purchase, and thankfully I did: '1, 2, 3, 4…'. I went straight to Downtown Records in Basildon and purchased *In The City*, receiving the full wrath of my parents on finally arriving home.

That led to a desire to witness The Jam live, and my opportunity came on the *Jam Pact* tour. I was on the fourth row at the Rainbow and was informed that when the lights went down, John Weller would be centre stage to introduce them, which is when I was to make my way over three rows of chairs in front of me. This I managed, and for my troubles received many broken parts of chairs bouncing off my head. I went on to see The Jam nine more times, including the infamous Paris gig, and at Wembley had a crap seat in the gods opposite the stage, but the moment the lights went down I made it into the main arena and got right to the front.

Ian Crabb (left) went straight to the record shop to buy *In The City* after hearing it at a mate's house

The Jam also had a hand in helping me fall in love with the only other band I listened to. I recorded their Rainbow gig off the radio and lent it to a mate, who recorded in a gap at the end of the tape three tracks – 'Stairway to Heaven' by Led Zeppelin, 'Closer to the Heart' by Rush, and 'Bomber' by Motörhead. The latter made me feel exactly the same as I did after hearing 'Art School'. I'm 61 now, and still love both bands.

I WAS THERE: DEBBIE DAVIES
I saw them at the Rainbow Theatre on Seven Sisters Road in 1979. I'd just passed my driving test, so I could drive my clapped-out Ford Escort with hardly any brakes!

I WAS THERE: GARETH GORDON-WILKIN
The Jam are in my view in the top ten British bands of all time. For many people they were part of the 1977 punk rock explosion, though wearing Mod suits they did not look the part. Initially I was much more interested in The Stranglers, The Clash and several others, but heard 'Down In The Tube Station At Midnight'

and really started waking up to this fantastic band.

I first saw them live at the Rainbow, May 1979. They were brilliant. Myself and two mates on the way home on the Tube to Brixton couldn't believe how a trio could deliver so much power. I next saw them at the Rainbow 50th anniversary show in April 1980, around the time the masterpiece 'Going Underground' single was released. Again, they were fantastic. In December 1981, they played the Michael Sobell Centre, just down the road from the Rainbow, where The Exploited and several other punk bands were playing. After the gig, punks and Mods were having punch-ups all around the Tube station, with chants of 'bash a Mod!' from some punks.

Gareth Gordon-Wilkin thinks The Jam are in Britain's all-time top ten

The fourth and final time I saw them was at Wembley Arena on the farewell tour. Their set was again fantastic. I felt sad when the music stopped. I firmly believe The Jam had several very successful years in front of them, but it was Paul Weller's choice to split The Jam at their absolute peak on their terms, with a fantastic last song, 'Beat Surrender'. I remember The Style Council being bottled off at Brockwell Park in May 1983, one of their early gigs, the feeling of animosity towards Paul that he had finished The Jam still raw with many. Personally, I thought The Style Council were quite good.

The 2015 *About The Young Idea* exhibition was absolutely amazing. I was amazed how much stuff was on display – posters, gig flyers, stage suits, gig footage, etc. It really brought it home to me what a fantastic, really important band they were. I've heard many people say it would be great if they reformed, but in my view The Jam were very special and called it a day without drugs, chaos and unfinished business. They openly declared their end and said goodbye with a farewell tour. Like a quality wine…they got better and better as they got older.

I WAS THERE: COLIN CUNNINGHAM, AGE 14

My autumn years may be approaching, but at least this means I was old enough, just, to experience The Jam live. My first Jam gig was my first ever gig; and what a way to pop that particular cherry at the age of 14. The Jam were by this time the primary musical 'buzz' among my friends and at school, and my mate Phil saw them the previous November headlining the *Great British Music Festival* at Wembley. Seeing The Jam live became our highest priority, so as soon as the dates were announced for the *Jam Pact* tour, the plan was hatched; I was to go with my cousin John, Phil and another friend, Aiden. I don't remember how we all managed to acquire tickets, but we got them separately and by different means, leading to the first of many lies spun to our parents that we'd all sit together and stick to each other like glue. Except we were sat in completely different parts of a venue with an audience capacity of just under 3,000, a venue that – by the middle of 1979 – The Jam were already able to fill to capacity over two nights.

I lived a few Tube stops from Finsbury Park in Bounds Green, and was allowed to make my own way, dressed in makeshift 'Jam gear', basically my school uniform, with my brother Dave's old red Fred Perry and a pair of Dunlop Green Flash. I met up with my cousin and pals (as well as various other familiar faces from school) in the foyer, and we bought whatever merchandise our meagre pocket money would allow, arranging where to meet after the gig to prove to the 'Designated Dads' for lifts home we had indeed stuck together like glue. Then off we went to find our randomly allocated seats.

I must have got my ticket a bit later, as I was up in the circle, about eight rows from the front. I exchanged a few nods and 'alrights' with anyone in the vicinity who caught my eye, but mainly sat staring at the empty stage, nervous, incredibly excited, extremely self-conscious. The first proper band I saw live was The Chords, who opened, making my mind up there and then I had to become actively involved in the Mod revival I'd been reading about in the music papers that did the rounds at school. In the aftermath I set about becoming 'the most rubbish Mod in North London' and there are still a few photos around as evidence.

It was towards the end of the set by the second support, The Records, about whom I remember little or nothing, that my first gig experience took a very surreal turn. To my left were four empty seats, soon occupied by two much older couples, very smartly dressed and looking more like the sort of people who'd be seen dancing in our living room to one of Dad's James Last albums after a dinner party. Once they'd taken their seats, the chap next to me seemed to anticipate the question on my bemused face I hadn't actually asked: 'You alright, son?' 'Yes, err, thank you, I errr…' 'We're with the band.' 'Oh, you, errr, know them?'

At which point he indicated the lady to his right: 'We're Rick's parents.' A polite wave from Rick's mum, and an 'oh crikey' to self. Then, indicating further along the row: 'And this is Bruce's parents.' More polite waves, another 'oh crikey' and probably a 'holy fuck' or two to self.

Fortunately, before I had time to ask any stupid questions, or just gawp at them in silence, The Jam came on, at which point the adrenaline and general bemusement overload almost made me throw up the sensible, stomach-lining dinner Mum had fed me a few hours before. My instinct was to follow the youthful herd, get as far as I could to the front of the circle to jump around, and sing along to a set that was over in a happy, sweaty, youthful haze of joy, before I had really let it sink in that it had begun.

The band had just three albums and some excellent non-album singles under their belt, the emphasis mainly on most recent LP, *All Mod Cons*, but with plenty of gems from the first two. Among my highlights was a rousing 'Mr Clean' – where I got to yell, 'And if I get the chance, I'll fuck up your life!' in my adolescent squeak with a chorus of like-minded kids. The most recent single, 'Strange Town', and live staples 'Down In The Tube Station At Midnight' and "A' Bomb In Wardour Street' really stood out.

The entire set was still making my ears ring days later (most memorably the following day, when I could barely hear the commentary on the FA Cup Final or the cheers of my Arsenal-supporting mum). To put a little personal icing on the cake, they even played the 'Batman Theme' as part of the encore.

I didn't see my distinguished seat neighbours again, during or after, but distinctly remember Rick's dad saying, 'Careful how you go, boys,' as we rushed to get a better view. Perhaps someone who reads this will be able to tell me it can't possibly have been Bruce and Rick's parents, stating various trainspotter facts as proof, in which case I'll hold my hands up and admit to having fallen for some elaborate and outlandish hoax. This hasn't stopped me telling the story to anyone willing to listen for the subsequent 45 years.

I went on to see The Jam four more times, each a unique, unforgettable occasion. They really were an electrifying band to witness live. I was a very lucky boy indeed that my first gig was courtesy of one of the greatest and most important bands in rock history. Long live The Jam. Pow!

I WAS THERE: IAN TRAYNOR

Hearing 'In The City' on a transistor radio in the school playground in 1977 at 14 genuinely changed what I listened to and what music really meant. As time went on, I realised there was a message, but was too young or too daft to understand it then.

I was saving all my pocket money to buy the albums and singles that seemed to be coming out every few months. The Jam were the first live band I ever saw. Not a bad start. I recall begging my parents for £2.50 so I could see them at the Rainbow. Once I started work at 16, I was able to buy my own.

One of the May '79 gigs would have been the first. Then three, possibly four more. I lived in Tottenham and went to school in Enfield, attending St Ignatius College. Quite a few of us were Jam fans, but my best mate, Tony Sheen, was, like me, a huge fan. He'd have been with me at that first gig. Very likely some of the others too.

I've got at least a couple of ticket stubs from the Rainbow gigs. If we only knew how precious they would become! Oddly, I only ever used to see them there, only living a couple of miles away. I assumed they would be around forever so never bothered travelling to other far-flung corners of London!

I WAS THERE: PAUL DUNN

My mates and I saw The Jam twice. Now, I often wonder why we never roamed further and more often to see them many more times. We were 16 or 17 years old and had no jobs, so perhaps it was a lack of cash and not having the balls to simply jump on a train, wangle our way into gigs and sleep rough wherever afterwards, as many fans did.

Our first gig was part of the *Jam 'Em In* tour. Three of us got tickets from the Rainbow box office. The queue was right round the venue and down the road. It being our first Jam gig, we decided to give it large so got kitted out in black suits, white shirts, black ties and Jam shoes, bought from Shelly's original shop on Seven Sisters Road. A couple of weeks before, we got new haircuts from Ron's barber shop on West Green Road to match Weller and Buckler. I have no idea what Ron really thought when we presented the *All Mod Cons* album cover, telling him 'I want it like that'. He did his best and although those not in the know would not have a clue, as far as we were concerned when we stepped out of his barber shop, we had two Buckler crops and one Weller crop that looked the business – the innocence (or stupidity?) of youth.

Paul Dunn saw The Jam twice at the Rainbow

Gig night arrived and we jumped on the 259 bus for just six stops to Finsbury Park, sitting upstairs 'at the back of course' with a mixture of feeling cool and pre-gig excitement – we were at last going to see The Jam live! I wore a cheap pair of Rick Buckler small shades to really set off the image. Sure enough, the way we looked ensured we got some interesting double takes on the bus and along the street. But once in the foyer of the Rainbow, there were so many new wavers, punks, Parkas, two tone jackets and suits, Jam shoes, etc. that it felt like we were at home.

There was an electric buzz around the place. Everyone had a common reason to be there – The Jam – yet was looking at each other with serious interest. Perhaps that 'interest' was a combination of checking out the clothing styles and trying to suss out where any potential trouble could come from. That all became the normal recipe for Jam gigs – paying homage to our heroes, to fashion styles and to potential violent flare ups!

The gig seemed to be over in a flash. We stood in the left lower circle and couldn't get down to floor level. They played most of the *All Mod Cons* album, various tracks from *Modern World*, most of the singles to date, including the most recent, 'Strange Town'.

The second and final time I saw The Jam was in December 1979 as part of the *Setting Sons* Tour, again at the Rainbow. After joining the queue (which we timed right this time as it was not so long) and getting tickets, a couple of us agreed to come early on the day of the gig to see if we could spot our heroes. We wandered around the back to the stage and equipment doors. There were two large lorries, seemingly having finished unloading, and a couple of fans were milling around. But nothing was happening, so after half an hour we gave up. Would we have got a chance to see a soundcheck if we'd stayed longer…?

Gone were the black and white suits, now replaced with two tone jackets, Sta-Prest trousers and Ben Shermans from second hand shops. Jam shoes were still the order of the day – I had no cash for loafers back then. My small Buckler glasses also made another guest appearance! This time we stood in the upper circle, which was a great view of the whole stage but lacked the buzz and jostling of the mosh pit – a sea of rough moving disciples paying homage to The Jam with a frenzy.

This time there were lots of new *Setting Sons* tracks played along with previous *Mod Cons*, plus recent singles 'When You're Young' and 'The Eton Rifles', the latter almost raising the roof. My ears were buzzing for a couple of days afterwards. Another great gig.

I WAS THERE: BARRY O'HAGAN, AGE 14

Five of us from the same class at Finchley High School attended this gig. Our hip young geography teacher was also in attendance, making it quite a turnout for one school. It was also quite a momentous period in time. Margaret Thatcher had come to power just days previously, and the gig was sandwiched between this and the up-and-coming FA Cup Final on the Saturday between a team a few hundred yards up St Thomas's Road from the Rainbow, against Manchester United two days later. 3-2 to The Arsenal.

It was my first time at the venue, the first indoor gig I'd attended. (My first was at the Rock Against Racism demo the previous year where The Clash made an appearance on the bill alongside X-Ray Spex and the Tom Robinson Band at Victoria Park.) It was also a venue that was to become a favourite as it was local to me and where I attended one of the last concerts there a few weeks shy of 1982 before it closed its doors for good.

We gathered on the left-hand side of the venue. The Rainbow had a passageway running around the back of the stalls and we plotted up there. Then we took up our seats before John Weller announced the band's arrival onstage, inviting the audience to come down the front of the stage. Which we did, of course.

Beyond that it's a blur. I was probably in a state of awe as Paul Weller was a few yards in front of me. I was 14 and in a sea of Parkas, testosterone and shouted lyrics. That was the only time I saw them.

My brother offered me a chance to see them on the *Setting Sons* tour later that year at the same venue but I'd joined a different musical tribe by then so I turned it down. But things move fast when you're young and Weller was spot on:

Life is timeless, days are long
When you're young
You used to fall in love with everyone
Any guitar and any bass drum

GREAT HALL, UNIVERSITY OF EXETER
14 MAY 1979, EXETER, UK

I WAS THERE: JON FLYNN, AGE 15
I am blessed that I saw The Jam four times. I've been to loads of gigs and seen some impressive artists, but none came remotely close to any Jam gig I saw. There was something really special, the bond between fans and band like no other in my experience. As we gathered en masse before a gig, there was an atmosphere that reminded me of going to a football match and being among fellow supporters. It was tribal, with passion that evoked extraordinary amounts of adrenaline. You had to be

on your toes – an underlying threat of violence often smouldered, but at the same time you felt you were among comrades and we were an unrivalled collective.

I was at school one Monday morning when a mate announced he had bought a ticket for the *Jam Pact* tour plus a spare. 'Anyone want it?' I snapped it up, spending my entire week's dinner money. The seller made a nice profit, some of my mates thinking I was mad, but I knew the chances of getting a ticket any other way was remote as I lived out in the sticks of mid-Devon. They could be sold out by the time I managed to get to Exeter that weekend.

On the night, excitement levels were out of the stratosphere. I lived in a village about 25 miles from Exeter, so my dear dad agreed to give me a lift. About midway, we picked up some mates in Crediton, where we went to school. I was still in my punk phase (it took a long time to seep into rural Devon!) and was wearing green combat trousers, ox-blood Doc Marten's and a red t-shirt I'd written 'The Jam' on with a permanent marker, *In The City* logo-style. My mates were dressed in their own version of punk, my dad glancing around at us all.

'Do the band wear that sort of clobber as well?' he asked. 'No dad – they wear suits,' I replied. 'Oh… like Bryan Ferry?' 'Um… not really, Dad!'

We got to the university and piled in. Drinks were served on trestle tables in a hall off to one side, and we managed to get pints in plastic cups with little problem. Then up the stairs to the Great Hall for the support. I don't remember anything about support act The Records, but I do remember the excitement mounting as we endured that endless wait before the main act, the roadies fiddling around on stage for what seemed an eternity, the microphones tested. Then the lights went down, this geezer with white hair, Teddy boy-style, coming on stage, the spitting starting. Shocking. He got covered. I later discovered this was the legend, John Weller. There's no way he deserved that. He introduced the band in that indomitable way with a roar like no other, three figures stalking hurriedly on stage.

Weller raised an arm in nervous salute, guitars plugged in, then… Pow! Straight into 'Modern World'. Pandemonium, continuing for the entire set. I pogoed, stage right, much of the gig now a blur. I remember being hugely impressed with the explosion and pyrotechnics at the end of "A' Bomb' and the fact they had the Tube train effect/affect (sic) at the beginning of 'Tube Station'. I was in love. This was *my* band.

After the gig, a group of us hung around near the stage, the band having a reputation for letting fans meet them. It didn't seem long before this big-built geezer with long straggly hair and a beard beckoned us forward with his index finger. 'Alright, you lot.'

In a daze, I followed the crowd behind the stage, down a corridor to a dressing room door, and we crammed inside. There they were, surrounded by fans who had got in ahead of us. I couldn't believe it. Eventually we pushed forward, in front of Bruce.

'Great gig, Bruce!' said one of my mates. 'Yeah, cheers, shame about the sound though,' he replied.

We were puzzled. It sounded great to us. Next, we approached Paul. 'That was fantastic, thanks, Paul!' 'Thanks a lot, ta, sound wasn't great though, was it?' he mumbled. 'Er... well, it sounded fine to us!'

Then we found Rick. 'That was great, Rick, brilliant! Pity about the sound though,' someone said. Rick looked up. 'What was wrong with the fuckin' sound?'

I WAS THERE: SIMON MESSENGER

I had bought *All Mod Cons* on release day with my hard-earned cash from morning and evening paper rounds. It had been on repeat on my cheap Pioneer turntable, and I knew all the lyrics by the time of my first of nine live experiences with what became my lifetime favourite band. The advantage of being the eldest of seven children growing up in a toxic blended family in the late 1970s is that no one cared where I was, even on school nights. Going to Exeter University on a Monday night to see a punk rock band wasn't going to be a problem. So it came to pass, having pre-purchased a ticket for £2 from the excellent Pitts Records shop in the High Street, that I was going on my own straight from school to see The Jam for the very first time.

I was wearing a white Ben Sherman buttoned-down shirt and my black ATC tie, done up in the opposite direction, the wide end tucked inside the shirt. The support band was The Records, who sounded like a second-tier sixties guitar pop band. I headed down to the bar area on the ground floor and was surprised by my luck at getting in without an ID check, taking full advantage and having two pints.

The ticket said it was 'The Pre-Exam Jamboree!' But, for Tory-voting upper-class Exeter Uni students – many of whom were and still are the offspring of landed gentry and wealthy business owners – it was a chance to celebrate Margaret Thatcher's General Election win ten days before. It's a damn shame that 'The Eton Rifles' was not yet recorded. It would have been a very appropriate inclusion.

They opened with a blistering rendition of 'The Modern World' and played almost all of *All Mod Cons* (sadly no 'English Rose' or 'Fly'), the rest of the first half a blur, blown away by the energy generated by the threesome, the crowd lapping it up. 'The Butterfly Collector' provided a welcome break from the ferocity and pogoing. 'Strange Town' was a must, followed by 'News Of The World', 'Tube

Station' and 'Wardour Street'. Two encores included 'David Watts'.

I was bloody knackered by then, and it was quite a long walk home to the Polsloe district of Exeter. School the next day was a real struggle.

UNIVERSITY OF LIVERPOOL
16 MAY 1979, LIVERPOOL, UK

I WAS THERE: COLIN MARSH

I must have been 16 when a friend offered to trade *This is The Modern World* for a worn copy of The Who's *Live At Leeds* purchased (or shoplifted) from a jumble sale a week before. I'd seen The Jam do 'In The City' on *Top Of The Pops*, liking what I heard. This was northern England, living at my parents' house on a council estate outside Chester, fashion and music taking a while to get to our neck of the woods, most new things passing us by. I was at a point in my life that I needed music, and the arrows taped on Paul Weller's sweater intrigued me. This trio looked like people I'd grown up with. I eagerly made the trade, taking the album home. I later found out my friend had shoplifted the album the day before from a local Woolworths. Fair deal!

Luckily, no one was home when I lifted the cover of Mum and Dad's stereogram, a Jim Reeves LP that they last listened to at Christmas still on the turntable. I put the album on, dropped the needle, and have never been the same since.

'Da da da de da, This is the modern world!' My life changed. This was what I'd been waiting for. 'London Traffic', 'Standards'… I loved them all, playing it loud over and over, entranced. I finally had something musically that was mine. After listening for weeks and also acquiring *In The City*, the next move was a live show.

A local newsagent stocked the *NME*. I read it in the shop, never having the money to buy a copy. I saw The Jam were touring in May, my nearest show at Liverpool University. Liverpool was a place I'd only been once. I didn't even know how I'd get there, but knew I had to go. A couple of months later, having saved enough delivering papers and hustling school dinner ticket sales to my friends, and with a few pounds I knew I'd get for my upcoming birthday, I talked a couple of friends into coming with me. We were set.

A train ride and a 15-minute walk put me and my friends outside Mountford Hall. We were early. I saw a coach, a truck and kids who looked like me. I was in the right spot. I saw a queue forming and joined. It was early and I wondered why everyone was lining up, then boom! A side door opened, a grey-haired geezer with a London accent and an intimidating bearded 'hit man' stood next to him beckoned us over. I heard music I recognised, we hustled in, and there in front of my eyes were the three geezers from the LP covers I'd stared at for months. I was in a soundcheck!

Five or six songs got a run through, some I didn't recognise as they were on the new album. I was still saving for that. The band were signing autographs, talking to fans and holding court. I pushed my way to the front, shook hands with Bruce and Paul, and we were then hustled out.

The doors re-opened at six. I found a spot in the middle, the lights dimmed and the same geezer who opened the side door earlier came on, announcing, 'Put your hands together for the best band in the fucking world!' The curtains opened and I found my addiction… I'm still addicted 44 years later!

I WAS THERE: JOHN WHALLEY, AGE 14

Christmas 1978 and my eldest brother (eight years older) received Blondie's *Parallel Lines* as a present. I was 13, growing up in a village 15 miles outside Liverpool. Up until then my musical taste was very much influenced by my cousin's love of rock 'n' roll, Showaddywaddy and Darts being regulars on my music centre. But things were changing.

My brother bought *Tonic For The Troops* by The Boomtown Rats, which became a favourite of mine. However, the LP he really wanted (but didn't get) was The Jam's *All Mod Cons*. The week after Christmas this much anticipated album hit the turntable. And what a sound – something hit us both about the music, the lyrics (the first time I'd really paid any attention to these), the passion and undercurrent of seething anger mixed with delicately beautiful love songs.

That was it – he had to see this group, asking if I wanted to join him, my other brother and their girlfriends to watch The Jam at Liverpool University. Roll on a few months and we arrived at Mountford Hall. I was dressed in my usual blue kagoule, beige Oxford bags and black trainers. It was my first gig, and the excitement was intense. As we walked into the venue, reggae tunes blasted out of the PA and I was greeted by the sight of hundreds of Mods in Parkas, Fred Perry t-shirts and sharp suits.

Rudi were first on and were good, but we were there to see the Holy Trinity – and this was like religious fervour, sweeping us all up, carrying us on an incredible journey. I knew nothing of Fire & Skill, but the power, ferocity of playing, the crowd singing, the heat and the volume are as vivid today as 45 years ago. Only having heard *All Mod Cons* and possibly 'Strange Town', many of the songs were unfamiliar, but that didn't matter. The songs may have been different, but the energy was the same!

The set ended with 'A' Bomb In Wardour Street', complete with pyrotechnic explosion to accompany the apocalypse crescendo. We left the hall stunned, ears ringing, discussing the highlights. I felt I was in a dream, unable to come down from the high I'd just experienced. And like any addict who comes down, the low of our mundane lives kicked in hard a few days later… a pattern for my subsequent Jam gigs. I was now 14 and life would never be the same again.

STRATHCLYDE UNIVERSITY
18 MAY 1979, GLASGOW, UK

I WAS THERE: PAUL MCBAIN, AGE 12

I first saw The Jam on *Top Of The Pops* in August 1978. They were playing 'David Watts' and it blew me away. I was twelve years old and that was me hooked. Prior to that I was a big Beatles fan. My dad was in the music industry so I was seeing bands live from the earliest age and he was booking bands locally, so music was a big thing for me. It wasn't until The Jam came along that I found my own identity. I still play The Jam every day. They still mean so much to me.

I've seen Weller in all his different guises about 60 times and he's still bringing out brilliant music. His decision to break up The Jam was 100 per cent correct. I thought that at the time. Obviously I was devastated but I can clearly remember seeing the newspaper and thinking 'this is the right thing to do because it preserves the legacy'. I was 16 at the time and I said, 'I am totally getting this. He wants to move on from the confines of a three-piece.' He was trying to do other things on the last Jam album and he needed to branch out. The whole Mod culture was and is about something new so I totally endorsed Weller right at the start. I remember saying to my mates, 'Look, he's doing the right thing. Sad as we are to see them split up, I think he's going to move onto other things. And we'll always have The Jam in its purest form.

There was a quote in the *NME* or somewhere that said something like: 'The Jam are our Beatles or our Elvis. Thank goodness they're not going to be our Rolling Stones.' Because the Rolling Stones were seen as a joke and an embarrassment in 1982, although obviously they turned out to be something a bit different now.

There's a lyric in the song 'In The City': 'Those golden faces are under 25.' Weller was 24 at the time they split up. It really meant something to him. In his last interview before the Brighton gig in 1982, he even mentioned the age of 25 being a big issue to him. Once you get past the age of 25, you have to get a mortgage and things. I attended the last gig in Glasgow in November 1982. They played 'In The City' and I

Brian Gibbard remembers singing 'Down In The Tube Station' on the Glasgow underground

Ed Silvester was an Epping punk

The Loft's guitarist Andy Strickland with his treasured copy of *All Mod Cons*

Colin Cunningham sat next to Bruce's and Rick's parents at the Rainbow in '79

hn Robb caught The Jam in Lancaster

John Waite saw The Jam several times

ark Hentall was at the Rainbow in 1979

Rezillos guitarist Phil Thompson with his most treasured Jam LP

remember Bruce Foxton looking over to Weller and smiling when they sang that line about 'the golden faces under 25'. I realised that was such a stigma for Weller and it was time to move on. So to me it was absolutely the right time for them to break up and that's why The Jam still get spoken about now. They didn't go on to become something old and embarrassing. Look at how The Clash ended up. I was a big Clash fan and that was awful. The last Clash album wasn't even The Clash. I didn't even listen to it. It was so bad. I think Weller's new stuff is brilliant. I endorse most of the stuff he's done, although he went a bit off kilter with The Style Council.

I first saw them when I was twelve years old. My dad's mate Ronnie was the booking agent for the Apollo and he booked all the bands for the Apollo. He also helped my dad get bands for his venue. I was begging and begging and begging my dad for a chance to go and see The Jam but in May 1979 they were playing Strathclyde University and I was only twelve years old so I was not getting into any over-18s gig. But Ronnie managed to pull some strings and I got a backstage pass and sat on the sound desk and me and Ronnie's son Richard watched The Jam live for the first time.

The gig is on YouTube and a few songs in, during the song 'It's Too Bad', Bruce Foxton got hit by a bottle on his face and the whole thing exploded. Bruce went off his head and Paul Weller did as well. It was just typical of these student gigs. Weller said, 'You asked us to not play the Apollo any more so we're here and look what happens.' About a year later, Clare Grogan from Altered Images got smashed by a glass at the same venue and that's why she's got a scar on her face, the same sort of thing. Just idiots.

The next time they played after that was 8 December 1979 at the Apollo for the *Setting Sons* tour and that was unbelievable. I was still a young kid but the songs started to mean something to me. I think a lot of Jam fans relate to the words and the songs on that album. Weller was talking about his kids growing up and all the things they would do and how they would move the part and that whole concept he was working on the whole concept just resonated.

It's one of those albums that Jam fans just go back to. All my mates dispersed to all the parts of the world? That's the album we still talk about. *All Mod Cons* was the album that I got into. I can't believe how good 'Down In The Tube Station At Midnight' was. So from August, when 'Tube Station' came out, until November, when *All Mod Cons* came out, I was just building up this absolute love for The Jam.

There were very few bands at that point which really mattered. You had The Clash, and a couple of years later The Specials came out, but The Jam were always the ones that ran through to me. The Loch Lomond Festival was a brilliant gig but there was a lot of violence. Glasgow Apollo on the *Sound Affects* tour was another memorable one. I saw them play at a sports centre in Irvine. I was on the crash barrier for that one, being crushed to death. I couldn't believe how brilliant it was. A year later, I saw The Clash there and I was just so disappointed. But The Jam were still full on.

   They finished the *Trans Global Express* tour with two nights in Edinburgh and two nights in Glasgow. I went to one gig in Edinburgh and both the Glasgow Apollo shows. I was lucky enough to get into a soundcheck and to get backstage and meet them on 7th April. Me and my mate were there when the door opened and we just got called in. I hadn't even turned 16. I was really nervous, and I was really worried it wasn't going to be any good, but they opened up the dressing room door and we went in and they were brilliant. Bruce Foxton's wife Pat was really good. She saw that the kids were really nervous and she was comforting everybody and encouraging us to go and talk to them. Weller was really good with the fans, just talking about clothes and the shirt he had on and stuff. Bruce Foxton was holding centre stage, signing everything and just chatting away to the fans. Rick Buckler was doing the same, but not many people were going up to him. I met him subsequently to that at a book signing he was doing. He went to the wrong Waterstones so turned up early, as did I, and I had half an hour talking to him and he was such a nice guy.

   In September 1982 they played the *Solid Bond In Your Heart* tour including this big old agricultural venue on the outskirts of Edinburgh, near Edinburgh Airport. We went early to see if we could try and get in to the soundcheck. I knew something was wrong because they weren't talking to each other at all. I've been in soundchecks before and they'd be chatting away and having a laugh. On this occasion I thought they'd fallen out or something. I knew something was not right. I didn't suspect the split, but certainly on that day they weren't in a talking mood.

   The last gig was November 25, 1982 at the Glasgow Apollo. They had announced they were splitting up at that point and it was obviously quite sad occasion, but I was quite happy. It was just getting over the finishing line to see them one last time and knowing that that was it and no one would come near them again.

   I was so sure they would always be my band and they always have been. They didn't let people into the soundcheck for that one, but Paul Weller did brush past me and say 'alright mate?', so there was still a connection with him. He was still being a nice guy. I think there's a lot of rubbish said about him. He was just quite introverted and trying to deal with the fame. He was never anything other than brilliant to the Jam fans.

   I've got a letter from Paul that he sent to me in 1980 after I wrote to him at his home address, which was in one of the tour programmes. He wrote back to me, telling me when they were playing Glasgow and he sent autographs. I got a letter back from Bruce Foxton, which was a very, very personal touch. At the Liverpool Exhibition a few years ago, my mate and I were talking to Nicky Weller and talking about writing letters and saying how it meant so much. It just felt like The Jam were your band, because they were just so normal and accessible. To this day, I hate my pop stars being pop stars.

My top ten favourite gigs are the ten Jam gigs I saw. One of my best mates, Pat, lives in Dublin so in October '22 me and my girlfriend went over to see Weller in this small venue in Dublin. The first time me and Pat went to see The Jam was in December 1979 and then we saw Weller in 2022. The two of us have seen The Jam, The Style Council and now Weller on several occasions. We're still hooked.

I've got several mates who are still saying, 'I wish The Jam would reform,' but that's the worst thing that could ever happen. The Jam were always about the young idea. That was then, this is now. It had to be that time, that moment, those five or six years. Let The Jam rest in peace.

ODEON THEATRE
22 MAY 1979, BIRMINGHAM, UK

I WAS THERE: PETER THOMAS
I only saw The Jam once, on the *All Mod Cons* tour at Birmingham Odeon. What a great gig! I think my seat was in a row about halfway back, but I managed to get right to the front. I had many a run-in with the bouncers there, but that time I got the better of them (well, dodged past them).

I WAS THERE: JONATHAN ROSE
Front row. Amazing! I remember Hell's Angels bouncers from Wolverhampton down the front, trying to stop people running to the front or getting on stage.

I WAS THERE: KEVIN SMITH
By the time The Jam returned to the Odeon, I'd made new friends through work. We were all apprentices at Rover Group. Myself, Chris Browne and Paul Deeley went along with Jude Pack and Maggie Shine, girls we'd got to know. My mother queued up and got us tickets. This time, we were in the stalls (thanks, Mum).

Although the Odeon was all seated, it was standard practice to abandon seats and charge down the front. Paul got told off by the bouncer for standing on the seats, but he was over six foot six and was sitting down! The girls found this hilarious.

Jude still talks about it. As the curtains drew back, Chris led the charge down the front. This was the closest I got to The Jam in person. I recall Bruce Foxton stopping playing, having a go at a security guard for having a go at a fan.

The five of us all went our separate ways. Jude worked in Denmark and got to see The Jam play the Falkoner Center, Copenhagen, while my next Jam gig was in November 1980 when The Jam played Bingley Hall.

GUILDHALL
24 MAY 1979, PORTSMOUTH, UK

I WAS THERE: ANDY LINTOTT

I was 16 when I first saw The Jam, inspired by seeing 'Down In The Tube Station' on *Top Of The Pops*, going on to buy *All Mod Cons*, my second LP purchase after *Saturday Night Fever*. I was hooked by the energy and power… better that than disco music!

It soon became a fashion thing, dressing in the early black suits, going on to follow Weller into his Mod culture fashion of nice shirts, Lonsdale t-shirts, Jam shoes/spats, and so on, even down to the haircuts. That first time was at Portsmouth Guildhall, my first gig. They had such a mixed fanbase, with lots of Mods, punks and skinheads, and that caused a few scuffles, to say the least.

I was completely hooked, going on to see them another nine or ten epic times, including the farewell at Brighton. For that last gig, general opinion and certainly mine was that it was a disappointing, flat evening, from the band and crowd. Whether it was just over-hyped or realism that this was very much unlike a Jam gig atmosphere, I don't know. But we were there to see 'the best band in the fucking world,' as John Weller put it, one last time.

SADDLEWORTH ARTS FESTIVAL
9 JUNE 1979, UPPERMILL, UK

I WAS THERE: PRENTICE JAMES, AGE 16

Oldham, Spring 1979. I was 16 and there was an intense buzz of excitement building in the sixth form common room at my grammar school. This was decades before the information immediacy of the internet and social media, most of my friends living in Saddleworth, where the rumour in the local villages was that The Jam were to play the Arts Festival that June.

For those of us already fully immersed in the immense late-seventies musical melting pot that embraced punk rock, new wave, 2 Tone, reggae and the

SOLID BOND IN YOUR HEART

Mod revival, this was an almost unbelievable rumour. Could The Jam really be heading to the picturesque but sleepy village of Uppermill to play in a marquee on local playing fields, part of the once every four years, very middle class, Saddleworth Arts Festival? Things like this just didn't happen in Oldham.

I can't truly recall how long it took for rumour to become reality, but The Jam's gig was confirmed for the second Saturday in June 1979. The excitement among my group of friends was uncontainable as we became obsessed with the emotions and logistics that surround a 'must go to' gig. The planning became a fixation: who was going? How would we secure tickets? How would we get there? Then there were pre- and post-gig arrangements, and so on.

Prentice James and girlfriend Rowena back in the day

How all this got ticked off is now hazy detail, but what remains vivid is that I and my group of friends all got tickets. We were in, and beyond excited. We knew this would be one of those gigs of a lifetime. That was the only real topic of conversation that mattered in the weeks that followed, helping the weeks pass.

Like all big events you look forward to, when the big day arrives the excitement of anticipation is replaced by the overwhelming euphoria of it actually happening… and 9 June 1979 was without doubt one such event and one epic day. So it was that Craig and Dave (co-members of our poor but very enthusiastic high school punk band, Sub-Life), Rowena (my girlfriend), Janet (Craig's girlfriend) and I gathered in Uppermill that afternoon. It wasn't scheduled to start until around eight, but Craig and Dave lived in Saddleworth so an early start seemed compulsory. The village was alive with excited fans and the pre-gig atmosphere was all I expected it would be. We savoured every minute.

By 7pm we were ready to start making it over to the gig marquee on the playing fields on the outskirts of the village. I don't know what the official capacity was in that marquee but I suspect there were around 2,500 kindred souls making their pilgrimage to the 'Jam Tent' that evening. Simply electric, the playing fields crowded with fans waiting to enter the marquee.

By 8pm we had all made it inside, and this was it… every single person there waiting to see one of the coolest (along with The Clash) bands on the planet. The Records were supporting, as they had been on the *Jam Pact* tour, and they did a great warm-up set to get everyone ready for Paul, Bruce and Rick. So to the main event… The Jam exploded on stage, the crowd erupted and we bounced relentlessly to tune after tune. And all pre-mobile phones, just soaking up every second. It was real, it was live, and we were living it. Immense.

I'd be lying if after 45 years (and a few beers on the night) I said I remember the exact setlist, but *All Mod Cons* featured heavily that night. Highlights for me were 'The Modern World', 'Away From The Numbers', 'David Watts', 'Strange Town' and absolute classic 'Down In The Tube Station At Midnight'. At the climax there was a big pyrotechnic finale outside the marquee (safety rules had forbidden it to be inside), the noise from which I believe caused many local residents to call the emergency services. A fitting, explosive end to a momentous day on my life's musical journey. The one and only time I got to see The Jam live, and it's maybe that fact plus the simple immense part the band played during my teenage punk years that makes this one of *the* gigs of my life. Unforgettable times.

I WAS THERE: DEAN KIRBY, AGE 17

We used to go watching them all around the North West, probably 15 or 16 times. I met the band. I met John Weller. I got guest passes. They were magic days. It was the energy that captivated me, just the energy of Weller, thrashing away on that Rickenbacker. And then you listened to the lyrics and discovered what the songs were about, plus they looked dead cool.

I first saw them at Manchester Apollo. I went to Blackburn, Bolton, Stafford. We'd go on the train. You'd meet the same people, single people on their own, going on the same journey. You'd get chatting. 'What did you think of the gig?' They played in a marquee on Saddleworth Moor. I was down at the front for that one, and I ended up sitting on the stage, picking plectrums off Weller's mic stand and passing them to the crowd.

It was dead easy to get tickets then. You just went to the venue. I remember getting a letter from the fan club saying that if you didn't have tickets to a gig, then if you took the letter along, you'd be allowed to get in. I went down to Birmingham, saw John Weller in the soundcheck and showed him the letter. He said 'alright mate?' and slapped a guest pass on me. But I was meeting an old girlfriend. I went to the station to meet her and she'd brought a friend along. There were three of us with no tickets and just one guest pass. So I wrote my name on it and 'plus two guests' and went back to the venue. I walked to the head of the queue and spoke to the security guy. He said, 'You need one of those each.' I said, 'Just ask John, will you? Just ask Paul's dad.' He didn't argue with me. He let us in.

There'd be a lot of violence after the gigs. At that one, we got chased through a pedestrian underpass by a gang of skinheads throwing bricks and stuff. These two girls were screaming their heads off. There were bricks bouncing off the walls. They were quite menacing days. I remember seats being ripped up at the Apollo. And there was a lot of spitting at gigs in the early days. They'd spit at the band and Weller would go mad. If you went down the front, as I always did, you'd get covered in it.

Another time I was on a second date with a girl. I met her at Manchester Piccadilly train station and within 45 minutes, I'd taken her in the back door of the Apollo and Paul Weller was autographing her copy of *Cosmopolitan*.

A guy in my local pub told me about the split. He knew I was a big Jam fan. He said, 'Have you heard? Have you heard?' I was destroyed. But as I got older, I understood why. Once the horns started coming in on 'Precious' and stuff like that, it didn't have the same energy as the earlier stuff.

Bruce played with Paul at the Royal Albert Hall in 2010. It was the first time they had played together in 28 years. They did 'Eton Rifles' and the cheer and the chill you got down your spine when he walked on stage was just fantastic.

PLAY INN RECORDS
SUMMER 1979, ECCLES, UK

I WAS THERE: PHIL THOMPSON, DEPARTMENT S

I was too young to see The Jam live, but got into them through my brother and cousin, four years older. I first got wind of the records they played in the summer of 1979, just before secondary school, including 'Strange Town'. I'd heard some punk stuff which I really loved (still do), but this was something different. I've always listened to music analytically and loved to play over and over again whatever singles I could nick off my brother when he wasn't watching, picking individual bits out. At the time I never knew what made a lot of those noises, but I loved to strain to hear things in the background.

'Strange Town' – bought from Pete at Play Inn Records, Eccles, where I spent all my pocket and paper-round money – was something else, the wall of noise behind the instruments in the intro which builds up then drops out as soon as the first verse starts, the little piano plinks after the guitar stabs in the second verse, the mysterious lyrics which meant so little to me but sounded so cool, the bassist playing a melody all his own which somehow fits, the weird drop-out near the end with the fast drum bit which breaks into a bit where he actually sings 'break it up!' (my jaw on the floor – is he actually singing *about the song*?), the dramatic outro and that fantastic noise at the end which I now know to be a whole symphony of feedback but at the time could have been Martians landing in the living room. It blew my mind then, and still blows my mind now, 45 years later.

I was twelve when I got *Sound Affects* for Christmas – the first time I heard a full Jam album. My parents didn't realise what they'd given me. Within the first 90 seconds of the first song, Weller sings, 'They didn't teach me that at school, it's something that I learnt on my own…' Wait, what? You can learn things about the world outside school? On your own? Then there's what turned out to be a stanza from Shelley's 'Masque of Anarchy' on the back cover: 'Ye are many- they are few.' My tiny mind was blown. I needed more… and boy, did I get it!

To this day, The Jam at their best are inspirational and disheartening almost in equal measure. Listening to it most certainly made me want to do it for myself, which I went on to do with varying degrees of success. But *really* listening to it still makes me realise I could never do anything quite like it. I'm 56 now and I won't be the only person to point out that The Jam were finished before Weller hit his 25th birthday. Incredible. The Jam, along with all those other songs and bands of that era set me off on a path which, for better or worse, I'm still on today.

TOWNHOUSE STUDIOS
15 AUGUST 1979, SHEPHERDS BUSH, LONDON, UK

The start of recording sessions for what becomes **Setting Sons**, *including 'The Eton Rifles'.*

I WAS THERE: BRUCE FOXTON

It was hard work. A lot of it was written in the studio, the Townhouse in Goldhawk Road, Shepherd's Bush. Certainly, some of the songs were just sketched ideas where Paul would lay down the bones of it during the day, then Rick and myself would stay up in the studio rooms – where you could crash out – and where we would work out what we thought would work on a track overnight.

Then we'd all crack on, kick it around the next day and record it. There wasn't as much pre-production, like going into rehearsals and knocking them all into shape before you recorded songs. It wasn't a cheap way of doing it, but I think we came out with a good record.

It was a very exciting time. I don't think we ever sat back on our laurels. We always looked to push on rather than stick with a proven formula. All three of us challenged ourselves in respect of what we did and what we played. With every record we tried something new, something experimental, to see how it would turn out.

I can understand why certain people would say it was a concept album, but I wasn't really that aware of that at the time. Three or four songs link together, but I don't recall anything more. Maybe Paul mentioned it, but if he did, I've forgotten it. I certainly can't hear him saying, 'OK, we're going to do a concept album!' But I might be wrong, it was all a long time ago.

What has really hit me is – and again this sounds conceited – what a great album that was or in fact is. I hadn't played that record in its entirety for quite a while. The lyrics are incredible. That's really hit home – how talented Paul was then. He's still going from strength to strength now, but the lyrics there are incredible for such a young man.

I WAS THERE: ALAN BUTCHER

The Jam were based at Townhouse Studios in Goldhawk Road from mid-August to early October, recording *Setting Sons*, and I went along to hang out with them. I'd been going to the pub regularly with Rick Buckler, having known the band since 1976. Peter Gabriel was also recording at the time and made me and Rick a cup of tea. It felt amazing having the lead singer of Genesis making me tea. I'd seen him with Genesis a few times.

One day Paul Weller asked if I still went to see The Merton Parkas. I told him I did and was given a mention on their album for handclaps and beer. Paul wanted me to get keyboards player Mick Talbot and X-Ray Spex sax player Rudi to guest on album track 'Heatwave'. I did my duty, The Jam were happy, as were the special guests. Rudi also appeared with The Members and The Boys, and of course Mick would end up playing with Paul's next band, The Style Council.

I WAS THERE: TRACEY SAUNDERS

My dad was Guy Saunders, a Woking cabbie with Johnny Weller, friends until he died in May 2000, John and Ann with our family at his bedside. I think Paul was in Japan, so he couldn't come to visit, or to the funeral.

Dad did a lot of driving for them, initially for free in the early days. I remember many trips to the studios, and gigs with him. The link with John was that he and my dad met hod-carrying in their early twenties, both going on to be taxi rank drivers in town.

He went on the first tour, driving the minibus, and I remember going to the studios when I had chicken pox. I was in middle school, so 1978 or 1979. I think it was Shepherd's Bush, West London. All I really remember was a stone-clad drum room, and the tea area where me and Rick were playing with the house cats and kittens!

I reckon I was in early secondary school – 11 or 12, 1980-ish, at Winston Churchill School, Woking – before older neighbourhood friends made me realise they were famous. To me they were just Dad's mates, who always joked about with me. I never liked their music!

I also remember an 'All Stars' charity match at Woking Football Club. The Jam were playing, and they announced it was my tenth birthday, so the whole stadium sang 'Happy Birthday'!

'WHEN YOU'RE YOUNG' RELEASED
17 AUGUST 1979

The Jam's eighth single reaches No.17 in a six-week UK Top 40 run. The promo video is filmed at Queen's Park, North West London. The B-side is 'Smithers-Jones', penned by Bruce Foxton.

I WAS THERE: BRUCE FOXTON

That ('Smithers-Jones') was seeing how my dad was treated by the company he was so loyal to for many years. That's just life, and happens to this day, where the boss deems them no use anymore, you're out, and all that past service doesn't seem to matter. At the time, he didn't even get a golden handshake. It was disgusting the way he was treated, but that happens to a lot of people.

I WAS THERE: NIGEL CLARK, DODGY

That line, 'I've some news to tell you, there's no longer a position for you'? For me personally, I wanted to be in control of all that. I didn't want that to be my life. I could see how easy it is to do it. People get trapped.

I WAS THERE: JOHN WAITE

I saw them several times between '79 and '82. My memories are now vague apart from being carried out from the front at the Queen's Hall in Leeds needing oxygen! A Jam gig was like losing your virginity with your ultimate 10/10 fantasy whilst watching your team win the FA Cup at Wembley. Trying to get your Jam fix on radio or television was such a rare treat. I recorded two hours of John Peel almost every night, and when he first played 'When You're Young' it blew my mind. I listened back to it all night. It was just the greatest – raw power pop with slashing chords, gruff harmonies and a military stomp back beat. Having just left school after turning 16 that March, the lyrics resonated beyond anything I'd ever heard before…

BOOKHAM BAPTIST CHURCH
AUGUST 1979, BOOKHAM, UK

I WAS THERE: ADRIAN CORBETT

I was aware of them from working men's club days, but somehow never saw them. My mate Steve Cripps mentioned them, saying their energy was amazing, going on to see them at places like the 100 Club. Looking at films of those early London dates, we really missed out. By the time I moved to the area, they'd moved up there.

I DJ'd at discos, Bookham and Leatherhead way, with a friend, Clive Wishart. We did Radio Jackie (Kingston-upon-Thames), Saturday evenings at Bookham Baptist Church, places like that, to around 200 kids, aged 14 up to 18 and 19. At one church hall disco, Clive said, 'Here's a new record from The Jam.' I looked at it and thought, 'This isn't the place for that, but bollocks, I'm going to put it on.' It was 'When You're Young'. It was the first time I'd heard it, and while part of me was thinking, 'God, not tonight,' everybody was enjoying it. It was then that I realised this funny group slightly on the side of things were on the way. Not because of any hype, but because that was actually a bloody good record. On the strength of that reaction, I'd play 'In The City' and others, and realised I could also play my Stiff and punk records to these kids.

TOWNHOUSE STUDIOS
10 OCTOBER 1979, SHEPHERD'S BUSH, LONDON, UK

The final Setting Sons *sessions are completed at Townhouse Studios.*

I WAS THERE: MICK TALBOT

I didn't meet them until a lot later – in '79. Paul rang me up and said he'd heard the B-side of our single, a piano thing, and said, 'I want something in that style.' He wasn't too specific, he just went, 'I like what you did on that, can you do something like that on this? It's gonna be the last track on the album. Do you know 'Heatwave'?' 'What, the Martha Reeves one?' 'That's it, yeah.'

'THE ETON RIFLES' RELEASED
26 OCTOBER 1979

'The Eton Rifles' enters the UK chart to become The Jam's first Top 10 hit, reaching No.3.

TOP OF THE POPS
1 NOVEMBER 1979, LONDON, UK

The Jam appear to play 'The Eton Rifles', returning a fortnight later.

THE MARQUEE
2 NOVEMBER 1979, LONDON, UK

I WAS THERE: HARRY SHAW SR

I saw The Jam as 'John's Boys' at the 100 Club. I'd seen them many times before, but as they became more popular getting tickets was next to impossible. They announced a secret gig in the *NME* and only true fans would get the hint. Next week, there it was in the gig section, 'John's Boys at the 100 Club'. We discussed it in school. Would it be them or will we be wasting our pocket money? We took the chance and went. OMG, The Jam at their biggest in a small club like that. And 45 years on, I still get a stir as to how good it was. I've never been to a better gig.

I WAS THERE: PHIL LEV

I grew up in South-East London and loved The Who. In May '74 I was spoiled rotten when they played Charlton Athletic FC, one of the greatest one-day festival line-ups I've witnessed. My best mate, Jim Woodward, was a massive Who nut. As punk developed, our tastes broadened and Jim became a huge Jam fan who thought Weller was God, along with his other fave performer, Pete Townshend. I wasn't a huge fan at first, but I liked the first two albums. I first caught them at the old Rainbow Theatre in Finsbury Park, in November '77. A great gig, with a very appreciative crowd. You could tell they were really starting to hit the straps. We also attended Reading Festival in '78, Quo headlining on Saturday and The Jam doing the same on Friday, that day given over to punk and new wave bands. The Jam played a great set, though the sound wasn't the best. I think it was worse on stage, Weller wrecking his equipment at the end of their set.

When *All Mod Cons* came out, I was blown away. Everything suddenly clicked. The pressure on Paul Weller turned out to be a good thing, bringing out the best, in mind and heart. It's one of my favourite albums of all time, chock-full of classic songs like *Who's Next*.

SOLID BOND IN YOUR HEART

As the late seventies and early eighties rolled by, the West End became my playground, all those fabulous venues so close to hand. The Marquee became my most regular haunt. By '79, I and plenty of mates frequented the place almost weekly. I met Shane MacGowan around then, spending many a happy night in his company. One of my strongest Jam memories was that secret, very memorable night there in November '79, not long before 'The Eton Rifles' was released. Jim heard a last-minute radio announcement that 'John's Boys' were playing that night and realised it was a code name for The Jam. He rang me at work, and we managed to get into the queue before it became a lost hope. The place was a sauna that night, with easily over 1,000 people inside even though the capacity was 400. Management often broke the rule, but being packed in like absolute sardines added to the atmosphere. Shane MacGowan's group supported. He was another Weller nut, so playing support to The Jam was a massive honour for him. Both bands played a blinder, The Jam previewing new songs.

I do believe they finished too soon. Of all the groups from the era, The Jam promised so much and were truly of a status equivalent to some of the greatest bands to come out of the UK's music scene. It's a real shame Weller didn't feel like continuing.

Photos by Phil Lev

A PEOPLE'S HISTORY OF THE JAM

I WAS THERE: PAOLO HEWITT

I saw The Jam a couple of times on the tour to promote *All Mod Cons*. By then I was a student at North London Poly in Kentish Town, writing for the student paper and doing small gig reviews for *Melody Maker*. Just prior to the eagerly anticipated release of the *Setting Sons* album, the band played a secret gig at London's Marquee venue, under the name John's Boys. Through my Woking connections, I got into that show – the only journalist present – and reviewed it for *Melody Maker*.

The paper was impressed and sent me on my first feature assignment, to interview The Jam in Manchester:

News travels fast. Even allowing for a quick midweek shuffle from the Nashville to the Marquee, come Friday night 'John's Boys' were the band to see and the Marquee the place to be at.

In theory, then, it sounds attractive, but was the reality of it all up to its promise? Well, to begin with, The Jam previewed a lot of new material, some of which was instantly attractive – 'Girl On The Phone' and 'Saturday's Kids' – and some of which will demand a bit more of your time, like 'Private Hell' and (I think) 'Thick As Thieves'. And whereas before Jam songs boasted a definite tautness, the new material often slowed down to leave just bass and drums and a lot more space for improvisation.

Another welcome addition was the fatness of Bruce Foxton's bass sound, which added so much more to the overall construction and sound and proved that it's not only Weller who's been pushing on.

Within the Marquee's small confines The Jam makes so much more sense, because you're near enough to understand why Weller attacks with such anger, why he'll suddenly start strutting on stage as he builds up the number to a whirlpool of crashing chords and gruff blazing vocals, and then finish the song with a curt 'thank you' as if nothing's happened. Honesty, pride and passion all come into it.

But the real bonus of the night was the gig's informality. The band missed chords, fluffed harmonies, Weller's voice gave out before the end, Foxton grinned at old faces, Buckler with a face like stone drummed as if there was no tomorrow (though he probably had an off-night), and the audience were just as active in making that rare kind of occasion when two-way communication becomes possible.

The only tragedy of the night came when, with 'A' Bomb in Wardour Street' ringing in our ears, we wearily hit the streets to be confronted by idiots who stank of too many right-wing meetings, in search of trouble. Ironies like that aren't too funny.

I WAS THERE: DEBSEY WYKES

I don't remember any trouble. I was going out with someone who heard about it, where from I have no idea. I found them stunning that night. I think it was being in a small club just watching Paul Weller up close, feeling his intensity… and he was quite attractive! I'd always considered them a bit of a boys' band, but that went out of the window that night.

I WAS THERE: TIM BOYLE

We were all Mods by the time the next album, *Setting Sons*, came along. There was a secret gig at the Marquee and they were billed as 'John's Boys'. I had a friend who was working in the music business and she said: 'You want to get yourself down the Marquee on such-and-such a night – The Jam are playing a secret gig.' So I told a few mates and we went down and of course it was sold out. It wasn't that much of a secret!

But I'd set my mind on getting in, although I didn't know how – and we weren't getting through the front. There was an NCP car park 100 yards up the road and you could get to the back of the venue through this car park, so me and five or six mates got round the back. There were a few other people there as well, but there were bouncers round the back as well. Some of the lads were trying to bribe the bouncers, but they weren't having any of it. But, all of a sudden, the bouncers disappeared because there was some sort of ruckus out the front with a load of skinheads. This wasn't unusual at the time, because whenever there was a Mod gig in London there'd be skinheads about wanting to beat us up for some reason.

So the bouncers were distracted and I decided to climb on top of the roof while my mates watched. I found an opening in the roof and I pulled the felt back and I could see the crowd inside, but it was too much of a drop so I climbed back down. I said, 'How else are we gonna get in there?' There was still no sign of any bouncers.

There were some boards on the window of the ladies' toilet. I pulled these back and I managed to get an opening so I said, 'Hey lads, I think we're in,' and we managed to squeeze in, one after the other. I don't know whether anybody else got in apart from our little crowd. But the biggest lad amongst us was a big lad then (he's a bigger lad now) and even he got in with his Parka on.

The feeling of actually breaking into the Marquee to see The Jam at a secret gig? That was great. It must've been five or ten minutes before The Jam came on and we managed to squeeze our way right to the front. They were playing a *Setting Sons* warmup gig and we didn't know any of the songs. It was after a dry writing patch from Paul Weller, but we got songs like 'Thick As Thieves'. The memory of that night and the feeling of that has stayed with me.

It became like a religion after that. Every year they played twice in London, once in the summer and once in the winter, and an album came out in the winter. That's how it was and you could set your clock by it. That was how you lived, looking forward to the Jam stuff. The writing was so in tune with what we were going through, although The Jam were a little bit older than us. Weller was about four years older than us. The way that Weller writes and the way that he was writing about relevant stuff to him was relevant to us too. He grew up in the suburbs? We were in the suburbs. The clarity of his writing fitted the life we were living.

My three favourite Jam songs I call 'the trilogy'. 'When You're Young' is about setting out and finding out what life's about and what it ain't about. You're a little bit naive and you want the world, you're trying for it, but you're not gonna get it really because the corporations have got you in their grip before you're born.

The next song in the trilogy is 'Strange Town'. To me, that's such a clever song. You realise that there's something that ain't quite right. You got so many people in a big city, like London, going around doing their bit and there doesn't seem to be any cohesion, but everything just works. You realise the place is a bit strange but you just get on with it.

The next one is 'Going Underground', when you realise it's just a load of bollocks and you gotta keep your head down and just do what you do. To me, that's the essence of The Jam in those three songs.

I was absolutely gutted when I heard they were going to split. It was like something had been taken away from me which I didn't actually own. It was the end of Mod. I had a Lambretta and I was incredibly into it. My friends had peeled off a little bit, and my best friend had been killed. I was kind of lost for a couple of years. It was like the end of our adolescence.

But there weren't any tears, because they left such a rich and fertile panorama to fall back on. I still play Jam stuff now. I didn't really like 'Town Called Malice' when it came out in 1982 – I thought it was too 'dancey' – but now it's one of my favourite songs. There's depths and charisma in the records and in the writing. I suppose Weller was writing it for himself really, but the people that latched onto it, the people like me that weren't particularly well educated and who needed to be led, we were happy to follow.

I WAS THERE: RICK BLACKMAN

Four days after my 14th birthday, on August 24th 1977, I watched the first episode in a new music TV series *Marc*. On it were The Jam, and I remember thinking they looked suspiciously like The Beatles, but much more explosive. Desperate to see them I tried in vain to get to a Marquee gig the following February, but my mum wouldn't forward me a loan on my pocket money, because it was a 'punk' gig. I lost track of how many times I saw them afterwards, but one gig remains solidified in my memory.

SOLID BOND IN YOUR HEART

It was the 'John's Boys' gig at the Marquee. Too excited to wait until the evening, me and my mate spent the day around Carnaby Street shopping and watching little groups of people milling around, waiting for the gig. We were seasoned Marquee attendees, so we knew to get into the club early doors to position ourselves right in front of the stage. That night The Jam were supported by The Nips, brilliant in their own right and doing a storming version of 'Gabrielle'.

Legally the Marquee was only supposed to hold 700 people, but there must have been twice that amount that night. Dangerously overcrowded, as I was later to find out, The Jam delivered a blistering set of mainly the *Setting Sons* album, and the passion of 'Thick As Thieves' and 'Private Hell' remain with me to this day. They were at the peak of their powers musically and with full on anger from Weller. Literally within touching distance, and on the verge of superstardom, I was never to be that close to the band at a gig again.

I had long dispensed with the need to dance or move about at Jam gigs, such was my devotion to Weller. I needed no distraction to stop my gaze upon him. Then, in-between the fourth or fifth song, he bent down to drink half of my pint that was sitting on the stage right beneath him. (A drink he still owes me!) It was customary to enter the cold winter nights from a gig saturated in sweat, but this night was completely different. The sheer volume of people in there was like being in a greenhouse. Being at the front of the stage meant being constantly pushed against it and unable to move or breathe. At some point about halfway through the set, crushed, I was so desperate for air I pushed myself back and collapsed, unconscious onto the floor. Considerately, as I lay there for a minute or so, everyone kindly danced around me, and I was not stamped upon, but it all happened so easily and quickly as it did with tragic consequences at Hillsborough years later. Once awoken, I was back at the stage and the rest of the set plus encores, but I can say, with no sense of irony, I nearly died for The Jam!

It's hard to convey now that feeling of euphoria and unity at a gig where the entire crowd is at one with the band. Every word of every song, spat out by Weller and with 1,500 people in imperfect harmony. I saw hundreds of bands around that time and since, but Jam gigs were totally unlike anything else I've ever witnessed, and this one was at the top of a very exclusive list. Not even the pitch battle that awaited outside, with skinheads attacking people from the gig up and down the length of Wardour Street, could sully the night.

I WAS THERE: TERRY SMITH, THE NIPS

All my mates were pop stars and I was getting nowhere as a drummer. I was in a little Mod band called Les Elite. Mandy Austin called me and said, 'The Nips are looking for a new drummer. You'd be perfect for it. They're supporting The Jam at the Marquee. Come and see them. I'll put you on the door.' My thing at the Marquee was to sit at the bar and look through these little wired-glass windows right on the side of the stage. I could see that the place was jam-packed with Parka'd Mods.

I was a bit 'meh' about the Mod revival because I was about ten when Mod first happened. But it was obvious that something very special was going on. The crowd knew all the words to every song and were singing along. It really made me pay attention. It was such a moving gig. The almost violent energy of Paul Weller was so powerful and passionate. It made people get into it. It was obvious this was something big. I became a fan.

And the next thing I know I'm playing with The Nips and Shane (McGowan) and it's all good. But The Nips didn't have any management as such. John Hasler wasn't very pro-active. We were offered the support slot on The Jam's next tour and we went to meet them at St Albans or somewhere. I remember going backstage afterwards and meeting the boys and John, Paul's dad, and them talking about the gig. But they wanted twenty grand for us to join the tour and we couldn't afford it so that was the end of that. Shane's drinking problem was getting worse. I think I was one of seven drummers who had put up with it and then I got a better offer from another band and went 'bugger this – I'm off!' The next time I saw Shane he said, 'I've got a new band. It's called Up Your Arse – Pogue Mahone.'

The next time I saw The Jam was when a mate of mine, Giovanni Dadomo, a journalist with *Time Out* and *Sounds*, took me to see them at a BBC concert at Golders Green Hippodrome in December 1981. It was towards the end of their career and they did 'Heatwave' with the horn section they had. It just blew my mind.

THE NASHVILLE ROOMS
3 NOVEMBER 1979, LONDON, UK

Another secret gig (billed as The Eton Rifles and also La Confiture) follows, with another full house.

SETTING SONS RELEASED
16 NOVEMBER 1979

The Jam's fourth studio album reaches No.4 in the UK album charts, and No.137 on the Billboard 200.

SOLID BOND IN YOUR HEART

I WAS THERE: PAOLO HEWITT

('Saturday's Kids') was the kind of song that made The Jam unique. Paul wrote it as a poem which he published in the *All Mod Cons* songbook. No one was writing about such people, the council estate kids with their factory jobs, their routine lives of hard work and hard play, their fashions, their rites and rituals. Paul Weller did. He had wanted punk to be a genuine working-class movement, and in his eyes it hadn't been. He now set out to chronicle the lives of his contemporaries and in doing so stand up for them. The Saturday kids were his people, the ones he had grown up with, gone to school with, fought and played with; these were the people he knew back to front, the ones, in fact, who now bought his records and worshipped him so. He knew their ways intimately.

A year of my teenage Saturdays are summed up in the first verse of this song. It's all there in black and white: meet at the Albion pub midday, drink till afternoon closing time, off to the local Light a Bite, heady on alcohol, think the waitresses in their tight nylon uniforms and little white socks incredibly erotic, ask for tea and a date, get rebuffed, look for the football scores (the Spurs, of course!) and go home to prepare for the night.

I remember Paul remarking to me, 'I don't know why they make such a fuss about my lyrics. Everyone does, but all I'm doing is writing about what I see around me.'

Ah, but if it were that easy, we would all be at it. Weller has great observational powers, and knows the value of the telling detail. He sings about the wallpaper lives, the dipping into silver paper, the inevitable marriage, the baby on the way. The vision is hard-edged, realistic, as all Weller's songs tended to be when addressing such issues.

Moreover, this song lifts the lid on a set of attitudes and routines music rarely reflects, and accounts for Weller's high standing among many. I have no idea if the Saturday kids still live the same way, but this is their first manifesto, enshrined for ever.

FRIARS
17 NOVEMBER 1979, AYLESBURY, UK

The Jam start a 28-date nationwide UK tour to promote the Setting Sons *album.*

I WAS THERE: HOWARD SMITH, THE VAPORS

A girlfriend got me a copy of *All Mod Cons* for my birthday, asking Ed (Bazalgette, bandmate), 'What can I give Howard?' I'd been buying their singles before then. I think I'd also seen them at Guildford Civic. They were one of a dozen bands I really liked. When it came to us joining them on the *Setting Sons* tour though, seeing them play, there was probably not a better band I've ever seen. It was really stunning.

The *Setting Sons* tour was a real challenge. Before that it would be a gig every few nights in front of a hundred or something. Then suddenly we're 19 years old and the support band for The Jam, two and a half-thousand seaters night after night after night. We'd never experienced anything like that before. I was getting blisters on my hands. It was pretty intense. And I think there's always pressure on a drummer. The others could play a few chords, stop playing for a minute and no one would notice, but a drummer can't stop playing! If the drummer stops, everyone has to stop!

I WAS THERE: DAVE FENTON, THE VAPORS
That was brilliant – our first real dabble into life on the road, going from playing to 20 people or one man and his dog in a pub to 2,000 seaters with The Jam. We each had our own minibus and every time we got to a service station, we had water pistol fights in the car park. They'd tape our clothes to the ceiling while we were on stage, that sort of thing, while we'd put talcum powder on the snare drum. I've got really happy memories of all that.

I WAS THERE: JULIAN BROOKS, AGE 15
I was at Friars twice to see The Jam, on 17 November '79 and 2 August '80. I was also at Islington's Michael Sobell Sports Centre plus London's Embankment for the CND March – the band playing on the back of a lorry trailer – and finally Wembley Arena.

The first time I heard them was via my friend's older brother, Robert Woods, five years older (Paul Weller's age). We were all into the music and fashion, big time.

Robert, aka Pogal, was a guitarist and when he played *In The City* and *This Is The Modern World* to me, I played along a bit. Those LPs blew me away. I first saw The Jam on *The Old Grey Whistle Test*, then for the first time live at Friars when I was 15. We walked in, up to the bar area and could not believe Paul and Bruce were sat at a table talking to fans. I was starstruck.

After a couple of drinks, we headed into the hall. The atmosphere was electric, with soul music playing and Mods all over the place. Then John walked on, and the rest is history. Straight into 'Girl On The Phone'. The place went up and I never came down till I was hovering out that hall. What a buzz.

ARTS CENTRE
18 NOVEMBER 1979, POOLE, UK

I WAS THERE: PAUL NYE
My first gig. I guess in 1979 or 1980 at Poole Arts Centre, The Vapors supporting. I'm old now… my memory has gone!

SOLID BOND IN YOUR HEART

I WAS THERE: GAZ KISS-HERE

My brother was a DJ and a Mod since his own teens. I inherited a few records from him but never had my own. Thanks to a Saturday job I now had cash in my pocket, so headed downtown, having already decided on my first ever single thanks to Sunday night's chart list on the radio – 'The Eton Rifles'.

It wasn't long before I was in a line outside the Arts Centre for my first live gig, heaving with people in fishtail Parkas, complete with targets and Union Jacks. I had no idea what I was in for – I only knew the one song. The Vapors were

Gaz Kiss-Here only knew one Jam song

a perfect support act, 'Turning Japanese' getting the crowd moving. Then came The Jam.

Opening with 'Girl On The Phone', going into 'To Be Someone', I was among already well-established Jam fans, singing every word through contorted faces and gritted teeth, with the energy they were unable to release so fully while playing songs on repeat at home in the bedroom. People pogoed in unison, some with arms around each other in camaraderie – the awesomeness of the shared experience.

The Arts Centre was pretty new and we heard rumours about how the dance floor was suspended in the air, a mechanical creation where it could disappear and the entire floor of fixed chairs would come to the surface. I stopped jumping around for one moment and found I was still moving up and down several inches as hundreds of fans pounded the floor within an inch of its life.

'The Eton Rifles' ended the set, but there was no chance of anybody leaving. And we got a real treat – two encores. The moment Bruce started thumbing his intro to 'The Eton Rifles', the place buzzed with electricity. I too sang along word for word, Paul's vocals all killer no filler, and Rick hammering through without breaking a sweat. No fancy pyros, lasers or gimmicks, just a bank of white spotlights saved for the song, turned out facing the fans, blowing you away, timed to perfection to 'E-ton Ri-fles', welding your eyeballs to the back of your head. The experience lives rent free in my head even today.

I got to see the band two more times on other tours and regret terribly not catching the final gig at Bingley Hall. I watched that on video for the first time in my thirties and found it weirdly emotional, catching myself tearily mouthing 'thanks' to an empty living room in appreciation and the knowledge that The Jam and every single song I soaked in through cranked-up speakers as a kid got me through to adulthood sane, less fucked up and grateful. Due to the nature of Paul's writing on life, politics and social issues, I also remain active nonconformist from the School of Jam. Their influence lives on and there really was no one else like them.

I WAS THERE: RUPERT TRACY

I took in four or five shows in '79 which was really exciting because The Jam weren't that popular until 'The Eton Rifles' came out. They had very little radio play. They might appear on *Top Of The Pops* once but then the record would start going down the charts and you wouldn't see them again. It would just be the one performance. 'Eton Rifles' was the one that gave them loads and loads of air play.

I remember working out which gigs I could afford to go to and whether I'd have to bunk off school to get to them. It was just an astonishing time. I had two or three friends who were as fanatical as I was, and we went to most of the shows that were south of Birmingham. I think I went to 41 in the end. It was fucking violent around those times and it wouldn't take much to upset somebody from a different part of the country. I'm not a tough buy but I could normally defuse things with a bit of chat and a bit of humour, but it wasn't called the Jam Army for nothing. There were a lot of fights at these gigs, sometimes between skinheads or Teddy boys. Skinheads were the worst. I saw a Mod get set on fire once. That was terrifying. I still have nightmares about it now. But, generally, the camaraderie amongst Jam fans was amazing.

I just wish I'd lived in London and been able to go and hang out with them in the studio and that sort of thing. Apparently, there were a hundred Mods outside Townhouse Studios when they were recording *Settings Sons* and they let quite a few of them in.

Kenny Wheeler, The Jam's tour manager, was absolutely fantastic, as was John Weller. There was absolutely no divide between The Jam and their fans at all. I didn't know of any other band that let fans into the soundcheck. That was unheard of. The Clash were quite accessible, but not really into the soundcheck. You could bunk in to see them afterwards. But there was no nonsense with The Jam. After the soundcheck had finished, you were expected to go out again and come back when the doors opened.

Paul Weller did not behave like a pop star in any way, shape or form. And it was always really exciting to see what he'd be wearing at the next gig. And you'd be thinking, 'Christ, how many cool clothes have you got?' He never ever turned up in anything that looked shit. You could stick a bin liner on the guy and he'd look great.

Shelly's Shoes used to make the pointed black-and-white shoes and then they used to make those awful badger shoes. I say 'awful', but I thought they were fantastic at the time and got my mum to buy me a pair! But you'd always have a button-down shirt, a boating blazer and a nice three-button Tonik suit if you could. Carnaby Street was such a mecca. It's a shame the clothes were such terrible quality.

APOLLO THEATRE
20 & 21 NOVEMBER 1979, MANCHESTER, UK

I WAS THERE: ED BAZALGETTE, THE VAPORS

Another highlight? The first time we supported The Jam at The Apollo in Ardwick. We did two nights there in November 1979, and there was a pea-souper of fog across Manchester. I grew up supporting United, so it was so great to be kicking off in Manchester. That was an extraordinary voyage into the unknown.

I WAS THERE: DEN DAVIS

I was a half-decent footballer and played a couple of years up so was welcomed by the older lads, and my brother reluctantly let me go along to see The Jam on the *Setting Sons* tour in November 1979. I managed to crawl my way to the front against the stage, the night Paul Weller wore that infamous black and white suit. I just remember not being able to breathe. I couldn't wait until the end of the show when the mass of bodies moved back. A gig's simply not the same if you're not among it all at the front and I still do that to this day. I saw The Jam 39 times between then and the end in December '82. Having different groups of mates, inevitably there was always someone to go with, further afield. We'd get the coach from Aytoun Street in Manchester. I then followed The Style Council, seeing them 52 times. I've seen Weller more than 100 times in the last 25 years.

I WAS THERE: MOE WOOD

I saw them twice, both times at the Manchester Apollo, on the *Setting Sons* and *Sound Affects* tours. The atmosphere was mint, so electric. It was so long ago, I can't remember much about the set, or who was supporting them. But the buzz before, during and after was epic. It was a very sad day when they went their separate ways, and I just wish it was The Jam reforming instead of Oasis!

GAUMONT THEATRE
24 NOVEMBER 1979, SOUTHAMPTON, UK

I WAS THERE: NICK MARLOW

I caught the *Setting Sons* tour in Southampton and the final concert in Brighton.

HMV
25 NOVEMBER 1979, NEW STREET, BIRMINGHAM, UK

I WAS THERE: PETE JOGLE

I began working at HMV towards the end of 1979 and was incredibly excited to discover there was an in-store signing session for The Jam to promote their *Setting Sons* album. There were loads of fans queuing to meet them and get records signed. We waited for the first to be let in down the stairs to the lower ground floor, and I found myself shoulder-to-shoulder with the 21-year-old Paul Weller (I turned 21 a month after). Being a naturally easy-going guy, I decided to make small talk for a couple of minutes, asking how the last American gigs had gone. That's when I wished the ground could have opened under my feet. Paul instantly referred to the support slot they were given – opening act for Blue Öyster Cult – and a tirade of swear words cascaded from his lips about the reception most nights from heavy metal sci-fi fans. He wasn't a happy man and I tried to change the subject as soon as I could think of something else to say. Things definitely improved as he met the fans though, and Bruce Foxton and Rick Buckler were charming and easy to get on with.

The other memory occurred the following day. During the signing session, Rick decided to sign a beige-coloured telephone on the counter, used to communicate within the store. I thought it was a nice touch. However, our lovely cleaning lady had other ideas. I recall her proudly telling me that soon as she discovered 'someone had written all over our phone' she made sure to wipe off the offending signature with her cleaning products!

The crazy thing is, I'm not sure if they did another signing later. I definitely recall us having the band behind the counter, and we decked out the rack of Top 20 singles with all the reissued double-pack seven-inch singles to make it look as though they were in half of the Top 20. Yet I can't find any information about when those were released.

TRENTHAM GARDENS
26 NOVEMBER 1979, STOKE-ON-TRENT, UK

I WAS THERE: JOHN TIDESWELL

My next Jam show was at Trentham Gardens, again in Stoke, The Vapors supporting. About eight of us went, including our girlfriends. We had suits made at Burtons, and felt pretty cool dancing down the front as they sang 'Billy Hunt'. Paul Weller had a throat infection, but still gave it his all.

I WAS THERE: PETER BOWERS

It was to be nearly two years before I'd see The Jam live again but in the meantime I'd been devouring the terrific *All Mod Cons* and the majestic *Setting Sons*. The latter was huge for me and it was with the anticipation of hearing the songs from that album performed live that I drove my dad's Austin Vanden Plas to the venue, with my student friends Colin and Rob in the back. We took up our places near the front of a packed Trentham Gardens ballroom and, after John Weller's introduction, The Jam appeared with Weller sporting a dapper half and half black and white suit and black and white Rickenbacker. 'Girl On The Phone' started a fantastic set and I was knocked backwards and forwards in the wave of dancing Jam fans. The set was drawn mainly from *All Mod Cons* and *Setting Sons* and it felt like heaven.

DEESIDE LEISURE CENTRE
29 NOVEMBER 1979, QUEENSFERRY, UK

I WAS THERE: CHRISTINE HARRISON, AGE 14

I first heard The Jam on *Top Of The Pops*, circa 1977, playing 'In The City'. My brother recalls me laughing at their suits! I got into their music not long after, and was soon hooked. I loved their energy and the apparent anger in some of Weller's lyrics resonated with me. Naively, I even wrote to him to tell him what I thought he was saying in some of his songs. Fast forward around a year, and their first gig at Deeside. I was only 14 and went on my own to my first gig. I told my parents I was meeting someone there. The gig was only about a mile down the road. It was amazing. The energy was mind-blowing. I remember the exhilaration of being there. One very tall guy put me on his shoulders, so I saw Weller up close and personal.

I also went to one of their last gigs at Deeside. Both were so amazing, and I can't separate them in my memory. I had the opportunity to go to another in Liverpool, but had begun my nursing training and was unsure what hours I would be working. It turned out to be one of their final gigs. I was gutted when they split.

I still have all their albums. I did have every single they ever released, but some were stolen. The Jam were a huge part of my teenage years. I liked that they were different. When I went to a Weller gig around 2001, two guys there were in awe of the fact that I'd seen The Jam live, and I regaled them with stories of how amazing it was to have been so lucky to have been there.

I WAS THERE: ALAN JONES

I saw them eleven times altogether and went backstage at Deeside once, where I had a good chat with the lads. I saw them there in 1979 and 1982. The Vapors supported in '79 and The Piranhas in '82.

I WAS THERE: NEIL CRUD, AGE 13

I'd just turned 13. My dad worked as a photographer for the *Evening Leader*, so I tagged along as his 'plus one'. My first gig, having been introduced to the world of punk rock a year earlier at Denbigh High School. The Mod revival was well under way and The Jam were one of those bands who straddled both punk and Mod. The music had the punk energy, but the fashion was most definitely Mod-orientated.

With half the ice rink filled by punks and the other by last year's punks, now Mods, there was always going to be friction, and it didn't take long to spill over. The whole evening was smattered with skirmishes as fist fights broke out. At one point Paul Weller stopped the show, calling someone in the crowd a 'cunt' and offering him out. I watched all this from the safety of the balcony, although I had to tell Huw Spew and Susan Forber (two of the school Mods) I was in the thick of it, otherwise they'd be calling me a coward.

A young Neil Crud with Paul Weller

The Vapors were up first; the first of the thousands of live bands I've seen. I remember them playing their hit, 'Turning Japanese' and its B-side, 'Here Comes The Judge'. As for The Jam, I have very little to recall; I don't remember the songs, just the fighting. One advantage of having a press pass was meeting the bands. Bruce Foxton legged it onto the bus, but Rick Buckler was happy to autograph my book, as was Paul Weller, who posed for a pic. I asked him what he thought of the show, but he just passed my book back and walked off. Unfortunately, that's the only pic my Dad has from that gig (albeit a brilliant one). Because of his work he had to surrender all the negatives to the newspaper, which will be long gone. He did print an ace full stage pic of the band, swallowed up by a teenage bedroom wall many, many years ago.

I also recall The Jam went to a club in Chester after this show. A band was playing and invited Weller, Foxton and Buckler to play a couple of songs, which they did.

I WAS THERE: NICK DAVIES, AGE 16

Leaving school in July, I begin working the next day on a building site as a pipe fitter's mate, on a new school in the hills overlooking Wrexham. Punk has happened and it has reached us. I am angry so it appeals to me – angry at the lack of jobs (YTS, stiffing most of my friends) and a lack of sex. Pretty much everything. All hormones and confusion. Despite this, 'Destroy' isn't really enough. My teenage brain says, 'Destroy, then what?' I find answers in two groups – The Clash and The Jam.

The Clash inform my politics and challenge me to look into what they're singing about. The Jam essentially describe my life. Their singer is only five years older than me. He's a lot cooler but he's like me. He's angry, he comes from a small town (small village, in my case). He knows how I feel and writes and sings about my life. Takeaway curry, Babycham, council houses, half-time results.

The band have style and swagger. I bus into Wrexham as soon as the shops are open to buy 'Strange Town' on the day of release. I've never heard it (imagine that). I rush home, play it a few times, love it, then go round to all my friends' houses so they can hear it. I belong to this as much as it belongs to me. Then I hear the news. The Jam are coming to North Wales. I've never been to a gig. I somehow manage to get a ticket for the princely sum of £3. Then the long wait.

Working on the day of the gig. I have to wash (no showers on site) and change. Jeans, claret and blue Fred Perry, khaki suede boots, fishtail Parka with target on the back (I've gone Mod now, oh fickle youth), bus into town and onto a packed train to Shotton.

Mods and punks are everywhere. They don't get on but they're tolerating each other. I have mates in both camps. I see them on the way to the ice rink, which is the venue. There are scuffles on the way. At one point the legendary Cloud 9 scooter boys make an appearance, with their distinctive silver helmets.

The support act is The Vapors. Their hit, 'Turning Japanese', means we've heard of them. Throughout their set there are punch-ups – punks vs Mods (some of whom, like me, were punks a short while ago), England vs Wales, old Mods vs plastic Mods. There's a tension building.

Then, The Jam. Fast, furious, incendiary. I'm transfixed. I can't dance but I jump up and down. It's like being at a football game. They're my team. I remember 'David Watts', 'Strange Town', 'Saturday's Kids', 'When You're Young', 'Down In The Tube Station At Midnight'. It's happening. I'm transported from all the crap in my life. Some idiot throws something at Weller, and there's a confrontation. It adds to the tension.

I wanna be like them, I want to be in a band. I want to write about how I feel and smash things up. All too soon it's over. There's no encore. We all march to the small train station. Two platforms. One to Liverpool, one to Wales. Large groups on both sides abusing each other, throwing things at each other. More carnage.

Six months later I joined the Royal Air Force and ended up sharing a two-man room with a scouser. You guessed it. He was standing on the opposite platform throwing stuff at me while I did the same to him. We're still friends.

I WAS THERE: JANE EVANS-JONES

It started in 1977 with the Sex Pistols. I grew up in a village in North Wales and it took a couple of years for the Pistols and punk to arrive. I loved them. I was 14 or 15 and school was as grim as any in the seventies. We started Punk Club at break, bringing our records and albums, the head getting wind of it – it was decided by 'the man' it would be called the New Wave Music Lunchtime Club or it wouldn't be happening! It was immediately disbanded.

Round about then I saw The Jam on TV and was very interested. The music, guitars, words, Paul Weller! My first album was *This Is The Modern World*, followed by *In The City*. I'd buy magazines, watch them on TV, the usual teenage stuff.

Madness were the first band I saw live, at Deeside. A friend's older brother organised it, with tickets, mini-bus, etc. I had a fantastic time, Madness were brilliant, live music was brilliant, and I got interviewed by Radio Deeside on the way out! I then went to see The Jam twice at Deeside. With the benefit of hindsight, I'd have taken photos and kept the tickets, but I was living in the moment. I danced, I sang, I met so many people. A friend from the infamous Punk Club was at the front, fighting! We met a few years ago and he confessed to being in the middle of it. I have no recollection of any fighting. The Jam split and that was okay, a bit of a surprise but… nothing lasts forever!

I continued to follow Paul Weller's career, seeing him a few times, but the pure joy of being young, in the crowd, with that energy, knowing it's your time, isn't the same. I still have all my Jam albums, they've travelled far and wide with me and I love to listen to them still. I think Paul is about seven years older than me and as an adult when you listen to the words and the music, he really is a genius wordsmith who definitely spoke to me and made me think.

I'm laughing to myself here. I've just wandered into the kitchen singing 'This Is The Modern World'. How is it I can remember the lyrics from all The Jam's albums but can't remember a conversation from yesterday?

I WAS THERE: STEVE CARROLL

Two months before the gig, I rode the eleven miles from Ellesmere Port on my bicycle to get tickets for me and my mate. There were 3,000 in there, a mixture of lads and girls from The Wirral, Liverpool and North Wales. The atmosphere was a bit lively, to say the least. The Jam came on and were brilliant, with loads of aggression and passion. Paul Weller had to appeal for calm at one point.

I WAS THERE: SCOTT NEWSON

In 1977/78, on the verge of leaving school, the punk era was taking off and because it was different to anything else and rebellious, I went along with it. But I didn't like the dress code – the safety pins, zips on t-shirts, DMs, the spitting… It wasn't long, however, before a good friend leant me the first two Jam albums, and I liked the cover of the first – three of them wearing black suits, sporting short clean haircuts. And when I got home and put the first album on, from track one, that was it for me – I wanted the suit, the lot.

I was only 15, with no money, playing those albums back-to-back for months. But when *All Mod Cons* came out in 1979, the same year as *Quadrophenia*, my direction from there on was to be a Mod – the music and the clothes. My mum and dad were going on a London trip, and I knew you could get the suit and Jam shoes in Carnaby Street. Now 17, and having saved a bit of money, I accompanied them, my first stop a tailor at Carnaby Cavern, with pictures of bands and The Jam on the window, saying, 'Buy your Jam suit today.' I was measured that morning and the suit was ready at 5pm the same day. Them were the days! A bit further up was Shelly's, where I bought black-and-white pointed Jam shoes. My suit was £60 and my shoes £15, my parents paying half, liking the idea of me wearing a suit instead of being a punk.

I couldn't wait to be the boy about town, posing around town (Oswestry) and the local discos, attending my first concert on the *Setting Sons* tour, taking the bus to Deeside Leisure Centre in Flintshire. It was £3.75 a ticket, the venue holding around 3,000. We queued for about two hours, and as the doors opened a surge of fans ran to the barrier. We went with it, my girlfriend and me (a first concert for both of us).

I don't remember the support because nobody took any notice of them, the crowd loudly shouting, 'Jam! Jam! Jam!' I remember a large brawl at the back between scousers and Brummies, which was quite frightening, but it soon calmed down with the lights going down and The Jam coming on. Paul and Bruce were in suits and Rick was wearing black trousers, a white and blue striped shirt and Jam shoes. Paul's suit was all blue, his jacket buttoned up to his neck, similar to a Beatles suit.

'Girl On The Phone' was the first song. I was on Cloud Nine, watching the only band I ever wanted to see. After 20 minutes, with the crowd pushing behind, it was getting unbearable, so we requested to be pulled over. They let us watch the majority of the concert at the side of the stage. The missus lost one of her shoes, but we were just happy to be out of the crowd, with everyone drenched in sweat. Mind you, wearing a suit and Parka you would be. On the way home and for weeks on end, I couldn't stop thinking of that night.

One night later, me and a few friends got invited to a house party (we didn't have a clue whose). They happened to like The Jam, so conversation was good. They said they had tickets to see them live. It was a mistake telling us that. Long story short, we nicked them, my friend and I and our girlfriends going to the gig.

We were sat upstairs, with a good view too, but ten minutes into the support band, the real owners of the tickets turned up. I couldn't think of anything to say. We had to get out of the seats but managed to watch the concert from the back. We had some explaining to do to the girlfriends regarding where we got the tickets from, but we would do anything back then to see The Jam.

LANCASTER UNIVERSITY
30 NOVEMBER 1979, LANCASTER, UK

I WAS THERE: JOHN ROBB, THE MEMBRANES

The Jam were still quite punky when I saw them but they weren't really a punk band anymore. They were seen as a Mod band by then. That's the interesting thing for me – they were a punk band dressed in Mod suits. They had the intensity and angst of punk. In 1977, the first time I read about them and heard them, they were definitely like a punk band, and everybody getting into punk where I was felt they were, their name was on the list – Pistols, Clash, Jam… That punkiness about them kind of dissipated as they went on, like most of those bands, getting into everything before punk, mixing that up with punk, but there was a point in time when I felt they were completely brilliant.

That first album was a great skinny punk record, but that run of singles like 'The Eton Rifles', 'Funeral Pyre' and – my favourite – 'Down In The Tube Station at Midnight', that's The Jam I remember. When the Buzzcocks played Blackpool, there was a massive fight in the crowd between punks and skinheads – Preston and Blackpool skins. It was one of those mad fights, with everyone about 15 and 16 not wanting to get in this massive fight with 20-year-olds. Then they played 'Tube Station' over the PA, and I remember thinking how those words really fitted that moment. I'd say every lyric in that song was completely brilliant: 'They smelled of pubs and Wormwood Scrubs, and too many right-wing meetings.'

Weller was a brilliant poet, writing really great lyrics which were snapshots of Britain at the time. I was disappointed when he got into that weird slanging match with Robert Smith, saying he shouldn't dress the way he did. I thought, 'Jesus, are you turning into your grandad?' But I got to interview him a couple of times, and he was alright.

So many of the bands in that era came from those satellite towns of London, beyond the suburbs. Bands like The Jam, The Cure, The Members, The Stranglers … that whole 'outside looking in' thing is really key to that period, and that 'outsider' status really resonated with people like us, growing up outside the big cities – they weren't cool, they made their own version of pop culture.

'Tube Station' is for me probably their greatest song, lyrically and musically. The tension in the verses and the way the chorus explodes… a brilliantly written song. And how dark those lyrics are for a Top 20 pop single… wow!

RAINBOW THEATRE
2-4 DECEMBER 1979, FINSBURY PARK, LONDON, UK

I WAS THERE: PHILIP BRIGHAM

My first time seeing The Jam was May 1979 at the Rainbow. The ticket cost £2.50 and we were in the circle. The second time was that December. We didn't have tickets this time but got the train from Stevenage to Finsbury Park early in the morning and hung around the Rainbow, sneaking in the back door for the soundcheck. On the way out, we bumped into Nicky Weller, Paul's sister, selling programmes and memorabilia in the hall. We ended up buying tickets from a tout for £8, with the face value £3.50, but they were great seats, three rows from the front. The gig was amazing, being so close to our idols. It's always been my favourite gig. We left covered in sweat, exhausted from jumping around to classic Jam songs. A night to remember.

Philip Brigham & his mates bought tickets off a tout

I WAS THERE: STEPHEN BEECH

It's summer 1978, I'm 15 and only two things matter, The Arsenal and The Jam. Let me rephrase that; only two *people* matter – Liam Brady and Paul Weller. Courtesy of an older brother, 'This Is The Modern World' had been blasting out for the past year and I was hooked by the sound and the look of the group on the picture sleeve.

Not many boys at my school were really into music – it was girls and football, or football and girls – but a few would talk about the latest band on *Top Of The Pops* or a record they'd heard. One mate, John, said he would lend me a particular record he thought I should listen to. That record was *All Mod Cons* and, hyperbole aside, my life changed. I thought it was the most special sound I had ever heard. That I still love it and play it 46 years later is testimony to its seismic influence on me and thousands of others.

Gigs were still an unknown to me. I had seen The Clash at the 'Rock Against Racism' rally in Victoria Park but really that was to support the cause and because it was near home.

Every fortnight John and I travelled to Highbury to see The Arsenal. Coming out of Finsbury Park and looking left, we saw 'The Jam' up in lights and three dates in December being advertised. We went to the box office and, using John's Access card, got two tickets for the Sunday. In the interim we went to a few other gigs but nothing could have prepared us for that night. The anticipation of getting there, the excitement of getting in and then actually being there with thousands of like-minded young people all going mad was unforgettable.

Then the moment arrived, and the band rushed on stage and launched straight into 'Girl On The Phone'. Pandemonium ensued and continued for the next 90 minutes or so, Bruce playing brilliantly, jumping in the air and waving to fans in the crowd, Rick rock solid behind his drum set keeping immaculate time, and Paul a blur of anger and fury, singing his special, special lyrics to *me*.

It seemed like everyone there knew every song (even the new ones, which I couldn't work out) and they sang their heads off and hearts out. There was genuinely something unique about being in a Jam crowd and sharing that experience. I was lucky enough to see The Jam many times, but nothing quite compares to the first.

I WAS THERE: GARY WILLIAMS

It must have been 1978 when a mate suggested I listen to The Jam, telling me I'd like them. I went out and *bought All Mod Cons* and it blew me away. Never has an album affected me like that. I went out and bought *In The City* and *This Is The Modern World*, loving them too. The music was right up my street.

Having gone to Northern Soul all-nighters, we now had someone singing about them too. It changed my life. To this day they remain my 'go to' sound. Obsessed with music from a young age, it headed me in the right direction, *All Mod Cons* is still my favourite album, along with Marvin Gaye's *What's Going On* and Blondie's

Parallel Lines. Being into scooters and football, it showed me the way.

We saw them at the Rainbow in December '79, and when they played my home city of Norwich in February 1981. We'd been to West Ham for football and on the train home, loads of other West Ham were on their way to that University of East Anglia gig. It was brilliant and we ended up having a party after. (Later, eight of us got nicked for running away after not paying for a meal!) I also saw them in Skegness on the *Bucket and Spade* tour.

Loads of my football mates knew Paul Weller personally, and ended up inviting me down to Brighton for the final gig in December '82, saying they would get me in. I never went, and have regretted it ever since. I've seen The Style Council and Weller solo many times since, even New York in 2007 for his three nights at Irving Plaza, but nothing comes close to seeing The Jam.

I WAS THERE: MARK HENTALL, AGE 17

I started following The Jam after the release of *In The City*, aged 15. I loved the rawness. Songs like 'Art School', 'In The City', 'Away From The Numbers'… At the same time, you had The Clash and the Sex Pistols, but to me they were too heavy and dirty looking. I loved the style – the Mod thing. I was hooked. Having grown up on a council estate, the words to songs such as 'Saturday Kids' also meant a lot.

When I finally got to see them at the Rainbow, I'd left school and was working in London. I remember yet again the rawness and had started to understand the politics behind their music. I loved Rick Buckler's solo – the sound of an underground train – during 'Down In The Tube Station At Midnight', and was intrigued how a three-piece band sounded like a four-piece. It kicked off after with skinheads outside the Rainbow, but what a concert. The late seventies was a great time for music – punk, Mod, skinhead, ska, etc. They were also dangerous times on the streets, but I cherished every moment.

I went on to see them a few more times, including the last concert in Brighton. I still see Paul Weller all these years later, and I still play their music. I must know every word to every song. My partner says, 'It's strange you remember all the words to Jam songs but can't remember our anniversaries.'

I WAS THERE: MARK BUNYAN, AGE 14

Myself and my best mate Gary Simmons begged our parents to get us tickets as we were only 14, and they did. Dressed like little Mods (Fred Perry, Sta-Prest and Parka), trying to look like our heroes, we got the 106 bus from Bethnal Green Station to the Rainbow. We stood at the front of the stage just where Paul Weller stood. It was a brilliant night watching The Jam and enjoying the music and atmosphere of the whole evening. The conductor kicked me and my mate off the bus going home because we were quite loud, singing the songs that were played that night. Luckily for us, he kicked us off only three stops from Bethnal Green!

I WAS THERE: ALAN WISE

Me and my mate Richard Leonard (he was from Guildford, I was in the nearby village of Peasmarsh) got free tickets and backstage passes because we're both musicians and knew some of the Buckler family. I used to play gigs at places like The Cricketers, Westfield, Woking Liberal Club, Woking Working Men's Club, etc., the same sort of venues The Jam played before they were famous. Richard played with Peter Buckler (Rick's twin) in a band called Static. He was a very good bass player. I remember Peter coming to my 40th birthday party. And Peter and Rick's cousin, Alan Buckler was a very good acoustic guitarist. He'd had private lessons with Anthony Philips, Genesis' original guitarist.

Peter Buckler got us in. I recall us chatting to Rick and Bruce whist Paul Weller was having an argument with somebody on the stairs. The gig was great. A week before, *Setting Sons* had come out and I remember buying it. The support were The Vapors, also from Guildford. Most people know the story that John Weller (Paul's dad) and Bruce Foxton went to Scratchers, Godalming and saw them play, both thinking they showed great potential. The Vapors played places like The Wooden Bridge and The Royal in Guildford, and Steve Smith of the band was also a good bass player. When he met me backstage at the Rainbow, he said, 'How did you get in here?'

Bruce Foxton and Steve Smith were often in The Royal, Guildford, drinking and checking out the bands. On the night of the Guildford pub bombings by the IRA in October 1974, The Jam were due to play Bunter's Club, Guildford. As you can imagine chaos was all around the town.

CITY HALL
6 & 7 DECEMBER 1979, NEWCASTLE-UPON-TYNE, UK

I WAS THERE: FIONA BUSBY

I was lucky enough to see The Jam a few times when they came to Newcastle-upon-Tyne, the first time on the *Setting Sons* tour. I also saw them at an event on the day of that first gig, at a record shop near the venue. I bunked off college for that! And I saw them in Carlisle one summer.

SOLID BOND IN YOUR HEART

I WAS THERE: DAVE PRATT

In December 1979, the usual suspects travelled up to Newcastle on a minibus to see both nights of The Jam's *Setting Sons* tour at the City Hall. The Vapors were supporting, and they played a blinder, half of which set we knew by heart because we'd listened to their John Peel session loads of times during the summer. By now, The Jam were at the top of their game. Tight as anything you will ever hear, anywhere and at any time. They pounded through a fantastic set of absolute classic songs, playing tunes that would stand the test of time and which still get requested at every bloke's 60th birthday bash in this day and age. The new album featured greatly, but the set was also full of the singles and the best of *All Mod Cons*. Simply magnificent.

I WAS THERE: GEOFF THOMPSON, AGE 16

I don't know what the connection was. Maybe because I was young and Paul Weller was young as well. They looked the part. I was into The Clash and especially the Pistols, but you didn't hear the Pistols much on the radio. The Jam got a lot of airplay. Mike Read played them a lot on his Radio 1 breakfast show, John Peel played them, and Kid Jensen played them on his early evening Radio 1 show.

I was brought up in a small market town where public transport was terrible. I found out an old form teacher was organising a minibus up to Newcastle from a youth club to go and see The Jam at City Hall. Me and my mate Steve went down and paid our money upfront.

I had the day off work. Steve and I spent the day listening to The Jam and memorising stuff. Newcastle is a big, big city compared to where I'm from. I remember getting there and thinking, 'I'm a 16-year-old boy stood on the steps of the City Hall and I'm going through them doors to see The Jam.' We were two rows back from the balcony but it didn't feel like that. It felt like we were down the front. That was my first proper gig and it just grabbed me.

After that, we went to see them every time there was a tour. We went to Bridlington on the *Bucket and Spade* tour. It was the beginning of July and I had learnt to drive. As soon as I learnt to drive that was it. We knew we had transport to get to gigs and we used to borrow my dad's car. The gig was brilliant, a bit like a football match, with all the surges you get on the terraces and the crowd going backwards and forwards like waves.

That night I got the closest I ever did to the front for a Jam concert, within about three rows of the front. I can remember being stood in front of the mic and thinking 'this is incredible'. But it was the middle of summer and we were in Parkas. After two or three songs we were battling to get to the back!

A PEOPLE'S HISTORY OF THE JAM

We went to Carlisle on the *Bucket and Spade* tour as well, although how Carlisle got on a *Bucket and Spade* tour I'll never know. They were going to do a light show, but the Market Hall had skylights. The Jam came on really late, trying to wait until it got dark, but it was the beginning of bleeding July so it was never gonna get that dark and certainly not dark enough for a light show! I don't think they had a support band that night. It wasn't very often that support bands got any support from the crowd. Some got absolute dog's abuse. I remember The Questions didn't go down very well. Same with The Piranhas.

Whitley Bay was a good one. There were about 3,000 people there and all they'd done was put boards over the ice. The ice rink nearly started melting. The worst one I went to was the Queens Hall in Leeds, a horrible venue. It was an old bus station. To this day, I'm not sure if I watched The Jam. I only heard them. There were concrete pillars everywhere. And the last one was Manchester Apollo. They finished on 'The Gift'. A cracking gig.

I can understand Weller wanting to stop and I'm glad he did. They stopped when they were at the top of the pile. They were never going to crack America and you could tell his music was changing.

I used to buy two of every release, one to play and one that's never touched a needle. You had to be first in the queue when you knew a release was coming out. It was the same with the badges. I'd go to some gigs and I'd see lads and they must've had every badge going all over their jackets. They're probably worth a bit of money now. I threw away all my press cuttings from *Sounds* and *NME* and such like a few years ago. But back then if you didn't buy those magazines, you wouldn't know The Jam were touring. It was the only source of finding out, although you might hear John Peel on a night say 'XYZ' and you'd be sending off cheques to PO boxes to get your tickets and always waiting for the ticket to drop through your letterbox.

Looking back, I'm gobsmacked that The Jam did places like Carlisle and Whitley Bay and Bridlington, because it's very rare that a band does them now. When I was 16 and 17, I went to gigs with a couple of mates. But I started courting in 1980 and the girl I started seeing, who later became my wife, had seen The Jam the day before I did, at Newcastle City Hall on December 6, 1979.

APOLLO THEATRE
8 DECEMBER 1979, GLASGOW, UK

I WAS THERE: TOM MASON

I was at the Strathclyde Uni and the Glasgow Apollo gigs. Energy comes to mind!

At Strathclyde a fight broke out and Bruce stopped it, right in the middle of 'It's Too Bad'. But the best Apollo gig for me was on the *Setting Sons* tour. They were really tight and for me that was the best period for the band – they played from *In The City*, *Modern World*, *All Mod Cons* and *Setting Sons*. They were a big part of my early life, and great live! There will never be another band live for me – only The Clash on a good night produced that energy.

I WAS THERE: DAVIE QUINN

I first discovered The Jam in late 1978, aged 15, hearing 'Tube Station' on the radio. I wasn't really into a band but had been to my first gig that year at Glasgow Apollo – Elvis Costello supported by John Cooper Clarke and Richard Hell and the Voidoids. We had crap tickets and were in the upper circle, the stage seemingly miles away… but live music had me hooked.

After purchasing *All Mod Cons* I set about getting all their previous releases in the all-important picture sleeve. I succeeded. I was unfortunate to miss the *Apocalypse* tour but determined I would be there next time they came to Glasgow. For the *Setting Sons* tour, I sent for tickets in plenty of time, as was the way in those days, being rewarded by two tickets in the stalls, a few rows from the front on the right, Weller's side.

That day we boarded a minibus for the one-hour trip to Glasgow. When we arrived, there were posters on every wall – the iconic image from the rear sleeve of *This Is The Modern World*, Bruce Foxton in mid-air. Me and my mate managed to peel a couple from walls and stash them, to be retrieved after the gig. That poster adorned my bedroom wall up until I left home to get married. How I wish I still had it! The gig was mind-blowing. I still can't get away with the height of the Apollo stage, having to crane our necks to see the band after leaving our seats, joining hundreds of fans dancing at the front.

A highlight of my week at that time was our Thursday night youth club disco, where the DJ – a massive Jam fan – played whole album sides at a time, me and my mate having the floor to ourselves, coming off soaking in sweat but absolutely buzzing.

My next gig was on the *Sound Affects* tour. I sent for tickets early and managed to get the first two on the front row on the left, Bruce's side, and again at the Apollo. We queued inside for the must-have tour t-shirt. I remember a whole pile toppling to the floor and an ensuing scramble to grab a freebie. I'm not ashamed to say I got one and still have it. It still fits too. Collecting any badge with the band's name on was also compulsory, and I still have my collection, my favourite being a 'Tube Station' one – Weller's finest song.

My next Jam show was on the *Bucket and Spade* tour in Irvine, eight miles from my home in Kilmarnock. Eagerly waiting on tickets at our nearest record shop, a newspaper reporter turned up as the band were staying at a hotel in our town, asking a couple of lads in front of me their names. They replied 'Paul Weller and Bruce Foxton', the reporter heading away none the wiser. I continued to be greatly affected by The Jam's music, playing their records constantly, much to my parents' consternation.

Next up was the *Trans Global Unity Express* tour, once more at the Glasgow Apollo. The music had lost the rawness and energy of the first four albums but it was still a great gig and they were always brilliant live. I couldn't take my eyes off Bruce, my hero to this day.

Then the news that they were splitting... I couldn't get my head round it. Their final gig in Glasgow, at the Apollo again, was on Thursday 25 November 1982. I couldn't get a ticket but borrowed my older brother's car and travelled to Glasgow with my younger brother, who had never seen them but was desperate to. I managed to get a ticket outside the venue and headed inside to look for one for my brother. I got one but the bouncers wouldn't let me back out to give it to him, so he spent the evening in a freezing cold car. The band received a standing ovation before they had even played a note. The gig was spoiled a bit by the horn section and backing singers, detracting from what The Jam were all about, a three-piece band giving their all for the fans.

I still play them regularly and am lucky to own vinyl jukeboxes where I can play all their 45s as they were meant to be played. Last year I purchased and customised a Rock-Ola jukebox, dedicated to The Jam, that holds a lot of my 45s from that era.

I was delighted when From The Jam formed. I've seen them several times, the first time with Rick on drums. The songs are still brilliant, but it's not quite the same.

I WAS THERE: SANDY MCLEAN, AGE 19

I turned 17 in 1977, leaving Port Glasgow High School, searching for my first job, music a must in my life. I liked The Eagles, The Beatles, disco and general chart hits. I loved The Sweet, Slade, Bolan, Rod Stewart and Wizzard, and recall Stuart Henry's Saturday morning radio show and the excitement of new releases from up and coming and established bands. But I never heard a sound or song that gave me the inner feeling and satisfaction I did the first time I heard 'In The City'.

We didn't have much money, but I bought the album of the same name on cassette to play on my battery-powered tape deck, and it began my interest in The

The Jam ticket stubs

The Jam PLUS SUPPORT
READING TOP RANK
Monday 13th June at 8 p.m.
Advance £1.00 Door £1.20
Nº 000302

FRIARS at MAXWELL (VALE) HALL AYLESBURY
SAT. NOV. 26
SPECIAL EXTRA SHOW 3·30 P.M.
This is the modern world
the JAM + NEW HEARTS
EARLY APPLICATION FOR ADVANCE TICKETS ADVISED
Tickets 175p From Earth Records Aylesbury
SUN Music H.W.C., Ellis Tons Amersham, Hi-Vu Buck
F.L. Moore Luton, Dunst. & Bletchley, Freds Leggy Home
OR 175p at door (I.s.) Membership 25p

GROBS PROMO
THE JAM
Cats Whiskers, Fishergate, York
Wednesday June 29th — 8 p.m. - 1 a.
admission

VICTORIA HALL, HANLEY
THURSDAY, 15th DECEMBER, '77
at 7.30 p.m.
Mike Lloyd (Music) Ltd presents
THE JAM
with guests
NEW HEARTS
THIS PORTION TO BE RETAINED BY THE PURCHASER
NO TICKET CAN BE EXCHANGED OR MONEY REFUNDED
Ticket Unreserved
£1.60 £2.00
IN ADVANCE AT THE DOOR
(including V.A.T.)
Nº 741
MLM NO PASSOUTS
Cameras and Tape Recorders will not be allowed in the Venue.
MIKE LLOYD (MUSIC) LTD.
5, Lamb Street, Hanley 24641
23, High Street, Newcastle 610940
109, High Street, Tunstall 84660

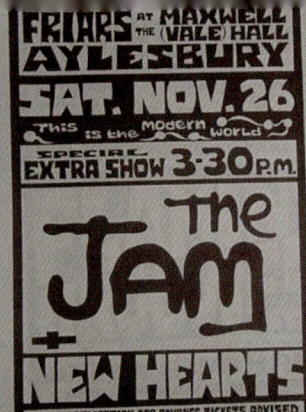

EMPIRE LIVERPOOL
1st PERFORMANCE
FOR TIME SEE DAILY PRESS
£2.00

RAINBOW THEATRE
FINSBURY PARK
Mel Bush presents
THE JAM plus SPECIAL GUESTS
at 7.30 p.m.
Friday MAY 11
CIRCLE
incl VAT
P 25

MARQUEE
90 WARDOUR STREET, LONDON, W.1. 01-437 6603
SATURDAY 25th FEBRUARY, '78 doors open at 7.00 p.m.
We Proudly Present
A Very Special Night With...
The Jam
£1-50
Plus various guests & DJ Ian Fleming
THIS TICKET DOES NOT PERMIT HOLDER TO RE-ADMISSION
THE MANAGEMENT RESERVE THE RIGHT TO REFUSE ADMISSION

489
CIVIC HALL GUILDFORD
Sunday 30th July 1978
JAM
plus Full Support 8 p.m.
Ticket £ 2-00

613
CIVIC HALL GUILDFORD
Sunday 30th July 1978
JAM
plus Full Support 8 p.m.
Ticket £ 2-00

587
CIVIC HALL GUILDFORD
Sunday 30th July 1978
JAM
plus Full Support 8 p.m.
Ticket £ 2-00

THE JAM
THURSDAY 23rd NOVEMBER
SPORTS HALL
Only £1·75 (adv)
£2·00 (dr)
8 p.m.
TICKETS FROM:- UNION SHOP
LONGPLAYER

RAINBOW THEATRE
NOV 16 — STANDING
Nº 29056

SADDLEWORTH FESTIVAL MARQUEE
"THE JAM" in Concert
plus The Records
SATURDAY, 9th JUNE, 1979
8.00 p.m. to 12 Midnight

Northumberland Road, Newcastle upon Tyne

Thursday, 6th December, 1979, at 7.30 p.m.

M.C.P. presents

THE JAM
Plus Special Guests

BALCONY £2.00   SEAT E 64

Booking Agents: City Hall Box Office
Northumberland Road, Newcastle upon Tyne (Tel 20007)

Northumberland Road, Newcastle upon Tyne 1

Friday, 7th December, 1979, at 7.30 p.m.

M.C.P. presents

THE JAM
Plus Special Guests

AREA £3.50   SEAT P 2

Booking Agents: City Hall Box Office
Northumberland Road, Newcastle upon Tyne (Tel 20007)

The JAM + Support
King George's Hall BLACKBURN
Wednesday December 12th 7.30pm
Tickets £3 (Advance)

THE JAM nº 4400
CLUB!
Ian McDiarmid
Paul Weller
B. Foxton

Best Wishes and Thanks for Your Support
Paul Weller
B. Foxton

MUSIC FESTIVALS (SCOTLAND) LTD. PRESENT
LOCH LOMOND ROCK FESTIVAL
24th and 25th MAY 1980
21 June
SATURDAY, 24th — Gates open 2 p.m.
Performance commences 4.30 p.m.

SATURDAY TICKET
£6.50 inc VAT (IN ADVANCE)
No 07709

SOLID BOND IN YOUR HEART

Jam. I also bought *Record Mirror* and the *New Musical Express* every week to follow the punk scene and growing bands, the Sex Pistols' 'Pretty Vacant' on first hearing giving the same vibes of energy for a young teen wanting all in life.

In '78 when *All Mod Cons* came out, I repeated over and over my favourite track on that album, 'To Be Someone', the lyrics and song style mesmerising and inspiring me daily. I idolised that album's powerful lyrics on youth life… and bang in the middle there was a secret track, 'English Rose'. I had to see them live. It took a wee while, but it finally happened at Glasgow Apollo in December '79.

Turning 19 that summer, we visited Great Yarmouth, wearing my shirt with the black Jam logo every day, wanting people to ask and comment on it. And 1979 for me was some year, growing up into a man, the music huge. We even had *Quadrophenia*, the movie of all movies. That gave you a lust for more. But while my Apollo gig experience was amazing, I never admitted to the guys I went to the show with that I'd been at the same venue a few years back with a bunch of girls from local bra and underwear factory Playtex, seeing the Bay City Rollers. That was mental.

The Jam gave local talent a chance, and I'll always remember The Questions, buying their single right after. Then came the headliners. One minute it was dark, then there was a beam of light and I recall the guitar sound for the first song, my favourite, 'To Be Someone', giving that inspirational feeling which remained to the end, us clapping and shouting, wanting encore after encore.

I saw The Jam twice at the Apollo. I still see the green lights and hear the sound of Foxton's bass and Buckler's drums for my first live airing of 'Pretty Green'. They also did the *Bucket and Spade* tour that year, and while I was only three days married, I went to the Magnum Centre in Irvine, Ayrshire, to see my heroes. My mother-in-law said, 'Start as you mean to go on, spending money on concerts and your record collection.' She meant well, my wife Jane five months pregnant then. That show was full of lads – I never saw many girls, not like the Bay City Rollers gig! Jumping and banging into one another, sweat, heat… fantastic!

My other Jam concert was on the east coast at Edinburgh's huge Ingliston Exhibition Centre in '82. By then The Jam were most definitely the biggest band in the world, especially in my mind. Who else could write songs with the energy of 'When You're Young', 'Funeral Pyre', 'Strange Town', and B-sides like 'Liza Radley'? Only Lennon and McCartney could match Weller's genius.

I was devastated when they broke up, but respected and understood that the genius wanted to explore… and boy, he did. The wife and I saw him with The Style Council and then the Paul Weller Movement at Glasgow's Queen Margaret Union in '89 or '90. I've never been let down. The songs live in my heart forever, and even that night he did two oldies. I live and love Weller.

On 5 November 2011, I found myself having to give up the booze, facing losing everything in my life, having hit rock bottom. I didn't know until a few years later that Paul gave it up around the same time. Ironically, I'd worked since 1999 at Diageo in Glasgow, home of Johnnie Walker whisky and other brands. I've been off the drink since, with a new life, having been through a divorce then remarrying the same lady, Jane, on 1 September 2018 on the Isle of Mull at Duarte Castle, home of my clan, McLean. I re-proposed at Edinburgh Castle that May.

We have a wee grandson now, aged five and autistic, James Alexander McLean… known as JAM. One boy among six granddaughters before him. I lived life well from '78 to 2011, but still thought I was in one of Weller's songs – 'life's a drink but you get drunk when you're young' was my motto. I don't regret too much though. I revisit the past and recall some fantastic music. It's a way of life is music, and I was lucky to see The Jam four times. I wish I could do it over and over again.

QUEENS EXHIBITION HALL
11 DECEMBER 1979, LEEDS, UK

I WAS THERE: MARK DOBSON, AGE 15

I went with my older sister who was 21, and everything that could go wrong did go wrong. It was a miserable, cold evening in a miserable, cold venue, the horrible old Queens Hall. I had some great nights there – Genesis, the Police, Lizzy – but if you wanted to go and see a gig in Leeds, you had to go to the Queens Hall. It was the only show in town. The sound was awful.

The support band were The Vapors. There was no sign of anything going on, but when The Jam came on there was a huge surge towards the front of the stage. I thought 'oh shit!' I'd been to a lot of gigs and I'd been in a lot of crowds. But there were people there who were deliberately agitated, piling into people. It's the only concert I've ever been to where I thought 'shit, I'm in above my head.'

Paul Weller didn't help. He was at the front of the stage and he wasn't trying to provoke trouble, but he was repeatedly hitting the microphone stand and knocking it over with the machine head on his guitar, and every time he did it there was another surge. And, all of a sudden, I've got my five-foot two sister at the side of me and literally screaming with fright: 'Get me out, get me out!' She was hysterical and she's not that sort of girl. We'd been to loads of gigs. We'd been to Stafford Bingley Hall, so we were used to big crowds, and she was used to handling herself in a concert situation. But it got really ugly. There was a bit of a brawl and it was scary.

This was eight days after Cincinnati (when eleven Who fans were trampled to death in a crush at the Richfield Coliseum in Ohio), and being a big Who fan, what went through my mind was, 'Shit, it's going to happen again, right here in Leeds.' And even as a youngster I was thinking, 'Hasn't anybody learnt anything in the past week? That you can't pen people in a space like this and then really have no strategy for crowd control?'

I hauled her out and we went back to a building called the Corn Exchange. There used to be a fish and chip shop next to it and I said to her, 'Come on, let's get some fish and chips and calm down and chill out.' And I said to her, 'My hand's hurting.' In the melee, and in trying to get her out, I must have hit somebody because I had a very, very swollen hand. But because of the adrenaline I hadn't noticed the pain.

It was a deeply unpleasant evening and it's still imprinted on my brain. We didn't go back in. We only stayed for two songs.

I WAS THERE: GARY COX, AGE 14

There was hard punk like the Pistols and there were other bands that were slightly different, like The Clash, The Jam and Buzzcocks. My brother, who was five years older, bought *All Mod Cons* and listening to that just blew me away. There was a whole variety of songs on the album, like 'Fly', 'The Place I Love' and 'In The Crowd'. I was learning to play the guitar so I was trying to learn those Jam songs myself.

1979 saw the Mod revival and I started understanding some of their influences. Weller would talk about The Beatles' *Revolver* and some of their later stuff so I started getting into that. I was saying how I liked 'Helter Skelter' when my friends were listening to 'Love Me Do' and 'She Loves You'. Then I really got into The Who, the Small Faces and The Kinks.

I went to grammar school, which was three bus rides away. I'd get home really late, at 6.15pm or 6.30pm. People would talk about seeing *Grange Hill* on the telly and I was like, 'Well, I'm still on the bus. I'm on my third bus journey.' I had a little red transistor radio which I'd listen to on the bus in the afternoon, but it wasn't great even with my earpiece.

Setting Sons was coming out and the tour was announced so instead of going to school that day I went down to HMV to buy a ticket. On the day of the gig, I convinced my dad I was going to my friend's house near school to play football and that his dad would then drive me home. After school, I changed into a military jacket I'd bought from the Army & Navy Stores and a pair of jeans. I might have had Adidas trainers. Then I got the bus from my friend's house into Leeds. I had my school stuff in a haversack.

I got in and went to the side near the front. I was quite tall, six foot one, so I could see okay. I remember the anticipation of just standing there, my first gig. The Vapors were on first and then John Weller came on to introduce the band like he did… and the magic happened! I'd never seen so much energy as I saw on that stage. Weller had this Italian-style jacket on and a paisley scarf and he just looked so cool. *Setting Sons* had come out the week before and I had got it, so I knew all the songs. I remember the crowd swaying. I could hear an organ sound; I think they had Mick Talbot behind the curtain. When they went off, the lights came on and I just stood there trying to take it all in. I was wet through with sweat and then it occurred to me. How am I gonna get on the bus, get home and explain why everything is crumpled? But I wasn't bothered. John Weller was throwing out plectrums and I got a plectrum – I don't know if it was Weller's or Foxton's or one from The Vapors, but I didn't care!

I went back home and was rumbled by my brother. My parents were concerned – they thought there was something up – and they were annoyed, but it was all right.

Rick Buckler and Bruce Foxton were more than just a rhythm section. And Paul Weller? Those songs mattered to him when he was singing them. I lived on a council estate and those songs resonated with me. He was only in his twenties and he was writing about social injustice, about a lack of social mobility and all the unfairness he was seeing in society. So it was, 'Right, I need to go and see them again.'

KING GEORGE'S HALL
12 DECEMBER 1979, BLACKBURN, UK

I WAS THERE: MICK SHEPHERD

My older brother had just passed his driving test, which meant we didn't have to run the gauntlet of public transport to get to Blackburn. Back then there was a lot of fighting between Preston and Blackburn punks, and a couple of friends had recently had trouble at a Buzzcocks gig. Rumour had it they'd send a few people down to see who was getting off the Preston bus before pointing them out at the gig!

Setting Sons had been released a month earlier and the gig showcased material from the new album. Support came from Guildford band The Vapors, who went on to score a huge hit with 'Turning Japanese'. My abiding memory of the night was the energy that went into those performances, from both bands. Weller positively spat out the lyrics and there was such fire and passion in the delivery it was hard not to get swept up in the moment. We all did! Raw, youthful energy with a political edge, it was all there.

As with lots of gigs back in the late seventies, there was the spirit of rebellion and a freshness to the sound, a feeling that we were all part of the music and a cultural revolution that was in full swing. The Jam delivered with such ferocious enthusiasm but there was also real quality in the songs. These weren't three-minute throwaways but stories with messages wrapped in infectious, well-crafted melodies. I was in awe of the power the three of them created on stage. The menacing heavy bass of 'The Eton Rifles', the vitriolic delivery of Weller's vocals… They had such presence live, and Weller was a new kind of frontman, with a nod to Steve Marriott but with that punk sensibility and anger at injustice that was so much part of the time. I can't be absolutely certain it was Paul Weller's plectrum, but I did find one on the floor near the stage after the gig. I like to think it was one of his.

I WAS THERE: JOHN WINSTANLEY

I went with John Jones, Michael Robinson and others who'd gone to Runshaw College, Leyland that September. I noticed John on day one of our Economics class as he wore a Jam badge, and we talked about every Jam release over the next two years. It was a freezing cold night. I think I got there by bus and know I had to go home on one as I needed to leave before the end to catch it in time.

As soon as we arrived, we piled in at the front of the stage in the middle. When The Vapors started with a drum intro, we erupted in a mass pogo. We had to move up and down as we were packed so closely – we had no choice. Frontman Dave Fenton stared straight ahead, the band powering through their set in no time. They were brightly dressed and, being that close to a live band for the first time, made my ears ring for days afterwards. I was dressed in a thick brown Parka and had to get as close to the outside as I could, sweating like a drowning man.

When The Jam came on, I hung back as the crowd went berserk. Weller was on the right, and I lined up to face him as best I could, with those slamming around me. He was so confident and commanded respect from the crowd, who came to pay homage to the trio's supremacy as *the* live band to see. 'Little Boy Soldiers' stood out as Rick Buckler did a mini-drum solo, his kit lit up like a searchlight while the rest of the stage was in darkness. Also, 'Strange Town' had been released, and got a rousing response.

CONFERENCE CENTRE
15 DECEMBER 1979, BRIGHTON, UK

I WAS THERE: SARAH HARWOOD, AGE 15

My first ever concert. My boyfriend had got my parents' permission. Paul had to stop a fight in the pit. I had a friend at school who asked nearly every day for my ticket stub. That was Russell Hastings, lately fronting From The Jam!

I WAS THERE: MARK TAYLOR

My first gig was at the Brighton Centre in December 1979, and my last was back there in Brighton in December 1982… with lots in between! I loved every minute, it was the soundtrack to my youth. I went backstage at the gig at Crawley Leisure Centre and had a few beers out of cans with the band. It was pretty chaotic, and God knows how we got back there! Jam shoes and a bit of blag, I guess.

I WAS THERE: STUART STEELES

It was 24 August 1977 when my sister, Kim, called me into the front room to see a band she thought I'd like. It was The Jam's performance of 'All Around The World' on the *Marc* TV show, and it was a pivotal moment. The energy, the haircuts, the suits and shoes, the red Rickenbackers, and the music and lyrics.

Five years older than me, Kim was instrumental in shaping my musical tastes. She introduced me to Slade and Bowie before I became mildly obsessed with early to mid-phase Beatles. That's when she decided I needed another steer, hence The Jam. She got me a copy of *In The City*.

Stuart Steeles (left) first saw Rick Buckler & the rest of The Jam on Marc Bolan's TV show

In 1977, The Beatles were viewed as hippies and were not at all fashionable. And it's funny to look back at 'All Around The World' on the *Marc* show and realise the impact that The Jam in matching suits and shoes had on me. Seeing Bolan in a leopard-skin jumpsuit open to the waist was what I'd got used to over the previous few years.

Fast forward to mid-December 1979, with three fellow 14-year-old boys in Brighton for the *Setting Sons* tour. Having got the train ridiculously early from Worthing, we found ourselves at the front of the Centre late in the afternoon. We weren't there long when an old bloke with swept-back hair opened one of the glass doors and asked if we wanted to come into the soundcheck. None of us knew what a 'soundcheck' was, but it meant we could get away from the freezing, driving rain so we followed him inside.

He led us into the main hall, where Bruce and Rick were already on stage, tuning up. There were maybe 30 people there, most taping down cables or something similar. Then, from a side door, in walked Paul. He came over, signed autographs and chatted. Completely gobsmacked, I couldn't think of anything to say, but finally asked if they'd play 'Art School'. Paul said he didn't think he could remember how to. Someone produced a football from somewhere and we joined the kickabout, as did Paul. It was very odd, being inside the Brighton Centre one rainy December afternoon playing football with Paul Weller. The football was taken away, and after making sure everyone was happy with their autographs, Paul joined the others on stage and they played three or four songs.

As the band left the stage, the same old bloke with swept-back hair apologised and said he needed to take us back outside. He checked we had tickets for the show and said he hoped we would enjoy it. A little before 9pm, the lights went down in the hall and the same bloke with swept-back hair came onto the stage. It was only then that I realised it was John Weller. What followed is the stuff of legend. And from such gestures of kindness and respect, lifelong solid bonds are forged. None of us will ever forget what happened that day. As the great man said, 'Put your hands together for the best band in the fucking world!'

GUILDHALL
16 DECEMBER 1979, PORTSMOUTH, UK

I WAS THERE: OWEN PARKER

In all I saw them seven times between Portsmouth Guildhall and Brighton Centre. I met them in 1979 after a gig in Portsmouth and they all signed the t-shirt I was wearing, albeit covered in sweat… which amused Paul! Great times.

I WAS THERE: DAVE CLARK

I got into punk and new wave in 1978, thanks to friends I made when I moved to Leigh Park, a big council estate on the outskirts of Portsmouth. I'd arrived the year before in flares with a bowl haircut. The Boomtown Rats were the first punk band I got into. Lots of people dispute that they were ever a punk band. To me they definitely were. Johnny Fingers in his pyjamas was so cool. Later, I bought myself a pair of black and white trousers, trying to get away with wearing them to school and getting sent home.

My new mates had a fantastic look. In a school with no uniform, wearing straight trousers, school blazers, shirts and (sometimes) ties, Jam shoes and sporting feather spike haircuts, we were proper Jam-influenced. *Setting Sons* was the first LP of theirs I bought on release (in London on a shopping trip looking for a Parka... with my mum). The first single I bought on release? 'When You're Young'.

I flirted with the Mod revival, which was quite a big thing in Leigh Park. I remember school discos chucking out and loads of people going up to Point 7 up the road, shouting 'We are the Mods!' Quite un-Mod behaviour, it transpires. There were also punch-ups with lads on their 'fizzies'. I remember, one night, proper bikers turning up at Broomfield, riding down Middle Park Way in twos, proper engines rumbling. When we realised, we legged it through gardens, over fences... not everyone getting away without a bit of a kicking. As for the Mod revival, I think my mum liked it more. I smartened up with some of my dad's old suits, tailored to fit.

I saw the *Setting Sons* tour at Portsmouth Guildhall, The Vapors supporting. I went in my Parka and got Paul Weller's autograph beforehand, on a Union Jack patch on the back. I'm pretty sure he was wearing a Parka... as were most people there.

A few of us photocopied tickets (not me, honest) and tried to get in with them. My mum sewed perforations in the fake tickets on her sewing machine. I think tickets cost about £3. As well as the autograph, I came away with a tour badge plus a Jam scarf, bought outside. I loved the gig, and The Jam have remained firm favourites. Later, I got into The Style Council and Paul Weller as a solo artist, and these days DJ with a friend, playing warm-up sets for Paul a couple of times.

I didn't last with the Mod revival. I felt a bit 'smart'. A school mate called Neil played a big part in me binning it off. While Parka'd up at Portsmouth & Southsea Station one day, I saw someone coming towards me in tartan bondage trousers, black leather jacket and spiked hair. I felt like a bank clerk in comparison.

I WAS THERE: STEVE MATTHEWS

I saw them twice in the late seventies at Portsmouth Guildhall, and then Guildford and then Hammersmith, in 1980 or 1981. I took my little brother and his mate to one at Portsmouth and they were invited backstage by the band… whilst I had to stand outside and wait!

PAVILION
21 DECEMBER 1979, BATH, UK

I WAS THERE: MARK FOSTER

My first ever concert, with The Vapors as support. I saw them again in Shepton Mallet on the *Sound Affects* tour and then one last concert, their finale at Brighton Centre. Happy days!

The year ends with Setting Sons *at No.4 in the* NME's *albums of the year and 'Eton Rifles' topping the singles list with 'Strange Town' at No.5. 'Down In The Tube Station At Midnight' features at No.4 in John Peel's Festive Fifty on BBC Radio 1.*

CORN EXCHANGE
11 FEBRUARY 1980, CAMBRIDGE, UK

I WAS THERE: JOHN GREENAWAY

I saw them at Cambridge Corn Exchange. Me and my mates went in the dressing room after. I remember eating half French stick sandwiches. I thought that was posh!

UNIVERSITY OF KENT
12 FEBRUARY 1980, CANTERBURY, UK

I WAS THERE: JON ABNETT

I saw The Jam many times, but this one stands out. This was the second of a four-night warm-up (ending with a gig at Woking YMCA) before they went off on a US tour. An earlier date in Portsmouth was cancelled, so I was on edge in case this was too. I attended with Neil Marsh, my good friend from junior school.

I was attending Maidstone College of Art for my diploma in graphic design and heard about the gig one lunchtime in the refectory. I thought it was a rumour, but the following lunchtime tickets were on sale in The Longplayer, a cool record shop in Maidstone town centre, at the top of Gabriels Hill. (Like most great record shops, it's long gone.) I bagged two tickets for £3.

Returning to college, I proudly displayed my tickets to anyone interested, keen to let them know. Like me, at first, they were sceptical. Now it was no longer a rumour. The course I was on was made up mainly of punks, but with a few other Mods, who also managed to secure tickets. Medway had a mini Mod population and a decent music scene spawning the likes of The Prisoners.

The gig was half empty, probably one of the emptiest I saw for a Jam gig – others I went to were rammed. The sports hall was cavernous and should have been filled to capacity, but that was the issue with 'student only' gigs, as technically only SU members were allowed tickets as it was promoted bvy the Students Union and only advertised in the colleges of Canterbury and Maidstone.

That was the first time I saw 'Going Underground' played live, or even heard it in any shape or form. Other notable songs were 'The Dreams Of Children' and 'Start!' and old favourites like 'Tube Station' and 'David Watts'. I was never one for getting down the front, but due to the poor attendance we were pretty close. And it was obvious that some non-student Jam fans found their way in.

The support was Kidz Next Door, with Jimmy Pursey's younger brother Robbie as lead singer and Grant Fleming (Sham/Cockney Rejects roadie, one of the main faces on the Mod revival scene) on bass. But I was only there for my beloved Jam.

Neither Neil nor myself had a car, so it was a train from Chatham to Canterbury, then blagging a lift to the uni off a like-minded fan in his Mini Clubman. Legging it back to catch the train home proved more difficult. Talk on the journey home was pretty much all about the gig, what Weller was wearing, his haircut, 'Going Underground'… After any gig, sleep deprivation was guaranteed, adrenalin still pumping. The next day at college was spent catching up with those who also went. It was always nice to hear people who had never seen The Jam live, hearing odd comments. The main one was always how loud they were for a three-piece band.

I started at the college in 1979 and remember a lecture theatre and at the back a control room with a state-of-the-art record deck, linked to mind-blowing (literally) speakers, with 'In The City' on rotation every lunch break along with The Clash, Ian Dury and the Pistols. The punks on the course were very elitist, soon turning their backs on the Pistols and The Clash, favouring Adam and The Ants, the start of the New Romantic movement.

Looking back, the crowd were very young, 14 to 18-year-olds really. There were the odd hippie types and punks in the early days, but when Mod hit big time crowds were 90 per cent Mod. It was mayhem down the front, with lots of fights. But there were some cool clothes and the start of the Weller clone thing. It was easy to get hold of the clothes, involving a trip to Carnaby Street for Carnaby Cavern, Shelly's or Melanddi.

WINTER GARDENS
13 FEBRUARY 1980, MALVERN, UK

I WAS THERE: CHRIS GREEN

All Mod Cons was the turning point. That album was outstanding. It was different to what punk had promised to be. Punk had all gone a bit nihilistic really, with caring for your fellow man being seen as some kind of weakness. Paul Weller turned his back on that completely.

I'd seen them the year before, in 1977, and I thought they were a bit of a mess to be honest. I wasn't overly keen on the first album. A lot of people think it's fantastic but I thought it was full of Dr Feelgood speeded up beat songs. But I liked the spikiness of Paul Weller and I liked the image.

I always remember the explosion at the end of ''A' Bomb'. I'd not seen a band do anything like that before. I'd been to other gigs, but not ones that captured that sense of excitement. I'm from Worcester and I first saw them at Malvern Winter Gardens. It's a wonderful venue in the Malvern Hills, in the least likely town you'd ever expect, but all the punk bands played there. The promoters went on to set up Cherry Red Records. It was a 1,000 capacity venue with a great bar in the reception area and a great merch set up.

I'd seen them on *Top Of The Pops* and thought 'he's a spiky young fellow, that guy; a bit angry but measured.' I came to punk a little bit late. I was aware of it in 1976, but I didn't go to any gigs. The Stranglers were the first band I saw, and I heard their first album, with the weirdness of Dave Greenfield's keyboards.

In The City is a fantastic record, but it felt like they were falling away a little bit with *The Modern World* and lots of other bands had caught up. Then they really hit their straps in 1978 with *All Mod Cons*, especially 'Down In The Tube Station At Midnight' which changed everything. There hadn't really been a single like that, with the drum pattern and the bass sounding like a Tube train waiting to come into the station. I was a West Brom supporter, and a lot of what The Jam and The Clash sang about was being played out at football matches. The supporters club would get a coach to go to away games and we were all into the same sort of music. 'Down In The Tube Station At Midnight' would be one of those songs we'd all sing on the way back from a game, when we've had a few beers.

After the *'A' Bomb* tour, The Jam became *the* band, and me and one or two others started following them around the country and even overseas. I was wholly into that and wholly into the Mod thing. I'd already had echoes of Mod, even during the glam thing, wearing a Ben Sherman shirt, because my brother had been on the back end of that first time round. A group of us just decided to become Mods from that point. We weren't aware of it becoming the bigger thing that it became in 1979. *All Mod Cons* summed that up really. The band had matured so much in that twelve to 18 months, and Paul Weller's strength and confidence and persona seemed to grow by miles.

I saw them 30 something times altogether. They played places like Barbarella's in Birmingham again in early 1978, but I was too young to go to those sort of venues until we knew we could get back home afterwards. I saw them again in April and May '79 when they went on tour, but the big year for me was 1980.

They did three or four gigs in preparation for the American tour and Malvern Winter Gardens was one of them. I think I'd read that people got in for the soundchecks so I said 'let's go along'. I had a good chat with Paul Weller before and after, because there's very little to do in Malvern in the winter, scenic place though it is. He said to me, 'Is there anywhere to go and eat?' and I said 'well, there's a Chinese up the road.' I remember having a good chat with him in the reception area about politics. There weren't that many people at the soundcheck.

They were touring in America when 'Going Underground' went to number one over here. They were slightly caught out by it going straight in at number one, so they flew back and they did all the *Top Of The Pops* things.

They played Malvern again in 1980, because they tagged it onto the end of the *Sound Affects* tour. For that tour, we went to a week's worth of gigs around the country and saw them in Bracknell, Poole, Cardiff, Birmingham and then a couple of gigs in Leicester. We stayed at the De Montfort hotel which I believe is where they stayed. I remember being in the bar with them afterwards and having a drink with them. That's how casual everything was. I met a girlfriend there.

The soundchecks started to get bigger, so you could have hundreds of kids just milling around. It would vary. When you went to Leicester or Birmingham or Cardiff, a lot more people would turn up.

I was a Mod in 1979 but by 1980 it was all over in that manifestation of it. It stopped being cool and ahead of the game and there was all this trouble between youth subcultures. To anybody else we still looked like Mods but we weren't wearing Parkas and we certainly weren't interested in fighting the rockers. There was none of that cliche stuff that came along with *Quadrophenia*.

I went to the infamous Paris gig where it kicked off. A lot of English went over there. There was a whole bunch of coaches which I think were organised by the band themselves. I got on the wrong coach – I had forgotten the number of the coach I was supposed to be on because I'd had a few drinks and stuff – and John Weller hauled me off it and put me on the right one.

EMERALD CITY
27 FEBRUARY 1980, CHERRY HILL, NEW JERSEY

The band embark on a 15-date North America tour. Supports include The Beat, The Professionals and Stax legends Sam and Dave.

'GOING UNDERGROUND' RELEASED
10 MARCH 1980

The Jam are staying at Hollywood's Sunset Marquee Hotel when, four days after its release, they hear that their new single has entered the UK singles chart at the top. The single spends three weeks at No.1.

I WAS THERE: RUPERT TRACY

Everything just exploded with 'Going Underground'. I remember sitting in my bedroom with my little transistor radio. The charts were on a Thursday in those days and I came home from school and I was listening to Radio 1 and it was getting to No.4 and they still hadn't played the new Jam single and I was thinking 'has it really not even made the charts?' I couldn't understand it. And then suddenly… Number one! And I was thinking fucking hell, yes! Everybody had gone out to buy the double pack single and by all accounts it sold over 250,000 copies in its first week. Which is unheard of now. And suddenly The Jam were the biggest group in the country. The Police may have sold more records. But they never had that fanatical and loyal fanbase that The Jam did.

I WAS THERE: GARY COX

There was a special edition of 'Going Underground' where you got an EP with a copy of 'Down In The Tube Station At Midnight', recorded in Germany with a special sleeve. Instead of getting the three buses to school that day, and knowing there'd only be so many copies, I went down to HMV, where there was already a massive queue. I didn't go to school that day. My mum and dad worked shifts so I was able to walk back from the bus stop about 6.30pm, saying 'yeah, just had a decent day at school' when actually I'd been home all day, playing the record.

I WAS THERE: JOE SHIELDS

My mate in the last year at school hated The Jam. He was a proper soul boy into the disco scene. He hated the punk sound or anything remotely shouty. He said The Jam were a load of shit. I said to him, "Going Underground' will go straight in at No.1.' He said 'no chance' and I said, 'I bet you a fiver,' which was my week's paper round money.' He said, 'You're on.' I used to go round to another friend's house for sandwiches at lunchtime, because it was about ten minutes away from school. We sat there waiting for the Top 10 countdown. They hadn't mentioned it and I said, 'It's got to be No.1, it's got to be No.1.' And it was. It went in at No.1. I went back into school and I was saying 'where is he? Where is he?' He went 'you fucker'. I said, 'Told you!' He said, 'I haven't got it on me. I'll have to bring it in tomorrow.' I remember him coming up to me at registration and saying, 'Here is your fiver.' I have never been so elated at winning a fiver in all my life. I still remind him about it every now and again, all these years later.

BBC TELEVISION CENTRE
27 MARCH 1980, WHITE CITY, LONDON, UK

I WAS WATCHING: ALAN BURROWS

I don't think anyone can ignore how much The Jam benefitted from *Top of the Pops*. To 'perform' 'Going Underground', they fucked off an American tour to fly back to the UK on Concorde to record the show. Dates in Houston, Washington and New Jersey were cancelled. They went straight in at No.1, the first band to do so since Slade in 1973, that news relayed across the Atlantic, the promo video shown that Thursday night on an iconic BBC chart show watched by more than 10 million people every week. But they were back in time to appear that following week.

It was *the* source of conversation for teens in the days of three channels, Weller sporting a Heinz tomato soup pinny turned inside out, confirming what fans already knew, spreading the word – The Jam were the 'best band in the whole fucking world'. The maddest thing about that night? It was the seventeenth time they featured on *TOTP* since 1977. They wanted exposure and got it from the start, at a time when The Clash were accused of selling out by signing for CBS. Don't forget, The Clash boycotted the show (in 1980 leading to a frankly daft decision to broadcast Legs & Co dressed up behind bars doing a routine for 'Bankrobber'.) Richard Jobson said the Skids' decision to play the show almost caused the band to break up, but The Jam dropped everything to be on it.

They were introduced at times by Tony Blackburn, who complained how it was 'disgusting the way punks sing about violence… why can't they sing about trees and flowers?' By the end of March 1980 change was underway, the line-up an eclectic mix – Liquid Gold, Genesis, Brothers Johnson, Dr Hook, Judas Priest, Siouxsie and the Banshees, John Foxx, and the Detroit Spinners. And The Jam.

It was later claimed that Weller was hitting back at anyone who thought the band had 'sold out', that Heinz apron in reference to 1967's *The Who Sell Out*. BBC bosses said he couldn't wear it – you couldn't advertise brands on the Beeb – hence his decision to wear it back to front. Others claim he was wearing it in contempt for the 'sheep' copying his clothes. The fact that a few fans wore soup aprons at Jam gigs after seeing that performance perhaps proves that. But forget all that, this performance sent The Jam into another league.

'And the public wants what the public gets, But I don't get what this society wants.'

Now I was getting what I wanted. No one else was singing lyrics that related to your life, that you could sing like a footy chant. The way he spits out 'rut' and 'plate' made this boy shout, made this boy scream.

Even after they announced the split, they hightailed up to Newcastle for the first broadcast of soon essential flagship Channel 4 music show, *The Tube*. Think about it now, 'David Watts', 'Tube Station', 'When You're Young' and 'The Eton Rifles' on telly at teatime, live from the North-East. And it wasn't just British telly. I spend nights whiling away hours online, looking at old footage. Some of it is amazing, in the days before wall-to-wall videos. Danish TV broadcast a 38-minute special on 19 April 1982 with twelve songs. The kids in the audience already have the wedge haircut and there's a brilliant version of 'Trans-Global Express'. And you can't say he'd lost his anger at that point – check out those lyrics!

RAINBOW THEATRE
7 & 8 APRIL 1980, FINSBURY PARK, LONDON, UK

I WAS THERE: RICHARD MUDD
Touring America with Blue Öyster Cult – God knows who put that bill together! – they came back for two gigs at the Rainbow that have almost become mythical with Jam fans. I went both nights and I was right in the midst of it at the first, jumping around. The energy and power that three-piece produced was amazing. And they were bloody good songs. Weller was still only 21, but some of those songs… wow! When they did 'Going Underground' that night, it was like your team had just scored a last-minute winner in an FA Cup final. There was always a good feeling among fans you met, and they had such a solid following. I was very lucky to be there.

I WAS THERE: PETER BOWERS
I attended the second of two consecutive nights celebrating 50 years of the Rainbow venue. We had seats on an upper balcony and as The Jam tore through their set, it looked like the entire downstairs standing area was a blur of

movement and energy. The band were wearing blue mohair suits and the whole spectacle of audience mayhem unfolding below us and The Jam on raucous form was thrilling to witness.

I WAS THERE: ALAN ALDER

My Jam story started with seeing them do 'In The City' on *Top Of The Pops*. They seemed so different to anything else that night. This was before many punk bands had been on TV. I was 13 and loved this wild new punk thing exploding across the country. I saw the Pistols on Bill Grundy – the funniest thing I'd ever seen. I was too young for gigs then, but that was about to change…

   I bought the next (and my first) Jam single, 'All Around The World', after seeing them on *TOTP* and hearing it a couple of times on Radio 1, loving the raw power, thrashing guitars and Weller's snarling delivery, hooked for life. The British music scene was suddenly really exciting, and I loved most of the bands that followed the Pistols in '77. The following year my elder sister and brother-in-law started taking me to gigs and by 15 I was going with older mates. I left school early and got a job, so had money for gigs and records, and that's pretty much what I did from '78 to '82. I was a big Clash and Buzzcocks fan too, but when The Jam put out *All Mod Cons* they became *my* band. From then, I barely missed a London Jam gig until they split, venturing out to other towns once I could drive.

   I saw them 28 times, and the gigs at the Rainbow, Finsbury Park and the Music Machine, Camden stand out. I saw them eight times at the Rainbow, and it was always great, but those two nights in April 1980 were extra special, with 'Going Underground' at No.1 and the America tour ditched. It was a homecoming celebration for the biggest band in the country, with the crowd and band at the absolute peak. One night they did the Four Tops classic, 'Reach Out I'll Be There' as an encore. I think that was the only time they played it live.

   The peak for me as a recording band and live was 1979/80. The big neon Jam sign would start flashing, John Weller coming out to introduce the 'best band in the fucking world… If anyone falls down, pick 'em up for The Jam!' The band would walk on, plug in, Paul would ask 'How are you, alright?' and we were off – two hours of mayhem.

POLYDOR STUDIOS
APRIL 1980, STRATFORD PLACE, LONDON, UK

I WAS THERE: BRETT 'BUDDY' ASCOTT, THE CHORDS

I was a huge fan from first hearing 'Art School' on a cheap compilation in '77 to seeing them live on a tiny stage at Stockwell College, Bromley that May, and all the way through the next two years until The Chords signed for the same label. After that, and all the unwarranted comparisons in the music press, we kind of became rivals, if not exactly competitors – they were years ahead of us in most areas. So, three vignettes, all in Dennis Munday's office at Polydor (we were *always* there, thieving records, drinking free beers, abusing the free phone).

9 April 1980: Paul Weller comes into Dennis's office. "Ere Buddy, you can play a bit of percussion, can't ya?' 'Er, yes, I never leave home without my maracas.' 'Come and give us a hand then!' The song is his demo of 'But I'm Different Now', destined for *Sound Affects* (for me, The Jam's best album). We cross the corridor to the in-house Polydor recording studio that's become Weller's temporary home. All that shaking and I never got a songwriting credit! Still, what an honour.

June 1980: Dennis plays us the acetate of 'Start!', the new Jam single, about to be unleashed on the public. Ten seconds in, all of us – huge Beatles fans to a man – look at each other and then Dennis and start laughing. 'Is this a wind up? It's a cover, right?'

August 1980: The Chords have recorded two potential A-sides for our fifth single at Townhouse Studios, West London, The Jam next door labouring over *Sound Affects*. One is Dexy's/Madness hybrid 'Empty Dreams' – a radical departure in approach and sound for us. The other is the more prosaic, Clash-inspired 'In My Street'. Chris (Pope) and Martin (Mason) opt for 'Street', Billy (Hassett) and I are 'Dreams' advocates, thinking a change in direction could provide a breakthrough. We're in Dennis's office again, but he refuses to cast a deciding vote in this impasse.

Weller pops his head round the door to talk to Dennis and is ushered in. 'We need a casting vote,' says Dennis. 'Sit down, have a listen to these two songs, say which is the better single.' Paul proves to be a 'Street' man. The rest is history. 'In My Street' peaks at No.50, ultimately proving to be Billy's last single with us. A sliding doors moment, one Billy and I often discuss with wry laughter.

Don't misunderstand me – we were labelmates with The Jam. Bruce, especially later, become a (heavy) drinking partner of Chris and I as The Chords petered out in late 1981. Paul was always supportive and encouraging, and though I hardly knew Rick back then (he's essentially a shy chap, I think), these days I'm proud to call him a friend.

PINK POP FESTIVAL
26 MAY 1980, GELEEN, THE NETHERLANDS

The band's performance is recorded for Dutch radio and captured on film, the band flying to Rome to record a TV appearance the next day.

KING GEORGE'S HALL
3 JUNE 1980, BLACKBURN, UK

I WAS THERE: GRAHAM WEBSTER

The Jam were very much a 'here and now, enjoy the moment' band. If mobile phones existed then, I'd like to think Weller would have banned them. I bought nearly all their records and still play them from time to time. The first album that really resonated with me was *All Mod Cons*. I was impressed that the lyrics were printed on the inner sleeve. The Clash didn't do that. Weller was a 'spokesman for a generation', but that mantle rested uneasy on his shoulders. The last two tracks on side two in particular changed the way I thought about music and the outside world. I don't think any album has had a better signing off. Punk told stories of real life and had a conscience. The Adverts sang about Gary Gilmore, The Clash had 'Career Opportunities', but nobody did it better than Weller.

'Do you wanna cut down on beer, or the kids' new gear? It's a big decision in a town called malice.'

The gigs were full-blooded affairs. Weller in particular took no prisoners in his delivery. It doesn't surprise me that he hasn't reformed the group or done much of their material live. It would be impossible to recreate that atmosphere again.

I was lucky enough to see them four times, the first time at Blackburn's King George's Hall in December 1979. In March 1980 I broke my leg and saw The Jam with my leg in a full plaster of Paris in early June back at the King George's Hall. After the gig I hung around and got Paul, Bruce and Rick to sign my cast, keeping the signatures after it was removed… long gone now. I was amazed by their chart success. 'Going Underground' was only their second Top 10 hit but the first single to go straight in at No.1 since the days of Slade. The Jam took on mainstream, daytime Radio 1 music and annihilated it. I also saw them at Preston Guild Hall on 5 July 1981 then Blackpool Opera House on 28 March 1982. It was an earthquake when the band split. I was only 18 but looking back I think he did the right thing. Like The Beatles or The Smiths, a reform was never going to emulate what had gone on before.

VICTORIA HALL
4 JUNE 1980, HANLEY, STOKE-ON-TRENT, UK

I WAS THERE: JOHN TIDESWELL
It was back to the Victoria Hall in Hanley with five Mod mates on a small tour after

'Going Underground' made it to No.1. A good gig, the band clearly pleased with topping the charts, and on top form, belting out all their best songs.

I WAS THERE: GAVIN JONES

My mate Steve told me at the tech about an unadvertised Jam gig he'd heard about in Stoke, a warm-up for Loch Lomond. We bunked off work the next day, picked up Mark, Trev and Cas in my trusty Beetle, heading off to Stoke on a screaming hot day.

At the hall we saw roadies load in and went to a record shop where we heard you could get tickets. Sure enough, they had some left. We were in, £4 each! We went back to the hall to see if we could get into the soundcheck. After about an hour hanging around, the tour coach pulled up, Paul off first, straight over to us (about 15 kids), asking if we wanted to come in. We followed and chatted to him, sitting on the floor in the hall while Rick went through his drums, one by one. Eventually they all got on stage and did about six songs. They tried to do 'Wasteland' but Paul kept cocking up the recorder, so threw it away! They also ran through a new song, 'Start!'.

Afterwards, we got chips and went to a pub with Charlie and his mate, locals from the soundcheck. We were knackered after walking around all day in the sun. That night, we bought 'Strange Town' shirts for £1 and watched the support Expressos, with a very nice girl lead singer. Eventually, John came on, 'Put yer 'ands together for three lads, The Jam!' It was a great gig, mostly *Setting Sons* and *All Mod Cons*, with 'Going Underground' and 'Start' in there, and two encores. We gave Charlie and his mate a lift to the station (seven up in a Beetle) and then drove the hour back home, knackered but elated. I fell asleep at the wheel once, going straight over a junction.

I WAS THERE: PETER BOWERS

This was one of a handful of dates on a short tour. It wasn't as manic a gig as the 1977 one and I got a place right at the front. The band played new songs from the yet-to-be-released *Sound Affects*, including 'Start!', which was the first time I'd heard it and possibly one of the first times the band had played it live. Bruce Foxton switched bass guitars for this one and it sounded terrific – like nothing else the band had done previously. Being right down the front and not knocked around in the echo and sway was a novelty at Jam gigs.

LOCH LOMOND ROCK FESTIVAL
21 JUNE 1980, BALLOCH, UK

I WAS THERE: DAVE PRATT, AGE 16

Mike Tinkler, Steve Thompson, Gordon Peden and I went to our first music festival. All just 16, Thomo's dad gave us a lift to the site on the Friday afternoon and quickly erected a little tent for us. The festival was due to start on Saturday. From our tent, we could hear The Jam soundcheck in preparation for a headlining show the next day. We decided to get a bit closer so we could hear better, ending up on a country road behind the stage. When the soundcheck finished, we were beginning to make our way back when a minibus pulled up. We spotted the band in the vehicle and to our astonishment we were invited aboard to meet Paul, Bruce and Rick and get autographs and photographs. I still have and cherish those photographs. The Jam were easily the biggest band in the UK and when we told our friends about the experience they didn't believe us; at least, not until the photos came back from the developers.

The weekend didn't all go smoothly. On Friday night a bunch of marauding, drunken Scotsmen went on a rampage in the campsite, wrecking hundreds of tents, including ours. We were unable to fix it, so at about 2am we abandoned it and walked to a beer tent, spending the night with loads of others who suffered the same fate. The festival itself was great, seeing lots of brilliant bands from the front, including Stiff Little Fingers, The Tourists, Bad Manners and The Chords. And The Jam were triumphant, despite crowd trouble apparently started by local skinheads. Thankfully, we managed to avoid this – we were on the front barrier all day. Saturday night was, again, spent in the beer tent with hundreds of other. We probably got about two hours' sleep the whole weekend. I think we caught a train back to Durham on Sunday morning, but my memory is a bit hazy.

I WAS THERE: JOHN CAMPBELL, AGE 13

My first time seeing the best band in the fucking world live. My first gig was the previous year, the Skids at the Odeon Theatre, Edinburgh, but I couldn't wait to see The Jam, with a big thank you to Tommy, a big brother of a mate who had the most amazing vinyl collection and took me to so many gigs afterwards, introducing me to some fantastic bands. He got the newest releases as soon as they came out and played guitar in a punk band, with us helping with their equipment any time they played locally. That was instrumental in giving me a love for live music that I have to this day. Through him I got a free ticket to Loch Lomond.

It was miserable Scottish weather and about a dozen of us piled into an old Bedford van for a 90-minute journey. The older teenagers had a carry-out and were looking out for us younger ones, supplying us with the odd can of lager. We were full of excitement as we'd been to gigs before, but nothing like this. We knew there would be a mixture of Mods, punks, skins and rockers, but felt safe with the

SOLID BOND IN YOUR HEART

Photos by John Campbell

John Campbell saw The Jam at Loch Lomond

older ones in our group. Highlights for me were Stiff Little Fingers and The Jam, who blew everybody away with a blistering set of about 20 songs. The festival was marred by lots of fighting, bottle throwing and horrendous weather – fights and mud everywhere – and there was a fire at some point. But I loved it, scared at times but growing up quickly that day, seeing the band I would love for the rest of my life.

I managed to see them four more times, wishing it had been so much more. Two nights at Edinburgh Playhouse, getting the service bus there, four of us with a bottle of Bull's Blood wine acquired from the parents' drink cabinet. This particular bottle had a cork in it. We all had turns trying to push it in, passing it around and around, then – my turn again – bang! In the cork went and with the force, out gushed the wine and covered my white Lonsdale t-shirt. Not a pretty sight – it looked like I'd been seriously assaulted. The walk back to the bus station in Edinburgh mostly turned into a run, as in those days there was always loads of Mods, punks, skins and rude boys in the city centre – you could always guarantee a fight on that walk or run to the station. But we were young and it was part of the fun and excitement.

There was also one at Ingliston, just outside Edinburgh, then Glasgow Apollo, with tracks from the Playhouse and Apollo later included on *Dig The New Breed*. By then I was heavily into the Mod scene, and the Ingliston gig was full of scooters outside. Not long after, I got my first scooter, and I love them to this day.

I feel so lucky to have seen The Jam live, by far the best band in the fucking world, and live even better. I wouldn't like to see them reform. I imagine most fans that saw them live would feel the same. I guess that those wanting them to reform are those that never got a chance to see them, which I understand. But memories are best from those gigs in the past, the way it should be. It would never be the same.

I wish for only one thing – for Bruce, Paul and Rick to get together for a photograph. Long live the memories of the best band in the fucking world.

I WAS THERE: PAUL BROMLEY, AGE 15

So many of the Jam shows I saw stand out, not least Loch Lomond Festival in the summer of 1980, my first ever festival. Saturday was aimed at the new wave, ska and Mod crowd, with the likes of The Tourists, Stiff Little Fingers, The Chords and Bad Manners playing, while Sunday was more rock-focused, including Saxon and Wishbone Ash. We didn't do much of the Sunday. Most of the bands played an hour set, but The Jam did nearly two hours. That was my first time seeing them north of the border, and I went on to see them in Glasgow, Edinburgh and Irvine. As for the audience, the reaction was pretty much the same as in England, although maybe the mosh pit in Glasgow was a little more tasty.

I WAS THERE: AMANDA AUSTIN

I used to work for Cowbell Agency who represented The Jam so I went to many of their shows. One that particularly sticks out in my mind is when they played at Loch Lomond. My friend was a business travel agent so sorted out our train tickets for next to nothing, but for some reason we didn't bother with a hotel. Everyone piled back to the band's hotel and stayed in the bar until really well into the wee small hours. Only when the band started drifting off to bed, Paul being the last, did the hotel staff ask us our room numbers and then unceremoniously kick a whole bunch of us out because we weren't guests. We somehow made our way back to Glasgow Central and ended up sleeping on benches around the station until we could get on a train home. Not something you can do anymore, as the stations won't let you in if you don't have a ticket for a train you are about to get on.

MAINICHI HALL
3 JULY 1980, OSAKA, JAPAN

The band begin a successful six-date mini-tour of Japan, taking in Osaka, Kyoto and Tokyo.

FRIDAYS, ABC TV
11 JULY 1980, LOS ANGELES, CALIFORNIA

I WAS THERE: BILLY DOHERTY, THE UNDERTONES

Michael (Bradley, bass guitar) was friendly with Paul Weller, and we were both in Los Angeles at one point, where The Jam were on a TV show. They gave us front-row seats – the band and crew, and were so good. There were only three of them, but the sound was incredible. Then, when they finished, we went to walk out, but the floor manager went bonkers, as every time the camera panned round there'd be an empty row.

I WAS THERE: MICKEY BRADLEY, THE UNDERTONES

In 1980, we were in the middle of a short tour of America. Well, it was short compared to other groups, but to us it was a whole month away from our front doors. In Los Angeles one morning, I was asleep, sharing a room with Damian O'Neill, and the phone rang. It was Paul Weller. I'd met him once before at a party in London. He looked only slightly less uncomfortable than I was, standing in the middle of a room of music journalists and record company people, gathered to mark the Ramones new LP *Road To Ruin* and their appearance at the Hammersmith Odeon. We'd just signed to Sire, he'd just released *All Mod Cons*.

I loved The Jam, from the first sighting on the cover of the *NME* through to hearing the 'In The City' single in O'Neill's front room and then hearing 'David Watts' one summer's day out in O'Neill's back yard, buying everything they did. Now Paul Weller himself was on the phone, asking if we would like to come down to a TV studio that afternoon, where The Jam were guests on a music show.

I remember it for two things – they did 'Start' which hadn't been released yet. And yes, we spotted the 'Taxman' thing, but 'Start' is a far better song anyway. I also noticed and loved the Gibson semi-acoustic bass that Bruce Foxton played.

I suppose in hindsight, the correct protocol would have been us going back to The Jam's dressing room to say hello, and to thank Paul for the invite. I can't remember if we'd something else to do or if it was another example of us not being that forward. I never really hung about backstage anywhere, anyhow, anyway. Which does mean that a close encounter with any of my musical heroes are clearly remembered and still make me happy years later.

'START!' RELEASED
15 AUGUST 1980

The Jam's eleventh single, 'Start!', enters the UK charts at No.3 and reaches No.1 the following week. It's their second chart-topper and spends five weeks in the UK top 10 and seven in the Top 40. 'Liza Radley' is on the flipside.

I WAS THERE: PAOLO HEWITT

'Liza Radley' is one of The Jam's greatest songs and another inspired by Weller's Woking experiences. In the same way that the Ray Davies song 'Two Sisters' is actually about the writer and his brother, it's very tempting to see Paul as Liza Radley, the small town's misfit, the one who says very little but is acutely aware of all around, the one people think is a bit weird, just as I did when he came into my consciousness as a fully-fledged mod in the year of the soul boy. 1975. Paul must have got a reaction from many in Woking simply because of his individuality. No one I knew rode a scooter around town and dressed himself in Mod clothes. Paul was a one-off and would have felt that disparity between himself and his peers just as keenly as Liza Radley does in this song. Like her, Paul said little, but in his own room probably expressed in words (and maybe tears) his thoughts on their lives. The lyrics are bright and concise, and the melody is as haunting as the song's central character.

This is Paul's most revealing song from this period, opening up the loneliness of the individual for all to see.

HMV
15 AUGUST 1980, DUBLIN, IRELAND

I WAS THERE: ADRIAN CORBETT

While on holiday in the Republic of Ireland, within ten miles of the border, I went all the way down to HMV in Dublin to ensure I got a picture cover the day they released 'Start!' If I'd waited to buy it back in England, I wouldn't have got it.

TOP RANK
26 OCTOBER 1980, SHEFFIELD, UK

The band open their sixth major UK tour, 22 dates over 25 nights, before a further three weeks visiting eleven European cities and then five more UK dates through to the end of December.

I WAS THERE: STEVE CARVER

Even as late as the *Sound Affects* tour, late 1980, the tour bus would still set off from Balmoral Drive, Maybury.

SOLID BOND IN YOUR HEART

CITY HALL
27 & 28 OCTOBER 1980, NEWCASTLE-UPON-TYNE, UK

I WAS THERE: ANTHONY SPENCER, AGE 15

My best mate was a Mod and I was a skinhead. He brought *All Mod Cons* to my house one night and that was it… I was a Mod! For this gig, me and my mate Mark sneaked out of school and went to the City Hall, because we knew John Weller would let us in early. We went to see them every time they were in the North-East from there. I was devastated when Paul announced the split.

I WAS THERE: GRAEME DAWSON, AGE 13

I was nine years old in 1977 when I first saw The Jam play 'In The City' on *Top Of The Pops*. I'd also heard them on BBC Radio 1, and read *Smash Hits* and the *NME*, recalling my school friends talking about The Jam and their songs. 'Strange Town' was my first Jam single, and my first album was *Setting Sons*. I'd go on to buy all 18 singles and six studio LPs plus various greatest hits compilations. I saw them six times

Graeme Dawson (right) saw The Jam six times

live and caught three soundchecks. My first gig was at Newcastle City Hall, not long after my birthday. I was with a school friend, Salvatore Pignataro. I remember being excited, standing in front of the stage. I saw the words 'Fire & Skill' and really remember the impact on me. During their set the PA vocal stopped, leaving the band without vocals. While the repairs were taking place, they played an instrumental version of 'In The City' and the crowd sang along.

I WAS THERE: EILEEN CORNER

I was 14 when I started to like them. *Modern World* was the first album I listened to. I still have the albums, some singles and a scrapbook I made. I used to wear boating blazers, Harrington jackets and Fred Perry polo shirts. I would write 'The Jam' on my wooden desk. I went on a minibus with all the lads. I remember seeing Paul Weller's dad in the crowd.

I WAS THERE: GRAEME SMITH, AGE 17

I'd been a Jam fan since first hearing them on a cassette someone brought into school after recording them on the John Peel show. Their sound and Paul's lyrics seemed to capture something about being a teenager that no other band had. Plus the look was so sharp. Myself and my girlfriend travelled on a coach organised by The Other Record Shop in Hartlepool. I distinctly recall John Weller introducing them in his usual manner, 'Put your hands together for the best band in the world, THE JAM!' It was the Sound Affects tour but I don't think the album had been released so people didn't know some of the songs. But that didn't matter – the atmosphere was electric.

Five songs in, the PA broke down, Weller cadging a ciggy off someone in the crowd while waiting for it to be repaired. It was a great night that inspired me to watch as much live music as possible from then on. And two years later, I happened to spot an advert in the local newspaper for two tickets for the first of five nights at Wembley…

I WAS THERE: JOHN SUTHERAN

I was in my first year of apprenticeship as a plater at Cleveland Bridge, Port Clarence in Middlesbrough. My older brother, David, went to the booking office to buy tickets for another band (The Skids, I think) but they were sold out so he rang from a payphone in the foyer and asked if I fancied tickets for The Jam instead. I wasn't really into them but bought four… and it was probably the best night of my life. (My wife wouldn't be happy with that comment, but it was life changing!) I've been massively into them and Weller since.

Fast forward to 1990. Married, and still in the North-East, in Hartlepool, I secured a job for Marathon Oil at their Marylebone Road office in London, catching a 6.30am train out of Darlington station on Monday morning and returning at 4pm on Friday from King's Cross. I subscribed to the *All Mod Cons* fanzine, which was delivered to my home address, and that weekend the latest copy arrived, so I dropped it into my suitcase for Monday's journey down.

An advert in the back mentioned that Rick Buckler was selling all his discs plus more. I saw the address – The Engine Room, Cleveland Street – and recognised it, digging out my *A to Z* on arrival and realising how close it was to the White Horse Hotel, where I was living.

I waited for a quiet moment then used the office phone to ring the number on the ad, explained myself and was invited down after work. When I rang the intercom, the door opened, and I went up a set of stairs into a recording studio. It was like walking into the Tardis. Sat at the mixing desk was Jake Burns from Stiff Little Fingers, who nodded and said hello. I was in awe and was led to a room full of Jam memorabilia, including discs, jackets and posters, all for sale (today's value would be £100,000-plus).

I had only just married and money was tight, but I'd received a tax rebate so used that to buy a seven-inch silver disc of 'Going Underground' which had been presented to Rick. I also learned from Jake that Stiff Little Fingers were doing some concerts in London and managed to get on the guest list with backstage passes, meeting Bruce Foxton for the first time, him and Jake signing my pass.

Six months later, the project finished and I was due to return to the North-East. Before I left, I contacted the Engine Room again, asking if anything was left. I was invited back to have a look and ended up buying gold and silver *Sound Affects* discs, a solid silver medallion and a green jacket… realising later that the flying jacket was the one worn by Rick on the covers of *Snap!* and *The Gift*. I also later found a photograph in the Jam fan club book of the band being presented with the medallions.

I remain a massive fan, although I later sold my memorabilia to help fund my son's first house purchase refit. In total I saw The Jam nine times from 1980 to 1982. I still look back at the best band in the world with great fondness.

I WAS THERE: ANDY MCMAHON

I was 14 in '79 and 'Strange Town' was the first record I bought. They never got much airplay before that. I started going out with a girl from school who had *All Mod Cons*. (I bought her *Sound Affects* for Christmas in 1980.) We were too late getting tickets for Newcastle City Hall on the *Setting Sons* tour and I didn't get to see them until Newcastle City Hall in 1980. Then I saw them at Whitley Bay Ice Rink in 1981. By '82 I had started working and had a few quid. I spent it all on going to see The Jam with my girlfriend. We went everywhere – Newcastle, Liverpool, London, Edinburgh. I saw them ten times in total. I've been a fan of Paul ever since.

I liked The Cure, The Stranglers and Buzzcocks, but The Jam were the main men. Jam gigs were on a different level to everybody else, atmosphere-wise. Some people thought the atmosphere was intimidating. But I loved it. It was chaos, it was mayhem. There were some incidents between rival gangs but you'd get Mods, skins and punks there and there was never any violence at the gigs I went to. They were just joyous occasions.

I saw them at City Hall three times and got into the soundcheck each time. John Weller would let us in. I saw them at Edinburgh Playhouse twice and got into the soundchecks there, and I got in at the Royal Court. We were hardcore. If The Jam were playing, we'd be there at ten in the morning. We'd skive off school and go up to Newcastle from Darlington on the train. And it wasn't just me and my girlfriend. There'd be 20 of us, and we each knew each other from gigs previously. There was a real camaraderie. It was a very big deal.

They were more than just a pop band. Weller was very intense, which we liked. There'd be times when he'd break a guitar string and take the guitar off and kick the shit out of it. We used to like it when he lost the plot. We liked the music, the clothes, the guitars, the look.

Being a Jam fan was like being in an exclusive club that other people didn't know about. And it was ardent. People loved the band. Their records went in at No.1 because Jam fans would all buy them the day they came out. But because Jam fans had bought the record straight away, they would go up the charts in record speed and leave the charts at record speed as well! You didn't get casual record buyers buying Jam records.

I thought the treatment of Rick and Bruce was a bit unfair. They'd been tucked up a little bit by Paul and John. But The Jam was Weller's band. He dictated the way they played and the way they looked and to pretend anything else is to kid yourself. Bruce and Rick were outstanding musicians but he wrote and arranged the songs.

I saw The Style Council a few times and it wasn't the same. The music was still great but there was no comparison with The Jam live. And I think that's what Paul wanted. He wanted something a bit more sophisticated, and not three young lads jumping around.

I think he got the hump with people hanging on his every word. There was an element of 'he's not the messiah, he's a very naughty boy' about it. Everyone thought he was the Dalai Llama or something but he wasn't. It weighed on his shoulders and he couldn't live up to it, which was understandable.

I can still put *All Mods Cons* on and listen to it without skipping any tracks. I love the last four albums. I wasn't that keen on *The Gift* at the time but I love it now. It's not as in your face as the other three albums but it's still better than anything else released that year by anyone else.

I'd go if they reformed, but it wouldn't be the same. Paul doesn't sing Jam songs the same now, he accents them differently. He doesn't play them like he used to. Everybody loves them when he plays them, but in the cold light of day they're not the same. You can't be the same when you're 60-odd as you were when you were 21. I've seen cover bands do them better than he does them now.

He was young and mental. That was part of the appeal. That was what young lads and girls liked about him. He wasn't polished. It wasn't an act. It was completely from the heart. There was an intensity about it. I've seen some great gigs, but there was nothing like a Jam gig. The Jam were different gravy.

SOLID BOND IN YOUR HEART

I WAS THERE: MARK RAILSTON

Me and my mate bunked off school and found out that The Jam were staying at The Crest Hotel. A handful of kids scoured the hotel for any sign of them and we were about to give up when we stumbled upon Bruce and Rick in the hotel café. They said it was cool if we wanted to sit down and have a chat with them and we couldn't believe our luck, but after a couple of minutes, screaming girls rushed in and Bruce and Rick apologised telling us they had to go.

We walked through the hotel foyer and found Weller on a settee in reception, looking very uncomfortable with kids either side and opposite him. We traded hellos but the vibe seemed subdued and weird, with hardly a word said and the kids just gawping. Weller still looked uncomfortable and so after a few minutes we got up to leave.

We got into the soundcheck and hung around after for autographs. At the gig, the PA went off – the amps were fine but the mics were dead. After a couple of minutes of frantic fiddling by roadies, it was clear it would take longer to fix. The band launched into a blistering 'In The City', the crowd happily supplying vocals.

Denis Munday, The Jam's A&R man, reckons these City Hall gigs were the best he saw them play. And those who attended Jam gigs over the years at the famous venue seemed to experience a special intensity and atmosphere that I honestly didn't find elsewhere.

Later, me and my mate Phil bought a bootleg of the 28 October show at a record fair. The cover carried individual shots of the band taken from the inner sleeve. We naively handed them to Bruce for an autograph, which although he was happy to do, he was concerned with the pics for copyright reasons. John Weller was nearby, and Bruce showed him. They said there wasn't a problem with buying the record but asked us where from. We told him it was at a student hall five minutes away, so he asked us to show him. We trooped off, followed by a small group of kids, sensing there was going to be some action.

Outside the hall, we felt guilty for inadvertently grassing the stallholder up. John's boxing background came to the fore – he burst in, shouting and swearing, scattering punters as he headed for the poor guy who sold us the bootlegs. John tore down posters, grabbed records and gave the poor bloke hell for five minutes. He was no shrinking violet!

Fast forward to 2016. Me and two mates were at the *About The Young Idea* exhibition in Liverpool. At the merchandise area, we had a chat with Nicky Weller, and then looked at some record rarities and bootlegs. The stallholder recognised our accents and said he was also from Newcastle. He started to tell a tale about how he had a stand at a record fair when John Weller had burst in, followed by some fans, and had to stop selling some gear for copyright issues. I said, 'Aye mate, sorry, that was me with John!'

I WAS THERE: KEN DENT

We were back again the following December for two nights, seeing them again at Newcastle on the *Setting Sons* tour. And that was the first time me and Davey met them. We went up for the soundcheck and we were down at a signing at a little record shop just round the corner from City Hall, called Listen Ear. We ended up going in there waiting for the band.

The band was so accessible. There were no airs and graces about them. We went to five or six soundchecks and it was always around 150-200 people, although it crept up to about 300 later on, as more people found out that you could actually get in to them. You'd turn up with your bootlegs and records and stuff and get them signed. I took the day off college to go to the soundcheck and meet the band on the *Sound Affects* tour. Bruce was up on the stage. Me and Davey were down the front with the rest of the crowd, about 200 of us. I looked around and saw this guy sitting at the back of the City Hall, feet up on the seats. And it was Paul Weller.

Me and Davey sneaked to the back. We were the first two down there, just sitting talking to Paul Weller. He pulled a cigarette out of a packet and it was the last one. Straight away I said, 'can I have your packet?' and I got it signed. John Weller was smoking a cigarette and I asked him for it, and I put the half-a-cigarette in the cigarette box. Then Rick Buckler was taking one of his drum skins off and Davey shouted, 'Can we have that?' and big Kenny Wheeler brought the drum skin over. We got it signed twice by all of the band. We were going to cut it in half so we'd have half each, but I've still got the full drum skin. I had it framed.

I've got a bedroom upstairs full of records and posters, all signed. I've got John Weller's cigarette stub, Paul Weller's signed tab box and Rick's drum skin. I've also got a few singles signed. My poster and my drum skin are my treasure.

PLAYHOUSE
29 OCTOBER 1980, EDINBURGH, UK

I WAS THERE: JOHN BATHGATE

I saw The Jam three times, all at Edinburgh Playhouse. The first time was my first ever gig. I'd started working full time two days previously, and a lad in the office with me was my age and a huge Jam fan, as well as a burgeoning DJ and a Mod revivalist, like myself. He attended the gig with me and 40-plus years later we remain friends, having reconnected before, during and after Covid.

My other Jam gigs were in 1982 on the *Trans Global Express* tour. We got the first bus to town at 6am to queue outside the Playhouse to buy tickets and there was already a queue round the block. But who cared? We were Jam fans together, the complete example of what the band meant to so many youngsters. I eventually got mine at half past one and was ecstatic.

Someone in the queue had a ghetto blaster and played Secret Affair, The Chords and The Merton Parkas. I'd heard a few songs before, but this cemented my love of the scene – that and the camaraderie, with no hint of trouble. I also recall us walking over to HMV to buy a just released twelve-inch of 'Town Called Malice'/'Precious'. I then got home, switched on the news and one of the first pieces was about how 'Malice' had gone straight in at No.1. I remember feeling so proud; this was 'our' band, the best of the best, at their peak, meaning anything was possible. I should know better at 59, but that shows the effect those guys had on us.

APOLLO THEATRE
30 OCTOBER 1980, GLASGOW, UK

I WAS THERE: CHAS BLACKIE

My mate suggested we try to get into the soundcheck, so we chanced our arm with a few like-minded fans. We met The Jam on the way in, Rick and Bruce enjoying the attention, signing autographs while Paul Weller seemed embarrassed and shy. He tried to get in unnoticed, with a gruff acknowledgement to those there. We hung around for a while, and then the stage door opened and a girl appeared and was conversing with us. Soon, a fire door was opened from the inside. We were in! The girl we believe was Weller's girlfriend, Gill.

That night after the show, we went back to the stage door. It was the same scenario, Buckler and Foxton revelling in the attention, Weller and Gill rushing shyly onto the bus.

APOLLO THEATRE
31 OCTOBER & 1 NOVEMBER 1980, MANCHESTER, UK

I WAS THERE: STUART GORNALL, AGE 16

I saw them 19 times, first getting into them in 1977 at 13. Some of the guys were getting into punk, and one of my friends had the first album, then *This Is The Modern World*. They were just another band – there was that much good music about. But by the time I left school in 1980, I saw how The Jam had progressed.

A PEOPLE'S HISTORY OF THE JAM

My first Jam gig was in Manchester on the *Sound Affects* tour and it blew me away.

I lived next to a caravan site in Scorton, Lancashire, with lots of people coming up from Manchester and Liverpool. Most where I lived were into heavy rock – AC/DC, Black Sabbath, etc. – but I had mates from Manchester and Liverpool into new wave, and soon was 'the only Mod in the village'! I had the haircut and the clothes – the boating jacket and Mohair suits. I dressed like The Jam, so I was labelled a Mod.

I later met the band next door to the Apollo. There was a little pub down the side, and after going to a soundcheck we went for a beer and The Jam were in there. Bruce recognised us as we'd been to a few gigs, and we had a beer with them. Paul was very quiet, but Bruce was very talkative.

I WAS THERE: GAVIN JONES

We didn't have tickets which my girlfriend, Helen, wasn't sure about but I booked time off work and picked her up at 10am. Two hours later we were outside the Apollo, in a car park, looking at a 'Sold Out' sign. We found a stage door, saw the roadies beavering away and asked when the soundcheck was. They said about 4pm. We went to a pub and once that closed at 3.30pm, we went back, asking the other kids if they had spare tickets. None did. I got talking to some scousers. A lad called Ray Finch said he'd stayed at Paul's house once, when he went to London for a gig.

When the group turned up, we got in, talking to Paul in the seats as Rick and Bruce went through their soundcheck. We were treated to our first hearing of 'Pretty Green', 'Dreamtime', 'Man In The Corner Shop' and 'Boy About Town', along with a couple of older songs. We had a quick chat with the group before Big Kenny kicked us out. I hooked up with Ray again, who said he'd got us all on the guest list, so we had to stay close to him. We went to the train station to hang around, going back about 7.45pm. Unfortunately, we got split up in the crush. Ray got in but we didn't.

I was desperate for tickets. An old boy jumped out of a taxi, asking if we wanted two for £9, only £1 more than face value. I snapped his hand off. We pushed our way in. Not long after, support act The Piranhas came on. They were OK, but I only knew 'Tom Hark'. After a long break, The Jam came on, ripping into 'Dreamtime', all in all doing about eight new songs and old favourites, with two encores, a brilliant version of 'Tube Station', 'To Be Someone' and 'David Watts', and ending with a booming "A" Bomb'. It was a great gig, and despite a difficult drive into the night on the way home, I had to laugh on Saturday morning. Looking at the ticket, it was for the following night. Somehow, we'd got in, no problem. Good job I hadn't noticed. I'd have shat myself!

I WAS THERE: DAVID PRATT

I travelled to Manchester on my own to see them. John Cant, Gordon and I also saw the band at Newcastle City Hall twice earlier that week. This tour was promoting the *Sound Affects* album, which hadn't yet hit the shelves. But by the time I saw the second show at Manchester, I'd heard the songs a few times and could sing along to a few.

On the morning of the second Apollo gig, the band were doing an interview on Piccadilly Radio, so I decided to wait outside. To my surprise I was the only person there and I enjoyed a good chat with Paul, Bruce and Rick when they came out. I don't mind admitting I showed off a bit, talking about the new songs and asking Paul about some of the words I hadn't grasped. I also reminded them that we had boarded their bus three months earlier at Loch Lomond. Bruce said he remembered it well. Whether he was just saying this to be nice was beside the point; I was chuffed to bits. That night as I got to the venue, the tour bus arrived at the same time. Walking past the backstage door, Bruce shouted, 'Oi Rat, do you want these?' He gave me two tickets for seats at the front. I gave a ticket to one of the Jones sisters I was staying with, and she was over the moon, as it was better than her rear balcony ticket.

Seeing The Jam four times that week was a great experience and a feather in the cap.

DEESIDE LEISURE CENTRE
2 NOVEMBER 1980, QUEENSFERRY, UK

I WAS THERE: PETER BOWERS

Two nights earlier, I'd had seats in the balcony at Manchester Apollo. Now came the buffeting and clamour of a Deeside Leisure Centre gig. It was absolute pandemonium. You'd be whisked forwards, backwards and sideways in the melee, having no choice but to be swept along in the crowd. There seemed no respite. The band played a blistering set and the audience responded with wild crush and abandon.

I WAS THERE: NIGEL FRAZER, AGE 16

My first time seeing The Jam. The support band was supposed to be Rudi, but it was The Piranhas instead. Paul Weller's dad came on, shouted 'we're not Mods' and encouraged people to go and fight outside. It was a Wales vs England thing mostly, involving Scousers. It was nuts outside.

The December 1982 concert at Wembley Arena, a Sunday, was much better... and safer. Supporting The Jam that night were Big Country. Women and men cried that night. A good night but sad. I felt sorry for Bruce and

Rick. Weller had his own ideas as to which way his music was going. The Style Council and the French theme? I didn't really get that. But 1977 had been an amazing year for music with all the punk and new wave acts coming through. I loved the freshness of it all and went to see quite a few, The Clash and The Jam being my favourites.

I WAS THERE: PHIL BOULTON

I saw a lot of bands in the seventies and eighties. I was 17 or 18 in 1977, an art student in Northwich and worked as a glass collector at a pub in the evenings. I remember taping *In The City* on cassette after buying it. I played it during an evening shift and one barmaid was impressed that we were playing 'punk' music, as she called it. Even though I was the right age, new wave passed me by. I was into Quo, Lynyrd Skynyrd, AC/DC and Dr Feelgood. The Jam was a great wake-up call. I loved the energy. I bought five or six of the first singles. I recall a photo of the boys in their pre-Jam days, impressed one of them was playing a Zenta Tele (a poor Japanese copy), as I also played one. It was disappointing when Weller ended The Jam for The Style Council.

I WAS THERE: LAWRENCE CHAPPLE-GILL

There was a coach trip organised by someone in Welshpool. There was a lot of fighting down the front. I kept well away. I was more into Sham 69 and Siouxsie and the Banshees. My brother got into them a bit more, and I think he came along.

I WAS THERE: JOHN TIDESWELL

I borrowed my dad's car to travel 50 miles to Deeside in snow for my next Jam gig, taking my girlfriend, Janet (now my wife) for an early birthday present. It snowed on the way there and on the way home. The Piranhas were supporting, playing their hit song 'Tom Hark' about three times, as every time they tried to play another song they got booed! It was a packed crowd, with lots of lads in Parkas and lots of trouble. A couple of young lads tried to snatch my girlfriend's bag but got a boot in return. I was at the loo when it happened. Stoke girls don't take to having their bags stolen.

I remember John Weller coming on stage, asking everyone to stop fighting. The Jam came on, kicked in with 'Pretty Green' and played a great set, which calmed things. But we were glad to get out in one piece.

Was I sorry when The Jam split? Yes, but in hindsight it was the right thing to do. The music Paul wanted to make required more than a three-piece band, and that would have affected the dynamic.

Britain was a mess in the late '70s, with manufacturing in decline, workers striking, unions and politicians fighting it out. As a young person you were expected to follow the path your parents took. For the most part, ambition or change was discouraged, your life carved out dependent on your defined class status. Weller eloquently spelled that out in a song from the first album, 'Away From The Numbers', and telling us he was 'gonna break away and gain control' – a sort of optimism within despair suggesting it's up to us to make that change. Thankfully some of us did. Not bad lyrics for a teenager.

QUEENS HALL
3 NOVEMBER 1980, LEEDS, UK

I WAS THERE: GARY COX

'Start!' came out, and because I'd been listening to *Revolver*, I thought 'this sounds a bit familiar'. I'd been buying weird secondhand psychedelic stuff like Traffic, which I'd buy on Leeds markets. Then *Sound Affects* came out, which is my favourite album. It blows me away every time I listen to it. I went to Queens Hall again. By now I'd heard that they let people into soundchecks so I took another day off school and I went down about two o'clock and there were lots of fans hanging about. About 4.15pm, a security guard and John Weller came out along with Nicky Weller and she said, 'Do you want to come in and listen for 40 minutes or so?'

There were no bodies in there to warm the place up and it was so cold in there that Weller had a coat on and Foxton was wearing gloves. They played 'Pretty Green', 'Set The House Ablaze', 'Boy About Town' and 'David Watts'. It was like a mini-gig for the people who had come for the soundcheck because they hadn't got tickets for the gig proper. I was too nervous to go and talk to the band. When it was finished, the security guard was trying to get people out and John Weller was really nice, saying, 'Don't be like that with them. Let them stay a little bit longer.' Afterwards, I went to the Wimpy Bar and was telling people, 'I've just been to the soundcheck and it was unbelievable.'

The Piranhas were with them that night. They played *Sound Affects* and it was just brilliant. You could see that the skill level had gone up. Weller is underestimated as a guitarist. He played rhythm and lead at the same time, his musicianship was really, really good. The sound was awful at the Queens Hall and he would apologise but nobody was interested in that. We were just watching them. They were so good to watch, they were so watchable live. Every song was played like it was a new song they had just written and which they were playing live for the first time. They were really getting into every song.

I WAS THERE: RUSSELL HIRST

I saw them four times in Leeds between 1978 and 1982, and also at Loch Lomond

Festival in 1980. I remember purple dust on the floor of the Queens Hall at one of the gigs. Badger shoes took some cleaning!

I WAS THERE: KERRY MORIARTY
I saw The Jam on six occasions, the first time at Queens Hall, Leeds, where I was surprised to hear them perform 'Liza Radley'. Amongst all the 'biff, bang, pow', that was a thrill.

I WAS THERE: GLEN HOLMES, AGE 17
I was 14 and still at school when I saw The Jam on *Top Of The Pops* performing 'In The City'. The next day at school, everybody was talking about it. From that day I bought every single and album they made, usually on the day of release. My first time seeing them was at Leeds' Queens Hall, supported by The Piranhas. 'Going Underground' had just been No.1. I went with my brother. It was a fantastic night and the whole place was rocking as they opened with that hit single.

The second time was on the *Bucket and Spade* tour at the Festival Pavilion, Skegness. It was only a small venue, but my God it went down well. The third and last time was in Birmingham, a concert that can still be viewed in its entirety online.

When Weller took the decision to split the group I was absolutely broken. I still play The Jam most days at home and think of my youth with them. Over the last ten years or so I've seen From The Jam many times, and while they're not The Jam they play all the old hits I loved – and still do.

I WAS THERE: PETER HOPTON, AGE 14
I was twelve when 'In The City' came out. I was at secondary school and had just started getting interested in music. I went to school in Harrogate and a lot of the kids there were still into rock 'n' roll. There were a lot of Teddy Boys in my class. I wasn't one of them. I wanted to be a bit different. I was a bit of a rebel. I started listening to The Jam and The Clash. I liked the punky beat and I liked a bit of reggae with The Clash. I thought, 'This is for me.'

I lived in a little village called Harewood. I was born and bred there, and my dad worked at Harewood House for 40-odd years. Liking that kind of music in that kind of village in that environment, I was a bit of a loner. I remember going to little discos in our village hall and dancing to The Jam, The Specials and Madness. I'd be dancing there on my own, and all the older lads would come and pat me on my back and say, 'Good stuff, lad. It takes some bollocks to do that.' I used to knock about with a lot of lads who were older than me. I've always done that. Even when I started boozing at 16, I was boozing with lads who were 23, although they didn't like my music. I used to brew my own beer at school and take it to the youth club and stuff like that.

I would've loved to have seen The Jam in a small venue. I tried to get to go to The Jam in Leeds when I was about 12 but I wasn't allowed in. I didn't have a ticket but I tried to get in anyway. When *Quadrophenia* came out, I wasn't allowed into that either. I went to Harrogate to see it and queued up outside and they were really strict, pulling people out of the queue: 'You're not going in.'

I used to work on a farm at 14 and I'd use the money to buy all the Mod clothes. I could afford a suit so I bought a suit, at 14. I had a Parka and all that lot, and I used to go riding about on the back of this lad's scooter because I wasn't old enough to ride one myself. It was all because of hearing that first song and saying 'this is it, this is good'. I just loved them all the way through.

The first time they were supported by The Piranhas and the second time by The Vapors. When they came out on stage it was just absolutely brilliant. Even though it was a tram shed it still sounded great to me at 14. I'm proud to say that I was lucky enough to see them live.

I'm not really into Paul Weller nowadays. He's too slow for me. I like a bit of oomph still. I sort of fell out with him. The Jam were too good to pack in. Why do it? But I put my AirPods in and I still listen to The Jam when I go walking. When books about The Jam come out, I still buy them, even though I've got quite a lot of them.

The Clash? If you picked ten songs off of *Sandinista!* you probably would've made a good album out of it, but then *The Gift*, the last album by The Jam, is a bit iffy for me. I still like wearing the Fred Perry's and I still wear my Doc Marten shoes but I wouldn't call myself a Mod even though I still dress accordingly. I've lost all my hair so I can't grow a Paul Weller.

If The Jam reformed and it was something stupid like £200 or £300 to see them one last time I'd say yes. They should just do it, do it once and make everybody happy. Have a massive gig at Wembley. Do it once and walk away. I'd love to go and I'm sure thousands and thousands would be following me.

I WAS THERE: MARK CROMACK, AGE 15

I had been listening to all my mum and dad's old records, whether it be ABBA, Sweet, Mud or Gary Glitter, when I wandered into this old newsagent's in Bramley Shopping Centre in Leeds. I started flipping through this box of ex-chart singles by acts like Blondie and Elvis Costello. I came across 'When You're Young'. I'd not heard of The Jam, but thought they looked cool on the cover. The records were something like 20 pence each and I thought I'd take a chance on them. I got home, played 'When You're Young' and then flipped it over and played 'Smithers-Jones' and that was it. I was sold.

Then it was a case of going to record shops and trying to get all their back catalogue, which I did with the help of my mother, a very generous woman. When my mother bought me *Setting Sons* for my fifteenth birthday, I had them all. It's hard to choose between *Setting Sons*

Mark Cromack thinks the three members of The Jam should get together & talk about the old times

and *All Mod Cons* in terms of a favourite, but *Setting Sons* just pips it because it was the first album that I got on release.

I saw them at the Queens Hall in Leeds. I went with two mates, Ian Finlay and Michael Graves. We got the tickets from a clothes shop in Leeds called X Clothes. We bunked off school, walked along the Leeds and Liverpool Canal and spent the day in the city going into record shops and cafes because we weren't old enough to go into pubs.

We kept bobbing down to the venue to see how the queue was going on. Four or five hours before the actual gig, we saw there was a bit of a queue so we started queuing up and got ushered into the soundcheck. We didn't know this was going to happen. There were just 30, 40 little Mods all just queued up.

They did a good ten or twelve songs. Paul Weller kept shouting out, 'Right, what do you want to hear next?' We thought he was shouting to us, so we're all shouting "Strange Town', 'When You're Young', 'Tube Station" or whatever. And of course he wasn't shouting to us – he was shouting to the sound engineer at the back!

After 45 minutes or so we were then ushered out. The queue now was absolutely massive and we'd lost our place near the front but that soundcheck was brilliant. You were right close to your idols.

I saw them again in April '82 on the *Trans Global* tour. I was working by then. I didn't go with my girlfriend – she wasn't into them – but I went with her friend, and we spent the day around the pubs. That second gig wasn't as good as the first gig, because they were promoting all the songs from *The Gift*, which is my least favourite album, although it's grown on me a hell of a lot more since.

I bought the *NME* or *Record Mirror* in the newsagent's, got on the bus and started flipping through it when I read 'The Jam are splitting up.' It was just heart-wrenching. Their musical direction was changing and it wasn't for the better. I didn't like 'The Bitterest Pill' when it came out although I absolutely love it now. And when I bought *The Gift*, I said, 'This isn't *Sound Affects*!'

A reunion would be three old men and not the three young men I remember from 40 years ago. But I'd like to see the three of them in a room, just talking about the old days.

CONFERENCE CENTRE
5 & 6 NOVEMBER 1980, BRIGHTON, UK

I WAS THERE: PETER CHAMBERLAIN

My first gig was at Brighton Centre, where they were showcasing the *Sound Affects* album. Weller was losing patience with his Rickenbacker, smashing it on the floor, Pete Townshend style! My next was on 8th December that year at Bristol Locarno, a brilliant gig. Weller dedicated 'Start!' to John Lennon's passing. It also included the best version of 'Thick As Thieves' live that I ever saw. Then there was the *Bucket and Spade* tour in 1981, when I saw them at Stafford. There was a big fight in the crowd for no particular reason, which stopped as quickly as it started. And Guildford Civic Hall that year, on a steaming hot day. I sneaked in via a side door to look at their guitars, before being discovered and 'advised to leave' by security. Weller wore a black Fred Perry with a red Levi jacket on top, black trousers and black Jam bowling shoes.

My best gig was at Liverpool's Royal Court Theatre in September '82. Weller wore a brilliant striped cardigan with light blue Sta-Prest trousers. Then there was December '82 at the Michael Sobell Sports Centre, where Weller ran on, jumped on a speaker and promptly crashed to the floor! He wore a white long-sleeved Lonsdale top and they were showcasing *The Gift* on a freezing cold night. My train back to Wiltshire broke down, with thick snow everywhere.

By the time I saw them at Shepton Mallet's Showering Pavilion, Weller had announced the split and Foxton seemed frustrated with the crowd, attempting to motivate them, saying, 'Come on, you won't be seeing too much more of us!' Then came two concerts at Wembley Arena. Weller sang 'It's Too Bad' and 'Away From The Numbers' brilliantly. More soulful. Also, he shared the microphone with Foxton to sing the latter part of 'All Mod Cons'.

For the finale at Brighton, I travelled from Swindon by coach and managed to get right to the front... until my girlfriend fainted! We got her to the first aid room, then I returned with her to watch the concert halfway back. There was a strange atmosphere, and numerous bottles were thrown at the lads. One narrowly missed Rick and another was close to Bruce, prompting him to halt the concert to remonstrate with the offenders and tell them he wanted to 'remember this concert for the last seven years, not the fucking bottles!'

I used to love dressing as a Mod – boating blazers and so on. I also used to take some great pics of the band as often I'd get to the front. Frustratingly, I've lost them. But I do have pics of the final concert.

I WAS THERE: PAOLO OZZIE, AGE 14

My second ever gig, the first being Gary Numan on his *Teletour* a couple of months earlier. I was really excited as The Jam were massive in Brighton, and The Piranhas, a local group I also loved, were supporting. I remember Weller wearing a white shirt and puffing on a fag when he came out. I had a side-on view in the balcony and we seemed far away. As a starstruck 14-year-old, Brighton Centre seemed so vast. But these days when I go to a gig there it doesn't seem so far away. The set was one continuous wall of sound and the energy amazing, with songs from *Sound Affects* and earlier material. I started liking The Jam in 1979, with 'The Eton Rifles' my first single, so I wasn't that familiar with some of the earlier stuff played. Now, in my 58th year, I know and love all their stuff.

I WAS THERE: RICHARD MURPHY, AGE 17

I first saw The Jam at Brighton Centre. I've a ticket stub somewhere. There were around ten to twelve of us attending from Crawley. I was more of a punk but briefly wore Mod stuff. My brother Paul was really into it – I remember him wearing his Parka with a big Union flag on the back. It was the first gig I attended with my younger brother, one of only two we saw in total (both The Jam). I was entrusted by my parents with looking after him. I was 17, he was 15. Tragically he was killed in a motorcycle accident six years later, so these gigs hold a special memory for me.

The support may have been the Purple Hearts, who were definitely supporting when we saw them next. A great gig and The Jam were probably our favourite band at that time. The next we went to was 23rd February 1981 in our hometown at Crawley Leisure Centre. It was the same crowd of us Mods. In the weeks leading up to the gig, my brother and I learnt the words to 'Down In The Tube Station At Midnight', our favourite Jam song then, by playing the single over and again, writing them down bits at a time! I treasure those times, managing to see one of the greatest bands at that time. When I tell people I saw The Jam I can see the jealousy in their eyes, especially younger generations.

I WAS THERE: RUPERT TRACY

I subsequently found out that Paul had shingles throughout the *Sound Affects* tour. That is proper commitment. I think Brighton was my favourite Jam gig ever. They just looked brilliant on stage. Paul looked amazing as ever. Bruce had this smoke blue mohair suit on that looked the absolutely business. And Rick was playing a slightly different kit at this point, which looked amazing. The only show that compares is Hammersmith Palais in Christmas 1981. It was bitterly cold, with snow on the ground, and trying to get from Southampton to London was a bit of a bitch.

SPORTS CENTRE
7 NOVEMBER 1980, BRACKNELL, UK

I WAS THERE: ANDREW GORDON

I saw the Jam five times, at various venues all over the country. Bracknell was some sort of sports centre. It was during the winter, freezing with lots of snow. We got to the venue hours before and there was a bar above. We were in there. When the band arrived, they kicked everyone out, but we said we were with the *NME* so they let us stay. After a while we went downstairs and The Jam were doing their soundcheck, so we stayed and watched. Paul Weller's dad tried to kick us out, but Paul intervened and told him we could stay!

I WAS THERE: JO BARTLETT

I started getting into The Jam when *Setting Sons* was released, having read a great review in *Smash Hits!* I was really into The Jam and The Police, getting *Setting Sons* at Christmas 1979. Every year my family would go to the Outer Hebrides of Scotland on holiday, as my dad was from the Isle of Barra. In August 1980, while there, my brother's friend Alistair had all the early Jam singles – in picture sleeves – and sold them to me for £5. I bought the 'Going Underground' double-pack the day it came out, earlier that year, and from then on got the singles the day they were released - 'Start', 'That's Entertainment', 'Funeral Pyre', 'Absolute Beginners', through to 'Beat Surrender'. And while we were all told by Paul Weller not to buy the 'Just Who Is The Five O'Clock Hero?' import, we all did, to add it to our collections!

From the first time I saw The Jam there was no looking back. I saw them six times. Like every right-minded youth in the early '80s, The Jam were my favourite band. I was too young to have been there in the early or even middle years, joining in the fun for the *Sound Affects* tour in November 1980. My God, what a gig. I returned sweaty and elated. Jumping up and down the whole gig, elbows in my face, using other people's shoulders to propel myself upwards. My older brother, Tom, was having his 18th birthday party at our house that night. We came back and played Jam records to pogo to, telling everyone what an amazing concert we'd just seen. If I hadn't been hooked by gigs and music before that night, I sure was after it.

Support band, The Piranhas, from Brighton, had one hit, 'Tom Hark'. I had the seven-inch and knew the words to all three tracks. Dancing in an '80s style either in my room or at parties, singing along at the top of my voice. I went with my boyfriend, Tom (Carroll, younger brother of JC from The Members). He was a couple of years older than me and could drive.

We also took Alistair, who came down from Scotland for the gig. I asked him what he remembered. He wrote:

Memories include Tom and I visiting your school, drinking giant cans of Tartan Special at the party and falling in love with this gypsy-like lady. The gig was brilliant, talking to the guy at the door who you said was Paul Weller's dad, getting right to the front and having to get the hell out before I died, and freezing to death outside, soaked with sweat. Oh, and the Piranhas getting booed if they played anything other than 'Tom Hark'. Your mum introduced me to chicken liver pate, which I loved, and gave me a box of crackers and a pack of pate for the train back to Aberdeen. Happy days indeed.

BINGLEY HALL
11 NOVEMBER 1980, BIRMINGHAM, UK

I WAS THERE: BRENDAN FINNEGAN

I was 12 in May 1977 when my sister bought 'In The City'. She never really got into them so I inherited the single. I was too young to go to gigs so had to wait until I left school four years later. My first was Birmingham Bingley Hall. I was very small and remember being carried around by my chest in the crowd because my feet were off the floor. Absolute mayhem, but I was hooked.

Brendan Finnegan (left) racked up ten Jam gigs in all

I racked up ten gigs up to their last one in Brighton, and would have done more if I'd had more money. Most are hard to remember in full, but I do remember mayhem at Stafford in June 1981, with different football firms killing each other all through the gig, and having to hold the train doors shut at Wolverhampton on the way back to Birmingham, whilst Villa and Wolves fought it out across the rail lines.

My next memory was going alone to London for the first time ever, to see them at Hammersmith Palais in December 1981. The train was packed with Police fans and it seemed I was the only one with any taste. I'd never been on the Tube, went the wrong way, got lost, asking people who were in the same boat. I went two nights running but travelled home between shows to do half a shift at work. That second night was rammed, Bananarama supporting. 'Malice' wasn't yet released but I'm sure they played it. Coming home I fell asleep on the train and ended up in Wolverhampton at 2am, with no trains back to Birmingham New Street until six in the morning. I missed work and my dad did his nut because he thought I was dead. No mobiles then.

My most vivid memories are of the last gig. We had no tickets but went anyway. We were in the pub all day, then went to the back doors, waiting for what seemed like an eternity before out came John Weller with a book of tickets. I was only in there ten minutes when, like a prat, I jumped on my mate's shoulders with over-excitement. The band hadn't even come on, and a rather large bouncer handled me straight out the front doors onto the street. Tears in my eyes, I thought I'd blown it but I returned to the back door and Mr Weller came to the rescue, so I was in again.

I cried my eyes out at the end, and probably did so throughout the Christmas period. My mum was dying at the time, and she passed on 2nd January, so I kept blaming it on the fact we were losing her. The day the split was announced, my family thought I was going to top myself. Truth be known I could have. I'm so glad I never did anything stupid.

I remain an avid Jammy. I was in and out with The Style Council, seeing them 33 times. I've been the same with Weller's solo career, racking up well over 100 gigs. But all that has never given me the buzz that The Jam did.

I WAS THERE: RUPERT TRACY

The Jam were unstoppable now. They were on the front of *Sounds*, *NME*, *Smash Hits*, *Record Mirror*. They were the number one band in Britain. We had to wait until the November for the next album, *Sound Affects*, to come out. But in August they brought out 'Start!', my favourite single. I thought this was a masterpiece. I know everybody thinks this ripped off The Beatles' 'Taxman', but it just showed which way they were going. Because every time they brought out an album they went in a slightly different direction. Polydor postponed the release date for the album so most of the tour was played to audiences that hadn't actually heard the album yet, which was a bit annoying. But 'Set The House Ablaze', 'Start!' and 'Pretty Green' were all amazing tracks and we sort of got to know them immediately, even though there was no record out.

This was when boating blazers became a staple Jam fashion item, because Rick was pictured wearing one on a 'Going Underground' video or photo shoot around that time, and Paul had one as early as '79 in the 'When You're Young' video. So we all trooped up to Melanddi's in Carnaby Street to buy our boating blazers. The quality of the clothes was terrible but we didn't care. Mod was only going to last a couple of years anyway so it didn't really matter to us.

I WAS THERE: KEVIN SMITH

Bingley Hall was the biggest venue in Birmingham. Huge, used for various exhibitions, standing only, and this time there would be 5,000 or more inside. I went with my girlfriend Andrea. Being November, it was bloody cold on that concrete floor. Our feet were like ice. Andrea bought Adam & The Ants' 'Dog Eat Dog' on her way to meet me from work. She worked at Barclays Bank, her branch very close to the venue.

There were two supports. The Piranhas were booed off. By now the room was rammed, our feet not as cold. The lights dimmed, John Weller taking the microphone to announce 'the best fuckin' band in the world'. A big crush forward began. This was around the time the *Setting Sons* album was released. I recall Paul Weller's guitar string broke, but he continued to play and the sound was the same. The Jam were to return to Bingley Hall on a regular basis, and we were always there.

I WAS THERE: GAVIN JONES

I went with my friend Lisa. We found the place after about an hour, parked up and went to suss out the hall in freezing November rain. We had no tickets and Lisa was sceptical we'd get in, but we asked the roadies when the soundcheck was (four-ish) then got some food and went in a pub, meeting Charlie from Stoke. We chatted with him until he bit his glass and it shattered, the landlord asking us to leave.

We had a long wait in the cold for the soundcheck, which took place about 5pm, having to stand back from the stage as they were still building it. They ran through about five songs, but we were kicked out straight away so didn't get chance to ask to be put on the guest list. We met Charlie again, going for a drink in the Brum Rep theatre across the road. There was no one in, but Charlie leaned over and poured us a couple of free pints. When we looked outside, the queue went all round the hall. We went for something to eat, and I bought a tour t-shirt then went back to the main door, looking for touts. Lisa had lost all hope, but I was confident I could blag it. I heard The Piranhas come on and do their set. Even I was losing hope when out of nowhere a tout appeared and offered us two tickets for £12. We only had £11 between us so I got them for that, £1.75 over face value. We were in, skint but happy!

The Piranhas had nearly finished, and after a short wait John Weller announced, 'If anyone falls over, pick 'em up. Here they are, The Jam!' A crowd of mainly skins and Mods led to a charged atmosphere, Paul not keen on the 'we are the Mods' chants. I don't know if it was because of the atmosphere, but the gig was a bit less charged than normal, a bit flat, especially when some twats threw beer cans onto the stage and hit Rick's kit just before the start.

When a pack of fags was thrown on stage near Paul, he picked them up, saying, 'This is for whoever threw these,' going into 'Set The House Ablaze'. It was an OK gig, just not as stunningly brilliant as usual. When we got back to the car, some twat had let two tyres down. Luckily a guy sat in his car had a pump. I got home about midnight, ready for a night's kip and more fun at Leicester those next two days.

DE MONTFORT HALL
12 & 13 NOVEMBER 1980, LEICESTER, UK

I WAS THERE: TIM FILOR

This was the third time I'd seen them, a Loughborough Uni date following our first De Mont gig. I went with Chris Lazzari. We were now living the Mod lifestyle. We had scooters and lived in Parkas and Mod suits. It all became clear why at the Loughborough University show we'd seen a Parka-clad boy take a beating. I'd had a few close calls myself.

The popularity of The Jam was on an upwards surge and they usually did two nights at Leicester. I worked near the ticket office so hadn't left getting the tickets that late, but I was disappointed as the only tickets left for both nights were sat in the balcony. The night before the show, Chris was taken ill and he didn't think he would be well enough to go, so I offered the ticket to Pete Barratt. We started off in the balcony but could see that it was more fun in the stalls. The Jam came on and it was crazy at the front. Pete had also been a punk and liked leaping about, so we decided we wanted a piece of the action. We went downstairs, sneaked into the back of the stalls and gradually weaved nearer the front. New songs from the *Sound Affects* album – released later that month – rang out as we slowly edged forward. We were getting pretty close to our objective when the opening riff of 'In The City' started up. It was like a catalyst. We started leaping about like madmen. I don't think it went down too well with those around us, but we didn't care – this was what we came for.

I can't remember how much more of the gig was left, but we bounced around till the final chords of the encore faded out. We were knackered, but as I started to make my way out with the rest, Pete grabbed me and suggested we hang around.

We wandered around the hall while it emptied, avoiding the stewards. I was getting nervy, but Pete persuaded me to hang on. Others in the hall had permits of one sort or another.

What happened next left me gobsmacked. Bruce and Rick came out, stood very close to us, and a small crowd gathered round them. We had to get an autograph, but all we had was our ticket stubs, so that's what we handed over. They kindly took them out of our sweaty hands and we managed to get both signatures.

We needed the full set, but where was Paul? We had a little wander and found him in another part of the hall, leaning against a pillar. He looked a bit sullen, a fan speaking in his ear, something about 'prima donna'. Pete very politely asked if he'd sign our stubs, and a few seconds later we'd got the full set, a magical end to a brilliant night. It showed how well the lads treated the fans. How many bands at that level of fame would have come out like that after a gig?

I WAS THERE: GAVIN JONES

We had a couple of hours to kill until a 3.30pm soundcheck, so we went for chips and then returned, joining about 40 kids. Big Kenny Wheeler came to the door and let us in, and we walked past Paul, resplendent in a long black corduroy coat and paisley scarf, playing an old piano in the hallway, Rick and Bruce stood drinking lager.

During a lull in the soundcheck while Rick messed with his drums, Paul came to the front and we asked if we could get on the guest list. As we'd been to a few soundchecks, he recognised us, saying he would but had none left, leading to trepidation on our part. But after a couple of hours in a pub, we went back. The queue was around the block, so we walked to the front, said we were on the list (fingers crossed), and there were our names. Thanks Paul!

After watching Dolly Mixture and The Piranhas, eventually The Jam came on, introduced by John Weller, and it was a barnstorming set. They were really up for it. Most of *Sound Affects* was played, mixed in with older songs and kicking off with 'Monday', Paul's Steve Marriott hairstyle blowing up as the stage fan kept him cool.

They encored with 'Tube Station', 'David Watts', 'When You're Young' and 'Billy Hunt', all brilliant! After dodging security, we waited by the backstage door, the group coming out to chat with us and about 20 other kids.

After talking with Paul about *Sound Affects* and politics, we went over to see Rick, who was on his own, asking for a guest pass that next night. He said he'd give us some at the soundcheck the next day, so I said Ray and Mick could stay at mine, and we returned. True to his word, at the next soundcheck, we called Rick over and he gave us three guest passes.

Talking to Paul, someone asked if they'd done any older stuff on the tour, and he said they did 'In The City' a couple of times. I said cheekily it would be great if they played that again as it was always great, with loads of energy. Later, we saw supports Kids Next Door, then The Piranhas, and then we returned to the foyer watching kids come in, seeing our mates Chillo and Steve, who paid a kid a fiver for his name on the guest list and couldn't believe it worked. Soon enough, The Jam came on, a slightly different set leading to encores 'Tube Station', 'David Watts', "A' Bomb', 'When You're Young' and... 'In The City'!

RAINBOW THEATRE
15 & 16 NOVEMBER 1980, LONDON, UK

I WAS THERE: MICK TALBOT
After I did 'Heatwave', I played live with them at the Rainbow when *Setting Sons* came out, but I didn't see them for around six months. Then he (Paul) said, 'We're going to hire a Hammond organ and want to do three or four soul tunes near the end of the set, and can you do a couple of other tunes that have got organ on them?' I played about half a dozen songs with them for a couple of nights, again at the Rainbow, just for the London dates, then didn't hear from Paul for probably 18 months..

I WAS THERE: AIDAN KEHOE
I started listening to and buying punk records and although I was into the scene, something was missing. Possibly the fact that my older siblings had been into Motown and The Beatles, and that still resonated with me. From a young age I'd played their records on my parents' stereogram. I was 14 when I walked into the local record shop in '77 and a video from *Top Of The Pops* was playing. It was The Jam doing 'In The City'. I was instantly hooked. The sound, the anger, the look – fire and skill, if you will. I carried on buying punk records, but The Jam were my No.1 band. As time moved on and I acquired more of their records and read whatever I could about them and their influences, I changed from being a punk to being an out-and-out Mod. I saw them 27 times.

My first gig was in Birmingham in 1978, hanging onto the shirt-tails of my mate's older brother and his mates, who had seen them live for some time. They got me in. I was 15 but looked about ten so needed older kids to cover for me.

The Rainbow Theatre in 1980 is a stand out memory. A mate and me travelled to London. We didn't have tickets but on previous occasions we'd managed to get in by hook or by crook or at least got into the soundcheck. The Jam were great about that. They often let us kids in, including this time.

When we had to leave the soundcheck, we sat in the George Robey pub across the road with maybe 150 to 200 other ticketless people when a guy ran in and shouted that the box office had opened, and they had 50 tickets left. A mass exodus ensued, and we found ourselves about 150 from the front.

While still in the queue we heard a huge noise coming up the street. Hundreds and hundreds of skinheads had just left a football match and had covered the whole street, cars turning around, etc. They saw a queue of Mods and it was like a red rag to a bull. They charged, akin to the scene in *Quadrophenia* when the Mods smashed up the cafe. Everyone started running. People were falling, some getting caught, noise everywhere.

I spotted an alleyway on the right, grabbed my mate and said, 'In here!' Backs against the wall, breathing heavily, the rest of the Mods carried on running. There was a slight pause and the skinhead horde followed, screaming abuse. We gave it a couple of minutes then poked our heads out. Queue gone, skinheads gone. We went up to the box office and got straight in. What followed was one of the best, if not the best, gigs of my life. They kicked off with 'In The City', something they hadn't done live for some time. The crowd erupted. They had seats in there and the crowd took to ripping them up, piling the broken parts either side of the stage. Dancing room was a must.

I WAS THERE: ANDY MILLER

Back in 1980 The Jam were at their peak, 'Going Underground' and 'Start!' both No.1 singles. I'd already seen them live in April, and towards the end of the summer the band announced dates to promote their new album, *Sound Affects*. I knew I had to see them again. A couple of my friends' dads got us tickets for the Rainbow on November 16th and Hammersmith Odeon three days later, the final night of the tour.

Anticipation and excitement grew as the dates neared. I'd heard about the band or management letting fans in for soundchecks and discussed with my friends whether to go up early afternoon. On the day I met Sheila, Sandra and Tracy at Uxbridge Tube station and we got the train up, arriving in North London about half three, not knowing what to expect. We walked down the side of the Rainbow and by the stage door were a group of people hoping to be let into the soundcheck. Around 4pm, John Weller appeared and told us we could come in, but that if any of us misbehaved Big Kenny Wheeler would throw us out.

We filed in and took up seats in the front couple of rows. Paul, Bruce and Rick

SOLID BOND IN YOUR HEART

were onstage chatting to the road crew and tuning up instruments. After a while they played 'Dreamtime' from the new album, then 'Set The House Ablaze', 'Boy About Town', 'Man In The Corner Shop', and a couple of others. Having finished, the three of them came down to the edge of the stage and signed autographs. I still have the autograph book they all signed. We were then asked to leave, and not long after Bruce and his wife came out and I had a brief chat.

That evening's gig was everything we expected. We met up with more of our friends and were treated to the majority of the new LP, tracks from *All Mod Cons* and *Setting Sons* and some singles.

Photos by Andy Miller

Andy Miller got autographs from all three of The Jam

HAMMERSMITH ODEON
18 & 19 NOVEMBER 1980, LONDON, UK

I WAS THERE: ANDY MILLER

Three days after the Rainbow show, myself and quite a few of my friends bunked off school and made our way up to Hammersmith and the Odeon again, with the intention of getting into the soundcheck (again). After a bit of a wait, John Weller appeared at the stage door and invited us in, with the same instructions as the Sunday before. We noticed broken seats by the side of the stage and watched the band run through three or four songs, including one of my favourites, 'The Butterfly Collector'. When they'd finished, they came down to the front of stage and signed autographs, and I got my *All Mod Cons* songbook signed. Paul Weller was in a bad mood, annoyed at how rough the bouncers had been with fans the night before. He said, 'They want to charge us for the damaged seats. They can fuck off. We ain't paying!' We then left the venue in search of food and drink, meeting up with more of our friends for the gig, which was fucking fantastic, like some sort of religious experience, seeing the greatest three-piece on that stage one cold November night in London Town.

Afterwards, we made our way to Hammersmith Tube station, with running battles involving Jam fans, Mods and skinheads on all the platforms. They really were exciting and dangerous times… I wouldn't swap them for anything though. Didn't we have a nice time? We sure fucking did!

I WAS THERE: SPARKS JOHNSON, AGE 15

My Uncle Roy was a Sixties mod that never let go and he took me to see them. He took me to see a few Mod revival bands. I just wish I'd taken a camera! The Jam were brilliant live. We went to London on his scooter, a big thing for a country boy from Chatteris, Cambridgeshire.

I WAS THERE: DARRON ROBINSON

I finally saw them again on the *Sound Affects* tour at Hammersmith Odeon, taken by my brother-in-law for my 15th birthday. Pete's dead now, one of the early Covid cases, bless him. He was about five years older. I don't know why he bothered with this little 'erbert, but he bought me the very first Jam biography, with the black and white cover. I wasn't used to getting presents. I took it to school, opened it, and on the first page was a ticket for that week's gig at Hammersmith Odeon. What a guy!

For the two Rainbow gigs before, my old man was chauffeuring again, twice, from the Parkside club. Bruce would get the tickets, and my old man would get money to fit as many as he could in his VW caravanette, staying the whole night in his van waiting for them. That night at Hammersmith Odeon, that's when my life changed… or was ruined!

When we moved to Parkside when I was eight, probably the only thing we did in the summer holidays – and we weren't any poorer than anybody else - was go to the cinema… once. Mum took me and my sister on the bus to Walton for *Bedknobs and Broomsticks*, and that would require a bath and hair wash the night before, nice crisp, clean ironed shirt, and in typical Robinson fashion, we'd arrive about three hours before, so got to see the support movie, The Beatles' *Help!* I still love that film. At the point where the four of them go into the four different terraced houses, what little boy isn't gonna be, 'Wow!'? From there it goes into John Lennon singing 'You've Got to Hide Your Love Away', and at that moment I fell in love. To the point where my heart raced, I was sweating, I had shivers. What is this? That beautiful Epiphone guitar, his hair, his eyes, the way he sang those words.

And when I saw The Jam as a 15-year-old, Paul Weller walked on stage with a polka-dot shirt and that John Lennon hair and they launched into 'Dream Time', I had the same feeling. I don't mean in a gay way, but I fell in love. And whatever that is, I can never get enough.

He was straight in with the 'streets I ran, this whole town…' line. Just thinking about that, having spent my entire adult life in and around live music both as a punter and a performer, nothing has ever come anywhere near that pure power. The sound they made live was incredible, the precision and passion. Like standing on a runway with a jumbo jet in front of you… and there was only fucking three of 'em! Mental.

To say they were local lads makes it sound a bit… but it still makes no sense to me how Americans could like them, or the Japanese. Unless you come from Woking, or… well, what does 'A Town Called Malice' mean to them? What do they know about Sunday's roast beef, Co-Ops and the kids' new gear?

From there, we went to so many gigs, with my brother-in-law mostly. When my sister met him, he worked in a record shop, Record Scene. The first was in Sunbury-on-Thames, then they opened one in Woking, and he got me a Saturday job there around that time. A little after, he worked for London Records as a rep. He wasn't highly connected, but he knew what was about to happen. We always got tickets because we were ahead of the curve.

I WAS THERE: CATHIE STROVER

My third Jam gig. I went up from Reading with two friends. I nearly fell out with one, who said she wanted to know why Paul got so angry on stage. I defended him… but she was right, it was partly the anger that drove the genius and intensity, even if anger was not needed for the sublime 'That's Entertainment'. The fourth time I saw them was not far from my Hillingdon roots, at the Hammersmith Palais for the *Setting Sons* tour in December 1981. My heart still flips when I hear 'Wasteland', 'Girl On The Phone', 'Saturday's Kids', 'Thick As Thieves'…

I WAS THERE: JOE SHIELDS

'78 was my year. I was 15. My mum and dad were mad rock 'n' roll fans and I was brought up on Elvis and Buddy Holly and The Beatles and the Stones. I used to wear out my mum's Buddy Holly and Rolling Stones records. The first record I ever bought was 'Gudbuy T'Jane' by Slade, and then I loved T. Rex. I remember the punk thing exploding in '77. After the Pistols appeared on the *Today* programme, I wasn't allowed to play the Sex Pistols at home. I borrowed *Never Mind The Bollocks* from a mate and my dad threw it out my bedroom window!

I'd heard 'In The City' but the Jam really grabbed my attention when they appeared on Marc Bolan's TV show. He didn't introduce them as 'The Jam'. He said, 'An amazing group called Jam!' They did 'All Around The World' and that's when I went 'wow!' I then went out and bought all their records.

All Mod Cons came out. We were all young little Mods then and approaching the age where we could get scooters, although I never did – I used to go on the back of various friends' scooters. One mate was Lee Harris from Benfleet who later became the drummer in Talk Talk. I flirted with the Mod thing for a while but I realised it wasn't me. There were a load of clones in Parkas and Jam shoes, but fashion changed very quickly. What was in one day was out the next. I remember saving up for a pair of Jam shoes with my pocket money and my paper round money, but they seemed to be out of fashion by the time I got them and I couldn't wear them anymore. So I created my own look wearing red tag Levi's (now called 501s) and a leather biker's jacket or a Harrington.

I grew up in Southend-on-Sea which was quite a prolific area during the '79 Mod revival. Our local Mod band, The Leepers, supported The Jam on a couple of occasions. They eventually evolved into Le Mat and landed a tour as the support band for Duran Duran. Sav the drummer went on to be Wilko Johnson's drummer.

I was always going to different gigs but The Jam's gigs were the ones. They were the band that spoke to us. You had to send off a postal order and if your Jam ticket came through the post, it was like Willy Wonka's golden ticket. You'd phone your mates up and say 'have you got your ticket?' 'Yeah, I've got mine, got mine.' There was just an excitement about it. We would count down the days to the gig!

A guy local to us in Basildon (Derek Clark) would organise coach trips and you'd buy your ticket through him. For the first gig, four of us got a coach up to Hammersmith Odeon and when we got on it, we knew everyone on the coach. It was obviously a money spinner for this guy, as he did all the Jam gigs after that. We would book the coach as a way to guarantee the ticket but we wouldn't necessarily use his coach facility. I'd ring him up and say, 'We're making a day of it so we don't want the coach up but I want the trip back.' So you could get the coach back afterwards and be guaranteed a lift home.

My friend remembers the excitement in the build up to the gig. 'We're going to see The Jam. What are we gonna wear tonight?'

We'd all take the day off work and go up, go for something to eat, go to the pub, have a couple of beers and then go to the venue. You got all the excitement of seeing all the scooters outside and bumping into people you might know and making friends. Everyone was there for the same reason – to see their favourite band – so you always bumped into someone you might know.

SOLID BOND IN YOUR HEART

We were up in the gods at Hammersmith Odeon but you could just about make them out. I can still remember Weller having a bright yellow shirt on. In those days, you couldn't take pictures as they'd search you as you went in, but I used to sneak my little instamatic camera in down the front of my trousers. I've still got all the photos from all the gigs I went to. Hearing 'Pretty Green' thumping out on the bass for the first time is a memory I'll never forget.

I WAS THERE: RICHARD HERRING

One November evening in 1979, whilst round a friend's house, will live with me until my days are done. I was aged 14 and it was the first time I heard the recently-released *All Mod Cons*. It totally blew me away (and still does!). It was flawless in every way; it had the lot, from fast aggressive tracks to romantic ballads, and so my lifelong journey following The Jam and everything associated with them began.

I wasn't the only one. Everyone I knew was into The Jam. To think that a young Paul Weller was only a little older than myself and could pen lyrics like he did was just mind-blowing. His lyrics hit every emotion and thought of a teenager living in that time, and was perhaps the main reason why the band were so popular. The fact that the tunes were awesome helped a bit too!

The Jam at Hammersmith Odeon was Richard Herring's first ever gig

The Jam at Hammersmith Odeon was my first ever gig. I opted for a ticket sitting down. I was a long way from the stage and I can recall seeing kids my age near the front going mental to every track. I had to see them again, and next time I'd be in the thick of it.

On the next tour I went to Guildford Civic Hall. Woking was nearby and the small venue was heaving, the crowd waiting for the local heroes to appear. I got a place right at the front, next to the speakers. The energy and noise were something I'd never experienced before. The band did three encores that night, something I've never seen since, and being next to the speakers, I couldn't hear a thing for two days after!

My love of the band continued tenfold. The clothes followed... every shade of Sta-Prest, Paisley shirt, Fred Perry polo I could find were purchased. White socks and Jam shoes (or bowling shoes) completed the look. Every male I knew wanted to be Paul Weller. He'd look cool in his grandad's dressing gown and slippers! I didn't quite pull it off with my mop of curly hair to mock his Marriott-style haircuts...

A PEOPLE'S HISTORY OF THE JAM

I saw The Jam at a few other venues. The Michael Sobell Sports Centre was a real strange choice of venue, as was the line-up. A very talented rockabilly band called The Rimshots got slaughtered by the mainly Mod audience. The choice of date for that gig wasn't great either. The Rainbow was nearby and The Exploited were playing the same night. Mods, skinheads and punks filling the streets of North London after a gig only had one outcome… trouble!

Probably the best gig I ever attended took place at the Hammersmith Palais. The place was buzzing and the support acts – The Ruts, the Fun Boy Three and Bananarama – got the show going before The Jam exploded into life. Half my school were there and word got round that if we hung around after the gig, the band would appear to sign autographs and have a chat. The band duly obliged, upstairs in a bar. I was too star struck to say much, although I did get their autographs. My only regret is that I got Bruce and Rick's on the ticket stub but Paul's on an empty Rothman's packet!

The night didn't end well. Totally lost in the moment, I'd missed the last bus and train home. I lived in Chessington and was stranded in Hammersmith. It was a long walk home in the rain and I got in around four in the morning and I had school the next day. Was it worth it? Course it was!

I had every single and album within hours of release and the queue outside Our Price in Kingston-upon-Thames when a new record came out had to be seen to be believed. It was no surprise when 'Going Underground' went straight in at number one, quite a feat back then.

In 1982, my world fell apart when it was announced that The Jam were to split. I cried for days but, looking back, that last album and the later singles didn't quite live up to the stuff that had preceded them. Now I'm a bit older and wiser, it was totally the right thing to do. It gave the band the legacy they have.

So I had to go to the last gig at Brighton. It was probably the worst gig I ever saw the band play. The atmosphere was flat, and when someone lobbed a beer glass at Bruce Foxton it marked the end of a horrid evening. Not the way I wanted to remember them.

Everyone was into The Jam, and mates from that era still are, as am I. What made them so great? You could relate to them. The lyrics hit the spot on every tune. They were never big wig pop stars who'd not have the time of day for the people who made them great in the first place. They were more like your best mates rather than pop stars.

I've seen Paul Weller (and From The Jam) many times since and he still is an awesome talent and songwriter. He's probably the best this country has ever produced. A few years back, Paul's sister Nicky put a post on social media saying she had a few copies of a Jam book for sale. Unbeknownst to me, my wife got me one for my birthday and asked Nicky if there was any chance Paul could sign it. The book turned up a week later, duly signed. It certainly made up for that last signature on a fag packet!

SCANDINAVIUM
22 NOVEMBER 1980, GOTHENBURG, SWEDEN

The Jam undertake a nine date European tour.

SOUND AFFECTS RELEASED
28 NOVEMBER 1980

The Jam's fifth LP, Sound Affects, debuts at No.2 and goes on to sell more than 100,000 copies, spending 19 weeks on the UK albums chart.

VREDENBURG
1 DECEMBER 1980, UTRECHT, NETHERLANDS

I WAS THERE: KORS EIJKELBOOM

This was the second time I saw The Jam live. I remember this mostly as noisy and not very good sounding. The room they played was designed for classical music and the sound systems (and engineers) of the time were not sophisticated the way they are now. Having large stacks of Marshalls for this tour probably didn't help... it was all a bit drowned in noise.

I've since seen Paul Weller as a solo artist many times. He keeps returning to the Paradiso venue, where I've worked since 1992, first as a stagehand and now as manager of the production team. When he played in 2017, we put a posh bottle of 1977 port in his dressing room, accompanied by a note to thank him for 40 years of service, not realising he was off the alcohol by then. Hopefully he either flushed it away or gave it to the next person!

CONFERENCE CENTRE
5 & 6 DECEMBER 1980, BRIGHTON, UK

I WAS THERE: STUART STEELES

I got into the soundcheck for the second show. They'd become much more commercially successful and them letting people into soundchecks was better known. There must have been a couple of hundred there. They would always hang around to sign stuff, but the staff at The Centre were keen to clear the hall after they'd finished.

I WAS THERE: PAUL TAYLOR

I first saw The Jam on Marc Bolan's TV show, performing 'All Around The World', Marc trying to be cool in his introduction. I was mesmerised by the burgundy Rickenbackers – Bruce's bass and Paul's 330 – and the black suits and white-top shoes. Before, punk to me was spitting and swearing, The Stranglers and the Pistols. I was 14. I wasn't a punk, but I was into the music, and it pricked everybody's ears.

I didn't have any money then, but 16 was a turning point, starting my apprenticeship, earning enough to buy fags and stuff. Before that it was a paper-round, delivering the *Evening Argus*, obtaining records just beyond my reach and not savvy enough to listen to John Peel. My first Jam LP was *This Is The Modern World* from Cloake's in Crawley. That was my foundation, songs like 'Standards', 'Here Comes The Weekend', the title track, and that real humdinger, 'In The Street Today'. 'London Girl' was brilliant live.

By 1979, I was buying all the records. *All Mod Cons* was brilliant. I'd learn all those guitar parts, getting to understand that Beatles influence better. I first saw them live for the *Setting Sons* show, in Brighton, and again just before *Sound Affects* came out. We ran into the conference centre soundcheck, let in by John Weller. 'Come on boys!' John and the bearded bodyguard, Kenny Wheeler, in his big bomber jacket. We stood at the front of the stage, Paul messing around with a Beethoven thing on guitar ('Für Elise') and then Bruce started playing the opening of 'Monday', us thinking 'That sounds good!' They ignored us, acting cool, then went into 'Saturday's Kids', which blew us away.

I saw them six or seven times, including Crawley Leisure in February 1981, when I met Bruce in the Goffs Park Hotel. We thought we'd go for a quick drink – and so did he! I met Kenny again and we bought Bruce a drink. I also saw them at the Rainbow or in Hammersmith but remember more about the train journey up to London.

I was 20 when they split, going through a rough time with my dad, who had a drink problem. I moved into a professional house – three of us - and remember Paul's interview on the seafront at Brighton, explaining his reasons. My immediate thought, 'Things just can't get any fucking worse!' I was unhappy where I was living, everything a little shitty, but I understood why he did it. I enjoyed *The Gift* and that tour, but it was different, thinking, 'This isn't what I saw on Marc Bolan's show,' the sound three of them gave, nice and raw. You could see a change in direction… which was fine, but it wasn't The Jam.

LOCARNO
9 DECEMBER 1980, BRISTOL, UK

I WAS THERE: PAUL GAMMON, AGE 15

We'd been Jam fans for a couple of years, but unlike some of my mates I hadn't managed to see them live, so I was excited to get tickets for the *Sound Affects* tour. The new LP was brilliant, The Jam at the top of their game, the biggest band in Britain.

I was never sure whether to be a punk, a Mod or a rude boy. I loved all the music, but for this one I donned my best Fred Perry shirt and Harrington. We got to the Locarno early, and being only 15, we weren't into beer yet (though I would have some later in the evening), so we headed straight to the front of the stage and chatted with the Mod girls already hanging around there.

A local band called Out of Order opened, so huge credit to The Jam for giving a platform to young unsigned artists. John Weller got on the mic and apologised that the Locarno was the only unseated venue they could get, and wasn't really big enough for The Jam. Not sure what the capacity was. Maybe 2,000. It was absolutely rammed. John announced, 'The best fucking rock 'n' roll band in the world… THE JAM!' and they came onstage to a tumultuous reception, playing a blistering set to a chaotic, pinballing scrum of a crowd.

It was the day after John Lennon's killing and Weller was quite emotional, dedicating the show to Lennon's memory. I remember in "A' Bomb in Wardour Street' the bass reverberating up through my ribcage, and the same with 'Strange Town', so intense and powerful. The sounds Weller was wrenching from his Ricky 330 were awe-inspiring. 'Down In The Tube Station' is a stunning song, and Rick's train-driving drum solo was amazing. They launched into 'Going Underground' and I swear the building shook. Looking up at the balcony I thought it might collapse, the way it was bouncing. I later learned that the Locarno ballroom was 'sprung' so was designed and built to withstand Jam audiences and 'Going Underground' moments!

For 'That's Entertainment', Paul and Bruce switched to acoustic guitar and the vocal harmonies soared. The songs spoke to us, in fact they shouted out to us. If you were 15 in 1980 and you didn't like The Jam, there was something wrong with you!

We stood at Paul Weller's feet like disciples. My mate Martin and I had recently started our first garage band. I'd switched from guitar to bass and we were trying to get a version of 'In The City' together. Like a lot of Bruce Foxton's stuff, the bass part is a bit tricky and I was nowhere near nailing it, so we were shouting 'In The City' between every song (probably to Weller's annoyance), so I could watch what Bruce was doing on his fretboard. When it came to the encore, Weller glanced down in our direction and said 'In The City'! I like to think he clocked that we were really young and wouldn't have seen them play it in the early days. Or maybe they were going to do it all along. Who knows?

At the end, he put his half-full can of Heineken down on the edge of the stage, right in front of us before walking off. I picked it up, necked what was left, and took the empty can home as a souvenir. I still have it. And for me, few evenings in my life have even come close to the sheer exhilaration of this. Youth Explosion indeed.

CIVIC HALL
11 DECEMBER 1980, GUILDFORD, UK

I WAS THERE: RICHARD WESTNEY

It was a year and three-quarters before we got to see them return to Guildford Civic, by which time they'd become massive, in a year in which they achieved their first two No.1 singles and played there three more times. *All Mod Cons* had taken them to a new level and *Setting Sons* kept them there, with *Sound Affects* released barely a fortnight before their 'special Christmas show' at the London Road venue that December.

CORNWALL COLISEUM
14 DECEMBER 1980, ST AUSTELL, UK

I WAS THERE: KATHRYN BARNES

It wasn't my first gig, I'd seen The Undertones in Plymouth in 1978, but they were up-and-coming and not well heard of at that time. Seeing The Jam was amazing. The first time I was starstruck, I couldn't stop staring at them! Ridiculous, I know, but I was only young. When I was in the sixth form there was a boy who was mad on them. We all became quite obsessed with them, playing them constantly on the common room record player.

I WAS THERE: DEAN LEGGETT, BOB

Me, Kev Downing and Tim McVay, both later of The Family Cat, went along. Our dads took it in turns to drop us and pick us up. It's about 20 miles from where we lived. It was our 'go to' for bigger bands, right by the beach, a couple of thousand capacity –

SOLID BOND IN YOUR HEART

it always felt big when we were little!

I bought the 'In The City' single and then the album when they came out. I read the music press, listened to John Peel, and Another Record Shop, Redruth stocked all the punk stuff and sold tickets for gigs. They'd have new releases and they had a Jam poster on the wall. I asked if I could listen to the LP and thought it was great. It sounded like punk to me. I then bought 'All Around The World', which I preferred, 'The Modern World', 'News Of The World'… I

Dean Leggett with his prized Jam vinyl

started getting into other bands then, like Stiff Little Fingers and Joy Division, but then The Jam hit back on 'Tube Station', 'Strange Town', 'When You're Young', *All Mod Cons* – my favourite period. *Setting Sons* and *Sound Affects* were also great, and they got huge, racking up No.1s.

Later, BOB signed with the same publisher as Paul and were set to join his first solo Japanese tour as support, but it didn't happen, all a bit gutting. But around 1990, me and (bandmate) Simon (Armstrong) had a tribute band, rehearsing Jam songs for fun. One night, maybe Nottingham on the *Stride Up* tour, the support didn't turn up, so we supported ourselves, with Arthur (Tapp) on bass (and a massive Jam fan) doing a set of Jam songs including 'Strange Town'. There's a tape in existence somewhere. That's one of the best. The drumming's fantastic, and it's got so much energy. I like all the tracks off *All Mod Cons* and 'When You're Young' is great, as is 'Tube Station'. But they're all great, aren't they?

Like in 'Strange Town', 'You've got to move in a straight line, you've got to walk and talk in four-four time. You can't be weird in a strange town.' Walking around Redruth on a Saturday with mohair tops, punk badges, hair stuck up at the front, creepers, tight trousers, when everybody else had long hair, we'd get chased or beaten up by Teds or regular lads. 'Greboes', we called them.

'Tube Station' really got me back into them. I'd play along on drums in my parents' front room, my first little three-piece kit, listening to my dad's record player. I was only allowed to play after school and before teatime though, otherwise the neighbours complained!

That night in December 1980 I had all the single sleeves from 'In The City' up to 'Start!' stuffed in a pocket – big enough not to bend them – of this big army overcoat, standing down the front sweating my nuts off on the off chance I might get to meet the band. After the gig and standing by this barrier, at the side of the stage near the dressing room door, where loads of us were waiting hoping to get a hello with the band, Weller came out and signed all my singles.

The second time I saw them there (25 June 1981), they did stuff off *Sound Affects*. I wasn't shocked when it all ended. They were doing stuff with a brass section, and you could see where he was going next – the 'Going Underground' days weren't coming back, and how much further could they go? *The Gift* was alright, but…

I WAS THERE: SEAN STRIBLEY

It was 1978 when I first heard The Jam, either on the Top 20 show on a Sunday evening or at school chum's house, Stephen Jelbert (guitarist, The Family Cat), on his Dansette record player. I was 13 and from Camborne, a tin mining town. I'd been taping music from the Top 20 since about 1975 on to an old reel-to-reel tape recorder, but it wasn't until the punk thing roused us that I was really interested. The Stranglers, Sex Pistols, Buzzcocks, The Clash, Ramones, Stiff Little Fingers… They all impressed, and then The Jam came along in 1978 with 'Tube Station'. Wow!

That was the first Jam record I bought, from the reduced section at Woolworth's in town, probably about 49p, with a picture sleeve. It was the first Jam song that truly resonated with me, and it's still my favourite.

I saw them live for the first time at the Cornwall Coliseum and got my copy of 'Tube Station' signed by the band. As teenagers living in West Cornwall, it was quite a mission to see bands live. Early days car-sharing with older fans, then motorcycles, then our own cars when we were still at school and college. I also remember meeting The Jam after another show and getting a seven-inch single sleeve signed.

I was surprised at Paul's decision to end it when he did. The Style Council was a clear direction change, but it wasn't for me. A couple of good singles, but radio music only for me. I was into the post-punk scene by then. I had my hair cut like Paul Weller in my teens (ha ha!), but the Mod scene was not for me. I preferred large Japanese motorcycles and the style that went with that.

I still listen to The Jam, mainly singles I pick up off YouTube. *Setting Sons* is a great album, and I like the raw feel of *This Is The Modern World*, which I had on cassette when I was about 13. I bought *Sound Affects* for my brother for his 13th birthday. 'Tube Station' takes me back to those days, sitting cross-legged in front of my parents' 1960s valve radiogram in the front room, playing it on a BSR record deck. It still plays on my Technics SL1210 today!

THE CRICKETERS
14 FEBRUARY 1981, WESTFIELD, WOKING, UK

The band are billed as The Jam Road Crew for a secret gig.

YMCA
16 FEBRUARY 1981, WOKING, UK

I WAS THERE: DAVE 'VOL' BOLTON, AGE 14

It was perhaps inevitable that as an impressionable 13-year-old growing up in Woking in the late '70s, my musical awakening would be powerfully kickstarted by The Jam. After hearing 'Strange Town' and 'When You're Young', quickly followed by 'The Eton Rifles', I was shaken into action and purchased the newly released *Setting Sons* from Boots. Life would never be quite the same again, the album mesmerising me with its raw power and singalong anthems, Weller's driving vocals providing social commentary on a changing Britain. I'd just turned 14, was word perfect on all the tracks, and seeing The Jam live was now a must.

In 1980, Britain was changing, Thatcher in power, social unrest and a rise in popularity for the right-wing National Front, resulting tensions seamlessly entwined into youth culture, in turn making football terraces and gig venues challenging places to visit. An edginess and fear of impending violence was tangible, and I was facing it on two fronts. I'd just started going to Arsenal on my own, and now had the prospect of facing the same experience at music venues. It truly was a time where the weak got crushed as the strong grew stronger.

I first saw The Jam at Guildford Civic in July 1980, and then again in November at Bracknell Sports Centre on the *Sound Affects* tour. The Jam were at their peak, with two No.1 singles. They were undoubtedly the biggest band in the country.

In January 1981, my Geography teacher, Miss Taylor, informed me that The Jam were to play two benefit gigs in Woking during February, at the YMCA and then Sheerwater Youth Club. Given the size of each venue, tickets were next to impossible to acquire. In desperation I turned to my dad, a Woking Borough Council environmental health officer, hoping he could pull a few strings. There was radio silence for two weeks, but on the Thursday before the gig, he came home from work holding two tickets for the YMCA. I could hardly believe my luck; I was going to see The Jam live in Woking.

The day arrived, a Monday, and me and my friend Jock were dropped outside. Woking YMCA was a non-descript building on Heathside Cresent's one-way system at the back of the railway station and we nervously entered through the main doors to find ourselves crammed into a dingy-looking hall along with 200 others. It was all quite surreal. I had no idea who the support was going to be so was pleasantly surprised when the Vaughn Toulouse-fronted Department S appeared, having heard them in session on John Peel a few months earlier. I enjoyed their short set, including the fantastic 'Is Vic There?'.

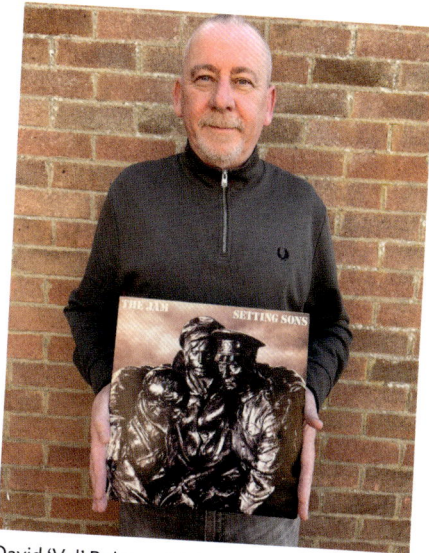

David 'Vol' Bolton with his treasured copy of Setting Sons

We didn't have to wait long for the main event, as enter stage left Gary Crowley to introduce the band. Out came The Jam. It became very quickly apparent that all was not well, the band looking like they'd enjoyed a few pre-performance beers too many. The sound was also an issue. Before long a very irate Paul left the stage, along with Bruce and Rick. In what seemed an age, during which time the atmosphere got distinctly edgy, the band reappeared, and with the sound marginally better continued with the set. I've no recollection of the setlist but vividly remember thinking, 'Here I am, hearing The Jam tear through 'When You're Young'!' I didn't care about the sound, only that I was there to witness it.

I was blessed to see The Jam live six times. I can't adequately summarise what it felt like to see them. I felt a belonging, an almost cathartic experience shared by band and crowd alike. It didn't matter what background you were from, your ethnicity, whether you were Mod or punk. Everyone was at one and for 90 minutes nothing else mattered. It was almost spiritual. The Jam were hypnotising, raw, powerful, uncompromising and energetic, with shout-along anthems and unrivalled lyrics capturing all modern life's challenges. The energy in the crowd was amazing, all word perfect with every song, a seething mass of sweaty youth pogoing as one, knowing they were part of something unique and special, determined to live every moment.

Those times live with me, an integral part of who I am. I never recaptured that feeling nor did I really want to. I cherish it to this day, finding it difficult to put into words how that period in my life felt. I didn't realise it then but came to understand that I received a dual education, the traditional state one in the classrooms of Winston Churchill School, and one as valuable from the pen and words of The Jam.

Above all else, The Jam gave you hope, a hope that allowed you to make your way in the world with the understanding that despite being chained and shackled by the establishment and inept leaders, with corporations putting profit before people, you had a self-belief and determination to be the best you could be.

Many still rue never seeing The Jam live, having a genuine regret, maybe thinking the band called it a day too early. I think the enduring legacy was partly because they finished at their peak. There was never a downward curve to the music they produced nor an embarrassing reform. They just managed to capture that magical moment in time and preserve it in pristine condition. Weller was right; why ruin something special?

Nostalgia occasionally allows me to reflect on those days, 43 years on, allowing myself to drift back to that cold February night where the 14-year-old me was present at an intimate hometown gig to see, at the height of their career, 'the best band in the fucking world'.

Thanks Dad x

I WASN'T THERE: DARRON ROBINSON

Our window cleaner had tickets. Did I want one? I had the ticket at school that day. But I was on a promise… and as it turned out, neither of those things transpired!

SHEERWATER YOUTH CLUB
17 FEBRUARY 1981, WOKING, UK

Another 'secret' gig for The Jam.

UNIVERSITY OF EAST ANGLIA
21 FEBRUARY 1981, NORWICH, UK

I WAS THERE: PETE KEELEY

It was a bit of a coup having them at UEA, as by that point they were playing much bigger venues. It was a warm-up for a European tour. UEA had Madness play on the Friday night and The Jam on the Saturday, two of the biggest bands around at that point. Tickets for both went on sale exclusively through Robins Records about a week before, on a wet Monday morning at 9am, with people camping overnight and the queues ridiculous. If you weren't in that queue, you weren't getting a ticket. Both sold out instantly, and that weekend became legendary. Fantastic gigs, both of them.

LEISURE CENTRE
23 FEBRUARY 1981, CRAWLEY, UK

I WAS THERE: KEVIN WATT

You know the song 'Pretty Green' from *Sound Affects*? The pause in Bruce's bass intro is where we felt some audience participation was needed, so myself, my brother, his mate and brother started it at Brighton Centre. Living in Crawley, Brighton was easy to get to. I saw them three times there, and when they eventually came to Crawley, one of us decided we'd shout 'oi!' if they played it… and we weren't disappointed. When Bruce started the song, we were ready, shouting at the top of our voices. To our amazement, everyone followed… We were so proud. Great days, great concerts, and we were at the last one at Brighton Centre. I'll never forget the atmosphere… before, during and after. Fucking electric!

'THAT'S ENTERTAINMENT' RELEASED
24 FEBRUARY 1981

Despite only being available as a German import, 'That's Entertainment' (backed by a live take on 'Down In The Tube Station At Midnight') reaches No.21 in the UK singles chart, in the third of its six weeks in the Top 40.

I BOUGHT IT: IAN SNOWBALL, AUTHOR

The first record I bought with my own money was 'That's Entertainment', when I turned eleven in 1981. The record hadn't been long out. I bought it with some birthday money. I marched off down to Woolworth's in Maidstone. It was a picture sleeve, and I remember getting home, realising – as with many seven-inch singles then – there wasn't a middle bit. I can almost picture myself racing back down to get an adapter so I could play the record. I'd have then played it over and over, as you did. The kids of today are missing out, aren't they?

   I was going to a youth club and the part of town I lived in was mod-heavy, rather than skinhead or punk, and the jukebox had three Jam tracks – 'Going Underground', 'Start!' and 'That's Entertainment'. They'd get played countless times every evening, and I was already aware of The Jam, with *Setting Sons* the album I first heard. They were soon my band, with the Mod thing important to me and my crowd. I've a photo of me at eleven, wearing a pair of desert boots,

SOLID BOND IN YOUR HEART

Sta-Prest trousers, V-neck jumper and buttoned-down shirt. Boys today of that age don't seem to have that passion for the music or surroundings. People were more old-headed then, and that was my gateway into finding out about bands like The Who and Small Faces. With songs like The Kinks' 'David Watts' or The Who's 'Disguises' I heard The Jam versions first.

PAVILLON BALTARD
26 FEBRUARY 1981, PARIS FRANCE

The Jam begin a ten-date Europe tour which concludes at Studio 44 in Rouen, France on 16 March.

I WAS THERE: AIDAN KEHOE

Apart from the Rainbow in 1980, the other gig that stands out of the 27 I saw is Paris in 1981. We noticed an ad in the back of the *NME*, £24 for transport there and back from London, including a ticket for the gig. It cost us a week's wages but there was no way we weren't going. We arrived in Paris early in the morning and spent much of the day on a diet of beer and biscuits. When skint, we made our way to the venue. Not long after getting there, The Jam's coach turned up and they let us and others into the soundcheck. When that was done, we spent a good hour or so chatting to the band. It was a brilliant gig as always, but it was again marred by violence, this time by French skins causing a huge fight which made the band stop playing briefly. After the gig was over, the band came onto our coach to personally thank us for coming. It was an amazing adventure for two 18-year-olds.

I WAS THERE: PETE EASTWOOD

I was 13 when punk came out and it changed everything. My best mate's brother worked in the local record exchange and one day he showed me the cover of *In The City* and that was it. I had to see this band, and from the second I discovered who they were to the second they split, they were my everything. I called them new wave, not punk, and as soon as I discovered Mod, that was it.

Pete Eastwood (left) caught The Jam in Blackburn and Paris

A PEOPLE'S HISTORY OF THE JAM

I saw The Jam 17 times. They played my home town of Blackburn three times and I went to all three. I saw them in Paris, Manchester (at the Apollo), London, Blackpool Opera House. The Michael Sobell Sports Centre gig stands out. There was a CND stall and because Paul wore a CND badge everyone wanted one. I went with Accrington Scooter Club. It was the coldest I've ever been in my entire life.

I'd seen the advert for the Paris coach trip in the NME. I went with a mate who looked more like Weller than I did, even though I'd take photos of Paul's latest haircut into the local hairdresser's – front, back and sides – to get my hair cut like his. I'd never been abroad. We went first class on the train and got thrown out (we hadn't paid for first class!). We arrived at Euston station the night before and had no money to stay anywhere. But if you had a ticket for the train the next day the police would let you sleep on the station so I slept on a bench in my Parka, Sta-Prest, Jam shoes, Fred Perry – all the works. My mate slept on the floor. I woke up to this Mohican asking me 'are you a Mod?' which was the most stupid thing I've ever been asked in my life. Normally I'd have answered with something sarcastic but he had two mates with him and I didn't think it was a good idea to take the mickey out of him.

They changed the venue because there was a rumour of French skinheads. I have a vague memory of the gig being in a makeshift marquee. The gig was amazing. There was a bit of kicking off inside the venue and Paul said 'get 'em out of here' and they were whizzed out. He tied a Union Jack to his microphone stand and that's when I proper felt part of something. You've gone abroad and your band are there, playing.

We walked outside the venue and there were 50 to 100 skinheads coming down the hill with batons and everything. To this day, it's the most violence I've ever seen in my life. The French police were just randomly hitting out at anybody who wasn't French. We managed to get on our coach but the coach next to us was fully burnt out and the driver was outside our window, being whacked with batons by police.

We'd paid for a tour round Paris after the gig as part of the trip but because of the trouble they just took us back to Euston. We got back to Euston where we were then arrested and taken into a back room at Euston police station. I thought we were going to get beaten up by them. They were that aggressive. But they'd pulled us in because they thought we were friendly with the Mohicans, who'd been causing trouble at the station. We grassed them up to protect ourselves. I then remember being sat on the Preston train, waiting for it to leave Euston, with the punks parading up and down the platform looking for us.

I was round at my girlfriend Yvonne's house when I heard about the split. We'd had a row – we always were – and she was sat talking to her best mate, Siobhan, when it came on the 12.45pm *Newsbeat* on Radio 1. It brought a tear to my eye. The argument with the girlfriend went out the window. I remember the interview he did in a mac and scarf on a windy seafront, possibly in Brighton, talking about the split.

They were everything to me. You had to buy the records on the day they came out. I'd have the local record shop save the windows displays for me. When they released a new album, they'd interview the band on the radio and they'd play every track, so you'd record the whole album off the radio. But you didn't want the adverts or the weather. It was a bit of an art to just get The Jam on the tape. When a record came out, you'd play it and play it and play it so that when you saw them live you knew every word. I didn't have loads of money. When gigs were announced me and my mates used to drive to wherever to try and get tickets.

I nicked off school one time when they were playing Blackburn and went down to King George's Hall. There were loads of people queuing up. I don't know what it is with me and Mohicans but a punk came up to me and very aggressively said, 'I want your ticket.' I blagged it, saying, 'I haven't got one mate. That's why I'm stood here, queuing up to buy one.'

A reunion? It'll never happen. Paul hasn't spoken to Rick since 1983. Rick told me he was at an event and Paul just walked past him and ignored him. And Paul doesn't need it. He's got an amazing band. They're all brilliant musicians. There's no egos. And I wouldn't want it to happen. But if it did? Then, yes, I'd want to be there.

METROPOLE
8 MARCH 1981, BERLIN, GERMANY

I WAS THERE: VINCENT PARKINSON

I was a huge Stranglers fan back then and didn't really take to The Jam like my friends did, but I went along to a packed-out gig. They played a good set but Weller was having issues with his Rickenbacker so instead of just swapping it he decided to smash it into his amp. After that he became a tad snotty with the audience, especially those at the front. They were mainly squaddies – so not the best idea!

After the gig Foxton and Buckler came to talk to the audience members who'd stayed behind. Foxton was very relaxed and engaging. He told us that because of the age difference he occasionally felt a bit 'old' on some of the songs. Buckler was also very easy going – they were just regular blokes – but the burning question was 'where's Weller?'. Then he sheepishly appeared with his minder, a big mixed-race guy who looked for all the world like boxer John Conteh. We approached him expecting a chat but he was having none of it. A few German kids asked if they could have a photo with him. He agreed but the kid who did the peace sign behind him was given short shrift by Mr Conteh and told to fuck off! It left a bad taste in the mouth and Weller kind of slunk away. To this day I've never forgotten his rock star tantrum.

ROYAL COURT THEATRE
27 APRIL 1981, LIVERPOOL, UK

I WAS THERE: PAUL MEREDITH

A Jam gig was an event. The anticipation in the weeks leading up to it, counting down the days, the journey in with the boys, singing the songs, guessing the set list, guessing the clothes… unreal!

This was the first time I was in the same room as my heroes. 'Put your hands together for the best band in the fuckin' world,' said John. He wasn't lying. First chord, bedlam. I was in Jam heaven. 'That is actually The Jam, my Jam! What's he wearing? That guitar! That attitude! That sound! Unreal, mate, kill me now. I'm ready, life can't get any better than this.'

So much energy, so much connection, tears to my eyes even now, reminiscing. They meant so much to us, still do. My dad had The Beatles, yeah, but I had The Jam, I still feel that way about my band. Not sure he still feels the same about his.

Take me back for a gig, I beg you. They really were something else. No one's ever come within a thousand miles, never will. Hope they do but, nah, they were the pioneers: the clothes, the Rickenbackers, the great white hopes, the lyrics to our lives, but most importantly the tunes. I loved them then and love them now. Imagine if I never found The Jam in '77. My life would be so, so different.

Thank you for the music, boys, you made me so aware of the times we live in, musically and politically. I can't thank you enough, you made me what I am today. I knew people who never got it. They were soon banished. I'm 60 now, still an avid collector of anything Jam/Weller related. I've got a big gig coming in December. Bring it on. Me and my son (yes, I taught him) will both be front row, giving it large. So proud.

I WAS THERE: DAVE PRATT

Gordon and I met at the bus stop to go to catering college, lamenting the fact that The Jam were doing a one-off gig in Liverpool that night. Wouldn't it have been great if we'd been going? Next thing we knew, we were dashing home to get changed and were on the 213 to Darlington, not for our day at college but to catch a train to Liverpool. I've no memory of how we got tickets. It was surely a sell-out, but we saw that gig and it was quite possibly one of the best Jam performances we ever saw. They played a barnstorming set and debuted 'Funeral Pyre', which was to be the new single. We made it back to the train station with five minutes to spare to catch the last train back home.

I WAS THERE: WARREN MEADOWS, AGE 16

We classed them as a punk band… but then everybody started wearing green Parkas. Ha! I only saw them once. In Liverpool, 1981. I don't really remember anything significant apart from it being a lot tamer than The Clash at the same venue – those gigs where you were thrown sideways, backwards and forwards.

It was about Weller's attitude for me. He sang with venom to get the message out there. Like Strummer, he had the punk ethos. 'Tube Station' was the first seven-inch I purchased and I played it to death. I had a good idea of the lyrics, and there are many great lines in there. However, it wasn't till I saw Russell Hastings of From The Jam sing it that I caught the closing lines, as Paul sang it with such vengeance.

'They took the keys, and she'll think it's me.'

That really resonates. How the hell did a 19-year-old come up with that? He wasn't married. To have those thoughts about his wife (I know it's third party) as he's lying on the ground, getting a kicking, staring at British Rail posters. Simply brilliant. McCartney couldn't have penned it better. Those lyrics need framing and hanging somewhere.

I was in Birkdale, Southport at the time, and had a friend, Paul Rimmer, four or five years older, who lived over the road. Luckily my parents trusted him to take me to gigs and return me home safely. He was a great influence and had a massive record collection. He'd buy records every Saturday with his wages, then play them to me. Like 1977 singles 'ROckWrok' and 'Young Savage' – I'd never heard Ultravox! sound so good.

We always got the train. I think it was underground then. It was good to see the bondage trousers build up, boarding the train, as we got closer. The trouble with the train was that the last one back was 10.45pm. I don't think they had curfews and fines back then, so after a sweaty gig, we got even more sweaty running for the last train. Staying for an encore was a gamble. I think the only train we missed was for The Clash (it was worth it though!), when we had to get the next train to Ormskirk and walk seven miles home.

AICHI KINRO KAIKAN
13 MAY 1981, NAGOYA, JAPAN

The Jam begin a four date tour of Japan.

A PEOPLE'S HISTORY OF THE JAM

LE CLUB
21 MAY 1981, MONTREAL, CANADA

The Jam begin a five-date North American tour, their fifth so far.

CONCERT HALL
22 & 23 MAY 1981, TORONTO, CANADA

I WAS THERE: IVAR HAMILTON

This was the go-to venue in the late sixties, when Led Zep, The Who, Procol Harum, Zappa and countless others played there, before it fell out of favour. Bands started to appear again in the eighties, mostly booked by indie promoters The Garys. With a wooden floor, a close-proximity balcony view and no air conditioning, it never took long to get the 1,500 capacity place roaring when there was a sold-out show. By 1981, the town's major concert promoters, CPI, had begun to regularly book the venue as well as emerging acts.

To the dismay of radio station CFNY, who didn't have as big an audience, CPI aligned itself regularly with CHUM FM, the No.1 rock station in the market. That seemed good on paper, but CHUM only spun Jam records occasionally. Their audience also had very little idea who they were. There's a live recording of the second night where, towards the end of the set, Paul Weller said he'd been in Toronto three days and was appalled by what he'd heard on local radio, urging the audience to pester radio to play them. Regardless, both shows sold out and it was filled with CFNY listeners who knew what the band were playing.

THE RITZ
26 MAY 1981, NEW YORK, NEW YORK

I WAS THERE: DAVE WRIGHT

I was lucky enough to see The Jam a few times in 1981/82 in New York City and New Jersey. I was a teenager in love with the excitement and intensity of punk rock and live music, and the band that spoke for me was The Jam. Their punk/no bullshit aesthetic and coolness grabbed me by the shirt collar and lifted me off my feet.

At the Ritz in New York, anticipation was off the charts. I wore a white buttoned-down shirt and black tie, waiting in line for the doors to open and the rush to get close to the stage. I was just a few feet back, right in front of Bruce. The sold-out crowd moved as one, the floor absolutely heaving. It sounds crazy but it moved with the crowd! Every song was a sweaty singalong. It was stiflingly hot, Paul's shirt dripping.

After the show I snuck up to the balcony and was amazed to see Paul, Bruce and Rick hanging out, greeting fans. I'd brought pictures of the band and got them signed. In over 40 years of going to shows I'd say this was my favourite, with a video included on the *About The Young Idea* Blu-ray.

'FUNERAL PYRE' RELEASED
29 MAY 1981

The Jam's 13th single enters the UK chart at No.4, staying there a second week before leaving the Top 40 two weeks later.

GRONA LUND
10 JUNE 1981, STOCKHOLM, SWEDEN

The Jam play the first of two shows in Sweden.

RAINBOW THEATRE
17 JUNE 1981, LONDON, UK

The twelve-date Bucket and Spade *tour kicks off at London's Rainbow Theatre.*

I WAS THERE: RICHARD NOBLE

Myself, and it seemed most of the school I went to, were Jam fans and had been for a couple of years or so, but no one had seen them live. It wasn't long before I was due to leave, and a local entrepreneur was adverting a ticket and coach deal to see them at the Rainbow. A guaranteed ticket, no mucking about with trains to and from London, and at a very reasonable price. Too good to miss, so my friend Kevin and I booked our places. Although all those on board were locals, there wasn't any chatter amongst us. There was a lot of eyeing up each other, checking out each other's style. Kevin stood out a bit, sporting a haircut based on Foxton's, whereas everyone else copied Weller's style, him saying 'my 'Brucie cut' is being checked out.'

When our tickets were handed out just before getting off, I stared at mine. It had The Jam printed on it and we were actually going to see them! Outside the venue we were met by a sea of people dressed like us. I could sense passers-by looking at us, even though they most likely saw a similar scenario every time a gig was on. First on were Apocalypse, which years later I found out was writer Tony Fletcher's band. Like everyone else, to my shame, I was too one-eyed for The Jam. I understand why Weller was frustrated with this and later commented about people not really taking notice of the supports.

Soon after, the lights went down, John Weller came on to introduce The Jam and we were off. And my God, we certainly were, as they kicked off proceedings with 'Going Underground'. I don't think anyone was expecting that. We were upstairs in the seats but standing at the front of the upper circle. Below us was sheer movement, which I'd never witnessed before. The set was mainly a mix of *Sound Affects* and *Setting Sons*, with one or two tracks from *All Mod Cons*.

I was disappointed they didn't do 'Tube Station'. I was looking forward to singing along, just like on the live EP that came with 'Going Underground'. There was also one song neither myself or Kevin recognised. I can't say to this day what it was. After the gig, waiting for the coach, a couple of lads who travelled with us managed to get in downstairs, even though our tickets were upstairs only. Soaked in sweat, they said it was totally mad from start to finish. I made a mental note for next time.

The days after I was on a high, wearing a *Sound Affects* t-shirt bought on the night for about a week. The noise, power of the band, unity of all the people… it captured me. I was never one of the cool kids at school but by seeing The Jam live, when no one else had, my credibility went up a few notches.

FESTIVAL PAVILION
20 JUNE 1981, SKEGNESS, UK

I WAS THERE: JONATHAN BILLINGTON

A fantastic gig on a fantastic midsummer day. We got the train from Kings Cross and changed at Boston or Grantham, and I remember sitting in the last carriage, being able to look out the back at the track behind us. By then we'd realised if you turned up early you could get into the soundcheck. We got off at Skegness and there were Redcoats on the platform greeting visitors to Butlins. We found the venue then went for a fantastic walk along the beach, the tide out. We went back to the venue and John Weller came to the door. There were probably 30 Jam fans waiting and they were let into the soundcheck. We watched them do three or four songs and it was great to be so close, with such a small number of fans.

By this time, they were playing *Setting Sons* and *Sound Affects* songs, but always went back to 'Tube Station' and songs from *All Mod Cons*. if you were lucky, they'd do 'In The City' as an encore, and 'The Modern World' kept turning up, always good.

We didn't have anywhere to stay, with Skegness in the middle of summer chock-a-block. We went to the pub after. I had a couple of whiskies. We then found a cricket ground with trees around the boundary. There was an estate agent's opposite, with free newspapers on the rack outside advertising houses for sale, so I borrowed some

Sandy McLean got a buzz from 'In The City' he'd never felt before

Brett 'Buddy' Ascott with The Chords in 1981

Photo by Marcus Ascott

John Campbell's Mod-ified Mini

The Undertones' bass player Mickey Bradley was so sold on The Jam

Darron Robinson got a Jam ticket from his brother-in-law

Laura Mauer, these days in Brisbane, has certainly kept the faith, for her love of music and scooters

The Jam at Guildford Civic in 1982 was True Deceivers frontman Graham Firth's first live show

Laurence Weight has met all three members of The Jam in recent years

and stuffed my clothes with them. We then went back to the cricket pitch and slept under an oak tree. By three in the morning, it was freezing.

I'd brought insulin with me as I'm a Type 1 diabetic, but both phials had broken, presumably while I was jumping around. First thing in the morning we looked for a hospital. We found a police car, explained our situation and were told there was a hospital just up the road. We were in at six in the morning, then walked down to the seafront amongst Mods, scooters and Parkas to sit outside a little seaside café for a bacon sandwich. It was like a scene from *Quadrophenia*. The proprietor was also Type 1 diabetic and allowed me in his front room for my insulin.

A few days later, a friend drove us to St Austell for the Cornwall Coliseum show, and from there we went to Stafford's Bingley Hall. By now venues were more like aircraft hangars, not so much fun. I preferred the earlier smaller venues. Shepton Mallet was another big one with not much atmosphere, but tremendous songs as always. We saw them two or three times at Guildford Civic Hall and a few times at Brighton Centre. It was mostly southern gigs, and although the presence of Mods sometimes attracted skinheads who'd get in the way, events were generally friendly. People just loving the music, harmonies, great tunes and energy in the five years I saw them.

I WAS THERE: ALAN WHITE

I didn't get into The Jam until the autumn of 1980, when someone lent me *In The City* and *This Is The Modern World* as a double album. It blew my mind, and within a month I'd bought all the LPs and singles. The more I listened, the more hooked I became, and in June '81 I saw them live for the first time on the *Bucket and Spade* tour. They opened with 'Going Underground' and were even better than on vinyl. It's still up there in my top-ten life memories.

I saw them five more times over the next year or so before Paul pulled the rug from under us, and was lucky enough to get tickets for the second night at Wembley, which at the time was going to be the last night. I still watch tribute bands, especially From The Jam, and even local bands that play the odd tune get my attention. I'm not angry anymore… just happy I was there and able to say, 'If you've never heard 'Tube Station' live, you've never lived.'

I WAS THERE: BOB MILES

I saw The Jam a few times, starting to take an interest at 17. I switched from Status Quo to the Sex Pistols around then, having started college in 1978, aged 16, and they had a sound studio there. After buying records like 'Hong Kong Garden' by the Banshees, I progressed to The Jam. I'd buy singles and play them at college, and at 18 I had a Lambretta and was firmly into Mod.

My first Jam gig was in 1980 at the Top Rank in Sheffield, stood on the upstairs balcony, wearing my Fred Perry and boating blazer. It was a fantastic gig, with lots of atmosphere. The next gig and probably the best I've ever seen by any band was on the *Bucket and Spade* tour. A dozen of us went to Skegness from Alfreton. Some stayed in digs, and we were in a bus shelter until we crashed their digs. We got into the soundcheck, went backstage the morning after, and I discovered my first bottle of Perrier water in the changing room, which would have been drunk by a band member. If only I'd kept it. There seemed to be double the allowed capacity in the venue, with steam rising from the crowd. I was wringing sweat out of my t-shirt on leaving.

I WAS THERE: GRAHAM BOWDEN, AGE 16

I first saw The Jam at Skegness, which was one of only a few seaside towns featured on the *Bucket and Spade* tour. I had left school after O-levels and the friend I went with, Jo, was 15. Skegness is only about 40 miles from where we lived so we decided to get a local service bus. Unfortunately, it stopped at every village between Spalding and Skegvegas, as it's now known, taking about three hours.

It was about lunchtime when we arrived, and there wasn't a lot to do but wander around to pass the time, and it wasn't the warmest June day. We eventually made our way to the venue and hung around there, other Jam fans having started to gather. We soon noticed something going on at one of the side doors and made our way over, seeing people being allowed into the hall. We decided to join them and what we saw amazed both of us. Paul, Bruce and Rick were on stage, and we realised we'd been allowed in for free to watch the soundcheck. There were only about 50 of us there but it was a privilege to see them for the first time in our own private gig. They only played about three songs, one being 'Thick As Thieves', before we were told to make our way out again.

When it was time for the gig proper, we joined the queue early and went straight to the front (neither of us are the tallest). Eventually they ran on and played 'Going Underground', after which a massive surge from behind us made us retreat to the quieter side to somewhere we could see okay.

As the venue was only small, the heat became unbearable. We went out to the foyer for water while they were playing 'Move On Up'. When it was all over, it was time to find mum and dad's car as they were waiting to take us home, having heard a lot of the gig whilst parked outside. It was an amazing experience to see such an iconic band at a young age. I also saw them in April 1982 on the *Trans Global Express* tour in Leeds and at Birmingham's Bingley Hall on the *Beat Surrender* tour.

SOLID BOND IN YOUR HEART

I WAS THERE: CHRIS GREEN

Thereafter, we saw them every time they toured. We saw the *Bucket and Spade* tour in '81. There was no album. Skegness was the furthest north I went to see them. A band of that size should not have been playing a venue like that. It was totally unsuitable. It was a sprung dancefloor and it was moving. I thought the floor was going to go through in the venue. It made that tour quite exciting really!

I don't know how I fitted it in around the job. I worked at Longbridge, the big car factory, and I was a bit cocky when I was younger. I used to say things like 'they pay me for what I know, not for what I do,' and I used to take time off work all the time. I said that they wouldn't sack me because I knew where all the bodies were buried. If they'd sacked me, they'd have had to bring somebody else in and train them up, so they tolerated me taking time off.

I WAS THERE: SIMON CARTLIDGE, DAD OF THE MOLOTOVS, AGE 15

It was the first time I'd actually been to a Jam gig but I thought I had a fair idea of what to expect. My mate Vinny and I were 15 and had travelled down the east coast from our hometown of Scunthorpe in eager anticipation. We spent the afternoon at Butlin's holiday camp, drinking pints of bitter and playing snooker on the full-size tables. We were suited and booted with regulation white Fred Perrys underneath our jackets. Vinny was wearing an Ian Page haircut, while I was sporting a spiky look, more Foxton-sans-mullet than Weller.

When we arrived at the venue, we were surprised at how small it was considering The Jam were the biggest band in the land at the time. There was the expected array of scooter boys and Mod girls hanging around outside and there was the whiff of potential violence in the air. We decided to make our way into the venue so as to get as close to the stage as possible. Fortunately, it was a standing only gig and we managed to bob, weave and finally push our way towards the front, stage right and in front of Paul's mic. When we finally couldn't get any closer than about two rows back, we stood chanting 'Jam, Jam, Jam' in unison with the rest of the crowd.

Suddenly, the lights dimmed and manager John Weller took to the mic. 'Put yer 'ands t'gether for the best band in the fucking world, THE JAM!' Our heroes bounded onto the stage, Paul, the envy of every geezer in attendance, immaculately dressed in dogtooth check trousers, black and yellow Fred Perry and black and white Jam stage shoes. Bruce was in a light blue suit along with a dark blue shirt with button-down collar. I could only make out Rick's light blue shirt behind the kit. It was the first time I'd actually seen famous people – other than the odd pro footballer visiting the Old Showground – in the flesh and I was strangely surprised at how they resembled what they looked like in photos and on *Top Of The Pops*!

Without further ado they went straight into 'Going Underground'. The crowd erupted and Vinny and I were immediately swept off our feet as the crowd swayed from one side of the stage to the other. The heat and the crush were almost unbearable but we just sang along, pogoing whenever our feet found terra firma. Paul, ever the minimalist, rarely spoke to the crowd – ditto Bruce and Rick. They just blasted through their set at ninety miles per hour with only the occasional stop for a guitar change or a glug from the can of Heineken precariously perched upon the drum riser. I remember feeling relieved about three songs in when they slowed things down with the wonderful 'Monday'. Soon they were back up to full speed with classics such as 'To Be Someone', 'It's Too Bad' and 'The Modern World'. Highlights for me – they were all great, mind – were 'Funeral Pyre', 'Little Boy Soldiers' and 'Private Hell'.

The testosterone in the room that night was a testament to the aggression of The Jam's onstage performance and Weller's vocal delivery. There were calls throughout for 'Tube Station' but Paul characteristically, and never the populist, chose to ignore them. I cannot remember if they did two or three encores that evening but had they not bothered to have done one, I would've gone home a happy punter.

I have to say, that night was the best night of my life – sorry Olivia, sorry kids. I saw The Jam three more times before Paul – rightly, in my opinion – decided to call it a day. I was blown away by the band's intensity and the crowd's fervour. On 20th June 1981, The Jam were indeed 'the best band in the fucking world!'

GRANBY HALLS
22 JUNE 1981, LEICESTER, UK

I WAS THERE: MARTIN ALLEN, AGE 18

I saw The Jam at the tail end of their career, five times between June '81 and December '82. None were in my hometown of Nottingham; each required a trip with friends and relatives – to Leicester, Stafford or Birmingham. During those two years I was at college, working or unemployed, The Jam were the soundtrack to my life. They described how I was feeling, the complexities of life I was yet to really experience and showed a keen eye on what was happening in society. At our church youth group, their records were often played and 'Down In The Tube Station At Midnight' ended every weekly session while we tidied and vacuumed before leaving for the pub.

The journeys to gigs themselves were something of a pilgrimage. An eye was kept on the music press or local papers for announcements. One of us was nominated to get tickets, which meant having access to a phone at the time box offices opened – on the first day of sale. The Jam were one of the biggest live acts in Britain, so it wasn't easy. Once the day itself arrived we met up, piled into the back of a Morris Ital van and drove to distant towns with anticipation and adrenaline. Our uniform was simple: a Jam t-shirt, jeans and Doc Martens, with a change of t-shirt for afterwards.

The gigs themselves were all energy and passion. They were loud, they were gentle, English nostalgic and punky. The sound wasn't always great – Victorian exhibition halls don't have the best acoustics – but that doesn't matter when you're 18. There was also a feeling of togetherness. It didn't feel like you were dancing with strangers, and the band were just like us, the setlists mixing hits, fan favourites, covers and new music.

The final concerts had backing singers and brass. Not a surprise, as so did the final record. You felt things were moving on and knowing the fifth time would be the last time I would see them was emotional – sadness, thankfulness and hopefulness all mixed into one.

The Granby Halls gig on the *Bucket and Spade* tour was my first ever and ignited a passion for live music I have to this day. What I won't do is see ageing artists rehash past hits. The Jam split at the right time and integrity came out of every chord, drumbeat and lyric. After 40 years and hundreds of gigs, The Jam are still my benchmark for live music.

I WAS THERE: STUART GORNALL

By the time of 'Absolute Beginners' and 'Funeral Pyre', they were changing direction, and the *Bucket and Spade* tour that summer included the best gig I went to, in Leicester. They couldn't get them off stage. They did about four encores. Weller had a purple polka-dot shirt and that Steve Marriott haircut. It was very hot, and they were raw live, not like on records, still like a punk band, with all that energy and passion. They even played 'In The City', which they hadn't for ages.

I WAS THERE: GAVIN JONES

The gig didn't have a good atmosphere, not helped by a support band that sounded like The Shadows. When The Jam finally came on, they played more of a greatest hits set, including 'Pretty Green', 'Corner Shop', 'Monday', 'But I'm Different Now', 'Set The House Ablaze', 'Start!', 'Going Underground', 'Dreams Of Children', 'Butterfly Collector', "A' Bomb', and 'David Watts'. There was a great version of 'To Be Someone' as an encore, as well as 'Private Hell', 'Thick As Thieves', 'Heatwave' and 'Little Boy Soldiers'. It was surprising not to get 'Tube

Station', and Paul seemed to have trouble with his equipment throughout. He wasn't happy, jumping all over the stage, kicking things in a rage, ending the night saying, 'Thank you all for coming tonight, even if it is a fuckin' khazi!'

GUILDHALL
23 JUNE 1981, PORTSMOUTH, UK

I WAS THERE: STEVE AYLEN

I went with friends and my girlfriend Yvonne. As usual, the crowd was intense. There was no interest in the support, and the atmosphere was building as we worked our way to the front. The Jam came on and went straight into 'But I'm Different Now'. A manic crowd surged and I was well into it, not noticing until the end that my girlfriend wasn't with me. My mate said her brother had taken her out of the crush at the start. I wasn't popular. All was forgiven though, we've been married 38 years now, and she still puts up with me going to Weller gigs… but not near the front anymore.

BINGLEY HALL SHOWGROUND
27 JUNE 1981, STAFFORD, UK

I WAS THERE: PETER BOWERS

Another packed gig. Waves of jostling fans came from both sides as well as from the back. From a place near the front in front of Weller, within thirty seconds of the start of a song, I'd be shunted sideways, lifted forwards and jolted backwards, ending up thirty yards from the stage as the first chorus kicked in. By the end of verse two, I'd somehow find myself back near the front this time, over to Bruce's side. It was like that the entire gig.

I WAS THERE: GAVIN JONES

I couldn't get to the soundcheck, instead going with Debbie in the evening for what turned out to be a really good gig with about three encores. At one point the crowd started singing 'You'll Never Walk Alone'. When they came on again, Bruce said, 'This is for all you football fans,' and they did 'The Eton Rifles'. We met Ray the scouser and some of his mates, and again I put them up for the night, seven up in a Beetle. A great gig with a great atmosphere, unlike how it felt at Leicester.

I WAS THERE: MARK CUNLIFFE, AGE 15

I pegged off school for the day with three mates and got a coach from Manchester. Graham 'Titch' Schofield, who was quite small, disappeared. The next time I saw him he was being carried above the crowd to the front.

MAGNUM LEISURE CENTRE
30 JUNE 1981, IRVINE, UK

I WAS THERE: KENNY THOMPSON

I bought 'In The City' when it came out. My favourite Jam single is 'When You're Young'. I liked the style – two guitars and a drummer – and the clothing. Simon shirts, Ben Sherman, boating blazers, and bowling shoes. I was lucky enough to see The Jam three times – at Glasgow Apollo, Irvine Magnum and Ingliston. I was a teenager and my mate's uncle managed the Apollo and sneaked us in the side door. I went to the Magnum on the train with my mates. We dodged school to get there. Ingliston is near Edinburgh – planes, trains and automobiles for us. Good times, with the gigs as expected – absolutely fantastic.

I WAS THERE: ALLY WILSON

I saw The Jam playing 'All Around The World' on *Top Of The Pops*, then the following Saturday bought the single from Listen Records in Glasgow. In the window I also saw 'In The City' and bought that the following week. I then bought every single as it was released. The first album I bought was *This Is The Modern World*, just after it was released, then *In The City* a bit later. After that it was every album as it came out, along with every gig in Glasgow, all at the Apollo. I also saw them in Irvine on the *Bucket and Spade* tour. I remember being down the front at each gig, jumping around like a maniac. Every show I saw was raw passion, with a sense of belonging to something. I was 14 when I first saw them in '77 and 19 when I last saw them in '82. The gig at the Magnum Centre was one of the sweatiest I've been to. Afterwards, we walked back into the pub we had been in pre-gig. The barmaid said she thought I'd fallen into Irvine Harbour. I was soaked in sweat.

Photos by Ally Wilson

Ally Wilson was at the Magnum Leisure Centre but took these pics in Glasgow in 1982

ROYAL HALL
2 JULY 1981, BRIDLINGTON SPA, UK

I WAS THERE: DAVE PRATT

Gordon and I were joined by John Cant again to see The Jam at the Royal Hall in Bridlington. We caught the bus from Sedgefield to Middlesbrough, then on to Scarborough, spending the afternoon in the arcades and having the odd beer in the pubs. We caught another bus to Bridlington mid-afternoon so we could watch the soundcheck, and thoroughly enjoyed our night. After the gig, the three of us made our way back to Scarborough but hadn't booked accommodation so we spent a cold, boring night aimlessly walking around town and the seafront until we could catch buses home to Middlesbrough then Sedgefield the following morning.

I WAS THERE: GARY COX

'Funeral Pyre' came out and it was like 'where are they going with this?' I went to see them on the *Bucket and Spade* tour at Bridlington. It was a really small venue. Dolly Mixture were the support band and fans were throwing stuff and John Weller had to come on and say, 'The Jam won't come on if people don't let them play.' It got really rough. They were trying to play and people were throwing beer and all sorts, and then Paul Weller came on and said, 'Look, we're not playing if you don't let them play their set.' When he came on with The Jam, he was a bit angry. He was a bit annoyed with the crowd, but I think he was getting sick too of the cycle of writing songs and doing tours and being stuck in this image of what they were and what they were doing. They had no new material, so they played quite a bit of *Sound Affects* and a bit of a greatest hits set.

I WAS THERE: DAVE HEMINGWAY, THE HOUSEMARTINS & BEAUTIFUL SOUTH

The Jam meant so much to so many people. Young men (usually) who felt like the songs they produced were speaking specifically to them. All the pitfalls of love, youth and politics that seemed to describe what they were going through themselves. The fact that a very young Paul Weller wrote these songs and showed such understanding and anger resonated with them.

The band live were electric, spitting out the songs with excitement and energy. The albums were also excellent – *All Mod Cons*, *Setting Sons* (which many consider the finest) and *Sound Affects* especially. By that time, they'd also had their first No.1 single, promoted on Saturday morning kids' TV show, *Swap Shop*. Never have a band looked more out of place.

SOLID BOND IN YOUR HEART

The first time I saw them live was at Bridlington Spa on the *Sound Affects* tour. Weller's dad John came on to introduce them and simply said, 'If someone falls down, pick 'em up! Here's The Jam!' The place erupted as the first chords of 'But I'm Different Now' burst out of the speakers, and the place never stopped bouncing. A brilliant gig.

I was in a band called The Newpolitans at the time (with Dave Rotheray), and as a fellow drummer I felt Rick was indeed a great solid drummer, perfect for the band. I did feel he was treated badly when the band finished.

Dave Hemingway, there for The Jam at Bridlington Spa

The second (and final) time I saw them was at the Queens Hall, Leeds on the tour for *The Gift*. By then, the cracks were appearing to show… even to the point where they had a stand-up argument on stage. As we know, Weller pulled the plug on the band at the age of 24, while they were still the biggest band in Britain. A brave, maybe even selfish move, but obviously one he'd been wanting to make in order to move on musically. What was left behind was a brilliant legacy of music and style, created by one of the truly great bands.

MARKET HALL
4 JULY 1981, CARLISLE, UK

I WAS THERE: IAN WATSON

My first Jam gig, and the only time they played Carlisle. I also saw them at the SEC, Edinburgh and Bingley Hall, Staffordshire. Great times.

I WAS THERE: ROBERT STEVENSON

I was at the Carlisle gig, on the guest list. Weller was on my scooter before the previous gig at the Magnum in Irvine, so we done well with the soundcheck and after-show, talking to Weller's dad and so on. The scooter was fully signed by the three of them, then Jim Ross sprayed it after he bought it. Ha ha!

I SPRAYED IT: JIM ROSS

I regret that, big time! But those were happy days.

I WAS THERE: GRAEME DAWSON

My next date was at the Market Hall, Carlisle on the *Bucket and Spade* tour. Along with Salvatore and his mates, we travelled by train on a sunny summer's day. We also got in for the afternoon soundcheck. Paul Weller's dad opened the side doors of the venue and invited the teenagers in, which was really generous. I made it to three soundchecks in all – doing the same for my next Jam date at Newcastle City Hall, then at Whitley Bay Ice Rink. John Weller always let us fans in, and Paul was always generous with his time, talking to fans and signing autographs.

At the Market Hall soundcheck they played four or five songs then gave an invitation for some fans to go on the tour bus. Everyone made their way over and I got my shoe on the coach steps, only for Joe Awome (RIP) to say sorry, it was full. I couldn't believe I was so close but so far from getting on the bus.

After the concert we walked into town at midnight. Police saw hundreds of teenagers walking to the rail station and accompanied us to the station, sending us all back on a Royal Mail train to Newcastle. We were all sat on mail sacks and arrived back at three in the morning.

I WAS THERE: KEN DENT

After the two City Hall gigs in 1980, the next time I saw The Jam was at Carlisle Market Hall. It was the Wimbledon tennis final, John McEnroe and Björn Borg. It was a red-hot summer's day. My brother was at work, so we were waiting for him to come home because he was driving to Carlisle in a little H Reg Ford Escort. There was six of us crammed into the car. We set off about half past five and Colin did it in just over an hour, which was cool.

The gig was in a huge building, like a big cattle shed, with a glass roof on it. And because the sun had been beating down all day, it was absolutely red-hot inside. It's the only Jam gig I've ever been to where I was wanting it to end because the heat was virtually unbearable. But me and my mate Davey were down the front again, which we always did when we were downstairs. And it was one of them gigs where I was just singing. It was the last time I'd see them as a three-piece. Because after that, they brought that little brass section in.

CIVIC HALL
7 & 8 JULY 1981, GUILDFORD, UK

I WAS THERE: MALC SMITH

Sound Affects in late November 1980 was the first LP I could afford to buy at the time of release. The following summer I went to the first of two nights at the Civic Hall in Guildford, my nearest big venue. I'd seen a few bands there, but this was the first time I'd experienced a Jam gig. And they were different to those other bands. The sheer power and energy were mesmerising and inspiring. That's when a relentless fascination with the band began. I bought up the back catalogue and new releases whenever Saturday job earnings allowed and I searched out every interview and TV appearance. Trips to Carnaby Street also followed – Jam shoes and bowling shoes from Shellys, polka dot shirts and dogtooth trousers from Melanddi…

I WAS THERE: PETER CHAMBERLAIN
It was an absolutely sweltering night. I sneaked in a back door and clocked Weller's guitars in a separate room before being chucked out. Weller wore a red jacket on stage with a black Fred Perry underneath and black Sta-Prest trousers. Guildford railway station after the gig was a bit lively, with skinheads around. One lad lost his life, I believe, after running on to live railway lines.

I WAS THERE: JOE SHIELDS, AGE 17
It was the last night of the *Bucket and Spade* tour, a Wednesday, and it was a really, really hot day. There was a big Southend crew going and we met in our local pub for a couple of drinks first. We were all sitting in the pub, having a chat talking about what a great day it was going to be, seeing The Jam. Somehow, we got on to the subject of death and this guy, Eddie Cousins, 'Cuz', said, 'Well, if you're going to die after a good day out, after a few beers with your mates, a good laugh and seeing The Jam? It couldn't get any better than that, if you *were* going to go.' We all remember him saying that. Little did we know the tragedy that was going to occur that night.

We got the train from Southend up to Fenchurch Street, the Tube across London to Waterloo, and then Waterloo to Guildford. It was absolutely sweltering inside. I've got photos of that gig, with Bruce Foxton playing in shorts and Weller just stripped to the waist by the end. Afterwards, we went back to the train station.

In Southend, all the power cables for the trains are overhead. In Guildford, the power cables were all in the track. Hundreds of kids that had been to the gig were all sitting on the train waiting to go back to Waterloo and this guard said to everyone, 'You're on the wrong train. You need to be on that one over there.' So everyone got off the train. You had to change to another platform and the majority of people went over the bridge but a few kids ran across the track. They got off the train we were on, ran across the platform, got down onto the tracks, ran across the tracks and climbed up on the platform and onto the other train.

We were all sitting there on this other train when this other guard came along and said, 'Where are you going?' We said, 'We're going back to Waterloo.' He said, 'You're on the wrong train. You were on the right one before.' 'No,' we said, 'the other guard said this is the one that's going to Waterloo.' He said, 'No, no, it's that one.' So we got off the train again. We went back over the bridge but again a few people didn't and crossed the tracks again instead, and Cuz was one of the ones that didn't.

By the time we got back over the bridge, he crawled up onto the platform and we knew something was wrong but didn't realise the seriousness at the time. The police were there and they put a blanket round him. They said, 'Get on the train. You'll see your mate tomorrow. It will be alright.' We didn't quite know what had happened until we were on the train on the way back and somebody said that he had fallen. He'd tripped over the first rail and landed on the second.

Because of the accident, the train was stopped along the track and we ended up getting home at about three in the morning. A friend was staying at mine and next day I called in sick to the bank. I couldn't go in because I was tired and because I was waiting to find out what had happened to Cuz. Then we got a phone call to say he had died that night, at the scene. It was just a total shock. So sad. So young. Tragic. You don't expect to go to see you favourite band play and then see one of your mates get killed. It had been a brilliant day and a brilliant night, but I can't remember the gig or any of the setlist they played. It's all a bit of a blur. The only memories I've got are from the photos that I took on the night.

I wrote to the band and explained what had happened. I sent it first class. I was at work the next morning when Paul's mum, Ann Weller, phoned our house and had a long chat with my mum about it. They sent flowers to the funeral. I remember the funeral being absolutely mobbed out. He was our mate. We used to hang around in the same crowd and we all used to go and watch Southend United play and go and see The Jam. It was so tragic. I've got photos of him from that night in Guildford. Photos of all of us at the gig.

RIP Cuz.

I WAS THERE: GINA GUARNIERI

I was 15, in the fifth year of secondary school, when I discovered The Jam. My friends and I were going to parties around south-west London on Friday and Saturday nights. It was 1979 and the favoured band played on the parents' hi-fis was The Jam. We all loved them – that raw attitude cutting through the conservative cobblers of the time. We couldn't get enough; my friend Siobhan even painted Paul Weller for her O-Level art exam. I had an old dining room chair in my bedroom and recreated Bill Smith's spray-paint Jam logo on the seat with Tippex.

All Mod Cons was the first of what I regard as Mod albums I bought, having heard it at those house parties. Very near where I lived in Kennington was a great independent record shop, Page 43. Once the owner knew I was into the Mod revival he'd tell me about upcoming releases.

Jam lyrics seemed to provide a soundtrack to my life: 'Saturday's girls work in Tesco's and Woolworths… Saturday's kids live in council houses…'. I worked in Tesco and lived in a council house. This band was talking my language.

It was summer 1980 when we met a group of Mods and hung about with them at the local scooter shop to hear what was going on. The latest news was that Paul Weller and the band were recording their new LP at Townhouse Studios, Goldhawk Road, so we spent hours in Shepherds Bush trying to get a peek, from a distance.

Later that year I started working at *The Daily Mirror* and through a work friend met a Mod who was in the army, based at barracks near Guildford. We went to see The Jam in July '81 at the Civic Hall. As always it was a great gig but proved to be memorable for all the wrong reasons. Afterwards, waiting on the station platform with hundreds of other Jam fans, a tannoy announcement advised the train was now leaving from a different platform. A few people jumped down onto the train tracks and one bloke stepped on a live track and was electrocuted. My date was an Army nurse so tried to revive him, but sadly he didn't make it.

Unsurprisingly, the London-bound train was cancelled, which meant I had no way of getting home. but my date had an idea – I could stay the night at the Army barracks and get the first train home in the morning. Somehow, he managed to smuggle me past the guards and into a dormitory where I spent five long hours singing 'I'm up on the hills playing little boy soldiers' in my head to try and drown out the noise of a dozen or so squaddies snoring and belching.

One Tuesday night we were dancing at Le Beat Route, a brilliant sixties soul club in Greek Street, Soho, when three blokes from Woking turned up. I was starstruck and almost rendered speechless by their very presence. I pleaded with my boyfriend to get me

Gina Guarnieri was at Guildford Civic

Paul's autograph but that was considered way too uncool, so I conjured up the courage, grabbed a promo card and approached him. He said, 'Of course, what's your name?' I repeated my name a couple of times over the loud music before he put pen to paper and wrote: 'To Gena, Paul Weller'.

A few months later, April 1982, I saw them in Paris. I'd wanted to see the band in Amsterdam a year earlier but didn't have the money. Once in Paris we were taken by coach to a large, out-of-town tent in a square. The mood was dark, with running battles on the streets. A car caught fire, and we even got locked in a bar for a while. The afternoon's events overshadowed the gig and I don't remember much about it except seeing boys with Union flags climbing up tent poles. At the end of the night another battle started but soon petered out at the sight of French riot police with gas and guns. Not the trip I'd imagined, but an experience never to be forgotten.

I saw The Jam about six or seven times, and I agree with John Weller – they were 'the best band in the fucking world'.

I WAS THERE: MARTIN BEARDSHALL

I saw them twice at the Civic, the first time on the *Bucket and Spade* tour, which was like a furnace. The second time was the penultimate gig in December '82. I managed to get a ticket off some random dude who arrived just before they were due on stage. One of the best tenners I've spent in my life. Another strong memory is being in the bar before the gig in 1981 and watching a throng of Mods climbing up a drainpipe and through the window. A fair few got in before security cottoned on.

I WAS THERE: JO BARTLETT

The next time I saw The Jam, it was two glorious nights in a row at Guildford Civic Hall. A local gig for me. The first night they were supported by The Sleep, the second night by The Questions, who I had seen support The Undertones there a fortnight earlier. On the first night, I found an Outlaw 'access all areas' backstage pass, but lacked the courage to stick it on and saunter through… I think they'd have seen through this 14-year-old girl pretty quickly! We'd go to the stage door and then burst through, running into the dressing rooms. I did that for The Jam, but no one was there!

I've got my diary from 1981, the only one I still have from those days. It's as much amusing as it is painful, seeing my scrawly handwriting. The gist of most days seems to be that I took my dog for a walk, but every now and again I'd write what singles I bought, things like that.

For July 7th, my diary reads: 'Went to see The Jam with Christine.' That's my cousin. 'Found a backstage pass. Didn't use it.' There you go! Then: 'Broke up from school.

Bleached my hair.' And for July 8th, I wrote: 'Went to see The Jam with Tracy. Met Paul Weller afterwards, and Bruce Foxton.' I forgot that – I had a signed Paul Weller ticket on my wall for ages and learned to copy it – to this day I can do Paul's autograph!

I WAS THERE: RICHARD WESTNEY

I went to both nights. I remember the guy in the box office sarcastically telling me they'd be the same both nights. I knew they wouldn't be, and they weren't. There was always something special about the Guildford nights, the only decent-sized venue in Surrey and as close as they could get to Woking, so it always felt like a hometown gig. Different from London gigs, more intimate. By then, I was buying every Jam record on the day of release. The excitement of having something new, getting home and putting it on the record player was always something special. *All Mod Cons*, *Setting Sons*, *Sound Affects*, the special limited-edition double 'Going Underground' single. I remember buying them all.

I WAS THERE: IAN DOYLE

Two radically different performances and experiences. Stinking hot, and I remember it still being light when we came out of the venue. Many years later, the revamped *G Live* is under my auspices as a director at Guildford Borough Council. Funny old world.

I WAS THERE: CLIVE YOULTON

I was there for the July 1981 dates, but also April 1980 and July 1980. I don't think I've felt an electricity since at any other concerts I've been to. Maybe it was the era. I recall when tickets went on sale, they were like gold dust. I don't even know how I got them. I was 17 when I first saw them. I went to G Live recently, on the site of the former Civic Hall. Same stage. Brought back memories.

I don't drink but always remember being in the bar and moving to the floor nearer the time of the start. The lights dimmed and you knew they were coming on, with a charge from the bar to get on the floor. Then John Weller came on, announced them... then the unbelievable atmosphere. I remember they rarely did 'The Eton Rifles' live, but they did at one of those two 1981 dates. They sounded exactly like the records. Such quality.

I'm a Guildford lad, so it was great to see them in my hometown those four times. I know Maybury and Sheerwater, where they grew up. I worked in Woking and played for the football club so always felt that connection. I also remember being in the loo at a Vapors concert when Bruce Foxton came and stood next to me at the urinal. Heady days!

I was never into Mods and rockers and all that, but that music was superb. I'm

I WAS THERE: PAUL CARROLL
I saw The Jam at the Civic a few times. Bruce often parked his Jag by my loading bay round the back of Tesco at the bottom of town. He wasn't really supposed to, but hey, it was Bruce, who's saying no?

THE GOLDEN EGG
1980/81, HIGH STREET, GUILDFORD, UK

I WAS THERE: IAN HOOKE
I had a Saturday job at the Golden Egg, at the top of the High Street and North Street, and all three came in for breakfast on at least four occasions. It was amazing to serve them, although I probably had my chin on the floor in amazement each time, and the manager wouldn't allow any chatting other than taking the food order.

SOMETHING ELSE
2 OCTOBER 1981, WOKING & LONDON, UK

BBC 2 broadcasts a special edition of its magazine show, made by Paul Weller and friends Steve Carver, Anne Clark and Robin Richards, themed around class awareness, including performances of 'Man In The Corner Shop' and 'Funeral Pyre'.

I WAS THERE: STEVE CARVER
Paul just rang and asked me to jump on board. I'm guessing he approached the BBC and offered to make a programme for them. It was all his idea – the three different class kids. We actually visited Eton College… but I don't think they wanted to be involved.

SS UGANDA
OCTOBER 1981, MEDITERRANEAN SEA

I WAS THERE: GUY HELLIKER
Coming from a small village, outside a small town in what felt like the middle of nowhere where nothing ever happened, when I discovered The Jam everything changed… forever! Clothes, music taste, friends and even my future wife all came about due to The Jam.

It could have been my brother, Mark, six years older, bringing home the seven-inch of 'Going Underground' that planted the seed, but the thunderbolt struck me on board the SS Uganda, sat below deck in the Common Room on a Hampshire school cruise of the Mediterranean. There was a wall-mounted jukebox, and kids there from big towns like Portsmouth, Southampton, Aldershot and Winchester… and us bumpkins from Andover.

There were regular stand-offs over the jukebox, with Duran Duran and Spandau Ballet for the girls, Status Quo for some of the lads. One particular night, Stuart Law decided enough was enough, and at 50p for ten plays, he put in his Pretty Green and punched 80A in ten times for 'Start!' Or so he thought. We waited for Bruce's McCartney-influenced bass intro, only to hear the soft but beautiful opening of 'Liza Radley'. The single had been dropped in the jukebox the wrong way. But I fell in love to that song!

When I got home, I spent every penny I had on Jam singles and albums. I had to feed my new obsession. I wasn't alone. There were more of us at school. We shared records and thoughts on who was the coolest member, and I was always in the Foxton camp.

Occasionally, a few of us would take the train to Waterloo (peering out of the windows when we got to Woking) and up to Carnaby Street. We'd visit legendary shops used by our heroes; Shelly's for shoes (chisel-towed bowlers, red, white and blue stage shoes, never the black-and-white 'original Jam shoes' – they looked too much like the things Shakin' Stevens would wear!) and Melanddi for shirts (they never had the black-and-white striped ones like Bruce wore in my size). We'd look at Polaroids of the band visiting Carnaby Cavern for Sta-Prest and suits, and admire the photocopy of a cheque on the counter, signed by the band and John Weller. Then finally we'd go to Lonsdale on Beak Street in the hope of getting a cycle shirt like PW wore.

I looked the business! Red, white and blue stage shoes, Sta-Prest trousers, a boating blazer over a white Ben Sherman with a black inch-wide tie, red Fred Perry v-neck jumper, and a Parka, waiting around town. Wearing all that lot in July, I sweated so much that the dye came through from the shoes to my white towelling socks!

'ABSOLUTE BEGINNERS' RELEASED
16 OCTOBER 1981

The title of The Jam's 14th single is inspired by the Colin MacInnes novel of the same name. A Peter Wilson/Jam co-production, the single reaches No.4 in the UK charts.

CND RALLY, EMBANKMENT
24 OCTOBER 1981, LONDON, UK

I WAS THERE: JULIAN BROOKS

We used to go up to Carnaby Street and that's when we heard on the streets that The Jam were playing down the Embankment on a Campaign for Nuclear Disarmament (CND) march. When we got there, the first thing that struck me was seeing skinheads walk about with Tesco's bags over their ears… half full of glue. Vaughn Toulouse was on the back of the lorry trailer with Department S, singing 'Is Vic There?' Then Weller walks on with a beret on, going straight into 'Absolute Beginners' and 'Sweet Soul Music'. Absolutely brilliant.

I WAS THERE: DAVE PRATT

Our gang was attending a house party at the Leas in Sedgefield. At about ten that night, conversation turned to a big CND rally taking place in London the next day. The Jam were playing a free concert and it was likely they'd perform their new single, 'Absolute Beginners', for the first time live. Within an hour of the subject being raised, me and Mark Beveridge were stood at the top of the slip road at Bradbury, dressed in the clothes we wore at the party and hitchhiking, and it was bloody cold. We had about £10 between us. The half-cocked plan we put together during our lift off Fred Gibbins was to get to London, see the gig and hitch straight home. We had no money for accommodation and no contact numbers for anyone in the city.

We managed to make it to the capital without incident, although we arrived rather early. At 5am, we were sat on a park bench near the Embankment hungry, thirsty and freezing cold. We decided to spend the first part of our money on essentials, so it was off to the nearest paper shop to buy ten Embassy No.6. These fags would have to be rationed to last us at least 24 hours. We got a takeaway bacon sandwich and a cup of tea and started to make our way to where the stage was set up.

The stage was nothing more than the flat bed of a large lorry, surrounded by steel barriers. The first to arrive, we plonked ourselves in the middle of the barrier at the front. We had about six hours before The Jam were due to perform. The gig was good, but not their best, the set no more than half an hour. But they played some of the soul numbers which were part of the set in the early days. The new single and its B-side were duly performed, the gig completed with a cracking version of 'Going Underground'.

We made our way back to the motorway, grabbing a sandwich on the way. Our hearts sank when we reached the M1 at teatime. The hitch-hiking queue was long, about 30 people in front of us. However, utilising my experience of a Banshees tour earlier that year, I suggested retreating to the roundabout before the motorway to try our luck getting a lift before cars turned onto the M1.

Within five minutes we'd been picked up and couldn't resist giving V-signs to the poor souls on the slip road who began shouting obscenities at us for jumping the queue. However, this was pretty much our one and only piece of good fortune. The heavens opened that night, and we struggled to get any decent lifts. We eventually gave up at about 2am, near Derby, finding shelter under a motorway bridge, soaked to the skin and freezing and feeling utterly miserable. We eventually made it back to Sedgefield at dinnertime on Sunday. To add insult to injury, our final lift was from a fishmonger. We exited his van, cold, damp and stinking like Whitby harbour.

I WAS THERE: STEPHEN ELSDON

The back of the lorry on the Embankment; secret gigs following them as John's Boys and so on; the electric gigs at the end; *The Tube* for their final TV show; The Jam in Lille. Awesome nights, never matched.

I WAS THERE: LOUISE SMITH

I saw them at Sheffield Top Rank and also on a CND rally in the early Eighties. We were waiting to march, and they were playing down by the Embankment.

I WAS THERE: STEVE KINGETT

The Jam were the first band I saw at a London CND rally, on a lorry. But they weren't very good. I think it was called alcohol… from the night before! They were supporting Gang of Four. I was there, worrying that the world was going to be blown to pieces. (Nothing changes; the threat of World War Three remains.)

I was a big Jam fan, but only saw them that one time. I first heard about them at a Boys' Brigade camp in 1977 in St Agnes, Cornwall. Someone showed me a copy of the *NME*. I was 14 and, flicking through, I spotted an article on The Jam playing a couple of gigs in London, and saw that they were quite influenced by The Who. I liked that they were a crossover on the punk/new wave scene, and looked different. They were snappy dressers.

Living in Devon, I didn't know many people into them but for my birthday my uncle and auntie sent me a double cassette of *In The City* and *This Is The Modern World* which I played to death. In '78 I'd listen in on my blue transistor radio to John Peel playing The Jam. I wore my Jam, Who and Clash badges with pride. This went down like a lead weight with the so-called heavy metal Christians at my local church. No Rush, Meatloaf or (urgh) Jim Steinman for me, or for my Mod/punk mate and fellow Jam fan, Robert. I remember going into Boots, taking 'That's Entertainment' home to play it and having to nick the middle out of one of my mum's Perry Como singles to play my new purchase. I loved the lyrics: 'Lights going out and a kick in the balls.' Class!

Then came that accidental moment, seeing them live. Getting a train, 5.15am from North Devon. It took hours to get to London. I got to the rally at the Embankment about midday with fellow CND supporters Ben, Terry and Dave. There was a lorry parked up with a loud sound system at the front of the rally. A huge roar went up, with a shout from the lorry's stage. 'We are The Jam.' They only did a couple of numbers. As my favourite Jam song, 'Going Underground', was played I was in heaven! Unfortunately, they weren't the best, but it was my nirvana moment, my 'I was there' kind of thing. I think Mr Weller and his bandmates were seriously hungover! He apologised for being under par but said the reason we are all here was the threat of World War Three and nuclear war. I really thought it was going to happen. I was fucking scared. Shit, I wasn't even 16! The other highlight of the rally was Susannah York crossing my path, giving me the biggest grin ever. My mate exclaimed, 'Steve, did you see who that was?'

I remember the pros and cons of the split being discussed in the *NME* letters pages for weeks in early '83.

The only other time I saw Paul Weller was at Glastonbury Festival in 1986 with The Style Council. I wasn't a fan. Nor were the hundreds who gathered at the Pyramid stage, throwing mud when he came on in a white suit. He stormed off in a strop, covered in festive mud!

MICHAEL SOBELL SPORTS CENTRE
12 & 13 DECEMBER 1981, ISLINGTON, LONDON, UK

I WAS THERE: JOHN WHITE

I saw them at the Michael Sobell Centre, then in March '82 at Brixton Fair Deal and Alexandra Palace two days running, plus Granby Hall, Leicester that September and Wembley in December. Two nights in a row was exhausting, but so memorable!

I WAS THERE: STUART GORNALL

I was 17 by now and had my own money. I got a train down from Lancashire, paid for some digs and got the Tube there. They were great, supported by Department S, but there was loads of trouble as nutcase punk band The Exploited were playing the Rainbow and – really good planning – finished at the same time. I got the Tube back to my digs with all my Mod gear on and wearing a Man United badge. Two skinheads appeared and one asked for a light and clocked my accent. They were West Ham fans so I got a right kicking. One had a bloody Stanley knife. They didn't injure me too badly, but the knife went through my pants. The irony? I was down in the Tube station and it was nearly midnight when I got attacked!

I WAS THERE: JO BARTLETT

I turned 16 three days before. We caught the train to see them on the first night, with great support from The Questions again, Bananarama and Department S. An incredible night. They played some new stuff with a brass section. We got in at about 1.30am after hassle getting home. For the second night, it snowed and Farnborough station was closed. My 1981 diary says: 'There was a blizzard, and Dad said I couldn't go to The Jam. I was slightly annoyed.' That has brackets with 'understatement' and an exclamation mark! Evidently, some friends came over through the snow and we made mulled wine, so maybe my heart wasn't so badly broken! I've still got my ticket.

I WAS THERE: MARK RAILSTON

A bunch of us mates went down to London for this now infamous Saturday gig. We left Newcastle on the train and although it was cold, it was just icy. By the time we got to London we were surprised to find three inches of snow and it was still coming down. We got to the gig sober, too young to get into London bars, although a couple of cans on the train slipped down nicely. I remember buying some badges, getting served by Gill Price, Paul's girlfriend and future 'Beat Surrender' cover star. For once there seemed to be decent support – Department S and new band, Bananarama. After seeing The Questions five or six times on previous dates, they'd outstayed their welcome in our minds.

Weller was trying to create a revue-type vibe (with Gary Crowley spinning discs), concerned with narrow mindedness creeping in from an element of fans. He was trying to broaden horizons. With some Jam gigs it was like a football crowd. I was struck by the number of London fans with Parkas on, covered with the ubiquitous patches and Who logos. Ideal for outside, the weather rather Baltic, but inside they sweated like a dyslexic on *Countdown* as the crowd crammed further in.

The majority of the crowd seemed older than me and seemed to have had more than a few sherbets by the time Bananarama skipped on. After initially being well received, when the crowd realised Bananarama were miming to backing tapes, the atmosphere turned, with catcalls and boos ringing out, followed by the odd bottle and glass. It was later reported that Weller was disgusted with the crowd and that he thought this was because they were an all-girl group. But it was because they weren't playing live. Department S went down well – they could play and had some good songs.

Twelve months later I was in London again for the final round of Jam gigs. Despite what Weller may have thought, one legacy of The Jam is how they broadened horizons for thinking fans. How many working-class kids got to read George Orwell, got involved in politics and became firmly anti-racist, buying books of Adrian Henri poetry because he was name-checked on *Modern World*, got into the pop art movement through the likes of Roy Lichtenstein, or bought the collected verses of 17th century romantic poet Percy Bysshe Shelly because of a verse from 'Mask Of Anarchy' quoted on *Sound Affects*? Not many, I bet. But for me, The Jam and Paul Weller opened my eyes, in some ways like an older, intelligent surrogate brother, guiding me through treacherous teenage years. For that I'll always be grateful.

Now, 40-plus years after the split, there are still regular rumours about the band reforming. That wouldn't be for me. I don't want the memories tarnished and I'm sure many people would be appalled by the sight and irony of 66-plus-year-old blokes singing 'When You're Young'. I'm sure Weller would never do that – it would ruin everything they stood for and believed in. The Jam were our Elvis, our Beatles. Thank God they didn't become our Rolling Stones.

I WAS THERE: SHAYNE WEBB

I saw them three times. I was out of Islington, North London and moved to Essex when I was 14 in 1979. Listening to the usual crap, my parents bought me Leo Sayer and Showaddywaddy albums for Christmas. But then my older brother played an LP, me running in his room to ask what it was. *All Mod Cons*. I don't think those other albums got played again. I remember going to my new school and the uniform seemed to be Parkas and bowling shoes with stitched on badges of this exciting new band. Me and my mates had to see them in concert, so we got tickets to the Michael Sobell Sports Centre. It was a freezing December evening, but my first concert blew my mind. I felt grown up. It was brilliant to boast in school that we'd seen The Jam. I kept the ticket, £4.50.

I WAS THERE: JULIAN BROOKS

Snow was falling as we followed a gritter up the M40 into London Town. When we arrived, the place was buzzing, full of Mods, with soul music playing and Bananarama doing their stuff (I reckon they were miming!). They were followed by rockabilly band The Rimshots, who were subjected to cans being thrown and lit fags being flicked at them. But they carried on.

Paul had a word with everyone – he wasn't happy when he came on, but soon I was blown away. It was the first time I'd heard 'Town Called Malice' live. What a song – the passion of it all, the bassline, that Motown beat… Fucking fantastic tune! (Not like nowadays, when he gets a tambourine out and it's a singalong like a weekend at Blackpool Tower.) They followed that with 'That's Entertainment', Paul and Bruce with acoustic guitars, each side of the stage. At one point there was Gary Crowley stood next to me, enjoying it to the full. I was buzzing all the way back to Princes Risborough, Bucks… which took ages because snow was falling all night. I eventually got back to a party, which set the night and earlier hours off nicely. We all had Lambrettas back then, and I loved all that.

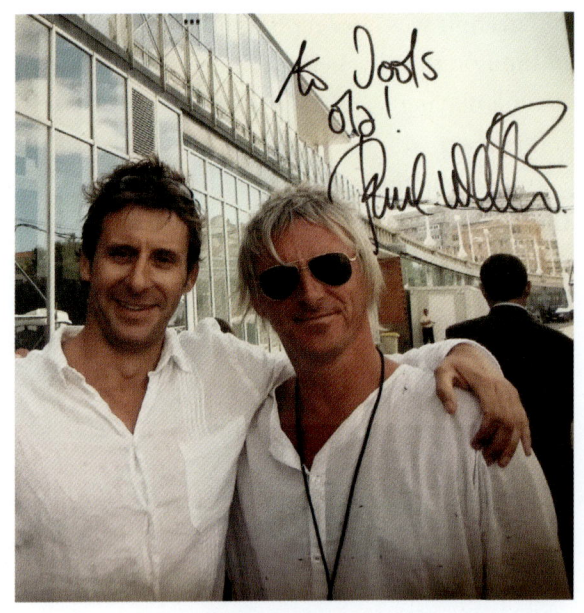

Julian Brooks with Paul Weller, signed by the man himself

Julian Brooks with Paul Weller in Barcelona in 2023

I WAS THERE: JOE SHIELDS

I remember having a row with my parents. We were invited to my cousin's birthday party and I didn't want to go. There was no way I was going to miss a Jam concert! The gig was near Finsbury Park and it was snowing. The Exploited were playing up the road at the Rainbow and trouble was brewing before and after the gig. I didn't see too much of it, but remember it all kicking off. There were kids with bloodied noses. I don't know whether they'd gone up to the Rainbow to have a go or if it was the other way round, but I remember thinking 'we've got to be careful'.

It was a great gig. Bananarama supported and they also had a band called The Rimshots supporting them, a swing rockabilly type of band who were really good. But some idiot Mods started throwing coins and shouting abuse at the lead singer, a big fellow in a suit. I like all kinds of music so I thought they were narrowminded pricks. Paul Weller was pissed off by this pathetic behaviour, and commented on it when he came on stage.

I WAS THERE: PAUL ROBINSON, AGE 16

I was born to be a Mod, although I didn't realise that until 1979 when I heard 'Strange Town' on the radio by The Jam, who I first saw on Marc Bolan's TV show in '77. Who were those young punks and why were they dressed in black suits and ties from Burton's? In Thatcher's Britain, we'd hang on every word of a young Paul Weller's manifesto. I was looking for something and I was hooked… suppose I still am. The Jam were our band, 'the best band in the fucking world', and the first time I saw them in concert was a sports centre in Finsbury Park.

A bunch of us teenage Mods from Bedford took the slow train to St Pancras and set about finding our way. It was a snowy day and treacherous underfoot. We met some very cool Mods on the way, all bedecked in Parkas, Sta-prest trousers and Jam shoes from Shelly's on Carnaby Street. I've a clear memory of one of them going arse over tit on the freezing slush. We tried really hard not to laugh…

With punk band The Exploited playing the Rainbow that night there were a few Mod vs punk brawls, although we managed to avoid all that. We arrived at the venue quite early, and for most of us, it was our first Jam gig and for some of us, our first gig ever. In the foyer was a merch table selling t-shirts and badges. I bought a 'Riverbank' tee. It was either going to be that or the 'Absolute Beginners' one… decisions, decisions. I still have my gig ticket and that t-shirt, which must be worth about £300 now. Wish I could still get into it. It must've shrunk.

We walked into an almost empty hall and made our way to the front for an unobstructed view of our heroes, although that turned out to be a big error of judgement. Supporting were almost unknown three-piece Bananarama, who sang along to a backing tape of their first single 'Aie A Mwana', twice, the tape failing first time around. Next was rockabilly band The Rimshots. We didn't give them the attention we possibly should have. Just one more act before the headliners, jazz-funk band Second Image. The line-up included Keith Thomas and Steve Nichol,

The Jam's horn section on their forthcoming LP, *The Gift*.

The Jam were introduced that night by DJ Gary Crowley, coming on to the title track of the next LP. Weller slipped over with a thud whilst running on. The place exploded. The crowd rushed forward and we were crushed like sardines in a tin. As the crowd went one way, we went with them. Without notice, the crowd then went the other way and we had no choice but to go with them. We were young lads, scared of being crushed, losing each other and being trampled underfoot. After what seemed like an age, we were able to prise ourselves out of the melee and get further back so we could finally enjoy the rest of the gig.

I WAS THERE: BILL ROCKETT

I might have seen them on *Marc* doing 'All Around The World' but I definitely saw them on *Top Of The Pops* doing 'Strange Town'. As soon as I heard it, I thought, 'That's the sound for me.' I immediately went and got *All Mod Cons* and then started catching up with *The Modern World* and *In The City*. I became obsessed. I remember racing to the record shop the day I knew *Setting Sons* was being released. I was only a young kid, only 14 or 15, and I was so excited when 'The Eton Rifles' got to No.3. It was a big deal because this was *my* band. I'd get my hair cut like Bruce Foxton. I had the black and white bowling shoes. There was a packet of Rothmans on the inner sleeve of *All Mod Cons* and I started smoking for a while because of that.

Me and my friend Pete Boothby went to see them at the Michael Sobell Sports Centre. They were debuting *The Gift*. We went on the first night and it was the first time anyone had heard 'Town Called Malice'. Gary Crowley compered and Bananarama were the first band on, possibly their first ever gig. They were miming away. Department S were really good. Everyone was familiar with 'Is Vic There?' so they got a good reception. This banner came down and it read: 'And Now The Absolute Beginners' and The Jam came on and they were playing away in front of me and I was absolutely gobsmacked. It was a fantastic night, although it turned a bit dark afterwards because The Exploited were playing the Rainbow and they allegedly told their fans, 'There's Mods round the corner – go and get them.'

The violence on the Tube was horrendous. They had to stop the trains and we got held in a tunnel. When we finally got to the next platform stop, they had all these skinheads lying on the floor under arrest on the platform. They were very racist skinheads so they were going after anyone black as well. Me and my mate were trying to hide our t-shirts under our jackets.

Rick would always throw his drumsticks out and Pete jumped to try and catch them but they brushed past his fingers. The Jam were the biggest thing in Pete's life. We were both devastated that they split up. He passed away about a year after The Jam split up, only aged about 18 or 19.

We went to see them in Stafford before they announced the split and they played stuff they didn't normally play, like the B-sides 'Disguises' and 'See-Saw'. I remember thinking that Weller looked a lot more into it than at previous gigs. It's because they knew they were splitting up and hadn't told anyone. A weight had been lifted off him and he knew the end was in sight.

Wembley was what it was. The sound wasn't great. Those final gigs were just thrown together. It was quite volatile, with quite a bit of trouble and it had a really off feel to it. Walking out I remember thinking, 'Well, that's the end of that then.' I saw them once previewing *The Gift*, twice on the *Gift* tour, and then that tiny six-date tour before they announced the split, and I'm so glad I saw them, because my other favourite band was The Clash and I never got to see them.

It was always incredible how much sound The Jam got on their records with just three people. I don't think Bruce gets enough credit for the depth and melody he brought to their sound. And Rick Buckler is a very underrated drummer. The Jam would not have been The Jam without the other two.

It was all kindred spirits. Everyone was there for the same thing. You did feel it was a closed group, being a Jam fan. If you saw someone with a Jam t-shirt it was 'alright mate?' and you'd start chatting to them. If you were into them, you were massively into them. People who weren't into them but liked the odd song would tend to like 'Start!', which most Jam fans didn't. For the real Jam fans, it would be *All Mod Cons* and most of *Setting Sons*.

I was massively surprised when they announced they were splitting. No one saw it coming. 'Going Underground' had gone in at No.1. 'Start!' had gone in at No.1. They were the biggest band in the UK by a country mile. Maybe the clues were there, but it was the first loss I'd had in my life. I'd never had anything taken away like that. It killed a lot of music for me. It was the end of punk, the end of new wave. And with that came in synth pop, new romantics, the dance scene. I didn't see decent bands come along until The Smiths and New Order.

If they'd reformed ten or 20 years ago that would have been great, but I don't think Weller's voice is up to it now. I've seen From The Jam at least 15 times and I saw them play a bullring in Spain recently. You could see that Bruce didn't look a well man. He looked very frail.

SOLID BOND IN YOUR HEART

I WAS THERE: GRAEME SPENCE

I was 14 when people at school started going on about punk. I remember seeing The Jam play 'David Watts' on *Top Of The Pops* and I heard someone say one of them was called Ray Davies. Then 'Down In The Tube Station' came out and I pleaded with my dad to be allowed go a concert at Newcastle City Hall. He said, 'You can go as long as I drop you off at the car park opposite and pick you up afterwards.' It was my very first concert and I went with a friend who lived across the road to us. That was in the days when they wore the black suits. I remember them playing 'Down In The Tube Station' and the concert finishing with 'Batman'.

The second time I saw them, I went with half a dozen kids from school. We came out of City Hall afterwards, turned left and were going down the side when the stage doors opened and John Weller was stood there. He said, 'Do you want to come backstage?' Six of us went backstage and the three of them were sitting there in their suits. I got them to sign my programme. Paul Weller drew a little doodle around his name and a few little dots linking them to his name.

The year after that, they did a record signing at a shop called Listen Ear, across the road from Newcastle City Hall. We took a load of stuff down to get it signed. You couldn't move. There were hundreds there. We watched as they came out of the shop and got in the tour bus and drove off, so half a dozen of us thought we'd chase the tour bus and see where they were staying. We lost them in the city centre, but we knew there were probably only two hotels they'd be staying at, the Swallow and the Crest. We went to the first one and that was the wrong one, so we went to the second one.

We went into the reception area and Paul was sitting there having a cup of coffee so we just plonked ourselves down next to him and started chatting away to him. I remember the concierge came up and said, 'Lads, you'll have to go, it's residents only,' and Paul saying, 'It's all right, they're with me.' And we got the stuff out of our carrier bag, a load of albums and singles, and he signed them all. Then the tour manager came and said they had to go to City Hall to do a soundcheck. Bruce and Rick came down and we hijacked them and got all our stuff signed by them as well.

I don't remember much of the conversation with Paul. He was quite intense but he wasn't unfriendly. He was smoking and when he put his cigarette out, someone pinched his cigarette butt. Then he stirred his cup of coffee and someone pinched the spoon. I remember someone asking him how long it took him to write 'Eton Rifles' and he said it took him about 20 minutes.

I next saw them in Carlisle at the Market Hall. It was a summer's day and absolutely red hot inside. I was right at the very front. I always used to go to Paul's side. He had the coloured bowling shoes on. That was the concert when they played 'Funeral Pyre' for the first time. I used to go with a girlfriend and another friend of mine. I would leave her at the back and run down the front, over the top of the chairs. I think my manners were left with her.

I went away to agricultural college in York. The first night I was there, I put a Jam t-shirt on before going down to the bar. And I met a couple of other people that had had the same idea. We knew we had something in common because we had Jam t-shirts on and we became friends.

We got tickets for the Michael Sobell Sports Centre. We got the train down to London from York. We didn't think about accommodation or anything. I remember watching the concert. That was the one when Paul came running on stage and 30 seconds later fell flat on his arse. We came out after and the snow was terrible. The Exploited had been playing at a venue nearby and there were loads of skinheads hanging around. Four of us were sitting in a carriage on the Tube and these kids were going between the carriages, getting more and more aggressive, asking people for cigarettes. I was saying, 'God, if they hear a North East accent, we've had it, you know?'

They went into the next carriage and there was a bit of a kick off there. And then this kid came running through the Tube train covered in blood. And we thought, what the hell has happened? Then someone said he had stabbed someone. The Tube stopped at the next station and he got off and legged it. The Tube carried on again and it was only then that somebody must have sounded the alarm.

We got to the next stop, which was King's Cross, and it was chokka with police. Everybody got pulled off the train and we all had to stand with our faces to the wall of the Tube station, while the police tried to find out what had gone on. Then they sent us on our way. So we had a bit of an altercation down in the Tube station, almost at midnight.

We went into London and said 'where are we going to stay?' It was bloody cold and everywhere was snowy. One of the kids in our group was from Darlington and he knew someone back home who knew someone who lived in at East Hounslow. So we found a phone box, phoned this lad back in Darlington who phoned this kid to ask if we could go and kip on his floor. So four of us ended up in East Hounslow sleeping on this kid's floor. When you're 18, you just go 'we'll just go down to see The Jam' and make no provision whatsoever for anything. Now you'd be thinking about the hotel straightaway, and checking how close it is to the venue.

I've seen Paul a few times since. He's a musical genius, the lyrics he wrote and still writes are amazing. People used to say to him, 'Do you not do protest songs anymore?'

and he said 'I've been writing them for years and nothing's changed.' And it's true. 'Kidney machines replaced by rockets and guns?' There's never been a truer line. That was written about 40 years ago, and it's exactly the same now. Nothing's changed.

I WAS THERE: PAUL WILLIAMS, AGE 16

I didn't pick up on them until '79, when I started branching out into my own music rather than my mum and dad's. A friend had a copy of *Setting Sons*, and then in January 1980, 'Going Underground' came out and I thought 'wow, this is fantastic.' I tried to go and see them on the *Sound Affects* tour, but my mum wouldn't let me. *Sound Affects* was such a contrast to *Setting Sons*. It was a lot cleaner, more stripped-back sound.

There was a guy in Corby, where I lived, called Franny Lanigan and he used to get 50 tickets for a gig and get a coach and we all used to go down to London. The gig before that he organised was Simple Minds and I was too slow to get tickets for that so I thought 'right, I'm not going to miss out on The Jam.' It was my first proper gig and I was so excited. I couldn't believe the atmosphere and the energy. It was electric. Everybody seemed so excited. A few people were a bit pissed and this was all new to me. When The Jam came on, I remember surfing across the crowd. I got completely wrapped up in it. I never realised you could have so much fun at a live music event. I managed to see them three times the next year, including at Granby Halls and then they announced the split. It seemed like a special event. Everyone was dressing up for it. And the pace of the gig… It was just bang-bang-bang. It didn't stop, from start to finish. Some of it's a blur now but you felt part of the band. I saw loads of other bands around that time. No one created the energy that The Jam did.

I WAS THERE: IAN HARVEY, AGE 15

I wasn't into the same music as my friends, who liked Adam and the Ants. Then I saw 'The Eton Rifles' on *Top Of The Pops*. We had a secondhand record store where I lived in Camden called Record & Tape Exchange so I'd hunt stuff out there. I bought *Setting Sons*, *In The City* and then *Modern World* and then I was up to date and bought stuff as it came out. They announced gigs at the Michael Sobell Centre, a short bus ride away. My mum wasn't sure it was a good idea for me to go but she sent off a cheque to MCP. Two weeks later it came back with a message saying 'sorry, sold out' and I was really disappointed. My mum phoned them up and they said, 'Oh, we've had a few returns. Send the cheque back and we'll hold the ticket for you.' So I went, on my own, to see them on the Sunday night.

I squeezed my way right down to the front. I remember John Weller coming on and saying 'best band in the fucking world'. The lights went out and my first image was of Bruce Foxton in mid-air because he'd come across the stage and jumped up as the lights came back on. I've been to some brilliant gigs since, but seeing The Jam was absolutely something else.

I saw them on my own again at the Ally Pally on the *Trans Global* tour, but in September they were doing the Brighton Centre and a friend's older brother, who worked in Holloway, got tickets for me, him and his work colleague. And then it was 'we're departing…' and it was 'oh no'. I didn't understand it at the time, but I do now.

I can see the progression from *In The City* to *The Modern World* and then the jump to *All Mod Cons* and then *Sound Affects*. If you compare *Sound Affects* to *In The City*, you're thinking 'is this the same band?' And there's parts of *The Gift* where you can see the Style Council influence coming in and the way Paul was going. I love *Modern World* as an album but I know a lot of fans don't. I've got a friend who's a big Paul Weller fan. He'll go and see him open an envelope. I like a bit of The Style Council and his solo stuff, but nothing compares to what The Jam were back then. If I didn't hear 'Town Called Malice' again, I wouldn't complain.

I went to Hyde Park because I'm a big Who fan, and Weller was on. We were stood next to these two blokes and when he did something by The Jam, the crowd just went wild. This bloke turned and said to me me, 'Do you think it drives Weller nuts?' If he does 'Boy About Town' now, it doesn't have the same oomph. There isn't that anger. His voice is different. *My* voice is different. I'd have to go if they got back together just to say I'd been. But it would tarnish a memory.

I'm a bit of a collector. A couple of years ago, a friend gifted me the big box set of albums they brought out. He had a spare and offered to sell it to me but I couldn't afford it. Then I was donating platelets and plasma around the same time as his grandson became ill. His grandson was having chemo and being treated for leukemia, so he was being given platelets and plasma. I was sat at home during Covid when this big box turned up at my door. When I realised what it was, I rang my friend and said said, 'Why have you done this?' He said, 'It's a thank you.' I said, 'No, no, no, my plasma and platelets aren't going to him.' He said, 'I don't know anyone else who does what you do.'

HAMMERSMITH PALAIS
14 & 15 DECEMBER 1981, LONDON, UK

I WAS THERE: CHRIS AVIS

Listening to the Top 40 on a Sunday evening, I taped 'The Eton Rifles' and it blew my mind. A few months later my girlfriend bought me *Setting Sons* for my birthday.

RAINBOW THEATRE 508
INSBURY PARK

M.P.P. presents
THE JAM
at 8 p.m.
Wednes JUNE 17
CIRCLE
£4.00
incl. VAT
M 16

The JAM
Michael Sobell Sports Centre
December 13th 6.30pm
To be given up
Nº 201

The JAM
Plus Special Guests
2nd IMAGE,
Bananarama and The Rimsho
MICHAEL SOBELL Sports Cen
Sunday December 13th 6.30
Tickets £4.50 (Inc. VAT)
Nº 201

The Jam
Plus Special Guests
T.V. 21
Bananarama and Rudi
HAMMERSMITH PALAIS
Sunday December 14th 7.00pm
Tickets £4.50 (Inc. VAT)
Admission will be refused to persons under 14
Nº 216

APOLLO THEATRE Manchester
MCP presents—
The Jam
Tuesday, 7th December 1982
Evening 7.30
CIRCLE
£5.00
U 46
No ticket exchanged nor money refunded.
No Cameras or Recording Equipment
Official Programmes sold only in the Theatre
A. B. Cooper (Printers) Ltd. Manchester

MCP PRESENTS
The JAM
SPECIAL GUESTS
AND A LOCAL BAND
ALEXANDRA PAVILION
Tuesday March 16th 7.30pm
Tickets £4.50 (inc. VAT) Stand

THE JAM
SPECIAL GUESTS
RUDI
AND A LOCAL BAND
Bingley Hall BIRMINGHAM
Sunday March 21st 7.00pm

DE MONTFORT HALL, LEICESTER
MCP presents
THE JAM
plus Special Guests RUDI
AND LOCAL BAND
MONDAY 22nd MARCH
at 7.00 p.m.
GALLERY £4.50 INC. V.A.T.
Tickets not transferable or money refunded
D 15
To be retained

THE JAM
+ SPECIAL GUESTS
BINGLEY HALL, BIRMINGHAM
Wednesday December 8th 7.30pm
Tickets £5.00 (incl. VAT)
Nº 2366

DE MONTFORT HALL, LEICESTER
MCP presents
THE JAM
plus Special Guests RUDI
AND A LOCAL BAND
TUESDAY 23rd MARCH
at 7.00 p.m.
GALLERY £4.50 INC. V.A.T.
Tickets not transferable or money refunded
B 17

THE JAM
+ SPECIAL GUESTS
BINGLEY HALL, BIRMINGHAM
Wednesday December 8th 7.30pm
Tickets £5.00 (incl. VAT)
Nº 0118

APOLLO THEATRE, Manchester
M.C.P. presents—
THE JAM Plus Special Guests
RUDI and a Local Band
Thursday, 25th March 1982
Evening 7.00
CIRCLE
£4.50
J 30
A. B. Cooper (Printers) Ltd. MANCHESTER

F 3
Opera House : Blackpool
.P. present THE JAM plus
ial guest & local group
ENING 7-0
ALLS
SUN.
MAR.
28th
1982
PORTION TO BE RETAINED
ne Tickets before leaving Box Office. Mistakes cannot be
ied afterwards. No ticket exchanged or money refunded

PLAYHOUSE THEATRE
Greenside Place
Edinburgh
Monday
5 April 1982
at 7.00 pm
Doors open 6.00 pm

M.C.P. Presents
"THE JAM"
Special guests THE QUESTIONS
Plus one LOCAL BAND
STALLS £4.50
NO Cameras or Tape Recorders Allowed
No ticket exchanged or money refunded—Retain this portion

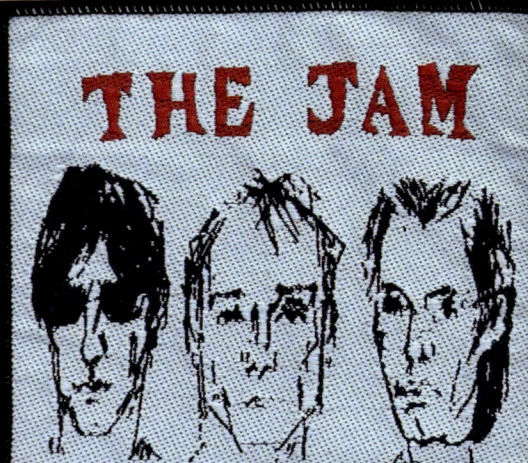

USTARD CONCERT présente
HE JAM
UEST STAR
KINI
UDI 29 AVRIL 1982 / 20 H
VILLON BALTARD / NOGENT-SUR-MARNE
VERTURE DES PORTES : 19 H
OF
000933
Droits de location en sus

THE JAM

EMBLEY ARENA
GOLDSMITH ENTERTAINMENTS &
MCP PRESENT
THE JAM
s Special Guests
in Concert
y, 4th December, '82
p.m. (Doors open 6.30 p.m.)
OUTH ARENA SEAT
£6.00
RETAINED

DECEMBER
4
1982
ENTER AT
SOUTH DOOR
SOUTH
A
S

THE JAM / DIG THE NEW BREED

GUILDFORD CIVIC HALL — THE JAM plus Support — Thursday 9th December 7.30pm — All tickets £5.00 — No 0585

THE BRIGHTON CENTRE
SATURDAY, 11th DECEMBER, 1982
at 7.30 p.m.
M.C.P. PRESENT
THE JAM PLUS GUESTS
SOUTH BALCONY £5.00
D 24
Skyline Restaurant — (Magnificent Sea View) Open two hours prior to most performances. Reservations: Telephone 203130
r the Council or their officers any responsibility for any loss age (howsoever caused or sustained to any property whatsoever ght on to these premises. kets cannot be exchanged or refunded.

CLIFFS PAVILION
STATION ROAD, WESTCLIFF-ON-SEA
THE NUMBER ONE ROCK VENUE IN ESSEX
M.C.P. presents
THE JAM
plus SUPPORTING BANDS
MONDAY, SEPTEMBER 20th — 7.30 p.m.
TICKET £5 (STAND-UP CONCERT)

WEMBLEY ARENA
HARVEY GOLDSMITH ENTERTAINMENTS &
MCP PRESENT
THE JAM
plus Special Guests
in Concert
Sunday, 5th December, 1982
at 7.15 p.m. (Doors open 6.30 p.m.)
UPPER TIER SOUTH

DECEMBER
5
1982
ENTER AT
SOUTH
ENTRANCE
58
ROW
O
SEAT

So began my obsession with 'the best band in the fucking world'. One of my mates was also into The Jam and through the fan club managed to get him and me tickets for Hammersmith Palais. I remember how excited I was walking out of the Tube station and seeing so many fans milling about.

Supporting were Rudi and TV21, the only group I saw get called back for an encore – us Jam fans were very harsh with support bands. The quicker they got off the quicker we'd get to see our heroes, seemed to be the attitude. In the centre a group of Mods started bouncing up and down, singing 'we are the Mods', a cue to start bouncing our way as close to the stage as we could. We ended up three rows back on Bruce's side. Result. Those 20 to 30 minutes between TV21 exiting and the boys coming on took an age, the tension and excitement growing with every passing minute.

Then the moment came, the lights went down and on walked the group I'd idolised for the past year, a moment I'll never forget. I screamed back every word of every song except the new ones played that night. We walked out soaked to the skin, ringing in our ears, no voice, overjoyed at seeing the best band I ever saw live. And I've seen over 300 since.

I WAS THERE: DAVID WIMMER

Having first bought *All Mod Cons*, I and all my mates were hooked. I finally got to see them at one of the pre-Christmas gigs at Hammersmith Palais. What an amazing gig! They're still the best band I've seen live.

I WAS THERE: GAVIN JONES

On Tuesday morning we congregated outside the Loco in Burton-on-Trent, waiting for Dave and Bruno to turn up with a hired VW van. We got Reaction's equipment downstairs and some cans of beer in. We'd be staying in London for the next three days; Reaction not only had a date supporting The Jam, but also another in Hammersmith Clarendon's basement bar that Thursday. The van turned up and we started to load in, including clothes and sleeping bags, as the van was doubling up as our hotel for two nights. We travelled down the M1 with Dave driving (he was the only one old enough to hire the van). Bruno was in the front seat and Steve, Andy and I crushed in the back with all the equipment, playing cards and drinking beer, all very calm considering in a few hours we had the biggest gig in Reaction's short history.

When we pulled up outside the Palais is when the nerves started to set in, with already about 200 people waiting to get in for The Jam's soundcheck. We'd all been to Jam gigs and witnessed soundchecks, but it felt different being part of it, pushing our way through, finding out where to unload. We blagged our way in, and as we walked across the massive dancefloor we saw Paul Weller on the other side, all but Dave laughing – he had almost exactly the same clothes on as his hero, having no argument against the ribbing we gave him.

Issued with backstage passes, we set about the task of getting the gear through the crowd. As we took an amp in, about five people tried to follow us. I'd have done the same if the roles were reversed. We had to wait our turn for a soundcheck, mooching in a corner of the Palais. We saw The Jam soundcheck and heard some new songs that would appear on *The Gift* the following year. They also played 'That's Entertainment' and 'In The Crowd', neither of which I'd heard live before. The kids were getting autographs and chatting with the band, one girl with a couple of decent black eyes telling Paul about being beaten up after the Michael Sobell Centre gig. Paul sympathised and eventually she went on her way with the rest as security guy Ken cleared the hall.

Next, we had to wait for Bananarama, making one of the first appearances with the Fun Boy Three, singing to a backing tape. The girls took ages as they kept messing up and mucking about, whilst Terry Hall skulked around looking like he didn't want to be there. Then it was Reaction's turn. Steve and I quickly set the equipment up and the band nervously ran through three or four songs, watched by Rick Buckler and John Weller. Paul was too deeply involved in a card game at the side of the stage with Ken and Joe, the security men, to take notice. And there was a lot of money in the pot! After Reaction, Ruts DC soundchecked in a very theatrical way, and then we waited for the doors to open.

At 7pm, around 2,000 people filed in. Reaction were on first, and before long DJ Gary Crowley was introducing them. As soon as they hit the stage, all nerves seemed to disappear. It was one of their best sets ever and got a great response. All too soon it was over, and Steve and I dragged the gear off before going backstage for a drink before going out to watch The Jam.

We thought we'd be cool, stand at the back and listen to the new songs, but they started with 'Man In The Corner Shop' and we rushed into a sea of people bopping away, fans once more. After a good set with a mixture of new and old favourites, the night was over. About an hour after The Jam finished, we got the van to the front door and started loading. Bruce then appeared at the door with his girlfriend, saying, 'Cheers, see you later,' walking off with kit bag under his arm, blending into the night.

In the morning, condensation dripping off the inside of the van roof on a freezing day, we soon had a rude awakening. We set up two camping stoves for breakfast, one for cooking and one boiling a kettle. When the gas ran out on one canister, Steve tried to replace it and promptly punctured the can. He panicked and passed it to me at the other stove. The next minute, the inside of the van was engulfed in a fireball, starting at the stove on the floor and circling around to the roof. Andy heaved the side door open and jumped to the pavement, the rest of us following. I was last out, the fireball remnants catching my trench coat as I tried to shed it.

We turned to see black smoke billow out of the van as our bedding burnt. We pulled the bedding onto the pavement and, having got our breath back, assessed the situation. The equipment was okay, but some of the hung clothes were singed and I had a nasty burn on my neck. While others picked through the burnt offerings, Kungy took me to hospital.

The main acts on Paul's Respond record label were on upstairs at Hammersmith Clarendon that night and we could check out the basement bar for our gig the following night. Dolly Mixture, The Questions, Apocalypse and The Rimshots were playing. We'd played with The Questions before, and there was a little professional jealousy as they seemed to be Paul's favoured band. It was a good, lively gig. Dolly Mixture were very good, the place about half full, the bands using some of The Jam's PA equipment and crew.

We spent another night in the cold van and the next morning sightseeing on Carnaby Street. We were caught in a bomb hoax and the streets were briefly cleared. At our afternoon soundcheck we started to get bad vibes. A doorman with a face full of scars and attitude to match told us we'd have to pay him out of our money for his services. It would have left us with nothing, so after an argument, and bearing in mind the week we'd had, we told him to stuff it.

Off we went, back up the M1 earlier than expected, after a week that felt like a month but one none of us would have missed for the world. It turned out to be the highlight of the group's career. After a few more gigs and no record company interest, it was over the following spring, one of thousands of bands that don't quite make it. But we got close.

I WAS THERE: BRUNO GALLONE, AGE 18

I was in a band called Reaction and a massive Jam fan. A month after our first gig, in December 1980, I began writing to John Weller and Dennis Munday at Polydor, asking for a gig. In late September 1981, I phoned up and in a mock London accent, pretended I was John's brother (I don't know if he even had one), saying I was set to be coming to a wedding but had lost his phone number. Bizarrely, Polydor gave me John's home number.

I phoned the number and couldn't believe it when Paul Weller answered! I composed myself and said, 'Can I speak to your dad please?' When John came to the phone, I pretended to be the manager of Reaction and said we'd spoken at a recent Leicester De Montfort Hall gig about Reaction supporting The Jam and he'd given me his number to chat about it. He must have thought it was true because he told me to ring back later. I'm guessing he then dug out the letters and tapes I'd been sending those last six months.

I called back a little later and, unbelievably, he offered a support slot at Hammersmith Palais. I was in shock. When I put the phone down, it struck me that the rest of the band wouldn't believe me, so I quickly called back and asked if he could confirm it in writing so I could 'get it in the diary'.

People always ask how they treated us, and in all honesty they were amazing. John Weller and the rest of the band were great to us and, because they treated us like a band it was very easy to chat with them before and after the gig.

One of my best memories is the soundcheck. As a fan I'd been to a lot, seeing them building from only six or seven people attending to around 40. By the time of ours, there were more than 500 – one of the biggest audiences we'd performed in front of. Once we'd tested the various sections, we played one of our songs, 'Can You See Me'. From the stage I could see John Weller standing with Bruce and Rick, watching. At the side of the stage, Paul was playing cards with roadies when he suddenly stopped, looked over to his dad and gave a nod of approval. What a moment!

I WAS THERE: BRIAN YOUNG, RUDI

We were on the guest list to see The Jam play the Michael Sobell Centre. It was the first time the other members of RUDI saw The Jam play and they were very impressed, and as we were supporting them at Hammersmith Palais a couple of days later, also somewhat apprehensive! To our relief, on the night we rattled through our support slot convincingly and without any mishaps. Better still, The Jam's audience seemed to accept us and we went down surprisingly well. We didn't know it at the time either, but the Jam crew were watching us closely to see if we could cut it on a big stage in front of a partisan audience. We must have passed the audition with flying colours as we were subsequently offered the main support slot on many of the *Trans Global Unity Express* tour dates the following year.

I WAS THERE: PAUL STEVENS

My first memories of getting into any kind of music was listening to my older brother's Beatles records in the early seventies. And he saw The Beatles live, a privilege of age... as is having seen The Jam.

Glam rock became my thing for a few years – The Sweet, Gary Glitter, Slade, Wizzard... Roxy and Bowie were too mature for my young ears. Then the Pistols arrived and changed everything. I was 13, entering my rebellious years. To my dad's disdain I went out and bought *Never Mind The Bollocks*, then got into The Stranglers. I had a few early Jam singles which my friend gave me – 'News Of The World', 'Modern World' and 'All Around The World' – but they didn't strike a chord. Then 'The Eton Rifles' came out and I was hooked, my tastes predominantly The Jam interspersed with Mod revival bands like The Lambrettas, Purple Hearts, Circles and Secret Affair.

Paul Stevens (left) did an interview for a fanzine with the band

I first saw The Jam at the Rainbow, Finsbury Park, in 1979. I took my girlfriend, which proved not to be a great idea – the crush was like being at a football match (and there always seemed a definite but indistinct connection between The Jam and football). In 1981, I got chatting to an old schoolfriend who started a fanzine and got a phone number for The Jam's office in Sinclair Road, near the old Polydor office. I tried to get an interview with Paul Weller. A gruff voice answered, who may or may not have been Kenny Wheeler. I gave him my details but never got a call back. I thought that was that, but a couple of months later, out of the blue, I saw Rick Buckler in HMV, Oxford Street. He revealed that the band were recording what turned out to be *The Gift* at AIR Studios, just down the road.

He didn't say I could just turn up at the studio, but he didn't say I couldn't, so two days later, armed with a cassette recorder and microphone, I did. It's generally a no-no to interview bands when they're paying for studio time and have other things on their minds, but I sat in reception patiently as Paul and Bruce wandered past, no one taking me seriously until Rick appeared, recognised me and said hello. To be recognised and spoken to by a member of The Jam was a big deal to me.

Rick was very pleasant and gave me an interview, then Paul posed for photos and they all signed my copy of 'Going Underground'. And that same year I managed to get tickets for their two December gigs at Hammersmith Palais. I was front row both nights and such was the crush that I could lift my legs and remain vertical.

After both gigs, I was drenched in sweat, but two shows just didn't seem enough.

The opening song was 'Going Underground', which I felt was a bad choice so early, the last song I think was 'The Gift', which also surprised me. However, Paul's spent his entire career surprising people, which probably contributes to his longevity.

I saw them again in 1982 on their farewell tour, an awful gig at Wembley Arena. It was all seated and The Jam just weren't an arena band, but they had to accommodate all the fans that wanted to see that last time, playing five consecutive nights. Then it was all over, their existence as the go-to band for so many people short lived.

Weller seemed to take his inspiration from The Beatles, always trying something new and pushing the boundaries, ultimately splitting the group to preserve the legacy and try new things. And for me nothing else has come close to The Jam in any aspect of popular music and fashion.

I was distraught when they split but fully understand and respect Weller's decision in my advancing years. So many bands of the time have reformed since and in most cases, it's been embarrassing, uncomfortable to see and pretty much meaningless. Thankfully, Weller's never even considered that. I believe Bruce and Rick would have in a heartbeat. If they did though, I'm sure every one of those people would gleefully buy the concert ticket and album. That's the conundrum. Weller seems to have accepted he's lost diehard Jam fans along the way, but it seems he'd rather plough his own furrow than pander to the masses.

I WAS THERE: RICHARD NOBLE

After the exhilarating experience of the Rainbow in June 1981, I was excited by the prospect of further London gigs at Hammersmith Palais and the Michael Sobell Leisure Centre in December. We chose the Palais and got tickets for the 14th.

It was in midweek, and I'd recently started a new job which involved a bus and train ride, taking over an hour each way. As I was on probation, I had to ask permission to have the afternoon off. On the bus, I couldn't wait to meet with my mates to make our way to Hammersmith. It was very cold and snowed a bit. Despite this, I decided just to wear a suit jacket, shirt and Sta-Prest trousers rather than a sensible coat.

At the venue we went straight in. Bananarama were on stage and we didn't pay much attention to them, but we were very near the front for TV21. I had their records, and they were excellent. RUDI were also great. I didn't know who they were then but Brian Young stood out a bit. Years later, living in Australia, I had a mate from Belfast who worked at Good Vibrations Records and knew all

SOLID BOND IN YOUR HEART

Photos by Andrew Clarke

Backstage at Hammersmith Palais

those bands and remains in touch with Brian. Funny how things turn out.

Gary Crowley provided MC duties and there were a couple of poets. Gary did impressions of musicians, including putting a hand over one eye for Phil Oakey of The Human League. Then came The Jam, kicking off with 'The Gift', which not many would have known, the LP of the same name yet to come. Bruce was right in front of us, and my friend Kevin, who was also at the Rainbow, had a camera. When the pics were developed it was like Bruce was posing for him.

I remember Paul windmilling during 'The Gift', releasing pent-up energy. Next was 'Tube Station' and I was ecstatic – they didn't play it at the Rainbow. The rest of the set was a blur, as it was such a melee. I'd not had experience of being down the front, totally underestimating what it was going to be like or how hot. During 'Funeral Pyre', still wearing my suit jacket, I was spun round amidst the pogoing. (I swear Paul announced 'The Eton Rifles' before launching into it, but there's no evidence – the heat must have got to me).

I recall a mic hanging over the crowd and wondered if it was being recorded. There was also a bloke in the middle, taller than us, taking photos, which was annoying as his elbows were getting in the way. Towards the end, the heat and sweat were too much to bear and I moved back to watch the last songs, 'Going Underground' and 'Little Boy Soldiers'. Like at the Rainbow, another song was played which I didn't know. It turned out to be 'Big Bird'. I'm sure the original was played after the gig, while I was standing next to a mate trying to chat up a girl from Hounslow who was going the next night too.

I wish I'd gone to more Jam gigs, but lack of funds and obstacles in getting time off work prevented that. I'm glad I chose the Palais though. It was later reported that the sound at the Sobell was dreadful. And purchasing the twelve-inch of 'Town Called Malice' in January '82, you can imagine my delight on finding that it included a live version recorded that night. I was also really pleased when the official audio of that gig was released.

I WAS THERE: RUPERT TRACY

The Jam had always played the Rainbow when they played London but it had closed down. The Michael Sobell Centre was a really odd choice for a gig. It was square, it was echoey and the sound was folding back all the time. But they did two shows at the much more intimate Hammersmith Palais, which I think only held 1,800 people.

And the 14th December show is where they recorded the live version of 'Town Called Malice', which they put out on the twelve-inch. That was a real buzz moment, to know I'd been there, and there was the extended version of 'Precious', which took them in a jazz-funk direction which I liked. It still had the guts. It still had the raw energy. It still had Weller's aggression.

The band claim Best Group in 1981's NME Readers' Poll, with 'Absolute Beginners' No.3 in the Best Single category. Meanwhile, 'Down In The Tube Station At Midnight' features for a fourth successive year in John Peel's Festive Fifty on BBC Radio 1, at No.13 this time, with 'Going Underground' at No.23.

'TOWN CALLED MALICE'/'PRECIOUS' RELEASED
29 JANUARY 1982

This double A-side single becomes the band's third No.1 and their second to enter the UK charts at the top, spending three weeks there in a seven-week spell in the UK Top 40. The Jam perform both songs on BBC TV's Top Of The Pops, becoming the first band since The Beatles to play two songs on one episode.

WEST BYFLEET
FEBRUARY 1982, SURREY, UK

I WAS THERE: NIALL BRANNIGAN

They'd already had three chart singles and were *Top Of The Pops* regulars. I knew what they looked like, sounded like and, through a couple of interviews, where they came from. Lumped in with the punk bands by the national daily press simply because they were new and sounded angry, it was obvious that they were nothing like those bands, who I disliked for bad-mouthing so many of the bands I loved. No, The Jam understood songwriting, song structure and where the music they were making came from, evident in Paul Weller's references to Lennon and The Beatles. Most of all, they could play; they were good musicians who had bothered to learn their craft. They also looked great on TV. The suits, Rickenbacker guitars, Rick Buckler's round shades, Bruce Foxton's haircut. There was a lot to like.

By 16 I was the drummer in a band, rehearsing mostly but playing occasional gigs, and this is how life continued for the next five years; music, records and the band, that was my life. Then I fell in love. I moved into a small house in West Byfleet. Woking became the place to go, shopping or for rare treats to take the kids to the cinema. To many people, it was the poor relation to Guildford's affluence; the runt of the Surrey litter. The huge Sheerwater council estate was on my doorstep and most of those I worked with lived there. There was an edge to Woking I hadn't come across much before; *Woking News and Mail* often featured stories of crime, fights and trouble in the town centre. And London was less than half an hour on the train via Waterloo and, for people like the lads in The Jam, a world of excitement which didn't exist in Woking. So close, so enticing, you could almost reach out and touch it.

By the beginning of 1982, The Jam had enjoyed five years of continuous success and 15 Top 40 singles marked them out as a special band. Then came 'Town Called Malice'. I remember hearing it in the car and being amazed at the sheer speed and power. I bought it the next day and was delighted when I got it home to find the house was empty so I could have the stereo up loud. I played that single a dozen times, back-to-back, eventually putting my headphones on because I wanted it even louder. I wanted to listen to Rick's right foot.

For right-handed drummers, the bass-drum is usually operated by the right foot; the drum is often called 'the kick-drum' by drummers because not only is it foot-operated but it kicks the band up the arse. It might be buried under all the other instruments but that's what makes your heartbeat faster when you hear a fantastic record.

On 'Town Called Malice', Rick Buckler's kick-drum is the song. It drives Bruce's bass, makes Paul go faster yet stay in time and fuels the aggression in his voice. It's recorded perfectly and is mixed to be much louder and higher in the mix. I'd go so far as to say Rick's kick-drum is the best sounding kick-drum in music. Ever.

The other thing which was obvious to me was that Woking was Malice. Unemployment in town had grown with each of Thatcher's new policies, exemplified by the boarded-up shops in the town centre, the growth in trouble and crime reported in the *News & Mail* and the steady stream of people looking for non-existent jobs where I worked. The lyric was angry. So was Weller's voice. Even though I was lucky to be in a good job I couldn't ignore what was going on around me. It was there when I went into town. It smelled, it festered.

'Town Called Malice' reflected the despair of a young generation. They wanted a glimmer of hope, a ray of sunshine in their lives. Looking around there was nothing but grey desolation, bleak skies and a burning frustration that there was nothing for them – no job, no life, no hope. They needed a voice to speak for them, to shout for them. And they found that voice in The Jam.

CENTRAL LONDON POLYTECHNIC
24 FEBRUARY 1982, LONDON, UK

I WAS THERE: JOHN BAINE, AKA ATTILA THE STOCKBROKER

In late 1981 I met Seething Wells (for many years, Steven Wells of the *NME*) when we both shouted our poems off the back of a lorry at a demonstration organised by the Woolwich Right To Work Campaign. That evening there was a 'Poetry Olympics' event at the Young Vic in London, headlined by Paul Weller, who at the time was dabbling in poetry. Swells and I decided to try and blag a spot, organiser Michael Horovitz kindly agreed, and we tore the place apart. Neil Spencer of the *NME* was there and gave us rave reviews. A music press movement (or rather a Warholian 15-minute fad) was born – 'ranting poetry'. Swells' phrase. Paul Weller was impressed, and Swells and I supported The Jam at the Hammersmith Odeon...

THE GIFT RELEASED
12 MARCH 1982

The Jam's sixth and final studio album goes on to top the UK album chart.

CONFERENCE CENTRE
13 & 14 MARCH 1982, BRIGHTON, UK

I WAS THERE: STUART STEELES

I saw them twice more at Brighton. I took my little brother Simon the first night. He was eleven. We sat on the front row of the balcony. We went to the soundcheck too, and they moved the queue to the road around the back as there were so many people. I also took my first proper girlfriend, Chloe, to the soundcheck as she wasn't allowed to go to the gig. They played four songs, including 'Carnation'. I stood holding her hand. It's a very fond teenage memory.

When I first saw them in 1979, I don't think I really appreciated what was happening. I'd never been to a proper gig before. It was loud and very exciting, but I had nothing to compare it to. I really enjoyed myself but didn't realise how good they were.

As years passed, I became more aware of the tension. Dangerous times. Going to football was tricky, and the same thing started to happen at gigs. If you had the wrong shoes or the wrong jacket, you were a target. I didn't notice it in '79, but I became aware of the challenges of getting back to the station, trying to avoid the trouble that would be waiting, several fights breaking out. When I took my brother along, there was a huge punch-up below us, the band stopping part-way through 'Heatwave'. Weller said, 'If you lot want to fight, fuck off outside and do it,' then carried on. Listening to the recording of the Brighton show from 1979, they abandon 'Heatwave' in the encore, but on that occasion it was because fans got up on stage.

I WAS THERE: ANDY NEWMAN

My first exposure was sat on my mum's stairs that led down to the kitchen when I came home one March lunchtime. We'd have Radio 1 on and I'd listen to the chart show. I remember being hypnotised by what had just gone straight in at No.1. I heard the rhythmic riffs of 'Going Underground', and I was hooked. I was twelve. I'm not sure my mum was as keen. Or my neighbours… unless the banging on the wall was a call to turn the music up.

My record collection grew quickly, as did my thirst for information. I also made the decision that I was a Mod. I loved what they wore, what they said, how they looked. It wasn't long before I was telling Mum I was 'just going into town'. But I was going up to Carnaby Street to buy clothes. It was £1.10 for a return, the Tube thrown in.

I soon stood out at school with my Parka and Jam shoes. I loved the sense of being a Jam fan; like being in a religion with a belief in all things Weller, Foxton and Buckler. But it wasn't until March 1982 that I got my first chance to see them.

I remember an electric mix of anticipation, nervousness, fear and excitement. I'd got into the soundcheck earlier, standing in a bass bin for the opening of 'Carnation'. My ears rang for about an hour after. There were scowling hairy roadies who didn't look as though they had any Jam link, moving amps, tuning guitars, looking busy. It was quite a learning curve. I wanted to get to the front as soon as possible.

The hall was smoke-filled and the smell of sweat drifted, like a heavy mist hanging low. It seemed an age before they came on, introduced by John Weller and straight into 'Strange Town'. Epic. I was soaked to the skin as I jumped up and down, the whole hall in a rhythmic trance. I was about a row from the front but couldn't maintain that for long – I couldn't breathe. I moved back a few rows but not far from the stage. It was like I could touch them – they owned us all. Fights broke out at random but soon dispersed, adding a little danger. Before long, it was all over.

It was one of the best experiences of my life. I loved it; every word sung, every beat jumped to, the drop at the start of 'In The Crowd' a stand-out memory. I left the hall full of myself, a bedraggled mess soaked in sweat. I walked home frozen, the night air colliding with my clothes. I don't think I slept a wink but resisted playing my Jam records when I got in. This would have been rectified in the morning. I always played an LP before school, to the distain of next-door neighbour Mrs Baker. (Sorry.)

BRIXTON FAIR DEAL
15 MARCH 1982, LONDON, UK

I WAS THERE: RICHARD WESTNEY

I saw them after *The Gift* came out. They were still good, but it felt different with the extra musicians on stage. In hindsight, things weren't quite right with the band, and while I thought 'Town Called Malice' was one of the best things they'd ever done, 'Precious' was one of the worst. I never liked it.

I WAS THERE: KEVIN MILLS

I saw The Jam at what was known at the time as the Fair Deal in Brixton, and is now the O2 Academy. It was just after *Sound Affects* – the *Trans Global Express* tour – and Weller had closely cropped hair and was sporting a short-sleeved grey Lonsdale t-shirt. It's the best gig I ever went to.

ALEXANDRA PAVILION
16 MARCH 1982, LONDON, UK

I WAS THERE: JOE SHIELDS

Whenever you go and see Weller over the years, it's interesting to see how many people copy every stage of his haircuts. At this gig, he came out and he didn't have his long floppy Steve Marriott-type haircut any more. He had cropped off all his hair. Almost overnight it appeared every Mod had done the same!

I WAS THERE: JO BARTLETT

They put on shows at the Pavilion while rebuilding the Ally Pally, where I later saw The Stone Roses. Main support act Dolly Mixture went on to release the first single on Paul Weller's Respond label, 'Been Teen', followed by 'Everything and More', a great song. I saw them a few times, once with The Chefs, when both bands did versions of The Velvet Underground's 'Femme Fatale'. I'd never heard it before, then got treated to it twice in one night. Of course, they ended up as Captain Sensible's backing band, having a No.1 with 'Happy Talk'.

I WAS THERE: RICHARD MUDD

I saw them for the last time around March 1982. I'd got to know Polydor's Jam A&R man Dennis Munday, and we chatted at the Alexandra Pavilion. By then, they had backing singers and a brass section. It had changed quite a lot. I then went on my travels and they split later that year. I do think they split at the right time, having peaked with 'Going Underground'. I understood Bruce and Rick's thinking, but Paul decided he was looking at a new direction. I reckon they lost their way a bit.

I've seen Paul on and off over the years and was lucky enough to catch a rather intimate gig in 2014 at Dingwalls, Camden Lock, to around 400 or 500 people at a time when he was also playing big arenas. I also saw The Style Council. He's done well for himself. I also saw From The Jam when they started in 2007, when both Bruce and Rick were in the band, and like the stuff Bruce and Russell Hastings have recorded since – that's been fantastic. Would I see them if all three of them got back together? If my boys wanted to go along and were willing to get tickets, they could drag me down, I suppose! But Paul's made it abundantly clear that he wouldn't do it. There's more chance of me standing on the moon.

I WAS THERE: RICHARD NOBLE

Another couple of London gigs were announced for March. I had a choice – Fair Deal, Brixton or Alexandra Pavilion. Coming from outside London and probably still a bit wary of places like Brixton – with common namechecks in the news following the previous year's riots – we chose Wood Green. And the venue proved excellent.

Dolly Mixture and local band 007 were supporting and went down well with the crowd. I decided to take a camera and get down the front to try and get decent pics. I was wearing a t-shirt and jumper, tied round my waist.

When The Jam appeared and to everyone's surprise, Paul Weller sported a very short haircut, to the extent initially that you wondered who it was. About a week before, I'd got my hair cut, a lot shorter than I usually had it. I wasn't happy then,

Richard Noble got a nod from Paul, possibly two

Photos by Richard Noble

but the barber must have known something I didn't.

To kick off they launched into 'Strange Town', and complete carnage ensued, during which I tried to take pics. I'm sure Paul saw my lone hand raised, camera attached, and nodded. Or was it my imagination? Next was 'Carnation', slowing down the pace. I took a few pics, which turned out really good. On 'Transglobal Express', Paul broke a string and walked off in a huff to get a new guitar, bashing the redundant guitar against a Vox amp. It looked so cool. Just as cool were Rick and Bruce, who carried on the rhythm waiting for Paul to return. When the gig finished, I realised my jumper was not round my waist and had to look around. I eventually found it. It had certainly been kicked around.

SHOWERING PAVILION
17 MARCH 1982, SHEPTON MALLET, UK

I WAS THERE: PAUL SAMMY THOMAS
I did Port Talbot and Shepton Mallet in 1982. My mate's dad drove us up in his old Daimler Sovereign. Great memories.

I WAS THERE: DEAN STANDERWICK, AGE 15
I had been waiting since mid-1979 and the first hearing of 'When You're Young' to see The Jam but due to being just twelve at the time I wasn't allowed to go to the following *Setting Sons* or *Sound Affects* album tours, so this was really built up to be a big, big thing in my buzzing little teenage mind! Fast forward three years and I'm 15 years old and sat aboard the organised concert charabanc from Bristol to Shepton Mallet. I'm now beyond excited!

I actually ended up seeing them twice in '82 at this venue, which was just a glorified cowshed. (The second time was for the *Solid Bond In Your Heart* tour.) I remember it being very loud and a bit of a football terrace-style forwards and backwards motion in the crowd, with the heat clouds rising.

The set list was fairly balanced, taking in some of the established crowd pleasers such as 'Butterfly Collector', 'Private Hell' and the opener 'Strange Town', alongside the as-then-new songs such as 'Running On The Spot', 'Ghosts' and 'Trans Global Express' complete with mind-blowing strobe lights! If I remember rightly, they ended with Start! and the aforementioned 'When You're Young'.

I WAS THERE: JEFF RYAN

I got the ticket for my 15th birthday. It was held in what was just a big shed at the showgrounds. I went with my older brother and a few mates, six or seven of us on the coach from Swindon, meeting a few more mates there who had gone straight there from a gig a couple of days earlier in London. They started with 'Strange Town', and then it was a mass of great tunes from *The Gift* plus some classics.

I moved to Australia two months after so followed the band's break up from afar. I liked the early Weller stuff with The Style Council, but not really what he does now. I loved his early raw social problem stuff and his almost political dislike stuff, which isn't so prevalent now.

I WAS THERE: ALISON DAVIS, AGE 12

I lived on a council estate in a village in Somerset. My dad died very suddenly in May the year before, leaving my mum, my older sister Lorraine and me. Mum did a brilliant job of bringing myself and my sister up and I am so grateful to her. But, without my dad there, she was quite lenient with me regarding being out and being friends with older boys. Thank goodness for that!

Me and my oldest friend, Lisa, made friends with some older boys who lived in the more affluent area of the village. Carson and Martin were four years older and totally obsessed with The Jam, buying records as soon as they were out and dressing like the band. We spent a lot of time sitting on their beds, listening to The Jam.

We went with them to see The Jam at the Showering Pavilion. It was my first gig. We booked with a company that provided tickets and a coach to the venue in the price. Because of the boys we were at the front. I don't remember many girls being there.

I loved all the albums, but especially *Sound Affects* and *The Gift*. I love the energy of 'Town Called Malice' and 'Precious', and liked the political references in lots of the lyrics, and could relate to them despite being quite young. I thought Weller was speaking for us! I also loved 'The Bitterest Pill',

'So Sad About Us' and 'I'm Different Now', for the romance and heartbreak.

We were all devastated when The Jam announced their split. I went around school with 'Weller is a Wanker' written on my school bag for weeks. But we went to see them at St Austell Coliseum. I expect there were tears!

One of the happiest days of my life was seeing The Gift in Bristol. Rick spoke to us all afterwards. I see From The Jam regularly and was lucky to see them during that short time that Foxton and Buckler played in the band together.

Alison Davis (right) was so devastated by the band's break up that she wrote 'Weller is a wanker' on her school bag

I also love A Band Called Malice for their raw energy and excellent choice of more obscure tracks. It takes me back to my youth, and a time when nothing mattered except for music and your access to it.

AFAN LIDO
18 MARCH 1982, PORT TALBOT, UK

I WAS THERE: JULIE BISHOP
I saw them twice in Port Talbot in 1982, in March and November. I've got photos of them leaving the gig and of me and my mates with the support band. Fantastic memories!

I WAS THERE: JEREMY GAGE, AGE 15
Port Talbot on *The Gift* tour was amazing. I'd broken my arm and it was in a plaster cast. The Afon Lido was a leisure centre, which with us all jumping around throughout made us sweaty. Towards the end, my cast disintegrated and fell apart, so it was back to the hospital the next morning.

This was only my second gig, after Budgie in Mountain Ash. I went on a large bus from the Cynon Valley, about an hour away, organised by others at Mountain Ash Comprehensive School. It was full of 15 to 18-year-olds… anyone who could afford a Fred Perry polo shirt was wearing one. I had a lesser-known polo shirt on, but by the age of 40 I must have had 40 Fred Perry polo shirts.

I bought an unofficial tour t-shirt and programme outside. The programme became mush, pushed down the back of my Sta-Prest trousers. The t-shirt didn't last long either. I mainly remember the seat and the people I was there with, catching glances of them in the crowd – huge smiles passed back and forth. The people I remember at that gig are still friends and The Jam played a special part in their lives, the music remaining relevant.

'Going Underground' made me a Jam fan for life. That and hearing those three amazing albums in a row – *Setting Sons*, *Sound Affects* and *The Gift*… Then it all ended very quickly. It took me a while to go back and get full enjoyment from the first three LPs. *The Modern World* is where you start to hear The Jam develop their own sound.

I was lucky enough to have Bruce Foxton and Russell Hastings play in my village many years later, part of the launch of their first album. I was living in Singapore and paid for them to have a gig back home in Wales. As one of my school friends, Julie, died from diabetes in the build up, I invited more school friends who had been at the Port Talbot gig than would fit in my home, so at the last minute moved it to our rugby club. A great night.

I once arranged for From The Jam to play in Singapore. Since then, Russ has kindly arranged tickets and passes. I've seen the guys in Milton Keynes and Cardiff, but also Tokyo. I wish I took a photo of me driving Bruce, Russ and their drummer in the back of my BMW to the gig in Singapore, their guitars next to me on the front seat.

Or the time I had an hour with them after the Tokyo gig. They invited me out for dinner, but I had work the next day, having to turn them down. I left the stage door with them, fans still waiting outside looking at me thinking I was the drummer. My only rock star moment.

I have The Jam tattooed on my shoulder within RAF circles. On holiday in the US in May, I'll spend a few nights in San Francisco with Simon Williams, who was at the Afon Lido with me. The reason he learned bass was because of Bruce, and he still gets up on stage with a band. When it looked like cancer was going to take his life a few years back, Bruce recorded a video with a positive message. What a tonic that was!

BINGLEY HALL
20 & 21 MARCH 1982, BIRMINGHAM, UK

I WAS THERE: BRIAN YOUNG, RUDI

As support act, we'd bought a beat up 'new' van for the tour but only managed to get as far as Chorley before the engine seized. We were panic stricken until

A PEOPLE'S HISTORY OF THE JAM

John Weller came to the rescue, hiring us a replacement vehicle and paying for our engine to be fixed. What an absolute gentleman! We reached Bingley Hall in plenty of time and soundchecked. The first evening was to be filmed and we were perturbed to see that the entire audience seemed to be made up of Mods who were baying to see The Jam. As we walked nervously onstage, the chorus of 'we are the Mods' intensified and a few coins were hurled at us. It could have ended very badly – but as the 'we are the Mods' chant reached fever pitch, fellow RUDI vocalist and bassist Ronnie Matthews stepped up to the mic, grinned and joined in!

Somehow it broke the ice, defusing any hostility and we sprang into action. That first night was hair raising but we never looked back. From then on, the Jam audience accepted us and we made the most of it. Instead of getting bottled off as I'd seen happen to some previous Jam support acts, we ended up getting encores night after night.

Bruce, Rick and Paul didn't socialise much offstage. By this time Paul had stopped drinking and seemed more reserved and introspective. After shows he tended to keep himself to himself rather than relaxing with a beverage or two. Bruce was more affable, always up for a drink or game of pool. I think he enjoyed being in a famous band more than his colleagues! Rick was very quiet and kept himself to himself though he could often be found putting together and racing radio-controlled model cars. On tour their every whim was catered for too – even their suits were flightcased! But they still seemed to get on well together and I certainly didn't think anything was amiss in the Jam camp at the time.

In contrast the Jam road crew were always full of life, carrying on and ribbing each other constantly – just one big happy family. We got to know them all pretty well, especially Wally, Ivy and Dave Liddle, Paul's guitar roadie who insisted on playing 'Puff The Magic Dragon' on my Gibson Les Paul at every opportunity. They couldn't have been more helpful to us either. On the first night of the tour, it was obvious that my guitar lead wasn't long enough for the large stage we were playing on. Next day they made me an extra-long 30-foot guitar lead. They also offered to carry all our gear with their equipment, which meant that every night when we turned up to play, they had already set up our equipment on stage. And they loaded it back offstage for us after.

Many headline acts restrict support bands to a tiny portion of the stage, mess up their sound and refuse to let them soundcheck properly. This had happened to The Jam on the *White Riot* tour. But The Jam always ensured we had a full soundcheck, plenty of room onstage and they made sure that their own soundman manned the mixing desk for us every single night. Many support bands also have to buy their way on to a tour and rarely get paid for their performance. We didn't have to fork out a penny to tour with The Jam and we got paid every night.

Another example of their good-natured generosity was demonstrated in Leicester. We'd booked into a dodgy B&B in the red-light district. Also staying in the same dump were some Northern thugs who were following the Jam tour, selling bootleg t-shirts. While our roadie Lowrie was playing pool, they swiped his leather jacket which contained all his money and his passport. Of course, they denied any involvement. Lowrie mentioned this to the Jam crew and a couple of days later in Manchester his jacket, passport and all his money were returned intact. I don't know quite how they achieved this – but they really did go above and beyond for us.

It was customary for The Jam to allow any fans standing outside in to watch the band soundcheck. There's footage on YouTube of the fans all rushing in to Bingley Hall and you can spot us sitting at the back by the mixing desk. Hilariously many of the Weller lookalikes were proudly sporting his Steve Marriott backcombed cut with a long fringe. They were visibly crestfallen to see that their idol had now cropped his hair into a suedehead cut. Next day many of them returned for the soundcheck with new matching haircuts!

For us, unused to touring on such a scale, the whole experience was thrilling. Not only were we treated like kings but we also got to watch The Jam play onstage, close up, every night. Even with the new temporary members on board, Weller, Foxton and Buckler had a thrilling, unique, musical chemistry built up through years of playing together. Each of them knew instinctively what the other was gonna play and they locked together instantly. I loved watching them experiment with unfamiliar numbers during their soundchecks too. I've never seen a tighter band.

I WAS THERE: MICHAEL BUSHELL

Bingley Hall was a tatty, old-fashioned exhibition centre on the site of what is now the International Convention Centre. The Jam were great, augmented by a horn section. But my overriding memory was the violence. Apparently, there was a stabbing. The gig was filmed and I hid behind a camera as things were feisty. Re-checking the setlist makes me realise that they played pretty well all my favourite songs.

Michael Bushell remembers a stabbing

It's a shame that was my only live experience of such a great band. We really lost something when Paul called it a day.

I WAS THERE: ANDREW FROGGATT

I saw them at Bingley Hall in Birmingham twice and at Stafford Bingley Hall twice. I just missed the punk thing. There used to be a department store called Beatties and the first-floor record department was next to the toy department. *In The City* was on cassette in the cassette rack and I was fascinated by the spray paint and the men in suits. I was probably into Blondie and *Parallel Lines* at the time, after Elvis.

Andy Froggatt will happily take *All Mod Cons* to the grave

In 1979, I remember seeing 'Strange Town' on *Top Of The Pops*. I bought the single the next day and played it to death. And then I flipped it over and played 'The Butterfly Collector' and thought 'wow, what's that?' I just immersed myself in them after that.

Setting Sons was just coming out and the Mod revival thing was happening. The Jam led me into The Who, because they recorded 'So Sad About Us' as the B-side of 'Tube Station', and into the Small Faces and to the Kinks. And then I became as interested in the clothes as the music.

We went to Bingley Hall early and were hanging around the front and they let us into the soundcheck. I didn't know they did that. That must have gone off for half an hour at least. After the gig, me and my mate, also called Andy, were with two Mod girls. Waiting for a lift home, we walked around the back and an older security guard said to the two girls, 'Do you want to see the band?' Me and my mate were like, 'He's pulling your leg, girls, come on. Let's go,' and we started walking off. But we turned around and they were walking in back behind the stage. We were like 'shit!' and ran in after them.

The security guys pointed up to the balcony that ran all the way around and said, 'Up there, girls, up there and along the balcony. There's a door there – can you see it?' and we followed. As we walked up the steps, John Weller came out and he said 'through there, kids' and we walked in and there was the band. The two horn guys were there, and it wasn't easy to talk to Weller because he was surrounded by fans. But you could easily talk to Rick and Bruce.

I remember I was sat outside a disco at Dudley College with some other lads when someone said, 'Have you heard The Jam have split up? It's been on the TV.' We were gutted. It was the end of the era. I was 17. I got why Weller ended it. Towards the end, he was getting fed up with it, all the football chant stuff. And I thought 'Beat Surrender' was a bit weak.

I saw the Paul Weller Movement. I was sat in the Barrel Organ opposite the Digbeth Institute having a drink just before the gig and Ocean Colour Scene came in the pub. They were just going to the gig as punters but two years later they turned into his backing band.

You could bury me with *All Mod Cons*. That's peak Jam for me. And *The Gift* and *Sound Affects*? I probably haven't played them since I bought the records.

I WAS THERE: GAVIN JONES

I went with Marc from Reaction, going to the soundcheck hoping to get him on the guest list (I already had a ticket). They played 'Carnation' and 'Precious', but we were kicked out straight after so couldn't chat to the guys. I didn't recognise many people, and it felt different – you could tell they were getting very big.

We found the group's hotel across town and saw Paul in the bar. He put Marc on the guest list (written on a fag packet!). We had to run to the gig as we nearly missed the start and got in as they were playing 'Happy Together'. Paul was really aggressive, kicking amps over and windmilling, Bruce was jumping loads and it was a great atmosphere. They did all the songs from *The Gift* except 'Planner's Dream', some *Sound Affects* tracks and some singles. It was a great gig, with three encores.

I WAS THERE: LAWRENCE BRACKSTONE, AGE 16

My parents discouraged me from going to gigs so at the age of 16, I hadn't ever been to one. In early 1982 The Jam announced a number of UK dates to promote *The Gift*. Could this be my time? My friend Andy got me a ticket for Birmingham's Bingley Hall, an ageing, huge open space building in the city centre, built originally for exhibitions and now, owing to The Jam's growing popularity, one of the few places in town big enough to cope with 5,000 plus fans.

It was pretty busy when we pulled up outside, with Mods sporting all sorts of Weller haircuts, Jam shoes, boating blazers and many fishtail Parkas. We made our way as close to the front as possible. The building had a number of pillars that could obstruct your view. But then we realised that the gig was to be filmed.

The stage had a huge black banner strewn across it bearing the words 'Trans Global Unity Express'. It was dark and had two huge stacks of Marshall amps positioned for Paul and Bruce, while Rick's massive ivory drum kit sat up on the riser awaiting his presence. Gary Crowley was spinning Northern Soul and Motown classics as the warm-up act, but the crowd were there for one thing, and one thing only – the trio from Woking.

The crowd was noticeably impatient, with an almost football crowd-like feeling as people pushed to get forward. Soon the lights went down and John Weller appeared on stage to announce the now famous line of, 'Put your hands together for the best band in the fucking world – The Jam.' The band walked on stage and I thought, 'Oh my god, what's Weller done with his Marriott haircut?' He had trimmed the 'curtains' for a short French crew cut and was wearing a black mohair suit, bowling shoes and a white Lonsdale t-shirt. After a courtesy greeting – 'you' – to the crowd, they tore into my then most favourite track 'Strange Town' – I couldn't actually believe I was there.

The pushing was violent and constant while the power of the sound was completely amazing and very, very loud. I could feel the bass pulse beating in my chest. I had positioned myself in line with Bruce on the right-hand side, about ten people deep from the front. As a bass player myself, I watched his fingers moving up and down his Fender Precision bass with fascination.

The roar of the crowd after the first song was huge and the band moved straight into 'Carnation' without stopping for breath. Song after song was reeled off in high tempo bursts of energy. Weller had brought in a two-piece brass section to give a more soul approach to the sound. This was used to best effect when Weller announced, 'This is one of Rick's songs' with a real sense of irony and they played the Curtis Mayfield classic, 'Move On Up'. The set was a mix of popular live tracks, eight from *The Gift* and songs that have since turned out to be Jam classics – 'The Butterfly Collector', 'When You're Young', 'Private Hell' and 'Tales From The Riverbank'.

There's always a graduated divide between the mosh pit and the curious bystanders at the back of a gig. Not at this one. Everyone was dancing (more of a 'pogo') and I mean *everyone* – front to back, side to side – all 5,000 of them. And the haze of sweat rising from the crowd was visible in the strobe lighting. Although it was seriously cold outside – snowing – it was seriously hot inside. I was wearing a blazer and Hush Puppies and both were wringing wet at the end.

Two days after, I caught a monumental cold from the extreme drop in temperature outside the gig.

I WAS THERE: TIM EATON

I first saw The Jam live at Bingley Hall with my mate Dave. We had a day off school and my mum took us. We were there early and got right to the front, in front of

SOLID BOND IN YOUR HEART

Bruce. We held on to the barrier all night. After the gig, I queued up to see the band but never got in to see them. They left on a coach, and we got a wave. My mate Dave's dad picked us up a couple of hours later. To this day, we have no idea how he found us in that era before mobile phones and online maps. I've still got the ticket stub.

I WAS THERE: TONY COWDRILL, AGE 19

It's the best gig I ever went to. I was a fan since seeing them play 'When You're Young' on *Top Of The Pops*. I went out and bought the single the next day and started collecting all their albums. I went on the bus to Bingley Hall, meeting a work colleague there. The raw energy of the band and audience stood out and being a part of it was something I'd never experienced before, or since.

Paul's writing matured on *Setting Sons* and that album struck a chord. The Jam influenced my fashion sense, got me to notice politics and what was happening to the country, especially the miners' strikes, and *The Gift* got me listening to more soulful music. I was devastated when I saw Paul on the news announcing the breakup. The Jam were the only band I'd ever really bonded with and felt connected to. They were the voice of my generation. There's not been anything like them since.

I WAS THERE: KEITH HANNIS, AGE 15

I was fully submerged in all things Jam and Mod related. The gig was my first ever, catching a band I'd loved unconditionally for at least five years. I begged my parents to let me go, as did two other kids in my close. We went into town, queued and entered. What struck me was how loads of people were packed in, gas heating off the posts pointing down into the crowd. It was a surreal experience with like-minded kids, growing up in Thatcher's broken Britain, but I loved every minute.

One minute you were stood on the left and then you were on the right, loving it, fully suited and booted – Parka, Jam shoes, boating blazer, tie. Weller's 'curtains' hairdo. They were shaping the youth, and I was in for the long haul. It was a way of life and identity. The guys were providing much more than music. And the values The Jam installed in me? To appreciate soul music, new wave, and our version of Modernism. They've stayed with me.

I WAS THERE: MICHAEL COUCH, AGE 16

I'd just turned 16 and had the ticket for my birthday. I went on the Sunday as I was on a football tour before and couldn't make the Saturday. When we met the band, Weller asked if we'd come the night before and I explained I was on my own tour!

We went into Birmingham on the bus, taking a Sharpie pen and some single covers in the hope of meeting them. We headed to the Holiday Inn and waited patiently. The first coach arrived, Rick and Bruce came out and we queued to have Parkas signed and me my "A' Bomb' single cover. Paul was on the coach behind and came out, everyone swamping him for autographs. We walked round to Bingley Hall as we knew the first few fans would be allowed in to watch the soundcheck. When the doors opened, we

Michael Couch on his prized Vespa, aged 16

ran to the barriers. The Jam were already on stage, line-checking. Weller's hair was freshly cropped and both Foxton and Weller wore long black Crombies. Weller's was cord. It was freezing, like a huge cattle shed. They played Curtis Mayfield's 'Move on Up' and James Brown's 'I Feel Good'.

We were ushered out, and then queued patiently for the main gig. The DJ and support bands came and went and the surges in the crowd were like nothing I've experienced to this day. The steam from all those sweaty youths was unbelievable.

I WAS THERE: ROB BUTTAR, AGE 13

My two brothers are five years older than me. We'd been listening to ABBA and Elvis Presley and 10cc. But they both got into punk in a big, big way – X-Ray Spex and then The Clash, The Stranglers, The Jam and the Sex Pistols. The Jam didn't stand out for me at first. It was just another band they were listening to.

We lived in Birmingham and our cousins lived in London and my brother swapped a Jimi Hendrix album for *The Modern World*. When I saw the cover of the *Modern World* cassette, I knew they were the band for me.

Rob Buttar was introduced to The Jam by his older brothers

I was nine years old and I thought they looked really smart. They looked like they washed! (My older brother's abiding memory of me as a kid is Sunday evening and me constantly ironing my three pairs of Sta-Prest for school.)

I'd listen to the first three tracks off that album, rewind them and listen to them again. It took me three months to listen to the whole album.

We're Punjabi Sikhs and all the Punjabi Sikhs we knew thought it was really weird that we could listen to this music, and that Mum and Dad would let us watch *Top Of The Pops*, listen to the radio and play a cassette in Dad's tape player in the car. They allowed me to do whatever I wanted. Dad let me buy a guitar at 14. I can't play it! I even bought a black-and-white Rickenbacker 330 just because Paul Weller had one. It's not been out of its case in 15 years.

My brothers bought *Setting Sons* but I bought my own copies of *Sound Affects* and *The Gift*. I'd go into Birmingham city centre at nine o'clock, buy the first copy, go into school with it and then make sure nobody touched it. I wouldn't get it out of its sleeve until I got it home. I didn't want people asking to look at the inner sleeve.

I saw The Jam live five times. The only band I'd seen live before was The Stranglers, at the Odeon. Bingley Hall was totally different. And it wasn't just the gig. It was the build up to it. I knew I had to get new shoes. I knew I had to get new Sta-Prest I hadn't worn before. I knew I had to get something new on top I hadn't worn before.

In those days, if Paul or Bruce were pictured in a photo shoot wearing something on a Wednesday, shops would be stocking something similar by Saturday. There was Oasis in Birmingham City Centre for new stuff, or you could get secondhand stuff on the market. And Reddington's Rare Records in the arcade was where you'd queue up to buy tickets. And when you'd got your ticket, you'd keep looking at it, counting down the days until the gig.

My older brothers went to Bingley Hall with their mates. I went with four of my mates – Chris Pollard, Paul Ryan, Justin Pitt and my best mate, Raj Sagoo. They came round to my house on the Saturday afternoon and we listened to The Jam on the hi-fi for about three hours. To get to Bingley Hall you had to go round the back of the old Birmingham Library, which was a bit concrete-y with concrete pillars. It was dodgy. We always had to watch our backs. I'd had run-ins with rude boys and skinheads, but me and Raj were Mods *and* Indian, so it was almost like a double excuse for the skinheads to chase after us!

The sheer excitement of seeing The Jam was building up inside me. There was this mounting thing of 'get them on stage, get them on stage.' It almost got to a fever pitch, and as soon as they played the first note of 'Strange Town', it went absolutely nuts. There was a time during that first song when my feet weren't even on the floor. It was that tight that I was just moving around with the crowd. And you're looking for your mates and you've lost them, because the crowd has taken them in another direction. They played 'Heatwave' and Paul didn't sing the first verse. It was so loud that the crowd sang it and he just watched them do it.

DE MONTFORT HALL
22 & 23 MARCH 1982, LEICESTER, UK

I WAS THERE: ANDREW FARMER

At a time when money was tight and there was no spare money for concerts, my family's appalling musical tastes ranged from Deep Purple and Queen to Tom Jones and Mario Lanza. We had a record player with about twelve LPs, all terrible. I felt like the whole world was waiting for change. Something for the youth of the day to be part of, something that spoke to them and their lives. Along came Paul, Bruce and Rick in 1977 to save the world from musical malaise.

We waited all week in the hope that the Fab Three would be on *Top Of The Pops*, or sat by the radio as the charts were released, fingers poised by the record button, nervously waiting for Mike Read to say, 'And new in this week, The Jam!' with record duly pressed and – fingers crossed – if you were lucky you got the whole song, which you'd then play endlessly, every lyric listened to and learned.

In 1980 I left school and got a mindless job at Tesco. I needed money for clothes, records and concert tickets, and with a group of friends we hired a mini-bus complete with driver to go across to Leicester. That was only the start. What would I wear? What would the band wear? Where would I stand? By Paul's side, Bruce's side or down the middle? Then, with enough money saved, there was a trip to Carnaby Street to spend two months' wages on the obligatory three-button jacket, Sta-prest trousers, Jam shoes, and a black and red polka shirt. Paul was bound to notice me, right?

On the day, I recall that one of the lads from the bus got attacked by a couple of skinheads. He was wearing a high-collared cape.

When the lights went down, John Weller came on to introduce the band and they ran on and started with 'Strange Town'. A lot of *The Gift* was played, 'Running On The Spot' a particular highlight. I needn't have worried about where to stand. It was carnage, the whole place one massive mosh pit. I lost a shoe, which I later found.

The band played three encores and finished with 'Heatwave'. The energy from the hall could have run a small power plant. Then they were gone, and life would never be the same. Yet Weller remained with me. Longer than my wife of 40 years. I couldn't tell you who I love more.

I WAS THERE: ANDY WRAGG, AGE 14

I was at secondary school when 'In The City' came out. I was away with The Jam as soon as I heard that track and saw their suits. One bedroom wall was plastered with The Jam and the opposite wall was plastered with Arsenal posters. It used to drive my mum mad.

I went to see them at De Montfort Hall. We all had our Parkas on, and there were all these rockers outside. We also went down to the five nights in London. Rick threw his drumsticks out and one of my mates managed to get one, but another lad got the other end and so my mate only got half a drumstick because it snapped it half! But I got both Steve White's drumsticks when he threw them out at Nottingham Royal Concert Hall at the end of one of Paul's gigs.

I always used to buy the *NME* and *Record Mirror* and I went into the paper shop that morning and saw the headline 'Jam split'. I couldn't believe it. I was crying in the newsagents.

I tried copying Paul's look. He stood out because of his clothes. When The Style Council did the 'Speak Like A Child' video, Paul was wearing a cream trenchcoat. It took me ages to find one. I found one in a charity shop in the end.

I went to see Weller play in Oxford Street and I was walking down Oxford Street in my Jam t-shirt and my Jam shoes. I saw this fella sat outside and he said, 'Are you going to see Paul Weller play?' I said, 'Yes, are you?' He said, 'Well, I'm his guitarist today.' I thought he was having me on but it turned out it was Steve Cradock.

Tracie, who was on Respond Records, was putting out her back catalogue and she wanted to borrow my tape of a Japanese TV show that she was on. I didn't really want to let it out of my sight so she sent a courier to collect it. She didn't use it in the end because the Japanese record company wanted too much in royalties. But when she put the back catalogue out, I got a thank you in the sleeve notes.

I hope they never reform. I want to remember them as they were, how they stood for youth. If they were going to do a one off, I'd be there. But I think Paul has said his kids would have to be homeless and in the gutter before he'd think about it. I think we can take that as a 'no'!

I WAS THERE: GAVIN JONES

Similar to Brum a couple of nights before, they did a frantic, electrifying set. At one point Paul smashed his Telecaster into his Vox speaker, and they did three encores after playing most of *The Gift* and some of *Setting Sons* and *Sound Affects*. I hung around after, got my *Sound Affects* songbook signed by them all and chatted with John Weller about going to Brussels in April, having signed up for a coach trip.

Next day I got to the soundcheck early afternoon. They kept screwing up 'Dreams Of Children', getting it right on the third attempt but not playing it that night. Paul had a horrible pink Telecaster which I never saw him use again. Later I met my friends Hoppy and Mac, who were seeing The Jam for the first time. I hoped it would be a good one as they'd put up with me going on about them for the past few years.

It turned out to be probably the worst Jam gig I saw. At one point the sound packed up and they had to stop for a few minutes while it was sorted. Including an encore, it lasted just under an hour, and you could tell the band weren't happy. A lot of the crowd were pissed off as well. I assured Hoppy and Mac they were normally much better. But they still thought they were great. And a bad Jam gig was still miles better than most others.

I WAS THERE: TIM FILOR

I didn't have to wait long for them to revisit the De Mont. My old mate Steve kept me company again. I could only get balcony seats, a bit of a bummer, but we were near the stage. There was no chance of getting in the stalls, with security tightened. Looking down, we could see Mods sweltering in their Parkas. They seemed so young, probably 14 or 15.

The Jam came on and the room erupted. They were huge now. We didn't know it was close to ending – we just sat back, enjoyed the ride. A constant stream of little Mods were getting pulled out at the front as the crowd surged. They had a brief moment with their heroes on stage before being hauled off by bouncers. The band did 'Trans Global Unity Express' and 'Scrape Away', which seemed extra-long, 'Pretty Green', 'Man at the Corner Shop' and finally 'Happy Together'.

We left elated and made a quick dash to the Old Horse on London Road to catch last orders. I was full of adrenaline. As we supped our beers, we never thought that would be the last time we would see them live. I didn't get to any of the final gigs, having to be content with the final outing on *The Tube*. Once the boys unofficially expanded to five it wasn't quite the same, but with hindsight you see where Paul wanted to go.

Massive thanks to The Jam. It was good while it lasted and it inspired me to get back in a band with three other fans. I never found fame and fortune, but carried on in various line-ups until 1997. I met my wife, made lots of friends, and have two great kids and a lot of memories.

I WAS THERE: PAUL ROBINSON

After the Michael Sobell Centre gig, we got the bus after school from Bedford to Leicester for the first of two nights at the De Montfort Hall. I managed to sneak in my Kodak camera in and had a strip of flash bulbs. The support was a local girl, a punk poet, followed by RUDI from Northern Ireland, once Good Vibrations label mates with The Undertones. Then John Weller hit the stage and announced the imminent arrival of 'the best band in the fucking world, The Jam!' Paul, Bruce and Rick took to the stage and assumed their positions. Weller, fag in hand, looked sharp in candy-striped shirt, Sta-Prest trousers and bowling shoes. He plugged in his black Rickenbacker and launched into 'Strange Town'. My mates and I were almost inside the speakers. The crowd surged, and I lost my strip of flash bulbs. And my hearing for a few days!

APOLLO THEATRE
25 & 26 MARCH 1982, MANCHESTER, UK

I WAS THERE: MICK CLEE

I left school in '81. Back then the resources for listening to music were limited to *Top Of The Pops* on a Thursday, John Peel at 10pm from Monday to Thursday on Radio 1, and Radio Luxembourg, which had a programme on between 7pm and 8pm called *Modern World* which used to play the intro to 'Modern World'. Of course, the reception was shocking at times. But I relied on those plus the *NME* and *Melody Maker* for all my information.

I was getting interested in politics. I was listening to The Clash and I was listening to The Jam and I was listening to Weller. Weller dressed so sharp, and as a spotty 16-year-old kid I related to it. The first gig I went to was Stiff Little Fingers in 1981 and about six weeks later, The Jam announced the *Trans Global Express* tour. They were doing three nights in Manchester and I went on the Friday night. Shortly after 'Town Called Malice' came out, it was released as a twelve-inch single with a live version recorded at Hammersmith Palais. Listening to that knocked me senseless. I thought, 'These guys have got a power that I want to experience.'

I had my green flight jacket on, a Fred Perry polo shirt and a small slim tie with The Jam on, ready for the gig. I was taken aback when I walked into the gig and saw masses of people in boating blazers, Jam shoes and Sta-Prest trousers. It was like a convention. I was looking round and thinking, 'Jesus, these guys are sharp. This is what I want. I want to be a part of this.' On the Bingley Hall DVD they opened up with 'Strange Town' but on this particular night Weller walked on with a brown mohair suit, button-down shirt and a polka dot brown tie. They opened up with 'The Eton Rifles' and the first chords of that just blew me away. It was like, 'Jeez, this is happening. This is real.' I couldn't believe how intense they were. Weller was spitting the lyrics out and you were thinking to yourself: 'This is the guy who sang such great songs on *The Gift* album and live he's got this raw energy and he combined them both.'

That night changed my life. I came out of the gig all hot and sweaty. We were walking back into Manchester with a group of lads to get the train back and one of them said, 'Are you going to the underground market tomorrow?' I said 'what for?' and he said, 'There's a stall there that sells pictures of live gigs and there'll be photographs of tonight's gig there.' I went the next day and bought a photograph of Weller in that brown mohair suit. It was the church of Weller from then on for me. He became my new God.

DEESIDE LEISURE CENTRE
27 MARCH 1982, QUEENSFERRY, UK

I WAS THERE: ALAN BURROWS

Were The Jam a Mod band? For me, everything changed with the release of 'Tube Station' in October 1978 and that run of extraordinarily brilliant singles and the albums *All Mod Cons* and *Setting Sons*. And I was the right age.

Quadrophenia was only released in August 1979 to spark a Mod revival, and I'm not sure it reached the North West in any great numbers. Revival bands The Chords, Secret Affair, Purple Hearts and The Lambrettas were all southern and fizzled out very quickly, mainly because they were rubbish.

There were one-inch Jam ties, mail ordered through adverts in the *NME*, etc., and Jam shoes, but hardly anyone walked around in tailored suits – they were the Mr Cleans of this world. The Stone Roses were scooter boys – look online at the state of Ian Brown's ripped jeans and dyed pink quiff at a rally; a million miles from Carnaby Street. The scooter scene lived on through the eighties, but was very much dressed-down MA1 bomber jackets and Doc Martens.

You never saw a Mod at Goodison Park. But there was Dave the Punk. When you went to London for footy, especially Chelsea away (on the ordinary train, not football specials), you'd see classic skinhead 'bovver boys' – Fred Perry t-shirts, braces, etc.

When The Jam played Liverpool Uni in May 1979, the Right to Work benefit gig at the city's Royal Court in April 1981 and the night of bedlam at Deeside Leisure Centre in March 1982, the concerts were full of lads you'd see at the match, dressed in what became labelled Casuals style, but what we'd call scally or just consider normal.

I say 'the night of bedlam' at Deeside, but it turns out there was an even worse riot in 1979 between punks and Mods, when Weller stopped the show, calling someone in the crowd a 'cunt' and offering him out.

On the English-Welsh border and close enough to a lot of big towns and cities, in those days the cops policed matches with escorts, truncheons, horses, riot shields and violence, and that night scallies and football firms descended on the area, arriving by train and piling out of Transit vans. There were rumours West Ham's ICF were there and everyone on edge, with fights throughout the evening on what was normally an ice rink. It sounds mental now, but don't forget a man was stabbed to death in May 1978 at a Depressions/Vibrators gig during clashes between Preston and Blackpool hooligans.

Gigs then were like football terraces, especially for bands that came out of punk. Kids could go, so you'd have packs of teens who'd bunk in or pay a couple of quid for a night out after bunking the train. And it wasn't just nights. Eric's in Liverpool laid on afternoon shows the same day as the main gig for children. You could walk up and pay on the door, so mates got dragged along – totally different to buying months in advance online with a credit card. Both football and gigs have been sanitised, mainly for the better – I certainly prefer my entertainment without the lingering fog of violence.

Even though the streets were full of tribes, most of the post-punk/new wave bands in the North West weren't heavily stylised. If you think about The Fall, Joy Division, Teardrop Explodes and the Bunnymen, you couldn't guess what their music sounded like from a photo. The Fall and Joy Division looked like what they were, lower-level admin office workers. And in the wider scheme of things, while you still had heavy metal fans and Teds knocking about, it seemed like there was a new sound every other week – Squeeze got bracketed with punk – and then the 2 Tone thing came along.

The Jam transcended everything else – they were out on their own. I even know of one Everton lad who claims he once 'bagged off' following a discussion with a girl over matching badges given away with the 'Strange Town' single and sold on the *Jam 'Em In* UK tour in 1979. They go for £20 on eBay now.

I WAS THERE: LAURA MAUER, AGE 15

I was a young Mod and a massive Jam fan. I lived in Neston, a small town on the Wirral, where a big gang of us were Mods. I was one of the younger ones, in days when we'd go to each other's houses to listen to music. We also attended a youth centre and piled on the settee to watch *Top Of The Pops*. When The Jam were at No.1 it was the best. We had discos at the 'youthy' and the Mods would all be on one side waiting for 'our' music, then we'd invade the dance floor.

Dad lived in Pentre, North Wales, walking distance from Deeside Leisure Centre, where The Jam were performing on 27 March 1982, which is probably why I offered to babysit my five-year-old brother with my younger sister that night. We were locked in, as I 'couldn't be trusted'. The second he left, I 'borrowed' money from my sister and climbed out of the window, taking the short 20-minute walk to the ice rink. By the time I arrived, The Alarm were already on, most people having gone in. There were several ticket touts outside, with prices at £3.50. I told one I had £1.32, putting to him, 'Who's going to buy one now?' He could see how desperate I was and sold me a ticket. I had more money on me but wanted a t-shirt.

I'd been to the ice rink many times, but this was different. Expectation built. I can't describe the emotion when The Jam came on. The crowd went off. I was so emotional and knew how lucky I was to be there. Everyone was singing along and dancing. It was the best night of my life, probably still is. The song I remember most was 'Tube Station'. I still get goosebumps hearing it. The atmosphere that song brings… I imagine myself there, and all the sounds and smells.

I got home just before my dad. My sister was worried sick. I didn't sleep a wink that night, and no one at school believed me the next day… but I knew. I managed to get a programme, and 42 years and many moves later, including a big one to Australia, that and my ticket are framed and in pride of place on the wall.

Paul Weller was my first crush. I had posters all over the bedroom wall. He broke my heart when they split. I love *All Mods Cons* and 'English Rose' gives me goosebumps each time I hear it. I have an 'English Rose' tattoo and still love to dress a bit Mod, loving my Fred Perry tops. Paul wore Lonsdale and boxer boots, and so did I. I was too young to understand what was going on in those times, but I love the anger in his words. I truly believe they have not dated.

I WAS THERE: PETER BOWERS

My final Jam gig and another buffeting in Deeside Leisure Centre. The atmosphere seemed somehow more aggressive and less boisterous than last time. It was *The Gift* LP tour, and with a brass section the band's sound was evolving. The times they were a-changin'.

I WAS THERE: CHRIS BITHELL, AGE 12

It was ten days after my twelfth birthday, the ticket a gift from my brother and his girlfriend. We arrived reasonably early, which meant we got close to the stage. The first support was RUDI, followed by The Alarm. It was all going well until John Weller introduced 'the best band in the fuckin' world, The Jam!' The crowd pushed and my tiny body was unable to cope. We moved over to the left of the stage and I sat, side-saddle, on the barrier to the ice rink. I'm sure Paul kept looking at me. The gig was absolutely awesome. Waiting for our lift home at the car park entrance, the tour bus drove by and I got to see the boys again. That made a twelve-year-old boy very happy.

SOLID BOND IN YOUR HEART

I WAS THERE: ANDY REED, AGE 14

The first Jam song I remember was 'Tube Station'. I'd attempt to record the charts every Sunday, ending with a DJ's voice over the end. The next time I was aware of them was when 'The Eton Rifles' came out. When 'Going Underground' came out, I became obsessed. That song was a game-changer. By now I had a paper round and money to buy records. Throughout the next few years, I was mad on The Jam, buying every magazine with interviews and posters.

I moved in late 1979 to inner-city Manchester, changing schools and having to make new friends. My first new pal, Gordon, lived across the road. His older brother was a part-time DJ so he had access to a massive collection. I'd call for him on the way to school and ended up going in and playing records, ending up late for school. The week it came out, I played the drum solo at the end of 'Funeral Pyre' to death.

During 1981, we spoke about going to see The Jam. My parents were not keen. (I was under five feet tall.) In early '82 they announced the *Trans Global Unity Express* tour and I was determined to see them. We didn't get tickets for either of the Manchester gigs but caught them at Deeside Leisure Centre. My parents ended up ordering four tickets via my aunt's credit card and they allowed me to go because Gordon's older brother Trevor had a car and his friend John would be driving.

nd 5pm. There were loads of people already knocking around. We had a walk around and then went back to the car. It wouldn't start so we had to call a garage to come out. He took most of our money, so that he had enough to pay for the repairs. I'd intended to buy a t-shirt.

The support was Rudi, plus a local band, after which Gordon and John went to the front to get as close to Bruce as they could. I stayed about halfway back with Trevor. He was a huge guy who no one would have pushed around. Gordon and myself were 14, but my mate was much bigger and had a moustache when he was twelve.

There was a massive surge forward when The Jam took the stage. I nearly went over, but Big Trevor looked after me. The big shock was that Weller had replaced the centre-parting he had on *Top Of The Pops* a few months earlier by a crew-cut.

After a quick hello, they went straight into 'Strange Town' and the venue exploded. We were getting pushed backwards, forwards, left and right while jumping around. They went into 'Carnation' next, the rest of the set flying by, and it was over far too quickly. I remember a few fights. We met Gordon and John outside. They'd ended up close to the front and talked all the way home about the gig.

OPERA HOUSE
28 MARCH 1982, BLACKPOOL, UK

I WAS THERE: ERIKA WARD

In the late seventies, my boyfriend Ian, now my husband, was an avid Jam fan. As we left school in 1980, we were 'on a break' when my friend Angie said The Jam were coming to our hometown, Blackpool, in early 1982, playing the Opera House… did I fancy seeing them? I was hooked on *Sound Affects*, so it was 'count me in.'

After the gig we went to the stage door and whilst I talked to other fans, Angie was talking to their coach driver. We were on our way home when she said we'd be meeting the band the next day at the Imperial Hotel. 'Of course we are,' I said.

The following day she knocked on my door, saying, 'Quick! We need to catch the bus, or we'll be late.'

At reception she announced we had an appointment with The Jam. One of the session men saw us and told us to help ourselves to croissants as the boys were just having a swim. It was a 'pinch me' moment. After ten minutes or so, sure enough they joined us. We took a few photos and had a surreal hour-long chat about the night before.

All these years on, if ever The Jam are on the radio or telly, I say, 'Did I ever mention I met The Jam?' Sadly, my husband never got the chance. I often wonder if they remember the day they met me.

Erika Ward got to meet Rick Buckler, Bruce Foxton & Paul Weller

I WAS THERE: KAREN WINROW

I used to follow The Jam everywhere, even got to meet them all at Blackpool after a gig. I never spoke… I was that nervous. Bruce was my favourite. I got a pic of the two of us. It was in a frame on my bedroom wall for years.

I WAS THERE: PAUL BURROWS

The first ever record I bought was 'Crazy Horses' by The Osmonds. As I got a bit older, I delved into all sorts of stuff. I listened to quite a bit of heavy rock at the time, Deep Purple and things like that, looking for something that I'd like that wasn't quite chart music. My cousin picked up on the punk movement in probably '77, '78, and to begin with, I thought 'I'm not overly keen on this,' but then I suddenly really got into it. I saw The Jam and the Sex Pistols and The Stranglers on *Top Of The Pops*.

I loved The Jam because I could just relate to them, but it didn't really start until the third album, *All Mod Cons*, and then they had a run of singles, and I remember being at school, and buying 'Strange Town' and playing that in my bedroom and thinking 'wow, this is brilliant.' And then I turned it over and it had a brilliant B-side as well.

I didn't get to see The Jam until near the end of their career. I'll never forget the concert, because we missed the opening song. We got in there and I was going down the stairs, and you could hear them playing and I remember thinking, 'Oh God, we've missed a song here.' They had sax and brass players and things on stage, and I'd probably have preferred to have seen him without that really, but they were trying to move on a bit.

Because that was the music you grew up with, it'll always be with you.

TOP RANK
29-31 MARCH 1982, SHEFFIELD, UK

I WAS THERE: MATTHEW COLLINGTON

My first ever proper grown-up gig. I remember the feeling and the smell of 'Private Hell'. I've still got the t-shirt.

I WAS THERE: DALE MOSLEY, AGE 15

The Jam in March and September 1982 were my first two gigs. My older brother had *In The City* and friends at school also listened to them. There was no other music I really identified with. I borrowed £5 from a mate and bought a ticket for Sheffield Top Rank. The bouncers weren't going to let me in as it was over-15s only, and although I was 15, I looked about twelve. But some proper blokes behind told them to let me in. It was freezing cold, pissing down with rain, and these blokes were wearing short-sleeved Fred Perry tops! The atmosphere was unbelievable, so packed I couldn't move. John Weller introduced them. I lasted about an hour at the front then had to go to back to get some air. Before the encore, Paul Weller walked on and said he wanted to apologise for playing like a cunt!

I WAS THERE: ANTHONY JOHN, AGE 17

It was great finally seeing the last of three nights at the Top Rank. They had a brass section at the back and hearing tracks like 'Private Hell' with Bruce's thunderous bass and Rick's powerful drumming was fantastic. They had a soul DJ as warm-up. Along with The Clash, this had the best atmosphere of any gig I've been to. You can watch all the videos and DVDs, and listen to live albums, but you only know what the atmosphere was like if you were there. If you know, you know… kind of like being at a relegation decider or penalty shoot-out at the football. It lasts 90-plus minutes. Being there was priceless.

I WAS THERE: ANTHONY MILLER

My friend and I finished school early, put our best Mod gear on and caught the bus to Sheffield, making our way up the incline to the Top Rank. I bought a programme and t-shirt and tried to keep them straight during the concert. It was hot and sweaty, and my ears rang for the next few days, but I didn't care – I'd seen my heroes live, and they were amazing.

I saw them again at Leeds' Queens Hall in September. My first impression of the venue was that it was a shit hole. I later found out it was an old tram shed, very rough and ready. It didn't affect the quality of the concert though, and they played a lot of older songs.

I WAS THERE: NEIL SPRUCE

I saw them three nights running in 1982 – twice at Sheffield Top Rank and then at Leeds' Queens Hall. We ran the old man ragged, having him ferry me and my brother around! I'd seen them previously at Bridlington Spa, where I queued with my younger brother to ensure he got autographs. It was out the back and the wagons were running while they were being loaded with the stage gear. Now, every time I smell diesel it takes me back there.

QUEENS HALL
1 APRIL 1982, LEEDS, UK

I WAS THERE: GRAHAM CLARK

I always intended to see The Jam but didn't get around to it until the spring of

1982. The venue was not exactly perfect – during the day it was used as an indoor car park – but it was the biggest indoor place Leeds had and so was regularly used for concerts. It was hot and sweaty. You literally slipped around on the painted concrete floor. The band were tight as ever, though one could sense Paul Weller was going to call it a day for The Jam. *The Gift* hinted at the more soulful direction he was taking, as later witnessed with The Style Council. The gig felt like a final farewell, albeit a soulful one.

I WAS THERE: LISA HARTFORD
I'd lost my voice by the end. Afterwards, my friend Julia and I were sat on the steps of the Queens Hotel, our feet in the gutter, waiting for a lift home. We had to pull our feet on to the pavement when a coach pulled up… and they got out! We were gobsmacked. Sadly, by the time we'd got over our shock, they'd walked into the hotel.

I WAS THERE: BRIAN YOUNG, RUDI
Dave Liddle introduced us informing the audience that 'Crimson' was 'Single Of the Week' in *Sounds* that very day – and we went down an absolute storm and had to play it twice! As it was also our last date on the tour, The Jam held a post gig party for us and we were sad to bid everyone farewell. Typically, while The Jam stayed in a posh hotel that night, we kipped in student flats that one of our pals from Belfast who was now living in Leeds had gained access to. Next morning we woke to the sight of a line of policemen heading towards our accommodation. They were looking for the Yorkshire Ripper, not some scruffy Belfast punk combo… Phew!

Later that year Paul Weller rang me at home as he was keen to play in Belfast. The Jam had visited Galway and Dublin in October 1978 but some of the roadcrew had been in the British Army and were reluctant to set foot this side of the border in case of possible repercussions. In a bitterly divided country where you could buy Jam shoes in red, white and blue for the Protestants/Loyalists and green, white and orange for the Catholics/Nationalists, who could say those worries were unfounded? Paul mentioned that someone had suggested Windsor Park, a large football stadium, as a possible venue. I told him I didn't think it had ever been used for any concerts but that we'd love to see them play here. Sadly, nothing ever came of it.

I WAS THERE: TONY METCALF
The band played my hometown of Huddersfield twice in '77 but I was too young to go, or know, so it all started in 1978 for me when I heard 'David Watts' in the school youth club. This led to *All Mod Cons*. Chuck in an older cousin who was

going out with the lead singer of the Killermeters and the writing was on the wall… the Mod life beckoned. I was 15 years old in '79. I saw most of the revival bands but the holy trinity of Paul, Rick and Bruce evaded me until 1982 and the Trans Global Express Tour at Leeds Queens Hall. ('April 1st? These tickets best not be a joke… they cost £4.50!'). The whole of Leeds from the train station (via a few pubs) to the venue was a sea of green Parkas. The actual gig is a bit of a blur but I remember the crowd chanting for 'Tube Station' and getting short shrift from PW. With hindsight, this was definitely the tour he decided on the split. The gig was more akin to a football match and very hostile… Luckily, I got to see them once more in the September. It was the same venue on the *Solid Bond* tour (£5 this time. Are they taking the piss?) The details are sketchy but the memory and the influence are still strong.

The best band in the fucking world? Certainly in the top one!

I WAS THERE: PAUL CRINNION, AGE 15

Living in the North-East in the late seventies meant we were late to the party. *Top Of The Pops* and John Peel were our main link to punk, new wave and the Mod revival. From the first time I heard bands like Blondie, The Addicts and The Boomtown Rats I was hooked; this new wave of music was for me. What cash I could scrape together picking spuds and dishwashing in a hotel went on records.

The first time The Jam were on *Top Of The Pops*, in 1977, I had already heard them on John Peel and seen pictures in magazines, I loved their sound and look and seeing the passion, power and cool look started a lifelong love of the best band in the world. Being eleven years old, I had to make do with magazines, records, TV and radio to follow their progress. It wasn't until I was 15 that I got to see them live.

With my mate Peter, I managed to get tickets for a coach trip to Leeds to see the *Trans Global Unity Express* tour. We were probably the youngest on the coach. Listening to other passengers recounting their experiences of seeing the band live added to our excitement. There was a great mix of Mod fashion, which given how hard it was to get anything other than army surplus in the North-East was testament to the fans' commitment to the band and the movement.

The Queens Hall was huge. The floor was covered in a fine layer of grey dust that formed a fine paste as moisture levels from thousands of fans increased. My Doc Martens were ruined by the start and never quite recovered. The Questions played first, but no support act could have prepared me for the energy level that overtook the crowd when John Weller eventually announced the band. The crowd surged forward and at a number of points during the gig I was able to lift my feet off the floor and remain upright, such was the fever of the crowd to get close to the band.

Every tune, from 'Running On The Spot' to 'Funeral Pyre', further endorsed what I still believe today – at their best no band could touch them when it came to stage presence and energy. I could feel the drum and bass pass through me. It felt like I was part of an enormous living engine driven on by the relentless power of Rick and Bruce. Within minutes of the first song, my voice was failing as I joined the crowd in singing every word along with our heroes.

The atmosphere was fantastic. I saw very little if any of the trouble my worried mother had warned me to steer clear of. Moving and chanting in unison for sadly what seemed far too short a time was one of the greatest experiences. It cemented forever a love of Mod music, so much so I picked up a guitar and joined a band at my first opportunity. The show was over after what seemed such a brief time, not that we were short-changed, as the set covered all the latest tracks and many of what by then were classics. We found our coach after walking from the venue surrounded by excited voices, recounting every song and every movement.

At school the next day I was tired and hoarse, but proud of my now scarred Doc Marten boots and my still sweaty, damp donkey jacket. They felt like badges of honour. I felt part of something bigger, something for my generation, something I'd never truly ever leave. Now the challenge was where to get a Parka.

I WAS THERE: GARY COX

I went to the soundcheck and they only let a few people in. Weller had gone from a Small Faces look to getting it all chopped off. They had a poet supporting them, and Red Lorry Yellow Lorry. It was a real angry gig. Weller started swearing at the crowd. People were saying 'play 'Tube Station'!' and he said, 'If you wanna play 'Tube Station', go and play it at home on your fucking records.' It was the angriest I'd seen him at a gig. They had an organist and they had Steve Thomas on saxophone and somebody else to bring a bit more rhythm to some of the songs that they'd written on *The Gift*, but Weller wasn't happy. His head was down. He didn't introduce the songs properly. Introducing 'Circus' he said, 'This is one of the new ones. You probably won't fucking like it.' There was a bit of resentment towards the crowd. Perhaps he thought that his audience would grow up with his songs as he grew up, but he didn't like people shouting out for old stuff. Maybe he was thinking, 'I'm probably not getting through here.' I took a friend who had never seen them live and they said afterwards, 'I don't know why you really like them, because they were pretty poor.'

CITY HALL
3 & 4 APRIL 1982, NEWCASTLE-UPON-TYNE, UK

I WAS THERE: PETER SMITH

This was a very different Jam to the early angry young men. While Weller remained the quintessential young Mod, clearly influenced by his hero Steve Marriott in particular, the band had mellowed, becoming more chart heroes, and the crowd much more, dare I say it, middle-of-the-road pop fans. Perhaps this was a marker that the end was in sight. The band had run its course. It had successfully blended punk, sixties Mod and pop, and in doing so helping move punk forward. Whatever the reason, Weller was beginning to feel this was the end of The Jam, who were soon to disband. I'd see them once more on their farewell tour. Looking back, they left a legacy of great singles and incredible, intense, energetic live performances.

I WAS THERE: MARK RAILSTON

There's a group of about 60 kids waiting outside Newcastle City Hall for a soundcheck, hoping they'll let us in, despite ever-increasing numbers. The tour bus pulls up, the imposing figure of tour manager Kenny Wheeler stepping off and promptly blocking out the weak spring sunshine, followed by Weller sporting a very short haircut. He looks tense and apprehensive, but this dissipates as the crowd spots him, a spontaneous football-style chant of 'skinhead, skinhead, skinhead' going up, fingers pointing. He breaks into laughter, goes a bit red in the face, which in turn makes us laugh.

I WAS THERE: GRAEME DAWSON

My next Jam encounter was back at the City Hall for the *Trans Global Unity Express* tour. I also caught the soundcheck. I was with another school friend, Colin Mould (RIP). We ran to get to the front and were standing so close to the stage that we could have touched Bruce Foxton's shoes. There were 80 to 100 kids there. Rick Buckler signed my drumstick and the band signed my plaster cast, as I had a broken wrist. This date stands out among all the others. Bruce was getting cramp in his arm and had to keep stopping, waving his arm around as it was too painful for him to play.

Newcastle soundcheck

Photo by Andrew Clarke

I WAS THERE: DAVE PRATT

I saw The Jam for the final times on the tour to promote *The Gift*. Me, Canty and Gordon went to both gigs at Newcastle, travelling up early for the soundchecks each day. By then, I'd become a bit disillusioned with Paul Weller and hadn't even bothered to buy the LP – I felt their music was heading in a direction that wasn't to my taste, and that Weller had turned into a pretentious arsehole in his interviews with the music press. As a live act they were still pretty good though and, despite my misgivings, I enjoyed both gigs. Later in the year, The Jam announced they were splitting up and there was an outpouring of grief from their legions of fans. I, on the other hand, felt it was definitely the right time.

PLAYHOUSE THEATRE
6 APRIL 1982, EDINBURGH, UK

I WAS THERE: PATRICIA MACGOWAN

'Put your hands together for the best band in the fucking world, The Jam!'

APOLLO THEATRE
7 & 8 APRIL 1982, GLASGOW, UK

I WAS THERE: JOHN KERR, AGE 16

The only time I saw The Jam. I was gutted when they split.

I WAS THERE: STEPHEN HOUGH

The Jam meant everything to me when I was a kid. I first got into them when 'The Eton Rifles' came out. I'd seen them earlier on TV, doing 'David Watts', but was too young to appreciate them. Me and my mates were totally hooked. We'd save our money and twice a year go down to Carnaby Street to get our new gear. The Jam totally shaped my life, the music I listened to, and remain the loudest, greatest band I've seen.

I caught them on the *Trans Global* tour. They did two nights at the Apollo. They were brilliant nights, and created such noise and power for three men. It was unreal. I also saw them at Bingley Hall after that, and then on the farewell tour. Every night was an absolute event, never beaten to this day. I was on the front row at the Apollo and can still feel that energy today.

I WAS THERE: MICHAEL CONWAY, AGE 15

I saw The Jam twice in 1982 at the Glasgow Apollo. I was 15, going on 16. They were promoting the *Gift* album the first time, and then I saw them again for their

Photos by Andrew Clarke

final Scottish gig that November. I went with high school friends both times. In April, my school friend Mark O'Neill and I went up to Glasgow on the train from Port Glasgow. The final Scottish gig was mentioned in the *Daily Record* one morning, in those days before the internet and mobile phones. We found a place in Greenock that was running a 52-seater bus with a Jam ticket included in the price. I went to that one with school friends Christine O'Donnell and Alison Devlin. It was a very wet, dark Thursday night. I'll never forget that night. It was dead exciting seeing the best band in the UK but sad year too because, after that, The Jam were gone.

JOHANESHOVS ISSTADION
16 APRIL 1982, STOCKHOLM, SWEDEN

A ten-date European leg gets underway in Sweden followed by dates in Denmark, the Netherlands, Belgium and France.

PARADISO
24 APRIL 1982, AMSTERDAM, NETHERLANDS

I WAS THERE: KERRY MORIARTY

The best of six gigs I saw The Jam play was the third I saw, at The Paradiso, Amsterdam. It's a small venue and I was up against the stage, directly in front of Bruce Foxton. The intensity was off the scale and the surprise of the night was hearing The Jam perform 'David Watts'. Five months later I saw them at the Royal Court Theatre in Liverpool, a great gig as they performed a lot of older material (from *All Mod Cons* and *Setting Sons*), which was unusual as their sets were always bang up to date. Little did we know that the band had already agreed to split.

I WAS THERE: ERIC TRAA, AGE 19

My friend Bas was from Utrecht. We were 19 years old. He was a real Mod at the time and I wasn't. He bought my ticket. In 1981, we'd hitchhiked from Utrecht to Brighton in our Parkas. It was my first connection with the British Mod scene, including fleeing from the skins in London. Bas said that The Jam were a great band to see. I didn't understand him. Was this Mod? Soul? Anyway, we were going to the Paradiso!

I stood in front of the band and to the left and it was so loud and heavy. The first song, 'Eton Rifles', blew me away and I was impressed by how involved the people around me were, and not just the English members of the audience. We were jumping around for half the concert, hearing songs like 'In The Crowd', 'Town Called Malice' and 'That's Entertainment'. I'd never seen anything like this before.

That night The Jam changed my life. Their spirit, lyrics, clothing and style have taken me to where I am now. I've seen Weller more than 300 times, including many times at the Paradiso, one of his favourite venues. And I finally met Paul in London in November 2023. I told him I'd waited 40 years for this moment. He loved to hear it.

ANCIENNE HALL
27 APRIL 1982, BRUSSELS, BELGIUM

I WAS THERE: GAVIN JONES

The venue reminded me of a smaller, scruffier De Montfort Hall, with a stage at one end, a balcony all round, and no seats. I decided to go upstairs, next to the stage. There were lots of Belgian Mods, skins and punks, giving it a charged atmosphere, like some of the punk gigs a few years before. There were Union flags dotted around the crowd and stage, giving it a patriotic feel, more so when the Belgians started singing 'Argentina' to taunt the Brits. (The Falklands War was on at the time.)

Eventually The Jam came on and delivered a fantastic gig, similar to *The Gift* tour back home but with a few older songs, delivered with extra aggression, with Weller supreme! I was glad I picked the balcony – all the way through the skins were fighting downstairs, chants of 'England' keeping the atmosphere charged. At one point Paul said, 'Here's a song about fucking England,' and did new song 'The Great Depression'. They ended with five encores, including 'Butterfly Collector' and 'David Watts'. It was a fantastic gig and a great atmosphere, but then we had to go outside and wait for the coaches, the skins kicking off and the police going in with batons, hitting a few Brits. I ducked out of the way of one baton.

HIPPODROME DE LA PORTE DE PANTIN
29 APRIL 1982, PARIS, FRANCE

I WAS THERE: MICHEL GARCIN

The Jam's first records displayed such energy that I immediately appreciated them and linked them to the punk movement I opportunely discovered during the summer of 1976 and 1977, spent in London to improve my English. I didn't see the band then, but looked forward to them. When they came to France, their popularity was such that their concert was transferred to the Hippodrome de la Porte de Pantin because the room initially planned (Pavillon Baltard) was too small. What a success in this 'modern world'!

Michel Garcin wore his Jam t-shirt when he saw Weller solo in 2023

When the group split up, I had difficulty following Paul Weller, although I saw him at the Salle Pleyel, Paris in 2023 in front of an enthusiastic if seated audience. I miss the early years of the trio voted the best dressed group, and I couldn't resist wearing my Jam t-shirt at this show.

RICHIE COLISEUM
14 MAY 1982, COLLEGE PARK, MARYLAND

The Jam's sixth North American tour opens at Washington's University of Maryland, with a further 14 shows to follow. The Gift peaks at No.82 in a 16-week run on the Billboard 200 chart.

THE PALLADIUM
15 & 18 MAY 1982, NEW YORK, NEW YORK

I WAS THERE: RACHEL FELDER, AGE 14

It was a big deal to see these English bands in the US because their videos wouldn't air much here. Seeing them live was so precious because it was your only real chance to see what they looked like. The first Jam single that I remember coming out was 'The Eton Rifles'. By the time I got into them they didn't tour the States again until *The Gift*. It was about a month before I turned 15. They didn't have

SOLID BOND IN YOUR HEART

much of a profile here beyond these little pockets of British music fanatics who were mostly in the big cities. I knew about them from college radio and from buying the *NME*, *Melody Maker* and *Sounds* on import, so when they announced they were coming to New York I was just beside myself with excitement.

There was a bit of a tone in the British press that maybe the band's final days were clicking forward because of the shift in sound. I didn't love the shift in sound so much, and I was disappointed about that they didn't play any of the songs that I was most passionate about, like 'Down In The Tube Station At Midnight' or anything from *All Mod Cons*.

I was really excited about the show, thinking about what I would wear to the show and how I would look Modish. I went with my best friend and a mutual friend. We got there really, really early. The Palladium was a venue that the new wave and punk bands would play when they got on the road to being big. I saw Elvis Costello play there, the Ramones played there, the bigger bands of the alternative scene. The Jam had played CBGBs in 1978.

I remember the grit and bile in Paul Weller's delivery and voice. That was more subdued on the records and became more subdued as time went on, particularly on the album they were touring and the vibe of those songs. I didn't expect that magnificent anger and passion to come across but – boy, oh boy – did that come across from literally the first few bars. They didn't talk between the songs and that was disappointing. It was the only taste of The Jam in person I would ever get, and as an Anglophile in America the Englishness of the banter between songs was something I craved.

But the show was great. I floated out of the venue. It had seats but everybody was standing up and dancing. I was very hot and sweaty and dehydrated because we had got there super early and we didn't want to leave our seats.

There are certain bands I've seen since where I really feel there's a link between that energy of the jam and those more recent bands, the Arctic Monkeys being the big one in my mind. I saw them very early and I was just struck by that by that real kinetic energy, which reminded me of Paul Weller during The Jam days.

Although I was only 15, I'd already seen a lot of shows. I was a regular at CBGBs at the age of 13 as soon as I was old enough to get in. I saw all the New York shows by my faves, people like Echo and the Bunnymen and The Specials. The Jam weren't in their prime when I saw them, but they were still absolutely jaw-droppingly great, and I say that even though it wasn't my dream set list by the band. You'd see a lot of good bands, but not many *great* bands. The Jam were a GREAT live band!

A PEOPLE'S HISTORY OF THE JAM

I WAS THERE: BOBBY TANZILO

I became a Jam fan around the time of *Setting Sons* while growing up in New York City. I would wait for each new release (as an import), running to the record shops to get them. I saw them a couple of times, the most memorable being at The Palladium, which is one of the best concerts I've ever seen. We waited outside all day and when the tour bus stopped out front, Bruce Foxton appeared at the window, waving, and they let us in to the soundcheck. There must have been a few dozen of us outside. Everyone rushed to the edge of the stage, but I saw John Weller sat in front of the sound desk and went over to sit next to him. We chatted for most of the soundcheck. He asked where I was from. I told him Brooklyn. He said, 'Oh, we went to a party once in Brooklyn.'

The venue – the old Academy of Music, a traditional theatre setup – was rocking. It was packed and there was a metal railing in front of the stage. My friends and I were being pushed up against it so hard that one of my friends got a cut on her leg. But The Jam were on fire and played a great set. They were my favourite band and have pretty much always been.

The other most memorable time was in May 1981, around the time 'Funeral Pyre' came out. Someone got me a ticket to be in the studio audience of *The Tomorrow Show* with Tom Snyder at NBC in the Rockefeller Center. Somewhere I still have the cameramen's cue sheets from the show, which one of the cameramen gave me afterwards. I was wearing a *Sound Affects* tour t-shirt, but it was cold in the studio and about halfway through I put on a jacket. The cameraman said he'd planned to focus on me and my shirt when going to a commercial break until then. They played 'Pretty Green' and 'Funeral Pyre' and did an interview with Tom Snyder, who had also had The Clash, PiL and others on the show.

After the taping was done, I walked down to the front, where Paul was standing by his gear. I wished him a happy birthday and got a 'thanks, mate' back.

Being a fan in the US when they were still together was both similar and different to being a fan in the UK. It was a lot harder to find them here – you had to be vigilant to find the records and magazines. And they didn't often tour widely, so if you didn't live somewhat near a big city like NYC, Boston, Chicago or LA, you might never have had the chance. It's also different in that pretty much no one else knew who they were. My bedroom as a kid was wallpapered in Jam posters and my cousin and I jokingly convinced his sister The Jam were The Beatles after John Lennon died. But it was also similar to being a fan in the UK in that you felt a part of something. When we were outside that Palladium gig, there were a few dozen of us and while we weren't a huge group, we felt part of something together, and

40-plus years later it's still that way when I meet someone who has been a long-time fan. There's an instant bond. A Solid Bond.

I was lucky enough to interview Paul when *Wake Up The Nation* came out. I started out saying, 'I want to mostly talk about the new record,' and he said, 'Good!' Like Paul I'm not a fan of living in the past, so I've never wanted to see them get back together. It's a badge of honour that they've never chased the money and done a reunion or kept going when they shouldn't have (like The Clash did with *Cut The Crap*).

CNE COLISEUM
24 MAY 1982, TORONTO, CANADA

I WAS THERE: IVAR HAMILTON

In the eighties, this was the go-to venue between playing concert halls and arenas in Toronto, holding around 5,000, and where the band played their final show in Toronto before disbanding. At this point, The Jam had somewhat hit the mainstream in Canada, 'Town Called Malice' getting multiple station airplay. This final show was presented by both CHUM FM but also top 40 station, CHUM AM. But the audience that turned up were still CFNY; that would never change due to their overwhelming support.

The show wasn't great, due to a venue built primarily as a horse exhibition palace and hosting dog and cat shows for many decades. It hosted big names in the sixties, such as Jimi Hendrix, and The Doors, but was never ideal for concerts and the audio was terrible. Motörhead played there in May, bringing the *Bomber* light show with them. The sound for that had fans livid at how bad it was, so it wasn't a surprise that it happened for The Jam.

When CFNY changed over to CDs in the mid-eighties, I managed to keep some of the original 'in studio' 45s from The Jam. I began working for PolyGram at the end of 1988 (later bought by Universal Music) in promotion, then marketing, ending my career in catalogue marketing, retiring at the end of 2023. I was able to support The Jam, The Style Council and Paul Weller solo projects for over 40 years and even went to From The Jam's one local appearance. I'm proud to have been able to.

KOSEI NENKIN KAIKAN HALL
11 JUNE 1982, TOKYO, JAPAN

The band play what proves to be their final Japanese tour, taking in shows in Tokyo, Osaka and Nagoya.

A PEOPLE'S HISTORY OF THE JAM

I WAS THERE: MICK TALBOT

In the summer of '82, (Paul Weller) got in touch and said, 'Look, you've got to keep this under your hat but I'm wrapping up The Jam and I've got a few ideas, are you interested?' At that time, it seemed full of potential, but I wasn't quite sure how lasting or what it exactly would be, but it sounded like a good prospect. It was important for Paul to know you had some background in it. We were quite surprised at how many books we had in common and things outside music that influenced us growing up, so that helped us well – you didn't have to sort of explain things to each other. I was already aware of Colin MacInnes. My dad had some of those books from that trilogy. Paul surprised me with his depth of knowledge about stuff. It was almost like we were playing a game of chess, taking an examination on Nell Dunn, Ken Loach, French New Wave…'.

'JUST WHO IS THE 5 O'CLOCK HERO?'
6 JULY 1982

The import-only single reaches No.8 in the UK charts in a five-week Top 40 run.

'THE BITTEREST PILL (I EVER HAD TO SWALLOW)' RELEASED
6 SEPTEMBER 1982

The penultimate Jam single reaches No.2 in the charts.

I WAS THERE: KEELEY MOSS, KEELEY

'Fire and Skill', The Jam's much-mouthed modus operandi. Paul Weller's sonic ferocity, wielding his vintage Rickenbacker like a bloodied bayonet as fellow sonic squaddies, Bruce and Rick, brought up the rear with military precision. The angry jabs of seething social commentaries in Weller's peerless songs, the scorching shards of molten metallic guitar, the taut rhythmic brilliance of Foxton's basslines and Buckler's lock-tight tom-thumping. The best punk band that ever was and the best mod beat group to ever stride a stage.

Keeley Moss felt The Jam saved the best for (almost) last

But… There was another Jam to come, a different beast with a different beat. And

SOLID BOND IN YOUR HEART

– whisper it – it would be the best Jam of all. One that produced my favourite single of all-time by any artist, with the song that ironically more than any other divided the band's fanatical fans and for all its lofty UK No.2 chart placing has all too often been the subject of scorn, even derision, among their notoriously spiky fanbase.

'The Bitterest Pill (I Ever Had To Swallow)' was released seven weeks before Weller's shocking and controversial decision to call time on the band at their commercial and creative peak. But it would seal Weller's rise to the ranks of his heroes, spearheading the band's finest fusion of poetic realism and emotional grandeur with the creation of a modern soul anthem that would stand tall among the most lauded soul songs of any era.

Powered by a lead vocal that's not so much sung as sobbed, it's an exemplary example of the sincerity of Weller's new soul vision, one that would find fuller expression in the imminent formation of The Style Council. Everything about 'The Bitterest Pill (I Ever Had To Swallow)' is perfect – boasting magnificent guitar lines and an achingly-beautiful string arrangement that floats and weaves though the track, set to a gorgeous tune and the most painfully poetic set of lyrics Weller would ever write:

In your white lace and your wedding bells
You look the picture of contented new wealth
But from the onlooking fool who believed your lies
I wish this grave would open up and swallow me alive
For the bitterest pill is hard to swallow
The love I gave hangs in sad-coloured, mocking shadows.
When the wheel of fortune broke, you fell to me
Out of grey skies to change my misery
The vacant spot, your beating heart took its place
But now I watch smoke leave my lips and fill an empty room

In 'The Bitterest Pill (I Ever Had To Swallow)' Weller writes of a betrayal so savage, so viciously and callously inflicted by a relationship partner, the sense of injustice with which he seethes throughout is more than a match for the anger and bitterness of any of the more lauded class-war staples of The Jam's earlier work.

Weller is assisted ably on this stunning song by his supporting cast – Foxton and Buckler provide a rock-solid backbone, serving the song as sensibly and sensitively as ever. An unusual feature is the backing vocals – Weller is joined on the choruses in a duet with Jennie Matthias of The Belle Stars, who lends a feminine flourish perfectly in keeping with the song's soft power.

Weller's guitar chimes gloriously throughout with a crystalline glissando jangle. It would be my favourite element of the track were it not for the lyrics – the most agonisingly resigned examination of a broken heart ever set to music.

Now autumn's breeze blows summer's leaves through my life
Twisted and broken dawn, no days with sunlight
The dying spark, you left your mark on me
The promise of your kiss, but with someone else
For the bitterest pill is mine to swallow
The love I gave hangs in sad-coloured, mocking shadows
The bitterest pill is mine to take
If I took if for a hundred years, I couldn't feel any more ill.

With this single, The Jam saved the best for (almost) last. There would be one more single (strident, defiant UK No.1, 'Beat Surrender') and a farewell UK tour. But with 'The Bitterest Pill', Weller could bring a halt to the band, having accomplished the creation of a near-perfect discography – six albums and roughly 20 singles – while having secured their status as the biggest band in Britain… all in the space of just six years. But great as most of those other singles undoubtedly are, none possess the devastating drama and overwhelming outpouring of emotion of 'The Bitterest Pill'.

'The dying spark, you left your mark on me,' indeed.

CLIFFS PAVILION
20 SEPTEMBER 1982, SOUTHEND-ON-SEA, UK

The Solid Bond In Your Heart tour gets underway at Leas Cliff Pavilion, Southend-on-Sea, before a return to Shepton Mallet, Brighton, Leicester, Liverpool, Edinburgh, Whitley Bay and Leeds.

I WAS THERE: JOHN LYON

They were a great band. I saw them twice and wish I'd had the opportunity to see them more. A really tight three-piece all bouncing off each other. Weller was a master frontman and controlled the stage and audience, though he didn't have to do too much as his adoring fans would go wild. As usual at Jam gigs, the floor in front of the stage was a mass of youths pogoing to their favourite songs. The atmosphere was electric and they always did a mass of encores… usually coming back on at least twice, sometimes three times.

I saw them in my hometown at the Cliffs Pavilion. It was supposed to be limited to 500, but there were definitely more there. It was packed out. I also saw them at Wembley Arena on the farewell tour, supported by Big Country, and that didn't disappoint. I was gutted I'd never get a chance to see them again though. They were the band of the time and disbanded at their peak.

What got me into them was seeing them perform 'The Eton Rifles' on *Top Of The Pops*, and they really influenced me with their attitude and clothes, not just the music. Once I started researching them, I went out and bought their past albums and was hooked. The Mod revival was taking off, all my mates were into it, and I followed suit, eagerly awaiting next release, 'Going Underground'. Next thing was to save up and buy a scooter. I have six now.

I WAS THERE: RICHARD NOBLE

I couldn't believe it – The Jam were going to play my hometown! Buoyed with the success of the photos I took of the previous Ally Pally gig, I intended to take a camera again. But a week before, disaster struck – it malfunctioned, and although it was under warranty, Argos wouldn't give me a replacement immediately; it had to be sent off to the manufacturer and wouldn't be back in time. I had to use another option, a camera with square bulb attachments... which in a mosh at the front, unsurprisingly, turned out to be useless. In fact, after getting the pics developed (being film, you didn't know how good or bad they were until then) they were so crap due to camera shake that my boss saw them and asked if it was someone in the nude. It was actually Paul.

The support was local band The Cards whose singer, Mark Roe, I later found out was one of the red tunic soldiers for 'The Eton Rifles' on *Top Of The Pops*. The local paper, understandably, gave them quite a bit of pre-gig publicity. I'd just started to learn to play drums and knew what a great gig that was. A few years later, playing in my own band locally, Mark Roe did the sound.

The Jam kicked off with 'Ghosts', with a different bassline than on the record. It sounded great. Although it gave the song a different feel, I always wondered if Bruce wished he'd used that line instead of what was recorded or if he hadn't come up with it by the time it was recorded. They also did 'Away From The Numbers', which I wasn't expecting as mostly later songs were played. Someone behind me shouted out for 'In The City'. Good luck with that one, I thought. When the gig ended, the best thing was that it was only a short trip home. Next morning, after my mate picked me up for work, knowing I was a huge fan (obsessed, even) he let me drone on about how great it was all the way, a good 30 minutes. I even said, 'It looked like they enjoyed themselves and I reckon they'll come to Southend again!' What did I know – less than three months later, it was all over…

I WAS THERE: SEAN WASTELL

It was announced in the *Evening Echo* that The Jam were to add an extra date to the *Solid Bond* tour. Result! I borrowed £5 for the ticket off my mum and we agreed to bunk off school next day to get them. We purchased our orange cardboard tickets then walked back to my friend Watti's house, stopping a few times to look and check it was really happening, once asking some random lady to confirm, reading the name off the ticket. Rather strange.

On the night, I had a nervous can of Coke in Rossi's on the seafront, then walked up the steps to the venue. Schoolboy mistake – I had a cream golf jacket, white shirt and tie, soon sweat-soaked.

Watching support act The Cards, I couldn't help notice they had Weller's Rickenbacker, with The Boys sticker on it. This was my second proper gig, having been lucky enough to see The Specials two years before, also at The Cliffs, but I was twelve years old then and stood back from the mosh pit as all the skins seemed six foot plus. I was probably five foot five now though, big enough to look after myself!

Before they started, we were probably five or six rows from the front, and I was boiling in my jacket and tie. The boys came on and there was a massive push, which seemed life threatening. They kicked off with 'Ghosts', my friend Watti's favourite song. He shouted 'yeah!' and I then didn't see him for about half an hour. It was electric, and the band mentioned that it was a cracking gig. I spoke to Rick Buckler many years later and he confirmed as much.

After, we asked the roadies for Weller's cold tea, which he had to drink on stage. We all had a sip. They wouldn't give us a set list. I particularly remember 'The Modern World' and 'In The Crowd'. I didn't dream that Paul would soon split the band. I thought I'd see them loads after that. I didn't even try to get tickets for the final tour. I was too upset. What a dickhead!

I WAS THERE: JOE SHIELDS

This was my top Jam gig. My home town Southend, when they came to The Cliffs Pavilion the day after my 19th birthday. I had ticket number 19. I took the day off work. We were hanging around the lobby and the bar area. I was with Pete Helmer, guitarist with The Leepers, and my mate Gary. We saw John Weller and Kenny Wheeler and they let us in for the soundcheck and I remember sitting there in the Cliffs, which is quite a small venue, watching them do a ten-minute jam session of

'Precious'. It was like watching them in an empty school hall.

My mum had sent in a request to Mike Read on Radio 1 which he read out that morning on the breakfast show. He played 'The Bitterest Pill' and said, 'Have a lovely time at The Jam tonight at Southend.' He dedicated it to me and my two friends and she managed to tape it. I've still got that tape now, digitised. That whole day makes that my favourite Jam gig. My band was coming to my town, John Weller let us into the soundcheck and I got my name on Radio 1.

The soundchecks were great. It was like going to a matinee performance! The band would always come and say hello afterwards, have a quick chat and sign a few autographs. It was very clear they appreciated their loyal following – The Jam Army – and no other band had that loyal sort of following.

I WAS THERE: NEIL LANDS, AGE 17

It was four days before my 18th birthday. I hid in the kitchens of the venue for 30 minutes after the gig with my sister Sally and we sneaked backstage when the coast was clear. We met the band and they all signed a copy of *The Gift* I'd taken with me to the gig and which I still have – a cherished memento of an important and influential experience in my early life. I had a long chat with Paul – just the two of us. He asked me what I thought of 'The Bitterest Pill' video and I told him, 'It's okay, but let's be honest, it's not The Jam, is it?' He must have thought 'cocky little so-and-so', but some years later I read in an interview where he said exactly the same thing... I recall thinking, 'I told him that!'

SHOWERING PAVILION
21 SEPTEMBER 1982, SHEPTON MALLET, UK

I WAS THERE: GUY HELLIKER

Did I mention I was at *Live Aid*? It's a standing joke with friends, but the gig I'll never forget was three years earlier. And a bit like your first love, you never forget your first gig... especially when it was The Jam!

Finally, the day arrived after what felt like months since I'd got tickets. I was going to see them, my brother, Mark, 21, driving me from Andover to deepest Somerset in his pride and joy orange MG Midget... on one proviso, we leave before the end. His car was low and the tracks in and out of the venue were pretty agricultural – he didn't want to risk losing his exhaust.

The venue was less than an hour away, but it felt like a lifetime getting there. About 20 minutes from the showground, I could see more and more scooters, the smell of two-stroke thicker as we got closer. Almost there, the road was closed apart from a sign saying, 'Jam concert straight on'. When we arrived at the Pavilion it was rammed with a sea of green Parkas and some of the coolest people this 15-year-old had ever seen. Guys in sharp suits and shades, girls in mini-dresses and bob-cuts. I squeezed my way to the merch stand and did a supermarket sweep-type spree Dale Winton would later have been proud of. T-shirt, tour poster, playing cards, match book, badges… and that's excluding the unofficial tat plus a red tour scarf I found in the car, smelling of diesel.

The mood in the venue felt menacing, a tinderbox about to go off. After a ropey support band, who in fairness played on through a barrage of abuse, the time was getting closer. A flurry of crew dressed in black quickly worked on stage, but for this fan not quick enough – this moment could not come fast enough. Then it was lights down and strap in for the ride of your life! 'Ghosts' was the opener of an incredible set I saw up to 'The Gift'. I missed out on 'But I'm Different Now', 'Funeral Pyre' and 'The Eton Rifles' because of that early dart before the end, but BANG! Like a bullet between the eyes, I was hooked!

The power of the music, a smoke haze over the heads of the crowd, dazzling white lights blasting from above the stage into the audience, filling my every sense. I longed to be up on the mezzanine, down the front, along the sides, where I watched the band's reflection on the glass windows, anywhere to get a better view and be part of the gig.

Seeing a sea of green Parkas bouncing as one, the band performing classic after classic, I was here! Everything was perfect, until a brown cider bottle was launched from the crowd, the glass shattering on Rick's kit. A yell of 'you cunt!' followed from Paul as a punch up broke out further down the front. The atmosphere went from electric to threatening, but still the hits kept coming!

The next day at school I felt like a celebrity, showing my programme, sharing stories and discussing the setlist. It's scary to think just a few months later, still elated, the announcement came out about the split. Like with Kennedy for the previous generation, and Lennon for ours, I'll always remember where I was when I heard. I was lucky enough to see them again on their farewell tour, on the last night at Wembley, but this felt more like a sad occasion, saying goodbye to a friend.

Like many others, I couldn't get a ticket to Brighton for the last show. Instead, I was at home with my girlfriend, begrudgingly listening to a Duran Duran concert on Radio 1. On the bright side, I got a sympathy shag… Like I said, you never forget your first time! And having met so many fans who never got to see the Jam live I will be eternally grateful that I was there.

I'm now 57, having met Jayne, my wife, through Bruce Foxton and From The

Jam. I've run From The Jam's websites and social media since 2009, and attended hundreds of concerts. I'm still a fanboy at heart, and where possible I share my passion with fellow fans I meet from around the world.

I never forget how lucky I am, experiencing some amazing things and meeting incredible people. If someone told me one day my name would be on the credits of three Bruce Foxton / Foxton & Hastings / From The Jam albums and that by 2013 I'd be sat on a flight case on stage at Billingham Forum, Teesside, chatting to Bruce Foxton and being shown how to string his guitar (I very briefly did backline as a guitar tech – a very hard job but a dream come true and great insight!), 15-year-old me would never believe it. Thank you, Liza Radley! And yes, I still love that single.

I WAS THERE: NEIL SHIDE
I remember someone in the crowd throwing something at the stage. (I thought it was a glass, though somebody nearer the front told me it was a lightbulb.) Paul stared into the crowd and said 'cheers cunt', then continued with the set. I know it happened, because for many years the friend I went to the concert with would, when he thanked me, affect his best Weller voice and repeat the same two words.

CONFERENCE CENTRE
22 SEPTEMBER 1982, BRIGHTON, UK

I WAS THERE: JOE SHIELDS
Two days later, we went to Brighton. I phoned up the coach guy and said 'are you going to Brighton and have you got any tickets?' I bought a ticket off him but I didn't want the coach trip because we drove down in my friend's mum's Hillman Avenger estate. We had a great day out, met up with the coach guy to get our tickets, saw the band – they were doing a lot of *The Gift* stuff – and carried on having a few drinks after the gig, in one of the hotels along the front there. We had sleeping bags with us so we slept in the back of the car that night, down by the arches, driving back home in the morning.

I WAS THERE: RUPERT TRACY
There was a rumour going round that The Jam were going to split up and I thought that this was totally preposterous. 'Why on earth would The Jam split up? They're totally at the top of their game.' But when it was leaked I remember I was sitting in my college refectory reading the *NME* and there it was: 'The Jam Split.' There were probably 200 Mods at my college, all with a face like fucking thunder.

Nobody could believe it. Nobody thought it was going to end, but it was. And we honestly didn't know what to do. We'd spent the last four or five years thinking about The Jam from when we woke up in the morning and listening to their music all day. Apparently, even John Weller said, 'What the fuck are you talking about, breaking the biggest band in the country up?' But that's Paul Weller…

After the summer holidays, The Jam decided to book the *Solid Bond In Your Heart* tour, which took in virtually every city in the country. They were amazing shows, two hours long and brilliant set lists, hearing songs you hadn't heard since 1978. He started doing 'In The City' again, and 'So Sad About Us'.

GRANBY HALLS
23 SEPTEMBER 1982, LEICESTER, UK

I WAS THERE: GAVIN JONES

I went with Reaction drummer Marc and my brother Piers, his first taste of live Jam, aged 14. We got there about four and there was a crowd waiting for the soundcheck. Then the rain started. We were soon soaked, wondering if we'd get in, when Joe (Awome) opened up and said '40 people only'. We managed to muscle to the front. It felt a bit like earlier gigs, with just 40 fans in the soundcheck. They ran through 'It's Too Bad', 'Precious' and 'Move On Up' before coming down for a chat, Piers getting all their autographs. We went to a pub, then back to the gig. After the support group, Apocalypse (who weren't bad), there was the impatient wait. Eventually The Jam came on for what turned out to be a brilliant gig, starting with 'Ghosts', 'In The Crowd' and 'Away From The Numbers'. They did a lot of *All Mod Cons* stuff, and 'The Modern World' and 'Tube Station', with 'But I'm Different Now' and 'Funeral Pyre' for encores.

After, we went to the stage door, and were told, 'Only 20 people in,' but again got in and had a chat with them all. It was nice talking to Paul and Bruce, who said they didn't have the confidence to play 'The Bitterest Pill' live yet. Paul seemed a bit distant and Bruce a bit edgy, as if something was going down.

Granby Halls soundcheck

Photo by Craig Simmons

However, we put that from our minds as we chatted with John and booked to go to Belgium again.

I WAS THERE: ANDREW FARMER
The second time I saw them was at Granby Halls. You had to go to Leicester Town Hall to buy tickets in person, so I had a day off work and got the train to Leicester, having to go via Birmingham. I queued, with tickets purchased at £5 each. I must have been in a state of euphoria, however, because I got on the wrong train and ended up on a non-stop express to London and was met with a fine for having the wrong ticket.

ROYAL HIGHLAND EXHIBITION HALL
27 SEPTEMBER 1982, INGLISTON, EDINBURGH, UK

I WAS THERE: MANDY SCOTT
I saw them three times in 1982 in Glasgow Apollo and also at Ingliston. I was 14, 15 that year and really not even sure how my parents allowed me to go.

I WAS THERE: HELEN CRAIG
My first ever concert was The Jam at Ingliston, not long before they split. I was a Mod but, being only 15 or 16, we wore neutral clothes as we were worried about the punks. The crowd was 50/50 Mods and punks, but no one cared. It was an amazing concert.

WHITLEY BAY ICE RINK
28 & 29 SEPTEMBER 1982, WHITLEY BAY, UK

I WAS THERE: PETER SMITH
The last time I saw them play was at the cavernous (and cold) ice rink in Whitley Bay, the first gig to be held at a venue which was used for large gigs until Newcastle Arena was built. The Jam played two nights there and again showed what a great band they were. I saw The Style Council a few times but couldn't really get away with them. I saw Paul Weller in concert a few years ago, and he was great. But nothing compared to The Jam in the late seventies and early eighties. Role on the reunion (never say never!).

I WAS THERE: PAUL BROMLEY
The first Ice Rink gig was quite funny – I was wearing bowling shoes, and by the end of the gig I couldn't feel my feet. They were cold and soaking wet as they only

put a protective cover over the ice. I'm sure I wasn't the only one. The following night it was Doc Martens for me.

I WAS THERE: GRAEME DAWSON

For the first night, I went for the soundcheck in the afternoon with five classmates, including Colin Mould (again) and David Beale. I bunked off school for the afternoon – the only time I ever did that. They included all the hits and favourite singles and album tracks. I had my camera and was holding it high as I could to get photos above the heads of the crowd, when this tall man lifted me on to his shoulders so I could see better. At the end, I hung around in the back corridor and managed to get a signature on the tour concert programme. I also went along the next night, again with friends from home.

I WAS THERE: ANDREW CLARKE

When they did the *Solid Bond* tour, they played Whitley Bay for the first time. There was a lot of trouble at Jam gigs. People would trample down the seats trying to get to the front, and rows of seats would collapse and then everyone was on top of them. So I understand why they made the switch from the seated City Hall to the Ice Rink.

But I remember going there and it was like a greatest hits tour, which was really strange. Every year there'd been an album and then a tour, heavily promoting *Setting Sons* or *Sound Affects* or *The Gift*. This was a retrospective and perhaps they were playing this to unsuspecting audiences because they knew what was going to happen. And it was shortly after that that they announced the split. It was my girlfriend's dad who told me they were splitting up, and I thought 'what does he know about The Jam?' But he said, 'No, no, it's in the paper.' I couldn't believe it.

I got a ticket for the third night at Wembley, because the Wembley gigs were meant to be the final ones. I just remember feeling gutted. But it had become a bit like a football match, with the trouble. And you had the people who were infatuated, singing 'we are the Mods'. When Weller brought the brass section in and he was doing 'War' and 'Move On Up', you could see that soul influence that he carried on into The Style Council. Quitting at the very top is what has given them legendary status. I don't think them reforming would be a good idea, not even for a one-off, but I'd probably go.

I never saw The Style Council and they only played Newcastle once. But in 1991 I saw that the Paul Weller Movement were playing in Middlesbrough and me and a pal jumped in a car and went down. I've seen Paul 63 times now, 18 with The Jam and 45 solo. His lyrics introduced me to politics and I know he hated being called the spokesman for a generation and all that and he would play it down but I think there's a whole generation of people, like me, who've got the belief system that they have because of The Jam. They weren't just a pop group.

I WAS THERE: KEN DENT

I'm a chef by trade, so I had to do two years full-time City and Guilds at college. 1980 and 1981 were just the best two years of my life. And then 1982 came along. In May I lost a friend in a nightclub accident. Peter and I were best mates. A bouncer pushed him down a steep flight of stairs at a nightclub and he died a few days later in hospital from his head injuries. And September was when The Jam announced that they were splitting up. So '82 was probably one of the worst years of my life.

I sensed at the time that something wasn't right with The Jam. It was just different on stage. You didn't get the same vibe. Bruce Foxton would snap at the people in the audience. I saw them in the April. And then they announced the *Solid Bond* tour for September where they did two nights at Whitley Bay. Which we were amazed by, because they'd just done two nights at Newcastle, so to do another two nights at Whitley Bay was brilliant. But it wasn't the same sort of atmosphere. You could just tell that something wasn't right. And then, sure enough, not long after that tour, it came out that they were breaking up. It was absolutely devastating. I loved the band that much, you know?

But I never enjoyed the '82 gigs as much as I enjoyed the gigs prior to that. I think I saw them about eleven times, the last four being at the City Hall in April '82 and then twice at the Ice Rink. I did try to get tickets for the farewell shows, but never managed to get them.

Some pop songs just work. You might hate the band. You might not like the act at all. But there's just something about a song, which is why it goes up the charts. You find yourself humming it or whatever. And The Jam's best tunes came from around '78 through to '81. Weller wrote some great stuff.

QUEENS HALL
30 SEPTEMBER 1982, LEEDS, UK

I WAS THERE: DALE MOSLEY

Six months later I bought a ticket for the *A Solid Bond In Your Heart* show in Leeds. I basically walked out of school early afternoon, got a train from Sheffield on my own and, on arrival, asked a copper in Leeds where the Queens Hall was. Luckily it was a five-minute walk from the station. I expected a similar night to the Sheffield gig, but it was completely different, with them playing older stuff ('Tube Station' sticks in my mind). I read years later that they'd already started playing the farewell set to audiences before the break-up was announced. I just made the last train back, and a week later a letter from school saying I'd walked out was sent to my parents. I was really in the shit!

I've seen Weller live dozens of times since, from the first Style Council tour to Wembley Stadium last year. I've met him a few times, and backstage in 1985 he asked if he could take a photo of me and my mate, dressed in scooter-type gear. I've also got a bit of Jam and Weller artwork by various artists, driving the wife mad!

I WAS THERE: CHRIS WALTON, AGE 13

I started going to lots of gigs from 1981 on. I was pretty lucky that I looked older than I was, so me, my cousin and his mate would go to loads, mainly at the Queens Hall. I got into them in 1978, aged nine. They pretty much took every cent of pocket money, Crimbo and birthday money, and any other way I could get money for singles, badges, patches, Parka and clobber, etc. I sold my collection a while ago but made a deal with myself and kept all the CD pressings and all my books, so the passion's still at my fingertips when I need a fix.

I WAS THERE: LYNNE OGLESBY

One day my friends came to school and said they'd got tickets to see them. I was so sad. That night I played my Jam records and told my mum about my friends getting tickets. The next day at school, I was in the dinner hall when one of my friends came in and said there was a phone call for me in the youth centre, which was on the school grounds. It was my mum. She said, 'Are you sat down?' As a matter of fact, I was. 'I have got you a ticket to see The Jam tonight. Could your friends take you?' I burst out crying.

My friends were over the moon and said they'd make room in the car for me. I don't know how she paid for it, as she'd become a single mum just recently. She says she can't remember (conveniently). On getting to the gig, I dragged one of my friends right to the front of stage. I just stared all night at them. Couldn't believe I was in the presence of The Jam! The whole thing from start to finish is still so vivid in my mind. Apart from having my two children, that has to be the next best thing in my life. The best band in the fucking world. Excuse my French, I don't normally swear.

It would be lovely now to show my mum what she did for me and how much I appreciate the sacrifice she made. She probably didn't pay the rent or something, just so I could go see them before they split.

SOLID BOND IN YOUR HEART

I WAS THERE: GARY COX

And then they came back and they played the Queens Hall again, just before they announced they were breaking up, and it was totally different. It was the *Solid Bond* tour, which was greatest hits plus *The Gift* and some old B-sides like 'So Sad About Us' and 'Disguises', and they were completely different. I think by then Paul knew it was over. They were on fire that night. The Questions supported them, who were a pretty good band as well. And then they announced the break up...

NEW BINGLEY HALL
1 OCTOBER 1982, STAFFORD, UK

I WAS THERE: SIMON SMEDLEY

Our three heroes from Woking have played a mighty role in my life – though admittedly I didn't truly appreciate what they were all about until not long before Paul seemingly decided it was time to call it a day.

When 'In The City' was released, I was still at primary school. Trying to recall those days now,

Simon Smedley, here with his partner, Tracey Conley, soon knew the Mod scene was for him

I loved my music and *Top Of The Pops*, but more distinct memories had been of the Sex Pistols, listening to 'Friggin in the Riggin' in my mate's bedroom when his mam went to the shops. My earliest clear recollections of The Jam are when 'Tube Station' came out and that bass riff of Bruce's. Wow! Then 'Strange Town', 'The Eton Rifles' and of course 'Going Underground'. I definitely had a keen eye on *Top Of The Pops* each Thursday, but my whole life changed in early 1982, leading up to me leaving school. And Paul Lund is responsible.

He was in my class at the Radclyffe School, Oldham, and we chatted sometimes in the dinner queue or if we met in the school yard. One morning, my eyes nearly popped out of my head when this beautifully streamlined Vespa 50 special scooter purred into the school car park, covered in lamps and mirrors, and that was Paul Lund, right there. I couldn't believe the sheer class and look of this awesome machine. From that day on, I knew the Mod scene was for me. All the kids knew Paul Weller and The Jam were knitted tightly to the Mod movement so my hero worship zoomed significantly after Paul Lund's ride into that car park.

Much of my attention swiftly focused on The Jam's music, and it wasn't long before I'd purchased all their vinyl to date. By the summer of '82, The Jam didn't have long left, but I got to see them live before the fateful split. And what a night that was at the old Bingley Hall, a former aircraft hangar in Stafford. We went on an old banger of a coach, myself and around four or five other lads – a couple having joined me earlier in the year in pledging our allegiances to the Mod scene and sounds.

I recall a sea of scooters outside the venue, then a sea of sweat-soaked Parkas when the gig was going on, but although I can still feel the buzz and adrenaline rush when Paul, Bruce and Rick were on stage playing, I can't remember much about the set. But I'd seen The Jam live, and no one could ever take that away from me.

40-odd years later, I listen to The Jam almost every day. Paul has been a big influence on me in terms of his look and attitude towards the Mod scene, but the music of The Jam has stood the test of time more than any other band in my opinion. Power, skill, influence, talent, words – The Jam had it all, so it's little wonder there are still hundreds of tribute bands paying homage to those three humble guys from the suburbs who went on to play huge roles in the lives of so many – even those who were still twinkles in their mothers' eyes in the later seventies and early eighties.

During my journalism career I never quite met Paul, Bruce and Rick for one reason or another. That, along with not quite making it to working at football's World Cup, are two big regrets. But I'll always have The Jam's music at my beck and call, and thank God for that.

I WAS THERE: MICK CLEE

I turned 17 in February that year and then I discovered through the classifieds in the *NME* that there was a shop on Carnaby Street called Melanddi and it said 'we supply The Jam' so I talked my mum and dad into letting me go down to London on my own for the first time. I got off the Tube at Oxford Circus, found Carnaby Street, found this shop and it was like all my Christmases had come at once.

I bought Sta-Prest trousers, button-down shirts, boating blazer… I was floating, having bought all this clobber. I had about an hour and a half before the train back home, so I thought I'd head towards Tottenham Court Road and walk back to Euston rather than take the Tube. And I walked past HMV and the *Trans Global Express* video was being played on the screens so I walked into HMV and watched that for 30 minutes. It was like being at a gig and it just brought back all the memories.

A couple of weeks later, they announced the September/October tour. By this time, I'd joined the Jam Club, which was run by Nicky Weller, Paul's sister. I'd heard it made it easier to get tickets. And as soon as tickets went on sale, I got tickets for Liverpool and Stafford Bingley Hall. So my second time of seeing them was a Saturday night at the Royal Court in Liverpool, standing. And it was just a repeat performance of Manchester. This time I was part of the congregation. I had the boating blazer on, my polka dot shirt, my Sta-Prest trousers and a pair of bowling shoes. I felt part of a group but I also felt like an individual. It separated us from the rest of society.

The following Friday we went to Bingley Hall. We bought a coach travel and tickets package for this one but we had no intention of going on the coach. One of the lads drove. We got right to the front and were stood in front of where Bruce Foxton was going to be. There was a band called The Questions supporting, who ended up on Paul Weller's Respond label. They were a soul band and they tried their best with a 30-minute set but they didn't go down too well with the Jam crowd.

Then John Weller walked on stage and did his usual intro and Bruce walked on, Rick walked on and Weller walked on. He was wearing Sta-Prest trousers and a yellow jumper and it was just absolutely fantastic. It was absolutely heaving with Mods. That's the first time I heard 'Little Boy Soldiers'. Weller did a rant about Ronald Reagan and dedicated the song to him.

On the way back we broke down on a country road, miles from anywhere. We were listening to Radio Luxembourg and they announced that 'The Bitterest Pill' had gone to number one. And there we were, parked next to a farmer's field, mist on the horizon, full moon, still soaking in sweat from the gig and singing away to it.

I was absolutely devastated when I found out The Jam were splitting. I was down in Euston, having gone to watch Liverpool play. The train back was 6.30pm so I went into WH Smiths to buy the *Evening Standard* to read on the train going home. And there was just a small article on one of the inside pages saying 'Weller to go it alone'. It went on to say that, 'Rumours are spreading that Paul Weller is going to call it a day with The Jam at the end of this year.' And it was one of these 'is this serious, or is this just tabloid journalism?' moments. But it got the worst of me and I thought 'this can't happen'.

The *NME* ran the story the following Thursday and then Weller did the announcement, saying that they were going to do a live performance on *The Tube* on 5th November. I was shell-shocked. I talked to my mates and none of us could get our heads around it.

I got tickets from the Jam Club for the last gig. It's a bit of a blur. I can remember certain parts of it, like Weller giving that speech before he finished off with 'The Gift'. You're watching The Jam but there was an element of, 'Well, this is the end tonight. This is it.'

Paolo Hewitt brought out a book out in 1983 called *The Jam: A Beat Concerto*. I queued up at HMV to buy it. That night we all got invited to a party at a mate's house because his mum and dad had gone on holiday. There was free booze, lads there, girls there and there's me sat on my own in the back room. I wasn't interested in anything else. I just wanted to read that book. That's how much The Jam meant to me.

I'm now in my fifties and I've seen Paul Weller 84 times. I've been with my partner 26 years. I got talking to her in a bar after her friend said to me 'my mate says you look like Paul Weller!'

If 'When You're Young' or 'Strange Town' comes on at a wedding, even for a man in his fifties, you've still got to get up and do it on the dancefloor. You're 17 again. But I don't think a live gig would do it. It would have been okay if they'd got together for *Live Aid*, but not now. Some things are better left alone. They never lose their value that way. The Jam were special. I want them to remain that way.

I WAS THERE: GAVIN JONES

They did a set similar to Leicester, with exceptions like 'Move On Up' and 'When You're Young'. They did one encore, coming back on and thanking Jimmy the keyboard player, the roadies and the crowd, this being the last gig of a small British tour, before blasting into 'Dreams Of Children' and going off for good.

We tried to get in the stage door, Joe asking for 30 at a time. We missed the first batch and he never let anyone else in, so we decided to follow the bus back to their hotel. On the way, three female fans from Leeds were hitching and we picked them up. When we arrived, Kenny told us to 'fuck off!' The girls made for a phone box, one phoning the hotel, asking for Bruce. The Girl on the Phone got through to him, but he said they were all tired and would like to let us in but couldn't. So off home we went, the girls singing in the back, happy until Marc crashed down a hole in roadworks on the A38. We managed to get out and I fixed a puncture, dropped the girls off and finally got home at 3am. A couple of days later I got a letter saying our trip to Belgium was cancelled as Paul had shingles.

I WAS THERE: JULIE WALTON

I queued up after to meet them, and got almost to the front of the queue when my dad turned up and made me get in the car to go home!

GLOUCESTER HALL, FORT REGENT
9 OCTOBER 1982, ST HELIER, JERSEY

I WAS THERE: ANDY BAGNALL

Two days after my 17th birthday, I was working in Jersey on a market stall selling records and cassettes. The Jam had announced they were breaking up, their gig in Jersey had sold out, and I didn't have a ticket. I was gutted.

On the day of the gig, at two in the afternoon playing *The Gift* on my market stall, this guy starts browsing the cassettes. He turns and says, 'You going to the gig tonight?' I said I couldn't get a ticket, and he says, 'I'm a roadie for them and if I can choose three cassettes, I'll get you and a friend on the guest list.'

I was like 'WTF? Is he genuine?' But it was one of those 'fuck it, gotta go for it' last chance saloon moments, knowing they were breaking up, so I agreed the deal. He chose three cassettes and said, 'Be at the main entrance at 7pm and be on time – I can't hang around.'

At 6pm I'm in McDonald's with my girlfriend, explaining why I'm taking her brother and not her. It gets heated and she's really pissed off. At 6.45pm I'm still there, knowing I have to get out, eventually storming out and running, finally arriving at the venue entrance sweating like a shitting dog at 7.05pm.

There are about 500 Jam fans queuing outside, me at the back with my girlfriend's brother… and the roadie isn't there. Not only do I think I've been mugged off, but I also look a right twat to my girlfriend's brother. In my head I'm 100 per cent down the fucking road. Plus, I'm three cassettes down and probably going to get sacked in the morning. But this thought only lasts a few minutes. I look up and there's the roadie, waving us to the front. We push past 500 fans, all giving us the eye. 'Okay, lads, you're lucky. You're in. Enjoy the gig.'

And we're invited to the after-show piss up, backstage. Wow, dreamland. I'm already thinking about what I'm going to ask Weller.

The show was loud, powerful, and OMG, the energy! How can three musicians create this sound? (Okay, and a horn section at the back, but…). Seriously, thank God my ears are only 17. I can take this. Too young to be deaf though, I stand back.

Hit after hit. I know all the songs, but they don't play the current single, 'The Bitterest Pill' and I'm gutted… again.

The show ends with 'In The City' ringing in my ears. Wow, I've seen The Jam live! Dreamland. Then there's the invite to the after-show party. This is it. I'm going to meet Paul Weller. A thousand questions went through my head during the gig, but there's only one I really want to ask. 'Where the fuck was my favourite song, 'The Bitterest Pill'?'

We walk in and I'm scanning the room. Where is he? We head for the bar, order a free beer and stand there not wanting to look too keen. I'm talking to my girlfriend's brother or pretending to while I continue to scan the room. Then, boom, I see Bruce Foxton, then I see Rick Buckler, sat at a table in the corner with their partners. No sign of Paul though, and I'm a bit stressed – my one chance to meet my musical hero is going to pass me by. I walk over though.

'Hi guys, fantastic show, really enjoyed it. Hope you don't mind me saying hello – I know you're chilling, and I don't mean to be intrusive.'

Buckler: 'No, not at all.' Foxton: 'No problem, sit down for a chat.'

I sit down, but I'm thinking how the fuck am I going to get through a chat with these two without asking where Paul is.

'So why didn't you play the current single?'

Foxton: 'We can't recreate that sound live on stage. It's too technical.' Okay, nice one.

'Where's Paul?' I knew as soon as those words left my lips that this question was a bad idea. Bruce ignored the question and changed the subject to what our favourite songs were. Two minutes later it was over. I shook their hands, said thank you for the memories and good luck in the future.

The roadie told me before we left that Paul went straight back to the hotel after the gig, as there was a bitter feeling due to the split. I knew then I'd never meet the people's poet, but damn, how close can you get? I told the roadie I couldn't thank him enough for getting us in, and we left. And I'll never forget my episode with The Jam, and just how close I came to meeting one of my all-time musical heroes.

THE JAM ANNOUNCE SPLIT
27 OCTOBER 1982

The news is carried in that day's national newspapers and, soon after, the weekend's music press.

I WAS THERE: RICK BUCKLER

I don't think there was ever any bitterness as such… We were grown up enough to sort of accept the decision that Paul wanted to leave the band. Where the bemusement came, let's say, was the fact that we didn't really understand his reasons. Having known Paul, and that he can be a bit kneejerk at times, over his reaction to things, we thought, 'One minute you're saying this, the next you're saying something else.' Then when he was free of having to look us in the face, the reasons changed again. I didn't mind whatever his reasons were. It just became a little hypocritical that he said to us one of the reasons he wanted to leave was because he was on a treadmill. But he'd already signed another treadmill deal with Polydor before our last show. That didn't make sense.

I really think there was more going on in the background. A lot of it was to do with the way John managed the band. We were beginning to ask questions, like, 'Why aren't we earning any money, John? Why are you going around saying Paul is now a millionaire?' I couldn't afford to buy a car. Those sorts of questions were beginning to raise their head.

I think that had a lot to do with the demise of the band, which was a real shame, because things were creeping in that weren't anything to do with us, musically. It was to do with things like the money and the fame, which becomes a vacuous reason to throw things away. There were other things as well, and we always got the feeling that Paul didn't like touring America. And we were getting to the point where we were probably going to have to start doing very large shows. The last shows we did were like the Wembley ones – multiple nights at the same venue.

HIGH STREET
27 OCTOBER 1982, CHATHAM, UK

I WAS THERE: JON ABNETT

I'd heard a rumour through friends about the impending split, then one day – going to the bank in my lunch break – I bumped into my mate Eon, and we discussed what we'd heard. It became fact when it was published in the *NME* or *Sounds*. It was more disbelief than anything else. Why was such a successful band, probably the top UK band at the time, calling it a day? Of course, once Paul released his statement and was on the BBC news before the last gig at Brighton, it was clear. He wanted to move on to different things. But I had to be there at the Brighton Centre for that last gig… five and a half years after my first sighting at the Hope & Anchor.

GUNNERSBURY PARK
28 OCTOBER 1982, WEST LONDON, UK

I WAS THERE: KATE DALEY

I was on the Tube going to school when the split was announced. I was heading from

Acton Town to Boston Manor. No one else was mad for them like me, and a girl sat next to me and told me. I was so gutted I got off the train and sat in Gunnersbury Park all day. It was the only time I bunked off. I sat in the park, inconsolable.

THE TUBE
5 NOVEMBER 1982, NEWCASTLE-UPON-TYNE, UK

The Jam's last ever live TV performance is on the very first episode of Channel 4's brand new music TV show.

I WAS THERE: PAUL BROMLEY

By the time I was 15, I was travelling a lot by myself to gigs, using public transport. I was following tours, from the *Jam 'Em In* tour in '79 through to the *Trans Global Express* tour in '82, and of course the farewell tour. In early November 1982 I managed to get in the audience for the first transmission of Channel 4 show, *The Tube*. A friend, Stu Holmes, phoned the office constantly, until they put him through to Alistair Pirie, one of the producers, who also did a radio show.

We went down for the rehearsals, collected our 'access all areas' ligger passes, and it was fantastic, especially to be on the first show. We were all over the TV, and got backstage afterwards to meet the guys, Jools Holland and Paula Yates. And all because of my friend's persistence, phoning that office. I haven't seen Stu for over 30 years, but if it wasn't for him, I wouldn't have had the opportunity.

I WAS THERE: GRAEME DAWSON

The Tube was a showcase for many emerging 1980s bands. Filmed in Newcastle-upon-Tyne and produced by Tyne Tees TV, the hosts including Jools Holland and Paula Yates, and The Jam performed on the first edition. It was their last live TV appearance before they split at the end of the year. I can actually be seen in the crowd.

When the recording stopped, the band carried on playing for the people there, some of which later featured on *Guy Garvey: From The Vaults*. When it was all finished, me and a few others went to the Green Room. We just walked in there – hard to imagine now. We talked to all the bands. Bruce and Rick seemed very sorrowful and sad.

My favourite Jam song? I can't choose between 'When You're Young' and 'Thick As Thieves'. Paul Weller was just 20, 21, and so young to have been writing such great lyrics that are actually like poetry. If they'd used this in English Literature lessons back then, I might have engaged more.

I WAS WATCHING: JOHN WINSTANLEY

By the time Weller announced he was calling it a day for The Jam, I'd moved on to other bands. I was pleased they had achieved the commercial success and industry recognition they deserved but they were no longer my band. They were everyone else's, and a whole host of Mods who they seemed to have attracted. I made a point of watching their last TV appearance on *The Tube* though.

I knew it was the right thing to do – to draw a line under The Jam while they were on top. History proved this to be the case – too many carry on long past their best and at worse become a travesty of their former glory. Not so for these New Age Sons.

I WAS WATCHING: OWEN CARNE

The band that got away…

I was born in September 1967 and lived in Abingdon, near Oxford, a city The Jam sadly never played. I had a brother, Dave, three years older, and we both discovered The Jam's music around mid-1979. I was eleven. The Stranglers were my favourite band, but The Jam have been a close second ever since. The first Jam single I bought was their anthem of youth, 'When You're Young' and I still consider this their finest hour. *All Mod Cons*, *Setting Sons* and *Sound Affects* are a Holy Trinity of near perfect albums. What an amazing creative run. I even like *This Is The Modern World*!

I followed their career with interest and bought each new album and single, enjoying hearing their music develop and mature with each successive release. Although I listened to records avidly in my bedroom, at my young age I didn't consider going to see any band live. Sadly, The Jam never came near enough for me to ask my parents to give me a lift. My brother, although older, showed no interest in going to gigs until he headed off to college in Banbury in 1982. By then, he was a fully-fledged Mod and befriended a lot of the Mods and scooter lot from the town.

Then came the announcement – The Jam were splitting and their winter 1982 tour would be the last. I was gutted. I scoured the tour itinerary, hoping for a stop in Oxford. It wasn't to be. Devastated, I resigned myself to missing the final tour. Seeing their extended farewell TV performance on *The Tube* just confirmed what had now permanently come to an end.

Soon after, my brother returned for Christmas and let slip that he'd travelled on an organised coach trip from Banbury to one of the Wembley gigs, and how fantastic they were live. A real kick in the teeth. Never once did he think to ask if I'd want to tag along to seize a final opportunity to see them live. I've never forgiven him.

Once The Jam split, I never forgot about them or moved on, still regularly playing all their albums today, although *In The City* less so. I even wrote to Paul, via Polydor, pouring my heart out about not seeing them play, and was stunned when I received a handwritten reply in a Solid Bond Studios envelope soon after.

I wouldn't allow myself to enjoy The Style Council – I begrudged Paul splitting the band to produce, in my opinion, substandard music. I've also never been drawn to his solo stuff, having witnessed an early Paul Weller Movement show in Oxford (yes, Oxford!) where 'Carnation', one of my favourite tracks, was absolutely ruined. YouTube clips of his jazzed-up versions of classic Jam tracks continue to reinforce that view sadly. I do enjoy the nostalgia trip of From The Jam, especially anniversary gigs for any of the 'Holy Trinity'. I even occasionally see Jam tribute bands to keep the memories alive.

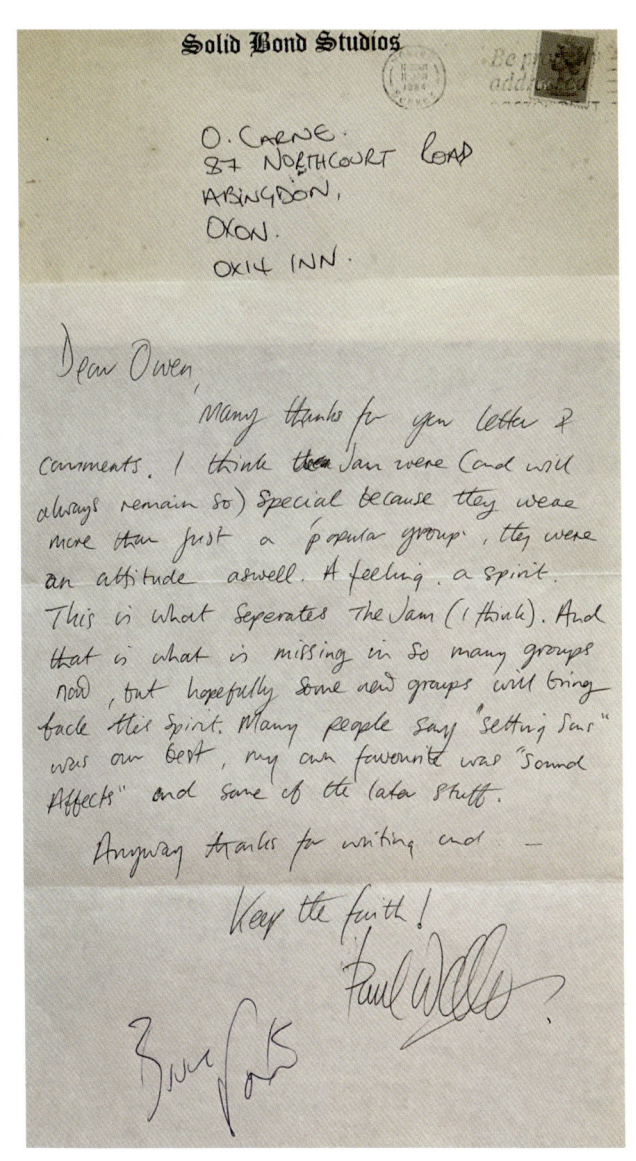

Owen Carne's January 1984 letter from Paul Weller

'BEAT SURRENDER' RELEASED
22 NOVEMBER 1982

The Jam's final single and Paul Weller's clarion call on bringing the band to a halt, is released, becoming their fourth UK No.1 single.

OUR PRICE RECORDS
22 NOVEMBER 1982, READING, UK

I WAS THERE: CATHIE STROVER

The news of their ending was very painful for me, but you hear Paul's new direction in 'Beat Surrender'. I didn't see any of the later dates. I was post-uni by then, working in Our Price, Reading, when that final single came out. The Jam were integral to my sense of self during those years. I grew up in Hillingdon but sadly never knew about what was happening in Woking, pre-*All Mod Cons*. I came a bit late to the punk revolution! But I loved them with all my heart, and still do. I can still sing 'Down In The Tube Station' word for word. Weller was a sublime poet.

'The Eton Rifles' and 'Town Called Malice' appear to be the constant favourites whenever The Jam are played, but for me it's always 'When You're Young', which captures the essence of the time – 'when the world is your oyster but your future's a clam'. Our youth really need to get that!

I was fond of The Style Council at the beginning, but the intensity was inevitably replaced by different musicianship. I've followed Paul's career, and I like his soul tendencies and the fact that he remains quite a prickly old cuss! He's true to himself.

In the last 15 years I've seen From The Jam seven or eight times, and they do a great job. It's been lovely to see Bruce still playing, despite all his heartache and illness, and Russell Hastings is an amazing front man… but much less grumpy! I can stand in the dark and pretend to be back in 1979. It fills me with joy.

APOLLO THEATRE
25 NOVEMBER 1982, GLASGOW, UK

I WAS THERE: GARY REID, AGE 17

This is still one of the best gigs I've been to, and I've been to a lot. I was in the top circle up the back with my wee brother. I too was quite wee for 17, so when everyone in front stood up, I had to as well, and when they stood on their seat I had to, or I wouldn't have seen anything. My seat was on the aisle and at one point The Jam started going sideways, so I was fired into the aisle, and when I looked around everyone in my row had fallen down. But after a heated debate with the bouncer, who wanted to throw me out, we were moved to the side rows.

ARTS CENTRE
27 NOVEMBER 1982, POOLE, UK

I WAS THERE: JOE REYNOLDS

I was at Poole and Wembley on the final tour, both great gigs. And then they played their last ever show on my 17th birthday. Cheers for that, Paul.

CORNWALL COLISEUM
28 NOVEMBER 1982, ST AUSTELL, UK

I WAS THERE: JON FLYNN

I saw The Jam three more times, all at the Cornwall Coliseum in St Austell, including on the final *Beat Surrender* tour. This venue was a weird, monolithic monstrosity, right on the beach, with an enormous car park. At the close of that final gig, I again hung around to meet the band as I had at Exeter University in 1979, knowing this would be the last time I'd see them together. The roadies on stage were beginning to clear up and one of them found a drumstick and hurled it into the thinning crowd. It was going right over my head, so I leapt as high as I could and managed to catch it in mid-air. As I landed, I felt other hands grab the prize. A huge tug of war ensued. I was aware of one of my mates grabbing on to help me out (thanks, Ian Pritchard) and together we managed to wrestle the others to defeat. I had my trophy! Then, as we milled around and spaces opened on the floor, I glanced down and there to my disbelief was a plectrum. Casually, so as not to draw attention, I bent down and picked it up and read 'Rickenbacker' on it. Two trophies!

Rick, Bruce and Paul (in that order) eventually appeared on the auditorium floor to meet us. Each was soon smothered by fans. I wasn't that bothered in joining the scrum. I had my drumstick and my plectrum. Still got them. Great times.

I WAS THERE: MARK JENKINS

Me, my brother Alex and his best buddy, Matt Knowles, were really into the Small Faces. The Jam came on from that. They were smart and tight. That first album was unreal. And their image just fitted with where our heads were at. We saw them on their final tour. The actual venue was a holiday centre sort of place with this big hall. They had a lot of good bands come down to Cornwall. Matthew drove and we got drunk in the car. We got

Mark Jenkins doesn't remember a lot...

SOLID BOND IN YOUR HEART

there just before they came on. It was packed, the most packed I saw it, that gig and the Ramones. I can't remember what songs they played – because I was pissed!

AFAN LIDO
29 NOVEMBER 1982, PORT TALBOT, UK

I WAS THERE: ROBERT FOSTER

I first saw The Jam at Shepton Mallet Showground. They were amazing live, with so much energy. And the lyrics were kicking against the system, so at the time they gave the youth something to shout about and something to believe in. I then saw them at Aberavon Lido on the *Solid Bond In Your Heart* tour. It was another great gig but by then they had announced that they were breaking up, and the reality that I would never see them live again set in.

I WAS THERE: MICHAEL DOWNES

We felt like this would last forever. I was a young Mod. I'd seen the band rise to the top of the music world and they led the Mod movement. What could go wrong? Well, our world was about to crash when Paul decided it was the end of the road, announcing the farewell tour. We just had to be a part of this. My friend's father made it possible by getting us tickets for the Port Talbot gig. He managed to get me ticket number 008. This being the very last time we would get to see them made it extra special and exciting, tinged with sadness. Now the planning had to start, with a trip to Carnaby Street to get a new outfit, Shelly's shoe shop for new bowling shoes (they had to be red, white and blue) and then over to Melanddi for a Jam striped shirt, matching the colours to the shoes.

We watched them on *The Tube* at the beginning of November playing their last live TV appearance. It all seemed so surreal. Surely, I was going to wake up soon, all this was going to be dream and we would still have them leading the movement forever? My birthday came just before the gig and having Jam-related items as gifts brought the loss home to me. I know people will say 'get over it – they were just a band', but to me and my mates

Michael Downes still rides a scooter

they were the driving force of a way of life. They put the Mod movement at the front of fashion, and we loved it.

All too soon the day of the gig arrived. We travelled down in my friend's car. There were already hundreds of fans there, some zipping around on scooters. More and more fans arrived until all you could see was boating blazers and Parkas. Finally, the doors opened and the mad rush was on to get the best position. Front and middle were the choice of all. On walked John Weller and, introduction done and with the blast of 'Start!', the whole floor went up as one and did not stop until the end of the gig. Being at a Jam gig was like winning the lottery, with non-stop dancing in a haze of sweat and beer. All too soon, the second encore was finished and so was the gig. We all stayed calling for more, as we knew this was the final time we would feel this buzz.

My new shoes had taken a beating and my clothes were soaked through. On the way home it finally sank in. This was the end of The Jam. What would happen? Would Mod fade and die? Well, 42 years later I still ride a scooter and still love the music. We were Young and, as in the famous introduction by Paul's dad, we had the best band in the fucking world.

I WASN'T THERE: ANDREW FOLLAND

For me, it was a case of not being allowed to go and see The Jam in the Afan Lido, Port Talbot, 1982. I still haven't forgiven my mother.

WEMBLEY ARENA
1-5 DECEMBER 1982, LONDON, UK

I WAS THERE: IAN SHAKESPEARE

I only saw them once, due to a lack of funds and an inability to find out dates, at Wembley. *All Mod Cons* and *Setting Sons* remain my favourite albums. How did Weller write 'Burning Sky' at the age of 20? Brilliant!

I WAS THERE: JULIAN BROOKS

The last gig for me was at Wembley Arena, which I thought was too big really. And the sound was shite. Awful… but it was The Jam, and they just stood out from everybody else. And oh my God, what a following they had.

When they split, I heard it on a Sunday evening from Radio 1 DJ, Kid Jensen. Shocked, shocked, shocked. But I loved The Style Council and Paul wrote some fantastic tunes with them. I saw them five times – in Ipswich the first time and the rest up London. Weller's solo years also blew me away. Yet again I honestly think he was on fire in the middle nineties, writing some of his best ever songs… 'Peacock Suit', 'The Changing Man', 'Wild Wood' and so on. I've seen him over 80 times solo, and my best gigs with him were at La Coruna, another in Spain on the beach and at the Razzmatazz Club, Barcelona. He's made my heart smile for over 45 years… and long may it last.

And long Live The Mighty Jam. We were so, so lucky to have Weller through our lives in our generation. I absolutely fucking loved it, and still do.

I WAS THERE: RUPERT TRACY

It was going to culminate in two nights at Wembley Arena, which quickly got expanded to five nights, and I managed to get tickets to four of them. Me and my pal Simon got to sit down and have a cup of tea with Paul Weller in the Wembley Arena canteen after one of the soundchecks. That was a big moment. It really, really was. He was a bit grumpy, if I'm honest. I think he was fed up with people asking him why he was breaking this great band up.

I WAS THERE: DEREK HERON

I lost my job because the boss wouldn't give me the weekend off for Wembley, so I told him to stick it. I got on the bus to London, stayed over for Brighton, and joined the RAF, mid-1983, staying on for 20-odd years. Cheers to The Jam!

I WAS THERE: GRAEME SMITH

I happened to spot an advert in the local newspaper for two tickets for the first of five nights at Wembley, and luckily I was the first to call. I shot straight to the fella's house and paid him for them. I don't think he charged any more than face value. Oh, how times have changed.

The same girl I'd been to Newcastle City Hall with travelled with me, even though we weren't an item by then. We got the train from Darlington, spending the day in and around Soho, Carnaby Street and Oxford Street before making our way to Wembley.

News that the band were splitting up had broken a couple of months earlier, but the place had an almost party atmosphere.

Gary Crowley did a short DJ set, followed by Big Country. Then it was time for the main event of the evening, and The Jam played a blistering set with such passion that it was hard to believe we wouldn't be seeing the again. Later, we made our way back to King's Cross, catching the slowest train imaginable back to Darlington, getting back around 4am.

I was gutted when Weller decided to call it a day, but I guess he didn't want The Jam to become one of those bands that tread the boards playing 'best of' sets for the rest of his life. That said, I wish he'd put them back together just for one more tour. That would make an old man very happy!

I WAS THERE: ANDREW FARMER

My third and final Jam show was on the farewell tour at Wembley Arena. I have mixed feelings about that. It should have been a celebration of the band and what they'd done and the lives they'd changed, but it was impossible to enjoy – we would never see them again, my life was over, the future uncertain. How could Paul do this to us? He'd better have something good up his sleeve. But Weller is always ahead of his time, and after 45 years, for me the torch is still burning as brightly as ever.

I WAS THERE: RICHARD NOBLE

Being the final shows, the demand for tickets was overwhelming and the date we originally wanted couldn't be guaranteed, so we ended up getting tickets for the Saturday. Which, fortuitously, meant I managed to miss out on some family gathering I would have been bored at.

My mate Kevin decided to drive to Wembley, as opposed to taking the train and Tube. It seemed to make it more of an adventure. Plus, all the way there, The Jam was being played on the cassette deck. Wembley was a huge, cavernous venue but our seats weren't far from the stage so we had a good view. At the merch stall, I bought a pack of cards, a keyring and a 'Beat Surrender' poster, all of which I still have. The poster cost about £3. With hindsight I wish I'd bought about fifty of them – they now go for £100 each. Then again, how was I going to carry them about during the gig?

Knowing it was Stuart Adamson from the Skids, we made a point of watching support act, Big Country, who I ended up seeing quite a few times during the 1980s. When The Jam started with 'Start!', we were coming back from the bar and towards the back, so had to make a dash to our seats, nearer the front. The song list seemed to be more of a trip down memory lane, with songs such as 'So Sad About Us' and 'In The City' included, as well as major favourites such as 'Going Underground'. At the end, they each said their goodbyes and left the stage.

On the drive back, the mood surprisingly wasn't sombre. It was quite upbeat, even though we knew we wouldn't be going to any more Jam gigs. In fact, when Kevin stopped for petrol and was paying at the kiosk, the rest of us got out and had a dance to The Jam on the station forecourt. I don't know what the petrol attendant thought of it.

SOLID BOND IN YOUR HEART

I WAS THERE: LAURENCE 'LOL' WEIGHT

Brackley today is known as the home of Formula 1 teams, but back in 1982 it wasn't known for anything apart from some tenuous link to the Magna Carta and one-hit wonder disco group Liquid Gold... although it did have the only nightclub in the surrounding area, The Bell Tower. On Friday 3rd December that year me and my best mate were in there, and I said, 'Hey Kev, The Jam are at Wembley tonight... and they are there tomorrow... and me and you are going!'

He replied, 'How can we? We haven't got tickets!' This small market town is in the middle of nowhere, close to the Northants/Oxfordshire border but not really belonging anywhere. That's how most of us teenagers felt. Our only sense of belonging was to the music that defined us. You had Terry the rockabilly and Cocker the punk, then me and Kev, the Mods, inspired by Paul Weller's style, and by *Quadrophenia*. We finally felt we belonged to something, yet that something was ending. Could we not go? 'We'll get some!' I told him. Whether I was being stupidly naive or supremely confident I don't know, but I knew we had to try or we'd never forgive ourselves. I've lived by the saying, 'You only regret the things you don't do,' and we were doing this.

Next morning, still hungover, we boarded the train at Bicester and set off for the capital. We got off at Wembley, found a tout and paid three times face value for two tickets – a staggering £15 each (and about the same as two pints would cost now). My memories of that night will live with me to the day I die. We were at the front of the circle at Wembley Arena, Big Country played their set (a great up and coming band, but not really the right audience), and as they left the stage you could feel the anticipation. Everyone wanted to see The Jam.

As the lights dimmed, John Weller's voice boomed out. 'Put your hands together for the best band in the fucking world!' The place erupted. A guy behind us jumped off the balcony to try and get into the crowd at the front of the stage, hit some sound wires and landed head-first on the floor. The last I saw of him he was taken out on a stretcher. He didn't even get to hear one song.

This was mine and Kev's first concert, and for a band we loved more than anything. The band we'd loved since we were 14 and 15, at school in '77. Our imaginations were ignited by 'In The City', the flames fanned by 'Tube Station', the inferno consuming us the day 'Going Underground' entered the charts at No.1. But they were also the band we were losing.

They opened with 'Start!' How else would they? And they finished with 'The Gift', although it didn't feel like we'd been gifted anything. It was the best and worst night of my life. I got to see my heroes, and my 'angry young man', for the first and last time. I didn't know it then, but those three musicians would stay part of my life for the next four-plus decades. I know they'll be there till I die. I've already picked 'Ghosts' as the tune I'll be carried into my funeral to, and 'Going Underground' as the tune they'll carry me to my grave to. Last year I was 60 and I set myself a challenge of meeting all three of them again. And I did. Like I said, 'You only regret the things you don't do.' But I'll leave the last words to Paul Weller. 'Oh, wasn't it such a fine time…'

I WAS THERE: GAVIN JONES

Here it was, the final tour, and once the disappointment of the split announcement had worn off, we were excited at another Jam gig. Off in the Beetle again, this time to Wembley with Marc and Steve. We all had tickets, getting there about half one, no one there other than touts. We went to a pub and returned about three to see if we could get into the soundcheck.

Stuart Adamson of Big Country came over for a chat, then the band arrived in separate cars. There was quite a crowd. We heard the soundcheck start, realising no one was getting in. We went with about ten London lads down the side, finding a fire door slightly open, opening more as we pulled it. We squeezed through to sneak in on the balcony. It was a massive place with just us in there! The Jam did a couple of songs, then were mucking about with soul covers, possibly a preview of Paul's new direction. Kicked out by a security guard, we sat in the car till the doors opened.

A good set opened with 'Start!', 'In The Crowd', 'Away From The Numbers', 'It's Too Bad', 'To Be Someone', 'Ghosts', 'Smithers Joncs', 'David Watts', 'In The City', and so on. They only did one encore, 'But I'm Different Now' followed by 'The Gift', then said thanks for the last five years. The set was good, but only lasted an hour and a quarter, a bit short for a farewell gig. Still, we went home happy, looking forward to Birmingham, as ever.

I WAS THERE: MARCUS MARSDEN

It's no exaggeration to say hearing The Jam for the first time changed the trajectory of my life. I grew up in the Midlands, in a middle-class family where music didn't really figure at all. My parents had a music centre and about a dozen LPs. It was 1979 and I was a sports-mad twelve-year-old. Then, on a trip to meet my aunt and uncle, my elder cousin – assigned to look after me – took me to his room, ignored me and started playing loud music. It turned out to be 'The Eton Rifles'. 'Strange Town' followed and I was immediately hooked.

Everything changed after that. All my pocket money was saved and spent on accumulating The Jam's back catalogue. My parents had no idea what was going on, but they never stood in my way. Of course, it wasn't just the music. Suddenly clothes became important too. The whole Mod look and way of life.

Over time, I collected all the singles and albums and plastered my bedroom wall with all the covers and pictures from the *NME*, *Smash Hits!* and so on. And 1980 was a great time to be a Jam fan. They were everywhere. I queued up to buy the 'Going Underground' single on its day of release and would be glued to the radio to hear the chart countdown. Going straight in at No.1 reinforced the belief that I was on the right track. It wasn't just me!

I loved the music, the clothes, the attitude and lyrics that spoke to me in a way nobody else did. Paul Weller not only seemed to understand everything I was going through, but also understand what was going on in England and the world at large. I didn't agree with all his politics (I still don't) but he made me think about things I'd never thought about before and read books I'd never have picked up.

I finally got to see my heroes at Wembley in 1982, after Paul announced that they were going to split. Such a bittersweet event. I'd never seen so many fans in one place before. I could not understand why they were splitting, but all these years later it's easy to see he was right. It's amazing that he had the guts to do what he knew was right.

The fact that Paul was so transparent about his musical influences also had a major impact on my life. I explored the 1960s music he talked about, from The Who and The Kinks to Motown. For some reason, The Beatles never stuck with me, but if you dig into the 1960s for any period of time, you'll eventually find Bob Dylan, who became my next musical obsession. But that's another story!

The Jam remain an integral part of my listening, songs like 'Thick As Thieves', 'Burning Sky' and 'Little Boy Soldiers' as potent today as in 1979, maybe even more so with the passing of time. I was never 'Billy Hunt' or 'David Watts', but never became 'Smithers-Jones' or 'Mr Clean' either, so I'll take that as a win.

I WAS THERE: DAVID PAWSEY

My first gig was at the Rainbow in May 1979, but the trip to Paris in '82 was the highlight. What a day and night! I then signed off with three nights out of the five at Wembley Arena. I was almost in tears walking away from Wembley on the 5th. I knew it was the end of an era.

I WAS THERE: MAT BERRY

I grew up in Oxford and was ten when 'In The City' was released as a single, a move to secondary school that September seeing my transition from child to youth, when I started to listen to music on Radio 1. And *Top Of The Pops* was a 'must watch'. That The Jam performed 'live' on there around 20 times is testament to the show's cultural impact and importance. The first topic of conversation at school on a Friday morning always related to the previous evening's show. It was a love for (any) music that bonded kids, where others were sharing a passion for football or Scalextric, stamp collecting or trainspotting. But when did The Jam come to mean more than The Boomtown Rats, Buzzcocks, Sham 69 or Public Image Ltd?

I became increasingly aware of the band as their popularity grew, generating more sales, higher chart positions, more radio play and more *TOTP* appearances… but then came 'Going Underground', as powerful today as on its release in 1980, as a song and as a message. Peter Powell – one of Radio 1's most middle-of-the road DJs – paused after playing it and then voiced what so many of us were feeling: what can you say, except 'that is just such a good single.' I was only 13, and while for some this may have been gig-going age, it wasn't something I thought of doing. A small amount of pocket money each week wasn't enough to regularly purchase records, but records were always being passed around, and taping from the radio could yield a compilation that was the envy of classmates, which itself would be copied.

I found myself listening to and seeking out more and more Jam music. A friend who lived in the same road lent me a C90 tape of singles, B-sides and LP tracks he himself borrowed from a friend. I played it constantly for days on end… that was it!

By the age of 15, I had a little more money available through various part-time jobs, and in January 1982, 'Town Called Malice'/'Precious' was the first Jam single I bought on release, as I did in March with *The Gift* (in its pink and white striped paper bag). That summer I managed to get hold of a tour t-shirt, with the LP cover on the front and tour dates on the back, and started buying one-inch badges (all of which I still own). I wore a different Jam badge to school every day and realised I now had to see the band live.

September 1982's *A Solid Bond In Your Heart* tour passed me by, but then came the split announcement, the end of year *Beat Surrender* '82 tour already announced, and my friend Dave came up with tickets for the final night at Wembley Arena.

The BBC's summer TV broadcast of the March '82 concert from Bingley Hall, Birmingham had whetted the appetite; the nine-song set on the first episode of *The Tube* showing us all what we were about to lose. So it was that Dave, my brother Ric and myself took an afternoon coach from Oxford to London's Victoria coach station, pausing as we descended the steps to the underground station, as featured at the start of the 'Strange Town' video, arriving hours before anything was due to happen.

Even then, there were people queuing. We joined the queue and watched as touts and hawkers roamed backwards and forwards, crowds building. We headed to the

SOLID BOND IN YOUR HEART

merchandise stall, where I bought as much as I had money for – a t-shirt, a tour programme (into which I later stuck my ticket – Entrance 58, Row O, Seat 88), a pack of Jam playing cards (which remain in their shrink-wrap) and a *Dig The New Breed* badge. I subsequently spotted a *Dig The New Breed* t-shirt: grey, with the treble clef, album title and caricatures on the front and the track-listing of the yet-to-be-released live album on the back – I wanted it, but with money already spent, I had to walk away. Despite searching I never found another until a work colleague turned up at five-a-side wearing that very shirt in later days. We chatted about the band, those concerts and the shirt, whereupon he took it off and handed it to me. Gurdev, wherever you are now, thank you very much!

I recall watching Big Country, but we were only there to see The Jam, and the cheer that went up when Stuart Adamson announced they had one more song is something I've never seen or heard repeated at any gig since.

It was time, my seat high up on the right, looking down and across to the stage. I could see the swaying crush of those standing on the arena floor but wouldn't take my eyes of the three members of the band that meant more to me than anything. Like all those around me, I rose to my feet when they took to the stage and didn't sit down for the next hour and a half. This might have been the band's swansong, but they were not a spent force – the set was full of energy. Neither did they perform to a script – the five dates at Wembley showed set changes every night.

They opened (for the only time on the tour) with 'Beat Surrender', the single at No.1 in the charts at a time when the charts mattered. While the set included songs from '77 to '82, the band steered clear of a clichéd greatest hits. Only six of the 23 songs were singles, with almost half of *The Gift* album played along with two unreleased cover versions – James Brown's 'I Got You (I Feel Good)' and the Small Faces' 'Get Yourself Together' – prompting Dave to shout in my ear, 'What's this?' 'Dunno,' I replied, 'But I love it!' Sure, there were songs missed out that I wanted to hear, but generally those would have been in addition to those played.

My recollection is of two encores. I tried to dig out the bootleg I later acquired to confirm this, but it's missing from my collection. I and those around me didn't stop clapping and cheering for a second while the band were off stage. I left elated (or was it relieved?) that I'd managed to see The Jam before their demise. There was no disappointment that I would never see them again, nor that there would never be any more music. The intensity of the show, even in a place as large as Wembley Arena, had been uplifting.

The following day at school I passed a kid in the year below wearing the same *Dig The New Breed* badge. We nodded our recognition, no words exchanged. It was a couple of weeks later that the vacuum left by the end of the band hit home… after the final date in Brighton, after 'Beat Surrender' had been knocked off the No.1 spot by Renee & Renato and after *Dig The New Breed* just failed to top the album charts.

I still listen to The Jam, and I still miss them. I got back in touch with Dave in 2023 after a 35-year hiatus, and the first thing we talked about was that trip to London. When conversations, as they always do at some point, get round to the first record you ever bought and first concert you ever went to, my combination of 'The Wombling Song' and The Jam at Wembley Arena is one I've yet to hear anyone better…

I WAS THERE: JO BARTLETT

I became a fan of Big Country after they supported The Jam that night. They cut the sleeves off their t-shirts, and I did the same when I got home! I went on to see them headline Guildford Civic.

I don't know that I was conscious of The Jam adding extra dates at Guildford then Brighton. I'm sure I'd have had a memory of hoping to get a ticket and failing otherwise. Those things tend to stay in your teenage brain. Those were the days of either sending a cheque in the post or turning up at the box office to pick up tickets. I'd get my mum to write a cheque and then give her my pocket money to pay for it.

I started a fanzine after The Jam split and I wrote to Bruce Foxton, with a 15-year-old's questions. Bless him, he replied, although the fanzine never actually happened. I asked if he was still in touch with Paul, and he said, 'Christmas cards.'

I WAS THERE: JENNY BARTON

I only saw The Jam once, due to funds being low. I went to one of the farewell concerts at Wembley Arena and they blew us away!

I WAS THERE: RICHARD WESTNEY

I was devastated on hearing the split announcement but also thought it was genius. I didn't want to see them get old and stale, playing stadiums like the Rolling Stones, The Who, and others of that ilk. I always said the day The Jam played a stadium would be when I stopped going to see them. I went to one of the Wembley Arena gigs under sufferance. It got too big. It was emotional, sad, exhilarating and horrible, all at the same time. I was so far from the stage, I hated it (I was used to being down the front) but remember the emotion of the crowd, the singing and chanting, and the band were superb. One of my mates went to all five nights at Wembley, but that was too rich for me.

SOLID BOND IN YOUR HEART

I WAS THERE: JOE SHIELDS

I went to the Saturday at Wembley. The Jam had the brass section at the final gigs and it was clear which direction Weller was taking. The final single was 'Beat Surrender' and it was released as an EP with 'Shopping' and 'Move On Up'. I love that cover! When The Style Council released 'Solid Bond In Your Heart' I remember saying to my mates, 'That should've been the last Jam single.'

When the split was announced we were absolutely gutted, like every fan. The rumours had been flying around but I didn't want to believe it. I wasn't shocked by the time of the official announcement, because I sort of knew already. It was one of the worst kept secrets. They were going for such a small space of time, from '77 to '82, just five years. I was 17 in 1980 and my first gig. By the time of my last gig in 1982, I was 19.

ROYAL HALL
6 DECEMBER 1982, BRIDLINGTON SPA, UK

I WAS THERE: MARK ROBSON

I saw The Jam four times – at Bridlington on the *Bucket and Spade* tour, Whitley Bay both nights in September '82 and then Bridlington again on the final tour. It was manic, and fantastic. I first got into them after seeing them do 'David Watts' on *Top Of The Pops*, buying the single, and that was it – I was hooked. I got *All Mod Cons*, then it was lift off. I didn't like The Style Council. They did some good tunes but weren't in the same class. Weller's solo stuff is great in the main, but there's some patchy stuff.

I WAS THERE: GARY COX

I tried to get into the soundcheck again, but again they only let a few people in. I remember being on the front wearing a boating blazer and staying in an old phone box for an hour just to try and keep warm because the breeze was coming in off the sea. They were brilliant there. The next night was Manchester Apollo and they were great again. They played a lot off *The Gift* and a lot of the old stuff. He had a couple of backing singers and they did melodic versions of things like 'That's Entertainment'. At Manchester, they did about three encores. And then it was over.

They still put lots of passion into the delivery. In Leeds in September there had been a bit of tension between Weller and Foxton and they weren't talking to each other much. But for those final shows you could see that they were still friends. They shared a mic for 'Town Called Malice'.

There was a massive connection with the audience. In the early days, they weren't new wave. You couldn't categorise them. Weller wrote stuff you could understand.

He made things simple for people. Going to see them live was such a great experience, and Weller was never scared to try new things.

It wasn't a surprise to me when they announced they were splitting. You could see from 'Funeral Pyre', 'Absolute Beginners' and 'Tales From The Riverbank' how they were pushing the music out in a different way. When I first played *The Gift*, some of the songs were very Jam-like and some were completely different. Some were more political, some were different like 'Carnation', which is a great song but not a typical Jam song.

I didn't think they'd go on forever. I think Weller just lost the passion to carry on doing it under the Jam banner. He wanted to have different types of musicians coming in pushing him. And I wouldn't have liked to have seen them doing the same things and continually turning out the same stuff. It was definitely the right thing to do, splitting them up.

Would I go and see them if they reformed for a one-off charity gig or something? If it was for the right reasons and the motivation was there for them then, yes, I probably would.

I WAS THERE: GORDON TOAL

I got into The Jam after hearing 'Down In The Tube Station At Midnight' on *Top Of The Pops*. The song just hit me; the aggression, the beat, the clothes. I was hooked instantly. I was just 15 years old and getting into the scooter scene, and thought 'this is the band for me'. I went out the next day and bought the first two albums and just about wore the vinyl out. So fast forward a year and The Jam are playing live in Bridlington, only 18 miles from my home town of Scarborough, I had to be there. I sorted tickets out, and went by car with some older mates. The first time seeing them live was electric, power, aggression, the music and lyrics were just fantastic.

I was lucky enough to see The Jam live four times, the last occasion being on Rick Buckler's birthday, again in Bridlington. I shed a tear or two when the crowd were singing happy birthday to Rick, knowing this was going to be the last time I would see this trio perform together.

APOLLO THEATRE
7 DECEMBER 1982, MANCHESTER, UK

I WAS THERE: MIKE LEA, DEPARTMENTS

I couldn't get a ticket for the last Manchester gig. It sold out as I was queuing. I was gutted. I went along hoping to buy one, but they were going for £20, way above what I could afford. I decided to go around the back and listen to the start of the gig. They came on to 'Start!'. The fourth song was 'Away From The Numbers'. I decided it was too painful to just listen and was about to go home when the stage door flew open and Kenny Wheeler, the tour manager, said, 'If there's no fucking pushing, you can come in!' I couldn't believe what I was hearing. There were around 15 of us stood to attention in front of him, me at the front. He led us in around the back of the stage and into the theatre, stage right. Paul, wearing a white monkey jacket, was singing 'Ghosts'. Every time I hear that – my favourite Jam song – I close my eyes and I'm transported back to that memorable night.

I WAS THERE: MICHAEL JOHN GILBERT

Tickets for their final tour were hard to come by. I was also in the middle of being made redundant. But then a friend asked if I'd like a ticket as he was unable to go. I jumped at the chance. The price was £5 but I had to bring him a programme back. The concert was at Manchester Apollo. I'd passed my driving test the week before so the prospect of driving 60-odd miles was quite daunting.

My girlfriend, Gill, insisted on coming along. On the journey it rained, then snowed, traffic very heavy for my first time driving on a motorway of any kind. Still, we persevered, getting to Manchester and the venue early, parking up and then going to get something to eat. Refreshed, we stood outside the theatre with a group of guys and girls and a coach turned up. We could see Bruce and Rick eager to get off, then Paul stood up and followed them off. He winked, said hello to us. Bruce was smiling but Rick looked a little more reserved.

Gill didn't have a ticket and along with about half a dozen other girls went to listen at a side door, until John Weller opened the door and let them all in. Ironically, she had a ringside view while I was seated almost at the back. I remember the atmosphere, and the energy of the music.

I WAS THERE: MICHAEL PORTER

I saw The Jam in Manchester on the last tour. I was offered £200 outside for my ticket, a fortune in those days. People were trying to squeeze through toilet windows to get in. I'd leave gigs in those days with a feeling of partial deafness from the noise. I don't seem to suffer that at gigs now.

I wanted to see them earlier on the tour in Leeds, but it clashed with one of my other favourites, Dexys Midnight Runners playing Ashton-Under-Lyne's Tameside Theatre. My brother, two years older, usually drove us to gigs, but he and his friends went to Leeds, so my mum had to drive me. We lived in Burnley, our main venues in those days Blackburn's King George's Hall and Preston's Guild

Hall, with occasional trips to Manchester. I'd just turned 17 and passed my driving test that week, but Mum didn't trust me out on my own in her Triumph Acclaim. She didn't have a ticket but somehow blagged her way in to stand at the back.

I had very few Jam records, but my brother had most, so I listened to his. He had a job while I just worked Saturday mornings, earning £4, coincidentally the cost of an LP. Saturday afternoons involved trips into town to the record shops. The first I bought was the Skids' 'Into The Valley', on white vinyl. I could buy four or five singles with those wages, while LPs were always on my Christmas list.

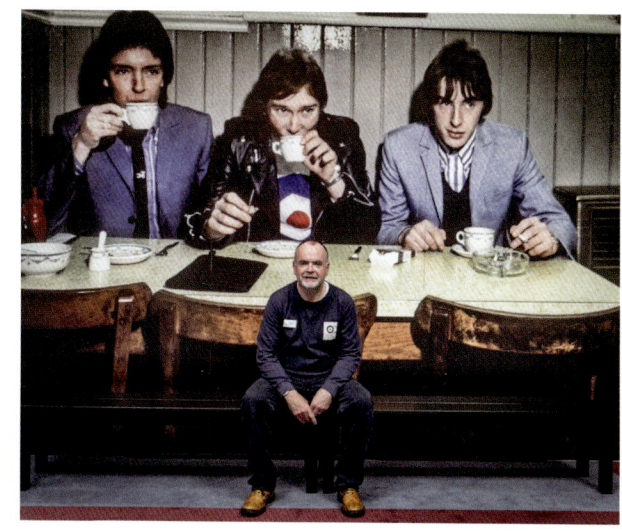

Michael Porter with his Jam heroes

I'd go to school in a donkey jacket, *Searching For The Young Soul Rebels* sewn on the back. I also wore Fred Perry t-shirts and made myself a pair of Jam-style shoes. I couldn't afford the real thing so had an old pair of red leather shoes, painting certain panels black. I eventually invested in a pair of loafers with tassels on top. In those days you either went with punk, ska or new wave or were into heavy metal. A bit of a dated comment but disco wasn't for the boys. I didn't and still don't like metal. The music I followed was socially relevant and meaningful, with lots of energy. You could tell the artists were singing, unlike metal. And I'd never have suited long hair!

I WAS THERE: ANDY REED

I was gutted when it ended. I read it in *Record Mirror* and knocking on my friend Gordon's door on the way to school. He refused to believe me and said it wouldn't happen. But all these years later, I think Weller did the right thing to protect the band's legacy.

I finally got to see them at Manchester Apollo on the final tour. Myself and my brother (two years younger) went with my cousin's boyfriend, who was around 20. The Apollo was an all-seater venue, so the gig lacked the chaos of the Deeside night, the atmosphere more sombre because we knew it would be the last time we'd see them. I don't recall a great deal about it. I caught up with Gordon, asked if he was there. He told me, 'I didn't have tickets but a few of us were going – including Stephen Hurst (RIP) - but my then just dumped girlfriend came round, rather worse for wear, so I didn't make it. I did however see them on 1st October at Stafford's New Bingley Hall.'

Now, the album I listen to most is *Setting Sons*, but my favourite song is probably still 'Tube Station', or maybe 'Private Hell'. It blows my mind how young Weller was when he wrote these songs.

Musically, for a few years I didn't get over The Jam. But following The Jam and reading their story gave me an outlook that nothing is impossible, and anything can be achieved.

BINGLEY HALL
8 DECEMBER 1982, BIRMINGHAM, UK

I WAS THERE: SHANE JUSON

I was listening to rubbish like Showaddywaddy (still don't mind them, to be fair). I had long hair, because that's what you did when you were twelve. I heard 'Strange Town' on the radio in 1979 but didn't buy it. Then, walking past the record shop in my hometown, Leominster, they had a 'When You're Young' picture sleeve in the window and I thought 'that looks good'. I hadn't heard the song but went in and bought it on the strength of the sleeve, Paul Weller in his Paisley shirt and turn-ups on his jeans. I'd just turned 13. I've loved The Jam ever since.

We lived in the middle of nowhere. Malvern was closest to us, about 40 miles away, and we didn't have a car. My first gig was The Beat at Malvern Winter Gardens. I had a ticket to see The Jam there about two months before, when 'Going Underground' came out, but my mum said I was too young. I was pushing it a bit – I was just 13 and a half – and no one went to gigs round by us anyway, so I'd have been on my own.

The first time I got to see them was on my 15th birthday at Stafford's Bingley Hall on the *Bucket and Spade* tour. My girlfriend also liked them, so we got tickets and her dad took us up in his car. He was a bus driver and produced his bus driver's licence and got in to watch them for free. The crowd were pushing and shoving. When they did 'Boy About Town', Paul and Bruce jumped at the same time where the trumpet bit is on the album. I thought, 'This is fantastic'. I wore a pair of white jeans that night and had a couple of plastic pop containers in my pockets. As the crowd surged, both exploded. I was absolutely soaked, my white jeans suddenly raspberry coloured.

In 1982 I saw them three more times, at Birmingham Bingley Hall in March, Stafford in October and back in Birmingham in December. I'd just turned 16 and was returning by train from an Outward Bound course in the Lake District with college when I found out they were splitting up. The train stopped at Carnforth and I thought, 'I'll pop in and get the *NME*.' I saw the headline and burst into tears. I got back on the train with about 15 other lads. They were all taking the piss out of me for crying. I was devastated. I didn't see it coming. People say there were rumours about them splitting, but I'd never heard any.

Birmingham was supposed to be the last gig, then they added Guildford and Brighton. I got into the soundcheck that day. I didn't know about soundchecks. We ran in and I thought, 'Well, we're not supposed to be here.' It was like our own private little gig. There were probably 50 or 60 people there. At the end, everyone was ushered out by security and we saw Paul Weller coming off the stage. I thought, 'I'm going to try and meet him', ran through all the security, said hello, shook his hand and ran off.

We were at the front of the queue to get back in. I was right in front of Paul. The atmosphere was fantastic, the audience fantastic. You hear all the stories about Brighton, people booing, throwing bottles, stuff like that – it couldn't have been further from the truth at Birmingham.

I managed to get backstage, and had a chat with Paul, Rick and John Weller. Bruce wasn't there. I asked Paul what he was going to do next, as if he was going to give a world exclusive to a 16-year-old country bumpkin. If The Jam reformed for a one-off gig I'd love to be there. I know it would be very nostalgia-y, but I'd be at the front of the queue, 100 per cent!

I WAS THERE: MICHAEL COUCH

I arrived in time for the doors to open for the soundcheck. This time, the atmosphere onstage was moody, the band not really communicating. Necessaries complete, off they went. When the doors opened for the gig, I ran as fast as I could to the front, hanging onto the front railing throughout. My ribs were bruised, but it was so worth it.

Having seen Foxton play, I was drawn to wanting to play bass but had no clue how. I was a semi-pro footballer, but a bad leg break left me with many weeks of recovery and borrowing a bass and small amp was the beginning of a journey… which is ongoing! I taught myself after a mate showed me the basics. My first band,

Newland, started in 1988, and was essentially a Jam tribute band way before that was a thing. We played a dozen Jam tunes and revisited Carnaby Street to see what clothes shops were still selling Jam-style stage gear. It was brilliant going back six years on, trying to find appropriate clothing.

Being a friend of Steve Cradock from our youth bands (he came to see Newland), I went to see his band The Boys, and we've stayed in touch. I've been very lucky to have been in Weller's dressing room on many occasions courtesy of Steve, and what a lovely warm, generous man Weller is – very accommodating to his fans, even sharing his rider as he wanted a bit of downtime after a gig, making sure we all had drinks while we waited.

I WAS THERE: STEVEN O'DRISCOLL, AGE 15

I grew up listening to my parents' record collection, consisting of the Rolling Stones, ABBA and The Beatles' red and blue albums, which I played endlessly in the latter half of the seventies. In 1979 I heard 'Strange Town', 'When You're Young' and 'The Eton Rifles' on the radio, and I was intrigued.

I'd just turned 13 when 'Going Underground' got to No.1. 'Start!' did the same and I knew this was the real deal. I listened endlessly to my friend's copy of *Sound Affects* until I could get my own. As 1981 came, I started to buy Jam records on release day as well as backtracking to buy all the ones I'd missed. Me, my brother James and mates Richard Beddall and Paul Wainwright decided to start a band. Originally The Slim Ties, we changed to The Four Faces. We began writing lyrics and I started learning guitar. Our band ended before it really started, but there was still The Jam.

But then Paul Weller announced they were splitting. I was gutted. A farewell tour was announced, named after the final single, 'Beat Surrender', their fourth No.1. My parents said I could go, as could my 14-year-old brother James, and we got tickets for Bingley Hall, Birmingham. They were £5. My two friends from our band also came, and my dad gave us all a lift to our first ever gig. We were so excited.

Apparently, Big Country were the support but we all just wanted The Jam. Then they began… Wow! Some grown-ups and older lads in Parkas and boating blazers said we could move to the front. We did but had no idea what a mosh was. Everyone behind us surged forward. Shit! That was a shock.

My mate Paul lost one of his loafers, asking fans around him to stop and help find it, which they did – Jam fans are simply the best. The music was amazing. We were all hot and sweaty, but we didn't care. To this day I treasure my one and only time seeing them live. I went on to see The Style Council and Paul Weller many times, and I'm still a massive Weller fan. To me though, Bruce Foxton and Rick Buckler were just as important. Those pounding drums from Rick and backing vocals and melodic bass from Bruce… Pow!

That month, the final album came out as a thank you to the fans, *Dig The New Breed*, a wonderful snapshot of The Jam over the years, only kept off the top spot by a new John Lennon compilation album. That didn't matter. He was a Beatle, Paul Weller was always raving about them, and it reminded me of my first musical love, listening to those red and blue albums. Long live The Jam!

I WAS THERE: GAVIN JONES

The final day had come. I picked up Trev and Tracy, heading on to Marc's. We got there about two, went for a drink, then to the hall when the pub closed. Soundcheck wasn't till five. We went to their hotel, chatting with Bruce and then getting on the coach, where Rick came and stood talking for a bit. Marc asked what he was going to do now. He said he had no plans, but he'd been back for his old job and was turned down! Then Paul came out, signing autographs before getting on the coach.

We went to the hall and were let into the soundcheck by a very cheerful Kenny. I smuggled a tape recorder in, getting a muffled recording as they played 'Beat Surrender', 'Precious', 'Planner's Dream' (a rarity, live) and 'Reach Out'. Once we were kicked out, we went to a café past the band's hotel, seeing comic Jim Davidson there.

At the gig we went right down the front. The set was similar to Wembley, but delivered with lots more venom. It was a great atmosphere, hot and sweaty. They finished with 'In The City' and then after ten minutes returned for 'A Town Called Malice', 'Butterfly Collector', 'But I'm Different Now', and the last song I saw them do, 'The Gift'. Then Bruce knocked his mic stand over and Paul threw his guitar on the floor and walked off. The end!

I grabbed a final tour poster and went back to their hotel, freezing as the cold air froze our sweaty bodies! Bruce was signing autographs and then went to bed, Paul and Rick coming down after half an hour. We chatted with them, thanking them for the last few years, shaping our lives with powerful music and inventive, insightful lyrics, never forgetting the fans. We shook Paul by the hand and that was it. John Weller said he'd get us into the Brighton gig if we turned up at the soundcheck, but I couldn't afford to go. I was skint.

They were great times. My whole life revolved around the next Jam tour.

I WAS THERE: ROB BUTTAR

By the time the split was announced, my brothers had moved down to London to work. They managed to get tickets for three nights at Wembley and I bunked off school to go with them. I took the whole week off. When I went back to school the following week, I forged my mum's signature on a sick note and said I'd had a cold. But the whole school knew I'd been in London to see The Jam! I ended up on report for six months until the end of the school year so I had to behave. I had to do my homework on time. I was being marked every lesson.

The Wembley gigs weren't like Birmingham. They were too big. On the first night we were standing on our seats on the floor. The other two nights we were in the bowl. The gigs were fantastic but you didn't get the same connected feeling.

When I saw them again at Bingley Hall in December, it was like that first gig again. You're connected, you're bouncing up and down with the crowd, there's nothing you can do, you've got to go with it, you're covered in sweat, your voice has gone because you're shouting out all the words… It was just nuts.

I think Ravi Shankar had been playing Birmingham Odeon that night. All these Buddhist hippy guys were hanging around the Bull Ring waiting for their buses. We'd come out of our gig bouncing, shouting and screaming, and these guys were looking at us and thinking 'these guys are aggressive, they're really, really weird.' The contrast between those two sets of fans on the bus home together was amazing.

The Jam were very different to other groups. There was power, passion, intelligence and style with The Jam. There was an air of respectability about being a Jam fan. There still is. My mates who are into George Michael and Wham! don't like talking about George Michael and Wham! but I'll happily talk about Paul Weller, The Jam and The Style Council. Everything Weller talks about makes sense to me. When he was talking about his kids, I had a kid. When he was talking about being separated from his missus, I was separated from my missus. We lived in Handsworth opposite what was called the Birmingham Dairies. You could look out of my parents' bedroom window and see the 'rows and rows of disused milk floats stand dying in the dairy yard' that he talked about in 'Town Called Malice'. It closed down within two months of him writing that song.

I'd come back from a school field trip to Malvern or somewhere and my mate Paul was really distraught. He said The Jam had split up and I said to him, 'I don't know what you're talking about. You're talking shit, mate.' But he was so upset that instead of going home after being away on this field trip, I caught the bus into Birmingham city centre and went straight to WH Smiths to find a music paper. The only one I could find was *Record Mirror* and in there it said that The Jam were splitting up. I was really upset for three or four days. All I could listen to was 'The Bitterest Pill'. But as soon as 'Beat Surrender' came out, I could hear something different, like with 'Shopping', and then I started to look forward to The Style Council.

It's a bit weird how some Jam fans haven't got past them splitting up and say 'he's been shit since'. My kids know The Jam, The Style Council and Paul's solo stuff and their go to music is 'My Ever Changing Moods', 'Have You Ever Had It Blue' and 'You're The Best Thing'. They'll say, 'Yeah, that's a track and a half.' They'll listen to The Style Council before The Jam. The Jam sound like an old seventies band to them, even though it still sounds fresh to me. But The Style Council lacked the energy and the power. Experiencing The Jam live was like being punched in the face and I've never experienced that high since.

Except I saw Paul Weller play Shepherds Bush Empire in December 1994 and he absolutely blew the roof off the place. Something must have pissed him off because he was so friggin' angry and it was just like 'wow, wow, he's got his mojo back!'

CIVIC HALL
9 DECEMBER 1982, GUILDFORD, UK

I WAS THERE: STEVE CARVER
The final hometown concert was a real family and friends affair. Alongside the balcony there were rows of seats, only about three deep. I remember 'the in crowd' got to sit there with Paul's mum and sister. It was a celebratory gig but tinged with sadness. Could this really be the end? For six years, The Jam were my life. There was always something to look forward to – a single, an album, a tour, video, and so on.

I WAS THERE: MALC SMITH
As quickly as it started, it all came to an end in 1982, Paul's letter from the fan club explaining why he was splitting the band. We managed to get tickets for what was – when we booked them – the final gig at the Civic Hall, and on the afternoon of the gig we skipped school… We didn't manage to get into the soundcheck.

Having fought my way to the centre of the stage a few feet back from the front, I was alarmed how quickly I was propelled first to the left and then the far right of the stage. And that was when the band had just walked on and were yet to play a note!

For the most part the atmosphere was high-spirited and good humoured. I managed to battle my way out and up to the balcony for a short respite. Most of the people on the balcony made their way down to the stalls, hence a crush of sweaty Weller lookalikes. I perched on the back of a seat as the band launched into the next song. In my teenage exuberance, I fell off the back of the seat, landing in the row behind.

I brushed myself down, grateful no one appeared to have noticed, but a woman approached from the wings, accompanied by a couple of bouncers (or security). Much to my embarrassment, she witnessed the whole episode and was concerned enough to ask if I was okay and if I needed a drink. I thanked her but declined the kind offer, before heading back to the heaving mass downstairs, ready for the final songs of the set.

Years later, having seen a few photos of Paul with his mum, I realised it was Ann Weller who was checking if I was alright. If only I'd accepted the offer of that drink, I may have even got backstage.

I WAS THERE: ANDY ORR

A school mate got hold of *All Mod Cons*. He played it and I sat there silently listening. I couldn't believe how good it was. When we'd finished both sides, we listened again. The following Saturday when I got my paper round money, I got my own copy. I was hooked.

My first ever gig was The Purple Hearts at the Marquee on Wardour Street and my first Jam gig soon followed, in 1979 at the Rainbow. I couldn't believe how big the Rainbow was, and the power and

For Andy Orr, Guildford Civic on the farewell tour was the stand out of the 20+ Jam gigs he witnessed

volume of The Jam was mind-blowing. Weller's passion was something else. I must have seen The Jam more than 20 times, but I didn't keep a diary. One of the best gigs was at Guildford Civic Hall during their farewell tour. It was a great set.

I never got backstage or into a soundcheck, but I met the band when they came to Le Beat Route, Soho for a Mod and Northern Soul night in 1982. In recent years I met Rick and I am currently on tour with Bruce. I've been with Weller at after-shows but I've not really spoken to him.

Like everyone else I was gutted when they split, but didn't much like *The Gift*, and as a hardcore Mod I was still seeing other bands. I still listen to *All Mod Cons* and *Setting Sons*, appreciating them like it's the first time I've heard them.

I WAS THERE: MARTIN WILLIS

I first heard The Jam at a friend's house in April 1977 as he bought a copy of 'In The City' on the day of release. Blown away by the sound and instantly hooked on the raw, aggressive melody, it was a lightbulb moment. I knew things would never be the same. My first gig was at Reading Top Rank in 1977 and I subsequently travelled far and wide, all over the country and even Reims in France in 1979. I was lucky enough to get backstage and meet the lads at Reading University that February – we drank, smoked and chatted.

Their penultimate gig at Guildford Civic Hall was a farewell to their Surrey fans. Having seen them 26 times since 1977, I was determined to go, although I didn't have a ticket, hoping for the chance to get in on the door. We left Reading in two cars. When we arrived, there was a massive crowd buzzing around outside, most of whom didn't have tickets, the venue being sold out and practically full to the rafters. My friends tried to push to the front to get to the main doors.

Thinking it highly unlikely that anyone was going to gain entry at the front, I slipped around to the rear of the building, made my way to some double glass doors, where I saw a large doorman standing. I gestured, 'Could I come in?' He slowly shook his head. I even waved some money at him, but to no avail.

I stood there for about 15 minutes. By this time The Jam were playing and the crowd was cheering. It was a freezing cold winter's night, and I was wearing my blue mohair suit. I was about to give up and walk back to my mates at the front when a stocky, silver-haired middle-aged guy walked up to the doorman. I knew straight away it was Paul's dad, John Weller. As he chatted to the doorman he glanced at me through the glass doors, suited up and looking cold. He told the doorman to open the door and let me in, which the doorman did, telling me it was my lucky night.

Once I was inside, John said, 'Come with me.' I followed him up to the balcony, directly off the side of the stage where family and friends of the band were sitting. He told me I'd be okay there and went on his way. I had a great seat, only a few feet from the band, and witnessed the most memorable Jam gig of them all. Sadly, my mates weren't so lucky, spending the evening outside the venue on that cold December night.

Paul's dad was such a lovely guy for giving me a night I will never forget.

I WAS THERE: ADRIAN JOHNSON

I'd just crawled out of bed after a week in bed with glandular fever, sleeping 23 hours a day and not eating. Pogoing at the front, I collapsed and had to sit at the side of the hall to recover. A fantastic gig otherwise!

I WAS THERE: STUART GORNALL

I got the train down. I went with my girlfriend. We didn't have any digs, but I got tickets, thinking it was the last one… then they added Brighton. I hadn't thought about getting home. I went to the train station after, and the stationmaster let me sleep there, in a little hut with a heater. In the morning, they woke me and I got a train back up to Preston.

I'm glad I didn't go to Brighton. There was a bit of trouble, I believe, and it was all a bit unsavoury. I was gutted when I heard they were splitting. Like someone had shot me. It had been my life. There had been rumours, but then my girlfriend phoned and told me. She was in tears. No one could believe it until that statement in the *NME*.

We lived our lives for it then – the tours, singles, albums. It left a massive gap. I packed two or three jobs in for The Jam, as it was clashing with the gigs! *All Mod Cons* and *Setting Sons* were the best albums, but by the end Paul wanted to go in a new direction, while Bruce and Rick were more rock based. It was horrible when they split, but looking back it was probably the right thing. And Weller's albums he brought out in the lockdown were brilliant. I particularly liked *On Sunset*. Before that, I felt he went a bit Phil Collins.

I WAS THERE: DALE HIGGS

I was lucky enough to get a ticket off a tout outside, just before the start. I watched two young girls from London pay £22 each for a ticket just before me. I only had £13 but he took it and gave me the ticket.

I WAS THERE: DARRON ROBINSON

I was at the last gigs at Guildford and Brighton. My brother-in-law, Pete, heard a rumour that the Wembley dates weren't going to be the last. He wasn't in a better place to get a ticket but was quick off the mark. I was a bit smug about Wembley, deciding instead to go half an hour down the road to Guildford. Then, that night, Pete said, 'I think I've got tickets for Brighton.'

I did think that was the wrong thing to do, finishing there. Come on, you're a Woking band! But Guildford was a brilliant gig. I got to the front as always.

By then I'd left school so had cash. I was a lorry driver's mate. If I wasn't going to football, I spent my Saturdays up Carnaby Street and the week before the Guildford gig I bought a very distinctive red, black and white Lonsdale cycling shirt from a proper sports shop around the corner in Beach Street. I was a bit unsure of wearing it to the gig but did so beneath a Fred Perry jumper. When Paul walked on, he was wearing the exact same shirt. I whipped my jumper off. 'Look at me! What he's wearing up there, I'm wearing right here!'

I WAS THERE: RICHARD AKEHURST

We were in the circle. It was so packed and humid that we were sitting on the stairs, and it was so hot inside that condensation was dripping down the interior walls. Great gig though.

A PEOPLE'S HISTORY OF THE JAM

I WAS THERE: RICHARD WESTNEY
I managed to get a ticket for the penultimate show. I heard it announced on the radio and took the morning off work to shoot down to Guildford to get a ticket. I mostly remember my sadness from that night, that it was pretty much all over and we'd never see them together again. It was just so important that I was there.

The Jam remain my favourite band of all time, even though I'm now in my early sixties. I've lived in New Zealand since 1997 and on a trip back to the UK a few years ago, I persuaded a couple of old mates to go and see From The Jam with me. They were doing a summer festival in Sussex, so we camped overnight. I loved every minute, was right at the front and briefly met Bruce. In 2019, they finally toured NZ and I saw them in Wellington in a packed small club. It was a very special night, reliving my youth.

I've read every book there is about The Jam, watched every documentary, and still listen to the music. It's never dated, it still sounds fresh and relevant. The whole ideology of that period and the punk attitudes inspired me and stayed with me throughout my adult life, along with the brilliance of Paul Weller's writing. I saw the Jam eleven times between '78 and '82, way more than any other band from that era. And I love that they never fully reformed and never will. And while I don't like everything he puts out, I love that Weller never compromises. He's still very principled, keeps moving forward, keeps pushing the musical boundaries, and does everything on his terms. I'd never expect anything less.

I WAS THERE: NEIL ATKIN
The last time I saw them was at Guildford, before the Brighton gig. I've seen From The Jam a few times since, but don't have the energy for it these days!

I WAS THERE: STUART MOORE, AGE 16
My first ever gig was the penultimate Jam show at Guildford Civic. I still don't know how I managed to get a ticket, as for most people that was the 'real' last one – It should always have been local, not Brighton. It's always been bittersweet that my first ever gig will always be my best one.

I WAS THERE: BEN DARNTON
I was outside the Civic Hall that night… unable to get in. There must have been 50 of us kids who walked back to Godalming from Guildford that night. I got back to my gran's in Meadrow around 11.30pm. I was in my Sta-Prest trousers, Mod shoes, all that, and because we'd been jumping up and down, she said that it looked like I'd been in the rain. But I was just sweating from walking back from the Civic.

SOLID BOND IN YOUR HEART

I was always a fan though. It was watching the Marc Bolan show that got me into The Jam. They had those black suits, white shirts, black ties, the Rickenbacker guitars, all that, Weller jumping around like Pete Townshend. I thought, 'Oh, I like that. They look like The Beatles.' I was only ten, still at middle school in Godalming. I always thought Paul Weller and Rick Buckler looked like proper sixties icons, But Bruce Foxton needed to get his hair cut – it was like he was with Pilot or Cockney Rebel!

Soon, I'd have the Steve Marriott haircut, the jacket, the Parka… all part of the jigsaw for me. And Paul Weller was a like mind in that sense. Later, I'd often see Bruce Foxton around Guildford with a chaperone, after the split. And like seeing Jimmy Pursey in Bonaparte's record shop in town, it was kind of, 'What's he doing in here? He's been on *Top Of The Pops*!'

I saw The Style Council at the Royal Albert Hall, maybe 1987 or 1988, and then the Paul Weller Movement. Did he play Guildford twice? First time it was only two-thirds full and he looked furious. A friend who worked in a record shop in Epsom asked if I wanted to go backstage after. I said, 'I don't think I do. He looks so grumpy. He won't want to talk to an idiot like me!' I've met him since though, and got to know his sister, Nicky. In more recent years, she came to me about two weeks before the *About the Young Idea* exhibition at Somerset House, asking what Jam stuff I had. I had lots of singles and a few albums in stock, lots of CDs… I got together more than I thought I had, which was then used for the exhibition.

Ben Darnton in his Guildford record shop

Photo by Dan Reddick

I WAS THERE: GRAHAM FIRTH, AGE 15

A friend brought a copy of *Setting Sons* to school on tape when it first came out. It was such a short album you could almost fit it on one side of a C60 tape. But it was the best thing I'd ever heard. I'd been into music for a few years, but mostly listening to my parents' record collection. The first album I owned was an Elvis Presley album, from my grandparents (my gran was a big Elvis fan). The first LP I bought myself was *Regatta de Blanc* by The Police, closely followed by all The Jam albums I could get my hands on.

Anything off side one of *Setting Sons* – possibly 'Thick As Thieves' – resonated with me, but I saw them just the once, catching the last gig at Guildford Civic Hall, December 1982. It was my first gig. I saw a ticket for sale on a postcard in the window of the newsagents at the end of our road. I did a paper round so rang as soon as I finished and bagged the ticket. My next-door neighbour, John Forster, in the same year at school, also got one. We lived about a 20-minute walk from the venue, so these two excited 15-year-olds headed off, not really knowing what to expect.

We managed to get into the middle of the crowd when The Jam came on, but then came the crush and my feet were lifted off the floor. The same happened to John, and as the crowd surged, we got carried in different directions. I was gutted that they booked an additional night in Brighton, so this wasn't their last ever show after all, as originally planned.

Was I surprised at Paul's decision to end it when he did? I was surprised, upset, angry. It was the first band I'd ever really been into. I really didn't want it to end. By this time I was also into The Undertones, The Clash, The Vapors, Buzzcocks. I bought everything The Style Council did and, whilst I enjoyed their music (let's be honest, The Jam were starting to head in that direction), I couldn't get anywhere near as passionate about it.

I used to dress in a Mod style for a few years, so I guess they (and The Who) may have influenced that. These days, I dip in and out of Paul Weller's music. I've got a few of his solo albums and he's still a class act – but it doesn't excite me the way The Jam did.

I WAS THERE: ALAN HILL

I saw them definitely twice, maybe three times. Pompey (Guildhall) in December '79 with The Vapors and the later Civic gig, but I saw them more than once at Guildford. I thought Steve (Miles) would have been with me and Mark (Wyatt) at the Civic. My sister, Gina came along, seeing one or two bands with us at the Civic when living in Stoke Road, Guildford.

'Tube Station' was the first Jam song that resonated with me. Many more have since, and I started buying their records when *All Mod Cons* came out. I bought all the singles and albums from then on, and later bought the first two albums.

It was definitely crowded at that last gig at Guildford. We could hardly get in the door. I wasn't that surprised when they split. I didn't think much of the last album. I quite liked The Style Council but haven't listened to any of their stuff for years. I haven't kept up with what Weller's been doing over the last few years, but I did like the early albums and still listen to them.

I still listen to The Jam now and again. Anything from the *All Mod Cons*, *Setting Sons* and *Sound Affects* period still sounds really good.

I WAS THERE: MARK WYATT

I only saw The Jam once… They packed the Civic out. I loved and still love *All Mod Cons*, *Setting Sons* and *Sound Affects*. I felt a bond with them (and still do) as they sang about places, local culture, and so on that I knew well, and I knew some of the older blokes who hung out with them in Woking (at the Lite-a-Bite, etc.). 'Saturday's Kids' felt very relevant. I knew loads of later-teenage shop girls who had Saturday jobs in town… I worked in their backyard, served Bruce a few times at a local builders' merchant (1976-81ish), and I knew Rick's Uncle John… but never knowingly saw Paul in Woking. It was John Buckler who introduced me to his nephew's music in late '76, early '77. Prior to that I'd drive past Jam graffiti on the Kingfield roundabout and wonder what it referred to.

I WAS THERE: KEITH WRIGHT

Six of us from West London headed to Guildford without tickets, in John the Nutter's (he ate a lot of peanuts) pimped-out van. Having failed in our normally successful effort to get in on the guest list, we retired to a quaint little pub across the road where time kind of flew by, with beers and conversation.

Suitably buoyed up several pints later, myself and John Mulchrone decided the open window we spotted earlier was indeed reachable, so wandered over to the Civic Hall. The window in question was about seven feet off the ground and just large enough for an 18-year-old to scramble through. So scramble we did.
'Take a pinch of white and pinch of black
Mix it together and make a movin' flavour…'
We made our way through the room we'd unceremoniously landed in.
'Move, move, we got the gift of life…'
Out into a corridor, turn right, turn left, into the arena…
'Thank you very much, goodnight!'

DIG THE NEW BREED RELEASED 10 DECEMBER 1982

A collection of live performances, recorded between 1977 and 1982, is released, entering the charts at No.2. It spends six weeks in the Top 40.

CONFERENCE CENTRE
11 DECEMBER 1982, BRIGHTON, UK

I WAS THERE: RICK BUCKLER

Quite early on, we realised where we did the last show was going to be of some importance. Initially it was going to be Guildford Civic, but for one reason or another we couldn't do multiple nights there, and as soon as we put shows up for sale, they'd be gone, almost overnight. The same happened with Wembley. We had to say, 'Stop, we can't keep adding nights on!' It was getting ridiculous. Brighton was no real home for The Jam. It was just this sort of frenzy for the Mod thing, the fights on the beach from the 1960s … which in itself didn't really exist. It was all a bit out there, really. But it was a good place to play, and a fairly large venue.

I WAS THERE: CRAIG SIMMONS

It was early December 1982 and brass monkey weather. I stamped my steel toe-capped boots on the icy tarmac in an attempt to warm my feet as I stood outside the locomotive build shop, chatting to a few of the fitters; keeping an eye out over my shoulder for the foreman, who took a dim view of my regular fag breaks (not surprising as I'd never smoked in my life and simply went out to chew the fat with those who did). A workmate from the heavy machine shop, Dave Muir, appeared behind me, waggling a copy of *The Sun* newspaper in my face… 'There's something in here about that bloody band you're always traipsing around after.' Having pinned him laughingly against the wall as he tried his best to hold the paper teasingly from me, I quickly scanned the, by now, screwed-up page.

I knew this was coming. A few weeks earlier, to the consternation of half of the right-minded youth of the country, Paul Weller had bravely/stupidly/suicidally announced that the upcoming December shows were to be The Jam's last. I won't go into my feelings; if you're reading this you probably went through the same agony, so I'll spare you this time. A shortish UK tour had been arranged, the original two nights at London's Wembley Arena expanded to five and sandwiched among regional dates at much smaller, sometimes remote establishments (St Austell, Port Talbot and Bridlington, anyone?). I'd already managed to get my ticket for what at the time was pencilled in as the final gig, 8th December at Birmingham's Bingley Hall (I always wondered how many folk inadvertently ended up at the better known Stafford Bingley Hall by accident, a fraught return to the car followed by a mad dash 20 or so miles down the M6 when they realised their error).

Once the initial tour dates were out in the open, the band announced, rather vaguely, there were to be one or two extra shows tacked on. Indeed, such was the haste with which the final tour was drawn up, several dates were missed from merchandise, including the gig at Glasgow Apollo which became the tour's opening night. There was a national outcry from fans at every location across the UK missing out, but to play no gig in Scotland would've been astonishingly cruel to a loyal fan base north of the border, so I think Weller begrudgingly relented, permitting an extra show, apparently one of the best.

Now, here I was, speed-scanning *The Sun* (I always despised that paper but needed the info it sadly offered). The Jam were to play their finale at Brighton Conference Centre on 11th December. Worryingly, tickets were already up for grabs at the box office. It was late afternoon, I was in Loughborough in the East Midlands, too far from Brighton to make the box office before closure, but still... 'Yeah, sorry Bryan, I feel terrible, I think I'm going to be sick, must've been something I ate.' Bryan Lilly, the machine shop foreman, glowered at me with disdain; he could read me alright. I clutched my gut dramatically as I staggered out of his little white hut in the centre of the huge hangar of a machine shop and quickly regained my composure as I got a trot on down to the adjacent railway station.

I made London St Pancras a few hours later but knew that whilst I'd make Brighton without a hitch, the box office would be long closed. My only hope was that tickets would remain the following morning and I'd be ready for them. As such, I dossed in a locked and dirty doorway at London's Victoria Station for some hours before being kicked out by the Transport Police. I found an all-night café and propped myself in a corner with a suspiciously opaque, flat Double Diamond and dozed off.

When I awoke, groggy and downbeat, I recall an older woman sat opposite, dressed up like a dog's dinner, clearly having missed a last train home from a night out. I reached under the table for my bag as I prepared to depart but on doing so, she let out an ear-piercingly loud cockneyish shriek: 'Ere, what you doin', knicker sniffing?' Every other inhabitant of this shabby little bar sprang instantly awake, staring as I sheepishly emerged from between her legs. It seemed futile to try to explain. I slunk out into the misty darkness, every pair of eyes burning into the back of my head.

I arrived in Brighton far too early for the box office's opening, killing time in the station cafeteria with a lukewarm, greasy, Traveller's Fare breakfast. As I pushed an anaemic sausage around the plate with one hand and propped up the *NME* with the other, I noticed a girl with long blonde hair, her back to me, ordering from the counter. I lowered my gaze and continued to read. Shortly, she came and sat opposite me. Aware there were plenty of vacant seats, I took this as a positive. It couldn't go any worse than the Victoria fiasco, could it?

'Hello,' she said coyly to the back of my music mag. I composed myself and gradually lowered the paper for dramatic effect. Wasn't this how so many black-and-white movies introduced lifelong lovers? My expectation of a modern-day Marilyn Monroe was soon quashed; a long string of snot dangled from her nose. I made my blustered excuses and jumped up from my half-eaten grub. 'I'll come with you!' she beseeched and despite my rapid departure I could feel her panting along behind. 'Why me?' Eventually I shook her off, finding my way down to the coast and the booking office.

I don't recall there being any form of queue prior to opening time. My initial delight at finding tickets were still available was somewhat tempered when all I could obtain were a pair of seated ones with a restricted view. Regardless, elated, I paid £10 for the pair and returned north without any further girl trouble. I walked out of Loughborough station and back to work, looking like a bloke who had left 20 hours earlier, slept in some of London's roughest doorways and returned without approaching a bed or a sinkful of warm soapy water.

I WAS THERE: ANDY MAYS

I was eleven or twelve when I first got into them. I used to sit next to my mate in art classes at school. I went around his house one day and he had recreated this image of Bruce Foxton in mid-leap from the back of the *In The City* album. It was this brilliant life-size piece of artwork right across his bedroom wall. I remember him playing the album and that was it. That image, and then the sound of it… that was it.

Another mate got into them and then the whole Mod thing came about and everyone at school had Parkas or two-tone trousers or a suit jacket or whatever. It was just part of being some sort of movement. You were either part of that or you weren't, and if you went out the same guys would be going to the same parties and stuff like that. It was just a group thing. It wasn't a case of having to be with others, it was that you all liked the same thing. You wanted to be part and parcel of that and you loved what was going on. And the music… Because all the other bands were then sort of flying around, like The Purple Hearts and The Chords and Secret Affair. It was just this absolutely brilliant time.

The first time I saw them, I went with a mate up to the Rainbow. It was a big theatre with rows of seats and when The Jam came on stage and said, 'We asked for a stand-up gig, we still want to do a stand-up gig, please now take your seats out,' everybody basically ripped their seats out. I can remember bouncers being at the side of the hall collecting the seats because everyone was just heaving their seats to the side. It was just mad. I seem to remember they got charged for the damage and the inconvenience.

Afterwards, I remember my parents were expecting us home by a certain time and I would be in trouble for getting home late, but I couldn't get anywhere near a railway station. There'd been loads and loads of skinheads down by the railway station and we ended up running back to the Rainbow, where all the older guys were now pouring out. It was just carnage, one of those nights of people chasing one another around.

It would just be a frenzy for tickets. As soon as you heard there was a gig it was all about trying to get tickets, and if you were the one that was going to go and get the tickets, you got tickets for you and two or three mates. And when albums came out, you had to be in the record shop the day anything was released. You went in with your little tab of paper to pick up your pre-ordered album or single. Just the excitement around it was massive. You couldn't wait to go and get it. There'd be people there that couldn't get a copy because there weren't enough copies to go around, other than those that had pre-ordered and gone in and paid in advance.

I remember the announcement of the split. I was 18 and working down in Brighton and I couldn't go to either of the last two gigs, which had been announced for Wembley, because of work. I was gutted. I had a day off. It was a lovely sunny day and I was walking along the seafront towards home when I looked across at the Brighton Centre. There's this guy up a ladder sticking letters on the front of the marquee, along the top of the Centre. He just had the 'JA' up and I remember stopping and watching him put the 'M' up and then a dash and then he started putting a date up.

I hurtled into the Brighton Centre and they said, 'Oh yeah, it's just been announced. We've just got tickets.' I'd not seen it in the press or anything and I wouldn't have known about it had I not happened to walk along and seen this bloke halfway up this ladder, putting the big black big black letters up. If I'd been there five minutes earlier, I would have missed it.

We made the normal attempt to get near the front. That was key, in the same way that your mates that hadn't got tickets would build up a group by a side door to the standing area that had a lady attendant on it. One of your mates at the back would suddenly run and push the group, and because it looked like 15 blokes were stumbling, you all just fell through the door into the darkness on the other side and kept going before anyone tugged you back.

I wasn't thinking too much about it being the last ever show. It probably hit me more when I came out. It was just frenetic and as lively as ever.

A PEOPLE'S HISTORY OF THE JAM

I WAS THERE: STEVE CARVER

Brighton. The last stand. I genuinely cannot recall anything about this gig. I was probably drunk, and an emotional mess. After the concert a girl asked me, 'What are we gonna do now, Tufty?' To be honest, I had absolutely no fucking idea. I can only imagine how Bruce and Rick felt.

I WAS THERE: IAN BURBEDGE

I saw them twice in 1981, in June at the Rainbow and December at Hammersmith Palais, at Alexandra Palace in March 1982 and two of the final shows, at Wembley Arena and then the last (and arguably the worst) at Brighton. There were a few fights, the band didn't seem up for it, and it all felt a bit flat. Everybody thought the same – 'Why is Paul doing it?' I get it now, and I get why he didn't reform the band. And I look with hindsight and say I'm glad he didn't – It would have been very difficult to recreate those halcyon days. Would I have gone though? Of course. After all, they were/still are 'the best band in the fucking world'.

I WAS THERE: JONATHAN BILLINGTON

The Jam were my everyday life. Sometimes we'd go to six concerts on a tour. It was easy to buy tickets. We sent blank cheques to venues and, lo and behold, we'd get very early tickets. I never had one-week or two-week holidays. I just took time off to see The Jam.

I came in from work and my younger sister, Lucy, told me they were splitting. I looked at her and thought, 'Don't be silly, this can't possibly happen.' I went up to my room, listened to the radio, and it wasn't long before I had confirmation. 'Blimey, this is going to be a bit of a change.'

Although it was sad, it was a lovely end to five absolutely brilliant years. By the time I saw them at Hammersmith Palais and the Michael Sobell Centre I wasn't jumping around as much. I was standing around watching, and songs like 'Precious' and 'The Bitterest Pill' I thought were dreadful, so I was pleased they were going to give up at the top.

I went to Brighton with Andrew, Glenn, Philippa and Dirk in Stephen's car. We parked on Madeira Drive. I don't think they let us in early, which caused a bit of frustration. Then we went into the Brighton Centre, with its appalling acoustics, and watched them for the last time.

I saw them 26 or 27 times altogether. Andrew saw them 32 times. I wouldn't want to be there if Paul reformed The Jam, not even for one concert. It was about the time, it was about being young. I went to see Bruce Foxton at Hastings' White Rock Theatre in December 2023, leaving after they did the *All Mod Cons* stuff. There's only so much an old man like me wants to be reminded of how much fun it was to be young.

I WAS THERE: KEVIN BONNOT

I was in the queue when Rick got locked out of the Brighton Centre. We had to tell the security he was part of the band!

I WAS THERE: JON ABNETT

I saw the five nights at Wembley but couldn't get tickets for Guildford, originally the last night. Apparently, the best night was at Glasgow Apollo, but for those I went to they didn't look like a group that were disbanding after it was all over. They were just as tight musically as any other time I saw them. There didn't seem to be any 'differences' on stage. All was friendly enough, despite rumours that Foxton had refused to go on tour.

Brighton was a mixed affair. The night was very tense for obvious reasons, but like all the nights I saw them play on that farewell tour, the band put everything they could into the shows. It was spoiled by someone deciding to launch a beer bottle at Bruce, narrowly missing him. He was ready to walk off stage. If you include everyone supposed to be there that night, the capacity would have been 8,000!

The band had been a big part of my life for five years, I was at school, I went to college, I had ups and downs at home… the only constant in my life was The Jam. Before the split, I knew where I was with them. Always great singles, LPs and live shows. Then on 11th December at 10.30pm, that had all gone, The Jam were no more. Little did I know that 42 years later, I'd still be listening to the Jam and anything else related to them.

I WAS THERE: ANDY NEWMAN

When news broke that they were splitting, I was gutted and blubbed like a baby. What was I going to do? Who was I going to follow now? Big questions for a 14-year-old. The only good thing to come out of it was that the last gig was back at the Brighton Centre. We got one of our older friends to queue around the block for us and secure the tickets.

It was cold on the day of the gig and there was a bit of a breeze. Learning from my previous adventures I now took a coat to gigs, deposited in the cloakroom. As was normal for the previous two gigs I'd attended, I went to the soundcheck. These were getting busier and busier.

There was an air of excitement in the hall. It seemed rammed. (Little did I know that they'd opened the doors to anyone left outside.) I positioned myself as close as I could to the stage, in the sea of faces waiting for the band to come on. My proximity to the stage was not the best idea, as when the lights went down, a hallful of eagerly waiting teens was not expecting the Eton Rifles dance troupe to come on. Anything that was not nailed down was thrown at them!

They trooped off (excuse the pun) and we were on. 'Start!' echoed out across the hall, every single person belting out the words in a fever-pitched echo. The Jam did not disappoint, most of the favourites played to a boisterous crowd. The band stopped at some point as bottles were flying about and towards them; maybe some people took the news worse than I did. It was a bittersweet affair, knowing in the back of my mind this was not going to happen again. I tried to make the most of what I felt was slipping through my fingers.

The show ended with two encores and the last song, 'The Gift'. The lights went up and they came back to say their goodbyes.

I was lost musically for a while and could not forgive Weller for what he had done to me. I bought 'Speak Like A Child' but couldn't get my head around it not being The Jam. Did he not know I had all the cuttings from the musical press? I knew when the singles were coming out and would be played on the radio. I had all the records and searched the shops at weekends, hoping to find rare Japanese import versions of unknown recordings.

I had my Parka and cycling tops that the guy in the bike shop could not understand me wanting. My mum had never understood why I wanted to wear bowling shoes to school or, worse still, Jam shoes that I snuck up to Carnaby Street to buy. I still look back on those days and feel it was such a big part of my life. I met good friends and moved through the most important parts of growing up listening to them. I still know every word to every song.

I've since forgiven Weller, seeing him loads of times, and am looking forward to taking my daughter to see him for the first time. I think she gets it. I've dragged her along to watch From The Jam, as I have my eldest son, who's embarrassed by my bouncing around at the front, eager to relive my youth.

I look back with fondness and a happy tear at those times. The Jam were my youth, when music was important. I lived, loved and cried then. I'm glad to say I was there!

I WAS THERE: ALAN NEWBIGGIN
I missed the last train home and slept under Brighton Pier. It was bloody freezing!

I WAS THERE: IAN TRAYNOR
Then came that fateful day. 'Fuck!' There was a mad scramble for tickets to see them on a farewell tour night at Wembley. Friday, 3 December. As good as it was, I didn't feel that was how it should end.

Me, a couple of mates and my girlfriend Maggie drove to Brighton. We had no tickets and no real idea why we were there. Touts were looking for £15 to £20 a ticket. We had about £20 between us! Wondering if there was a way to bunk in, we ended up at the stage door... just as John Weller came out waving a handful of tickets. I got within an arm's length of getting one, but they were all gone. 'Fuck!'

Then my girlfriend appeared out of a scrum of parkas and Harringtons. 'I've got three, is that okay?' 'Fuck!' yet again. We sprinted to the front of the Conference Centre and clubbed together to buy a ticket from a tout for £10. Result. We got to the entrance... 'Sorry mate. There's no stub on this ticket.'

A mad scramble followed, back through the crowd to find the thieving tout... who turned out to be genuinely sorry and gave us £15 back. Which was used to buy a ticket... with a stub! We got in just in time to hear someone (not John Weller) introduce the band. It was definitely edgy, with neither Maggie nor I brave enough to go near the stage. There was a similar tension to the football terraces back then... but I was unsure who wanted to fight who – we were all supporting the same team.

Ian Traynor in recent times with Paul Weller

And with Rick Buckler

Tony came with us, as did David Benjamin. We all got in. We were up in the balcony, just delighted to be there. It was somehow the best and worst night of my life. As the final notes of 'The Gift' faded out, that was it... My only achievement in life is being able to say 'I was at the last Jam concert!'

40-odd years later, my 60-something ears still listen to those songs with 14-year-old ears. I'm still too daft to understand the messages in the songs though. Oh, and Maggie became my wife... possibly on the strength of getting those tickets!

In the last year I've met (separately) both Rick and Paul. Both were lovely, but I completely lost the ability to speak when I met Paul. I only managed to shake his hand and mumble 'hello'. He must have thought I was an escaped lunatic.

A PEOPLE'S HISTORY OF THE JAM

I WAS THERE: PAUL BROMLEY
That Brighton Conference Centre finale was all very emotional. On the final song, 'The Gift', tears ran down my face. I couldn't get my head around Paul's decision to end it, as they were smashing it. However, looking back, what a way to go out, on top. The Jam influenced my path in life for a very long time – the clothes, the culture, and certainly the politics. The Jam have left me with an everlasting love of live music.

I WAS THERE: STUART STEELES
I was back at Brighton Centre for the *Solid Bond* tour and I saw them play the last night at Wembley. Then it was the final show, back at Brighton six days later. I was lucky to see them at a very special time. They had such an intensity that it didn't seem like it was a big venue. For the *Sound Affects* and *Trans Global* shows, we'd been to the soundcheck, so were able to be near the front of the queue and get down the front when the doors opened. These were very special gigs and my favourites. The Wembley Arena farewell was too big. Although it was a great set, I was far away in a balcony, feeling quite detached. It was also sinking in that this was all coming to an end.

When the final show was announced, I'd left school, started a full-time job and couldn't get time off to get tickets. Luckily a mate queued for hours at the box office. That final gig had a very strange atmosphere, more of sadness and disbelief than celebration. And there was tension. There had been trouble outside before, then there was the glass or bottle-throwing incident that caused Bruce to get upset. I had to get a drink during 'Precious' and realised they'd opened the doors to let extra people in. It was rammed and I stood to the side to watch the closing songs. When they came out and Paul held back, it all seemed a bit unreal that this was it. It was done. Beat Surrender!

As I got to see more bands and go to more gigs I got to understand and appreciate just what going to see The Jam was. They were always really intense and powerful, and Weller was very, very serious about it. I saw a few of their contemporaries, including The Clash, The Stranglers, Buzzcocks, and The Specials, but nothing was nearly as good as seeing The Jam.

I WAS THERE: LAURENCE ROLFE
I saw The Jam many times. At the last gig at Brighton, we broke in through the fire exit after pushing one of our mates through an air vent. It was mentioned in one of the music papers.

I WAS THERE: BRENT YEOMANS
I grew up in Horsham, West Sussex. I was into the punk stuff. My sister was a little bit older and into Motown and I listened to a bit of that. Then The Jam came

along. My mate said, 'Look, we're gonna turn Mods,' and I said 'what's that all about?' He said, 'It's like punk – but smart,' so I thought, 'I'll have some of that.'

After that I rushed out and got every single on the day it was released. I would queue up outside the shop and everything, and I'd go in the shops and ask for the displays when they'd finished with them. (I've still got some in the attic.) I queued up on the day 'Going Underground' was released. I remember being outside the shop at nine o'clock when it opened and them saying, 'No, it's not in yet mate.' So I stood outside and waited for every van to come past. When it arrived, I rushed in and I was the first one to buy the record.

I saw them about 20 times in London, Brighton, Guildford and in Crawley. As it went on, I got more and more obsessed with them. The lyrics were brilliant. I liked the clothes, the style, the haircuts, everything. I remember going to the gigs and waiting for Paul to come out and to see what haircut he had and what clothes and shoes he had on. It just dragged me in. They were *my* band.

For the *Sound Affects* tour in Brighton, we were down the front and everyone was crushed up and moving about. You went with the flow. Your feet came off the ground and you were swaying about everywhere. I got stars in front of my eyes and was starting to black out, so I pushed my way to the sound desk at the back. This fella came up to me and said 'do you need some water?' and I said 'yes please' and he went and fetched me some. It was John Weller!

The Crawley gig was when I was doing my O-levels. I was standing at the station with another lad from a different school, waiting to catch the train up to the venue, and my teacher was on the opposite platform. The guy I was with was started trying to draw attention to me, saying, 'Brent Yeomans, what are you doing? Why aren't you at school?' and I thought 'fuck'. But I went to the gig. At that time, seeing The Jam was more important than doing my exams.

I went to both of the Michael Sobell gigs. It was heavy snow and as we left Horsham, I remember them saying, 'We're going to get there but there's no guarantee you'll get back.' We thought, 'Sod it, we're gonna go anyway.' The Exploited were playing at the Rainbow and there were quite a few scuffles that night.

Another time, we'd got tickets but couldn't afford the train. We bunked the train and I spent ten minutes hiding between the back-to-back seats while the guard came to inspect people's tickets. But I had my Parka on and there was this bloody heater between the seats. I came out sweating like a pig. I was absolutely drenched.

I lost my shoe at Brighton, trying to get to the front. And when you went to look for your shoe afterwards, there'd be a dozen different shoes lying there and twelve different people hopping about with one shoe on!

I saw two nights at Wembley. I didn't have a ticket for Guildford but a mate did. He was worried about not getting up for his paper round in the morning. I said, 'You wanker. Give us your ticket!' Of all the times I saw The Jam, that was probably the best. It was pretty close to their home town, and the family were there, in the balcony. It was very emotional.

We didn't have tickets for Brighton and the tickets outside were expensive. I said to my mate, 'Let's walk up towards the station and see if anybody's got a spare ticket.' We were nearly at the station when we met this girl who said, 'Yeah, I've got two. You can have them for face value.' I think they were four quid so I gave her a fiver and a kiss on the cheek and that was it. We were in! I remember there was a guy flat out in the toilet. He'd spent 100 quid getting down from Scotland with his mates and he was unconscious. He didn't see The Jam that night.

I've seen Paul Weller 120 plus times now. I've been to Japan to see him and all sorts. I saw Bruce get up and play a few songs with Paul at the Albert Hall a few years ago and that was pretty amazing, but I wouldn't want to see the three of them get back together.

Over the years I've met loads of people and made lifelong friends, all because of The Jam and that camaraderie. We were like a big family in a way, and it got bigger and bigger as they got more famous.

I WAS THERE: DARREN LILLIS

Having done Wembley the week before, I couldn't miss Brighton, so I blagged a ticket somehow, but being 15 years old I had no money. I had to sell my mum's original Elvis record collection to a secondhand record shop. She only found out when moving house three years later. I wasn't popular! When I got there, the queue was very long at the main entrance. I took a chance there might be another way in, and the back entrance was open. Result. First ones in. Down the front. I managed to get in the book, the picture of them waving goodbye. Myself, and a few mates. Jaw dropped – I couldn't believe it was all over. The end of an era.

I WAS THERE: CHRIS BUSH, AGE 16

It had all started for me when they played 'Batman' on, I think, *Top Of The Pops*. I bought all the singles and albums. I bought the clothes from Carnaby Street, the Gibson shoes, Mod suits, Prince of Wales check jackets, bowling shoes, trench coats, Parka. I used to follow most of the retro Mod bands – The Merton Parkas, The Vapors, etc. Those were the days. The Jam probably influenced me in my passion for 1960s and my retro shop. I bunked the train fare from Redhill Station to go to the last gig.

SOLID BOND IN YOUR HEART

I WAS THERE: JOHN TOMSETT

When Paul Weller declared The Jam were no more, I felt abandoned. A failed golfer, at 18 I returned to school and found myself taking my A levels just as all my peers left. That autumn, I was reading Thomas Hardy's *Return Of The Native* while Weller was growling at me about a 'Philistine nation of degradation'. It was an unlikely mix.

And when it comes to unlikely mixes... the date of the final gig coincided with my final appearance for the Sussex County Golf Union. I'd given golf a good go, having been chucked out of school at 16 for being a general pain in the arse. We played at Worthing and my dad picked me up at 5pm and dropped me off on Brighton's seafront. I changed into black drainpipes and my top in the front of his Mini, jumped out and said I would find my way home, somehow.

I didn't even have a ticket. A few others were in the same boat. Asking prices were way beyond what I could afford. In desperation, one lad bought a dodgy looking backstage pass for a quid. When I met him inside, it turned out it was legit and he had full access to the post-gig shenanigans, the lucky bastard! Eventually I worked out that you had to stand on the corner of West Street and waylay potential sellers before they realised how much they could sell their tickets for outside the venue. I secured one for a fiver, from a naïve fan unaware of the fortune she could have made.

Whilst ecstatic at getting in, Weller seemed bloody miserable all night, more than usual if possible. I hadn't realised, but the band had been forced to play the Brighton finale after demand for tickets meant plans to finish at Guildford Civic Hall, on home turf, were not, apparently, commercially sensible...

Despite a morose lead singer, The Jam gave it their all. For the first encore, they played 'David Watts', 'Mr Clean', 'Going Underground', 'In The City' and 'Town Called Malice'... in a row! It was chaotic, and my black-and-white poster of Weller with his acoustic guitar got ruined as I bounced around the mosh.

Weller's misery was complete when someone lobbed a bottle. He found himself remonstrating angrily with the audience. In retrospect, it was a surprise he didn't just walk off. But this was the last ever time The Jam were to play together. As Weller said in his valedictory message, published in the *NME*, what the band created was something imbibed with 'honesty, passion and energy and youth.' Looking back, he made the right move, even if my 18-year-old self felt forsaken.

I WAS THERE: MIKE PHILPOTT

The Jam weren't the only band that taught me about how music can make you feel, but they certainly taught me how to be a fan. At the Brighton Dome, for my first Jam gig, as a 14-year-old on the *All Mod Cons* tour, I learned that if you're stuck with a balcony seat your parents bought you it's okay and actually quite cool to rush the doorman downstairs just as John Weller is making his customary understated introduction and sprint to the front of the stage. At the final gig at Brighton Centre, I learnt that, as a mature 18-year-old, it was okay to cry in public. In between? Well, didn't we have a nice time.

Those gigs in London at the Rainbow, at the Sobell Centre and at the Music Machine Christmas show, which I somehow got into with The Nips supporting (where I lost a shoe and waited until the place was empty before miraculously finding it nestled up against the side wall, dozens of yards from where it had been separated from my pogoing foot). The Wembley Arena not-quite-farewell show with Big Country, when we all knew the end was coming but still revelled in the glory of it all. Every single one memorable, every single one leaving a glow of satisfaction, knowing we'd all been a part of something special.

The Crawley Leisure Centre show where, with my eager fellow Modlings, we decided to start a fanzine after bumping into support act Purple Hearts at the pool table in the centre's café, proceeding to interview them with the assistance of a lipstick pen and a paper napkin to take notes (no fanzine ever emerged). And the *Sound Affects* t-shirt I got signed by Paul, Bruce and Rick that night before leaving it on my bedroom floor for just one day longer than my mum's patience lasted, and which she consequently put through the washing machine, leaving a sad blur of black ink-stained t-shirt and a sadder blur of teenage angst. (I'm talking to her again now.)

And all those hometown shows at the cavernous Brighton Centre. The *Setting Sons* tour with The Vapors supporting, the *Sound Affects* tour, by which time I was a dead cool 16-year-old (!), Dolly Mixture supporting and me and lifetime pal Kev hanging out at the bar with Steve and Ed from The Vapors before they persuaded us reluctantly to watch The Jam set from next to the sound desk with them rather than leap about uncontrollably in front of the stage. And, yeah, that bittersweet last ever gig.

Those Jam shows were different. Because they weren't just gigs, they were huge, full-on experiences. From turning up at the crack of dawn weeks before the show outside desolate box offices to take your place in queues for tickets you knew would sell out in hours, to turning up mid-afternoon on the day in the hope of getting into the soundcheck, Jam gigs were more than 75 minutes of sweaty adrenaline-fuelled emotion (although they were that too).

They were, for so many of us, a rite of passage, a coming of age. Turning up at 15, witnessing hundreds of cool scootering Londoners parading along Kings Road,

Brighton, where just two years previously I'd been a geeky 13-year-old queuing to get into *Star Wars* at the Odeon, had an effect. Sneaking into pubs with those guys, swapping stories and nascent teenage experiences, comparing notes on bands, music and life, all of that formed a significant part of who I am now.

And the songs weren't bad, were they? Millions of others have given their take on the music, but for me *All Mod Cons* remains the high spot, with *Setting Sons* close behind and *Sound Affects* in bronze medal position. The other three aren't far off and they can fight among themselves for position, but it doesn't really matter, because there isn't a weak song among them. And when I play any of those six classic LPs, they inevitably take my head and my heart back to a time of adventure, discovery, emotion and rapidly disappearing innocence.

I learnt a hell of a lot about life, as well as music, from The Jam.

I WAS THERE: JOE SHIELDS

We went to the last gig. Again, we went down in my friend's mum's Hillman Avenger. Face value for the tickets was £5 but the coach guy stung everyone that night for a quick profit. He wanted 25 quid. I said, 'Come on Derek, I'm always buying tickets off you.' But he said, 'No, 25 quid. It's the last ever gig. You won't be able to see them again.' That was big money then, because I was a bank clerk earning 45 or 50 quid a week, so half my week's wages. But I had to pay it.

That was a very sad night. It ended up with a bit of fighting in the crowd. I think someone threw a bottle at Weller. It was a very angry crowd because they were splitting. We were all pretty subdued and had a real feeling of emptiness that night.

I WAS THERE: CHRIS GREEN

I saw The Jam in the spring of 1982 when *The Gift* came out, and then in the summer or the early autumn when 'The Bitterest Pill' came out and then the final tour, I saw them all over the place then, venues like Birmingham Bingley Hall, Leicester Granby Hall and Shepton Mallet Showground, when we parked in what we thought was a back street in the centre of Shepton Mallet!

There was only a couple of times when we paid for hotels. Most of the time we just kipped in the car and moved onto the next place in the morning. I don't know why we gravitated to gigs down south but we must've seen them three or four times in Brighton. We knew the place like the back of our hand. We never thought about anything more than paying to park overnight in the multistorey car park at the back of the conference centre and then finding a loo to go and have a wash in the morning. We knew all the pubs and the cafés where we could get something to eat.

Sometimes I'd hire a minibus and we'd all pile into that. We didn't go and see them at the Michael Sobell Centre in December 1981 because, although we'd bought tickets, there was snow everywhere and we thought if we get this van stuck, it would've been horrendous. But some lads went and I think we had a bit of a fallout about why some went and some didn't. As the driver, I was always conscious of having a dozen guys in the back if something happened. I was just a little bit older than one or two of them and perhaps just a little bit wiser maybe.

The girlfriend I mentioned got very close to the group so we saw them a lot on the final tour. She ultimately left me for one of the roadies, a long-haired geezer, and I thought 'well, if she prefers him to me then fair enough.' But she did tip me off about them splitting up early so I knew that a few weeks before it was announced, and I was conscious about getting to all the final gigs and she did kind of help with that.

There was going to be a final, final, final gig in somewhere like Guildford or Woking and she was going to get me into that, but if it did happen, I didn't go to it. But I did go to the very final one in Brighton. It wasn't their finest gig by any stretch of the imagination. It was like watching the Cup Final, where teams very rarely play their best football. Seeing The Jam was always a very emotional event, and I don't know any other band where the fans sing every single lyric to every single song – most of the gigs in the last two or three years were like that – but that final gig was very emotionally charged and I think it was too much for the band. It can't have been easy for them, because Paul Weller had basically just told the other two: 'I'm scarpering, I'm doing something else now, I'm folding this band,' and that sense of togetherness that they always had usually was no longer there.

When you went to see The Jam, you stood up in the front and that was it and you were just away with the fairies for a couple of hours. But at Brighton the only tickets we could get were up in the seats. I tried to change our tickets but couldn't. One of the daftest things I've ever done – and I was lucky to survive it – is that when it got to the encore, I decided that I wanted to be as close the group as possible because they meant everything to me. So I went over the edge and jumped down onto the ground floor level. You could hear people shouting and screaming 'no, don't do it!' In that split second, I remember thinking 'I'll either break my legs or my back or I'll survive it.' Because of the adrenaline I was fine, but I took one hell of a whack. But I got as close to the front as I could.

It was the end of an era. And Brighton, with all that symbolism – because of Mod, because of bands like The Clash and others that movement, whether you call it punk or new wave – had come to an end. It all came to a final end. The spirit of that came to an end at that point.

SOLID BOND IN YOUR HEART

I WAS THERE: BRIAN TILLEY

Newcastle City Hall… excellent; Newcastle City Hall… good; Whitley Bay… worth a night out; Carlisle… worth a night out; Royal Court, Liverpool… utterly brilliant; Manchester Apollo… excellent; Loch Ness… ruined by bother; Skegness… worth a night out; Stafford Bingley Hall… worth a night out; Birmingham Bingley Hall… worth a night out; Paris… ruined by bother; Bridlington… excellent.

I WAS THERE: RUSSELL HASTINGS

I did know how many times I saw them – 26 or 36? Something bonkers. The Michael Sobell Centre with Bananarama, the last night at Brighton, obviously… I saw all the Brighton Centre and Portsmouth Guildhall shows, Guildford Civic Hall and Wembley as well, a couple of nights. The last night is always going to be too emotional, no matter what it is. It never meets up to expectations. There's always a lot of people on edge for whatever reason. And I understand that, all of a sudden people, felt abandoned: 'my football team's now been dissolved'. I understood that, but it was a case of 'something will come along'… although I didn't have the wisdom to know what back then. I did feel heartbroken. A strong word, but…

I asked Bruce what it was like, the night they came off at Brighton, and he said, 'We all split up into camps. Literally the moment we walked off stage, the camps were created.' Everybody was looking towards the future. And he said, 'Next day I woke up and I didn't have a job.' Lots of people have a problem with letting go all of that. Some of these real Jam-heads. They had something they hooked on to in their lives and they don't want to let it go. They can't deal with change. I get it. But I used to love marbles when I was a kid, yet I don't play with them now!

I stuck with Paul though. I was bang into The Style Council, and when I got friendly with Mickey Talbot a few years ago I told him a few funny stories, such as dropping acid to *Confessions Of A Pop Group* during my drug phase. He's a lovely man and doesn't take enough of his dues and credit for The Style Council. Most of that piano stuff was led really by Mickey T. We went to see Wilko Johnson once, and it was one of those moments – 'Fuck's sake! When's this dream going to finish? Is this my reality?'

I was gutted at the end of The Jam. But nobody knew he was going to come out with The Style Council next. It wasn't until the spring of '83 that all happened. I was 18 that July and it was a pivotal moment in my life, *Live Aid* and all that. I was working for Polydor by '85, displays and promotion, and got to work on the 'Orange' album (*The Cost of Loving*). I loved that and *Confessions of a Pop Group*. That was full of culture for me, turned me on to lots of things.

Later, Rick Buckler got me into classical music – 'Adagio For Strings', Erik Satie, all that. You'd never imagine that in a million years, would you, watching them at Brighton Centre – imagine how mental that sounds, watching The Jam for the last time play 'Tube Station' and the drummer, 26 years later, is going to turn me on to Erik Satie. And I'm going to be sat with a grown man who's crying because he's listening to classical music. My world is nuts!

We got backstage too, mostly down at Brighton Centre but also Portsmouth Guildhall. We'd arrive at three in the afternoon, watch the coach come in, Joe Awome would get off, and then John (Weller) would come out and let us all in and we'd watch the soundcheck. We'd get in somehow, sneak in or get on a guest list. Sometimes you'd be in there with 60 people at a soundcheck.

I had a white Levi's jacket and all three of them signed it. I spent the afternoon with Paul at the hotel back in '82 in the lobby. I told Bruce that, and he said, 'Why don't you tell him?' But I said, 'Fuck it! If people say that to us, I see sheer disappointment on their faces if we say, 'I can't remember that'!'

At that hotel, he pulled out these photographs, gave me and my friends three each. He said, 'Who's that?' I went, 'It's you, innit?' He went, 'No, Steve Marriott on *Ready Steady Go!* Where do you think I got it from?' And when you look at Marriott around '66, '67, and watch the body movements, where his guitar strap is, everything about him, Paul stole… but there's fuck all wrong with that!

I WAS THERE: RICK BUCKLER

I know myself and Bruce think we probably could have done a couple more albums. Looking back, we should have had the strength, probably of management, to say we're going to stop, take a break, do our solo things or put our feet up on a beach for six months – just step away from it. We were in a position where we could have done that.

I WAS THERE: BRIAN YOUNG

Like many others, I was shocked when Paul Weller decided to split The Jam at what was arguably their peak. It has been said he wanted to break away from the rigid formula of The Jam and explore new musical avenues. I can't see why he couldn't have done that alongside Bruce and Rick, as they were skilled and adept musicians more than capable of adapting to any style. Maybe they should have taken a career break and regrouped later? Who knows? I am sure that both Bruce and Rick were absolutely devastated – but, whatever the reason, it was obvious that once Paul had made his mind up there was no turning back.

I never did encounter any of The Jam or their road crew after 1982 – though I was saddened to hear of the death of Paul's father, John, and of Dave Liddle, both of whom I had great affection for and held in the highest regard.

Watching the most popular band in the UK play night after night was an education and an experience I'll never forget. None of the studio recordings come anywhere close to capturing the sheer adrenalin rush of excitement or untamed, frenetic power of the band onstage and it kinda goes without saying that their earth shattering run of hit singles is by far the strongest – and longest – of any by the class of '76.

Paul Weller was the only punk figurehead who tried to live up to his ideals, who tried to make a real difference on the ground where it mattered and who ultimately put his money and his efforts where his mouth was, for which I'll be forever grateful.

A post-split Jam singles reissue campaign leads to 16 Jam 45s back in the top 100.

The Jam clean up in the 1982 **NME** *Readers' Poll, securing best group and live act wins, best single ('Town Called Malice'), best LP (The Gift) and wins for Paul Weller (singer, songwriter, guitarist, haircut, best dressed, most wonderful human being), Bruce Foxton (bass) and Rick Buckler (drums). The Jam splitting also wins an 'event of the year' award, ahead of the Falklands War, Greenham Common, the World Cup and a papal visit to the UK.*

EMPIRE THEATRE
1 MAY 1983, LIVERPOOL, UK

Paul Weller unveils The Style Council, his first post-Jam project. Initially, it's a duo with keyboard player Mick Talbot.

MICK TALBOT: I WAS THERE

Paul was the one taking the risk. I had nothing to lose, having to reflect on the past three years. I did a normal job until I was 20, ended in a band that got signed, lasted a year, joined another that folded in about four months, got dropped by their original label, then another that lasted a year and got dropped by their label. There I was, 23, and maybe I needed to go back to the real world, this escape with the circus coming to a conclusion… and then Paul rang me.

In the same week, Kevin Rowland's manager rang to try and get me back on board. But Paul rang me personally while Kevin got his manager to ring – that might have influenced the way I felt about it. I thought, you know what, when I met Paul, he's about four months older than me, our reference points very similar, his background and family seemed to have lots of parallels with mine. I had more in common with him, even outside of music.

A PEOPLE'S HISTORY OF THE JAM

I WAS THERE: RICK BUCKLER

I was the first to get back out on the road. I found a songwriter, Jimmy Edwards, we were soon rehearsing, on the road quite quick – that was really what I wanted to do. I remember going to see Bruce that year when he did his solo thing. A difficult time, the style of things changing quite quick.

I WAS THERE: IAIN KEY

I wish I could say I was one of those cool kids whose older brother or sister sneaked them into a Jam concert while they were still a pre-teen, experiencing the electricity of the crowd and anticipation, waiting for John Weller to appear on stage to announce 'the best fucking band in the world'. Equally, I wish I could say I was one of those cool kids who purchased Jam shoes from those Melanddi adverts in the back of the *NME*, guaranteeing the genuine article 'as supplied to The Jam'.

Iain Key has sister Cathy to thank for introducing him to The Jam & letting him use her bedroom to play Subbuteo

But I wasn't. Although it was one of my older siblings who introduced me to the Woking trio, albeit not intentionally. During early 1982 when my sister, Cathy, moved away to do her nursing training I was able to set up my Subbuteo in her room and leave it down without going through the arduous routine of having to pack it up again each evening and trying not to put too many creases in the cloth which would be the pitch. This could easily cause issues and fights amongst friends if the slight 'bump' denied a goal-scoring opportunity or led to an inadvertent foul. One friend, Paul Woodman, a Liverpool fan, would react to such things, and happily, accidentally tread on one of his opponent's players if he felt he'd been cheated, which would then result in punches being exchanged and us being banned from each other's homes 'until you can play properly'.

As well as being able to have instant access to my favourite finger-flicking pastime, my sister moving away also meant I had access to her record collection. Over the following months, I shunned Shakin' Stevens and listened on repeat to three albums, The Clash's *London Calling* and The Jam's *All Mod Cons* and *Setting Sons*. The former was on cassette, so the latter pair got the most attention. I can honestly say those early weeks of 1981 changed my life. I'd pore over the artwork of the albums, soaking up the lyrics, writing quotes on my school books and singing along in a faux Cockney accent (as I was living in Birmingham at the time with a 'twang' I hate to think how that sounded). I'm sure many others will have done the same!

Due to a poorly timed parents evening, I missed the triumphant 'double-header' on *Top Of The Pops* of 'Town Called Malice' and 'Precious' (no videos in them days) and only had it described to me a couple of days later by a friend who attended another school. I saved my pocket money to buy *The Gift* (for some reason on cassette), played it until it got screwed up in the mechanism one too many times and eagerly waited for another release.

As a 13-year-old stuck between Redditch and Bromsgrove, with the closest city of Birmingham being too far away, the opportunity of collecting previous albums wasn't really an option, so other than listening to the records owned by visiting friends, the band's earliest couple of years' releases were just out of reach, as were the 'non-album singles' such as 'Strange Town' and 'When You're Young'. 'The Butterfly Collector' was spoken about in hushed tones by those who'd heard it. I was delighted by 'The Bitterest Pill' (perhaps, contentiously, still my favourite of the band's releases) but devastated (as much as a 13-year-old who had been into a band for less than a year) when they announced the split a few weeks later.

By this time, I'd started reading *Smash Hits*, mainly as a girl called Joanne Limbrick in my class did, and I fancied her so figured she'd be impressed if I did too. She wasn't… but it was through that that I learnt of the live album, *Dig The New Breed*, which I got for Christmas and then found the band were going to reissue all their singles in early 1983. With the begrudging agreement of my parents, I was allowed to withdraw all the money from my Junior Saver Account and hoover up everything that WH Smiths and Boots in Redditch's Kingfisher Shopping Centre had to offer (which turned out to be pretty much everything other than 'All Around The World', 'News Of The World' and 'Down In The Tube Station At Midnight').

I was a few years out of time, but I eventually caught up and those songs, especially those on *All Mod Cons* and *Setting Sons*, still resonate and take me back to a more innocent time. Through The Jam I took the natural step to The Style Council, from The Style Council I discovered Billy Bragg and my world was never the same again, but then I guess that's another story for another time…

I WASN'T THERE: TOM O'BRIEN

I was a latecomer in my appreciation for The Jam. I was 15, it was June 1983, and I was living in Southfields, Wimbledon, when I discovered the band for real.

Like many other kids I'd heard songs like 'Town Called Malice', 'Going Underground' and 'Down In The Tube Station', but didn't really appreciate these tunes. I was still discovering The Beatles, following John Lennon's assassination in 1980.

Brendan Hogan, a John Griffiths RC schoolfriend in Wimbledon, had a copy of *All Mod Cons* and asked if I'd listened to it. My older sister,

Tom O'Brien with his Jam LP wall art

Alice, had the *Snap!* double album and saw The Jam at Wembley Arena on the farewell tour, playing that compilation frequently. But when Brendan lent me his LP, I played it that night while reading the lyrics on the inner sleeve. And that proved to be the moment.

I was captivated by the quality of the songwriting, along with those fantastic melodies and the musicianship. I went out and bought that album, along with The Gift, which blew my mind again. 'Running on The Spot', 'The Planner's Dream', 'Carnation'… tunes that had me hooked. I bought all the albums and the Video Snap VHS (for £18). I started to learn more about the Mod movement, falling in love with the music, clothes and way of life. Living in South London, I was able to take the Tube to Oxford Circus at weekends and visit Carnaby Street, buying a blue three-but

I know the lyrics of every track they made, having many conversations and debates about which are the best songs with friends. The music Messrs Weller, Foxton and Buckler produced is quite astonishing and will live with me till the day I die.

SNAP! RELEASED
14 OCTOBER 1983

The double-LP compilation enters the charts at No.2.

I WAS THERE: ANDREW LINDSAY, MOD SHOES, 66 CLOTHING

In Christmas 1983 I received the VHS video *Snap!*, marvelling at so many great videos of the band, with 'Absolute Beginners' standing out for me. It still does and it's the song I probably listen to most. I really like the outfits as well as the playing. I love that striped top Rick wears. They look so cool.

My favourite Jam single is 'In The City' and my favourite LP is *In The City*! On the single, I love the way the guitar starts – you instantly know it's a classic and there are various chord changes that are like…wow! When he goes to E minor… brilliant. My favourite song on the LP is 'I've Changed My Address'. They started lots of gigs with it. That's the LP I listen to most. It's got a very sixties sound and lots of youthful exuberance, whereas others like *All Mod Cons* are progressively more mature. Some will argue that they got better and played better on other albums, but that's the one I enjoy most.

Looking at the album cover for *All Mod Cons*, Rick definitely liked a boot, but I'm going to draw attention to Bruce's shoes. The heel is really high. Of course, they were only referred to as Jam shoes because they wore them – you'd have those ads in the back of the *NME* or wherever where you too could buy them. What we do now is all because of The Jam. No Jam, no Mod Shoes.

I WAS THERE: RICK BUCKLER

I find it quite amazing, the longevity of everything – which we didn't plan for, I don't think you can. We must have been doing something right for that to be the case. Something for all of us to be very proud of.

I WAS THERE: BRUCE FOXTON

It hits home even more now how great Paul's lyrics are. Incredible considering how young we all were, to come up with those lyrics.

I WAS THERE: RICK BUCKLER

I look back with very fond memories, how we managed to do really good things, achieve a great deal. All the bickering and court cases, that sort of stuff happened after. A real shame but nothing to do with what people actually remember about The Jam or what actually put us on the road to where we are.

LITTLE CHEF, WOODALL SERVICES
31 JANUARY 1986, SHEFFIELD, UK

I WAS THERE: IAN WAXMAN

My sister worked in the Little Chef at Woodall Services. When she rang to say Paul was there I raced down there. I went straight up to his dad and said, 'Can I sit with you?' He said, 'Pull up a fackin' chair, mate!' They were heading up to Newcastle. I'd brought a bootleg LP with me, *The Jam At The 100 Club*. I passed it to Paul who said, 'I've never seen this LP in my fackin' life.' I said, 'Just sign it, please.' I had a good half-hour chat with them. John was really sociable. Paul was so cool.

A PEOPLE'S HISTORY OF THE JAM

THE WHITE ROOM
2 AUGUST 1996, LONDON, UK

I WAS THERE: MATHEW PRIEST, DODGY

I have my brother Chris, two years older, to blame. He was also into Japan and Bauhaus, and because he's a bit kind of OCD, he got every record The Jam and Japan released, imports as well – seven-inchers, albums, everything – so I was immersed in The Jam from the age of nine or ten. I loved them. It was part of growing up, my first immersion into proper music. I liked The Style Council's first album, but don't think he's bettered The Jam. God bless him. It was perfect. They were young, the complete package, they looked ace – the Jam suits, the shoes, the look, the hair, the politics… They made left-wing politics cool. We need another Jam around to stop all these fucking idiots you get now moving to the right. We need a 21-year-old Paul Weller guiding blokes with their politics. There must have been fucking thousands of kids who got their politics right because of Weller, Joe Strummer and Kevin Rowland. I met Paul when we did *The White Room*, We played opposite each other. We were sat on our stage, he came over, said, 'Alright, my name's Paul, you got any weed?' I was like, 'Yeah, I'll go and get you some.' That was it. Should have talked to him more, but I suppose I was star-struck.

A YELLOW CAB
FEBRUARY 2008, CHICAGO, ILLINOIS

I WAS THERE: RUSSELL HASTINGS

I've worked with all three, and when I look back I go, 'Fucking hell!' I've worked with Paul in the studio quite a bit, and I've travelled all around the world – you could say – with Rick and Bruce. I was in the back of a Chicago yellow cab with Bruce and Rick, heading for the Sears Tower, thinking, 'Fuck's sake, man!' That was 2008, playing sold-out shows in Chicago, New York and across. I count myself lucky to be involved, and I'm always proud of the three albums I've wrote with Bruce.

You couldn't really think about it too much - the enormity of it's pretty big. I'd really get nervous, even more than now. A sick nervous. But I had a way of dealing with that - remembering for the first five or six songs to keep my head down.

With Paul, we were on common ground. That's what was nice. We'd been in the studio all day, then he put the kettle on and said, 'Y'know what? You're nothing like I thought you'd be. I thought you were gonna be like one of them look-a-likeys.' Then at Nicky's 60th at Paul's house, he was there with the kids, the band was there, and it was all family, a really nice time, and you realise everybody's normal human beings – don't believe everything you see in the *News of the World*! I mean, the media blew the trouble up between Rick and Bruce too.

Playing a guitar part in Paul's studio, looking through the glass, I could see Bruce and Paul talking, looking at me. I had to try and concentrate on what I was doing, thinking, 'It's nice they're chatting after all I've read over the years.' When I got Bruce on his own, I'm going, 'What were you two fucking talking about when you were looking at me?' He went, 'Paul was saying you're a really nice guy and how much you remind him of Brookesy (Steve Brookes).' I'll take that as a compliment. I know Steve, a lovely guy… and he was Paul's best mate.

I remember Rick finding some old quarter-inch master tapes from the *Modern World* album, much brighter, different mixes and all that. We played them in the studio, those and loads of demos for *Sound Affects*, which no one'd heard. You'd hear Paul whistling over the back of 'Set The House Ablaze', stuff like that. It's amazing to hear.

I took an idea from an interesting guitar riff on a demo, changed it into the title track of Smash The Clock. A guitar line that never saw the light of day. We play 'Number Six' a bit live, and Paul played on piano with me on that. He's always there.

I ended up taking Wilko Johnson to Paul's studio with Alan McGee, overseeing him just after his operation. He came to play on a track. Paul's saying, 'Can you get Wilko to sign the wall?' I look at all Wilko's work around '74/'75 and that's 'In The City' all over. He mixed the Feelgoods with the Pistols… that is The Jam. I've spoken to Paul about that, and he's like, 'Well spotted!'

RADISSON BLU HOTEL
14 APRIL 2022, MANCHESTER, UK

I WAS THERE: PETE EASTWOOD

I've seen him 103 times but only met him three times. The first time was after a Jam gig in Blackburn. They signed my ticket and my autograph book. I met him with The Style Council and had a thousand questions but all I could manage was 'hello Paul, you alright?'. I ended up talking to Steve White instead. But in 2022 I was in Manchester with my mate the day before Paul was playing the Apollo. We were walking past the Radisson when my mate said 'that's Paul'. He was wearing a bucket hat and had pulled his Covid mask down. He was on the steps of the hotel having a fag. Steve Cradock saw us and said 'hello Pete'.

I told Paul I'd written a book, *But I'm Different Now*, named after my favourite Jam song. He said, 'Yeah, it's on my tour bus.' Two days later, he sent me a picture of him with it backstage in Newcastle and then, a couple of days after that, I got it sent back to me with a message in the front: 'Good luck brother, wish you all the best.' That made my year!

A PEOPLE'S HISTORY OF THE JAM

RIPLEY ROCKS FESTIVAL
9 JULY 2022, RIPLEY, UK

I WAS THERE: IAN 'GRIFF' GRIFFITHS

The Jam were the first punk rock band I saw. I was 14 and went with my brother to the Croydon Greyhound. Sadly, my brother's no longer with us, but that gig changed my life. I saw many punk bands from then on, going on to drum in Croydon punk band The Bad Actors. A recording artist and professional comedian, making loads of records, I'm now a host on 365 Radio. But my hobby and passion is playing drums in Jam tribute band Ghosts, The Spirit Of The Jam, with me pretending to be Rick Buckler. We were the headline act at Ripley Rocks, playing to 2,000 to 3,000 people, and there was an older lady – around the same age as my mum – down the front, singing and dancing to every song. She knew every lyric. Backstage after the show, we were saying, 'Did you see that older lady?' Then the stage door opened and she came in and said, 'You're brilliant! The only thing is, you're wearing the wrong shoes.' It was Paul Weller's mum!

Paul Weller's mum gave Ian 'Griff' Griffiths' band some fashion tips

The first thing she said was 'you've changed, son' to our front man, Lloyd. (He's from Jamaica.) She then looked at Pete Firmo, our bass player, and said, 'You've got the wrong shoes on.' We were wearing black suits and Lloyd had the proper black and white Gibsons on, while Pete was wearing The Jam trainers with white stripes. She said, 'They never wore those with the suits. I've got an old pair of Paul's if you want them.' That afternoon she had passed on the invite to Paul's barbecue and a chance to meet Noel Gallagher. She came to see us instead!

ST MICHAEL-IN-THE-HAMLET CHURCH
8 DECEMBER 2023, LIVERPOOL, UK

I WAS THERE: PETE EASTWOOD

I got a tip off about this church event (raising funds for Micah Liverpool Foodbank) and I couldn't believe it. I'd heard he was going to do a Jam song and a Style Council song. Steve Brookes was with him the whole set, and he didn't do any Jam or Style council. He even did a Bee Gees song. But to be with Steve Brookes and not do a Jam song blew my mind.

I WAS THERE: JOE SHIELDS
I now look back and think how lucky I was to be there at that time. The Earth is 4.5 billion years old and by a fluke of nature, thanks to the freezing cold winter of 1962/63 and my mum and dad having more than just a cuddle to keep warm, it resulted in me coming along and having my 18th birthday on September 19th 1981. I was officially an adult, a grown up. I could legally go and buy a drink in a pub, I could vote… and I was going to see the best band in the fucking world!

I WAS THERE: NICKY WELLER
I was a kid, selling badges and so on. I wasn't as involved until around the time The Jam broke up, working at Solid Bond Studios for Paul. But there was a hell of a lot of mail – crazy amounts! You sort of forget how big The Jam were, how quickly they became so popular. It wasn't an overnight success either. They worked hard to get there, but it was quite amazing the extent of it.

I WAS THERE: RICK BUCKLER
It had a big effect on my life as well as Bruce's and Paul's, but when I talk to Jam fans there's this real connection. It had an effect on them as well. They were part of The Jam as much as we were. That connection was really important. I don't think you see that with many other bands.

I WAS THERE: ALAN BURROWS
Bar The Pogues and New Order, very little of what played in the mid-eighties soundtracked my life. I went to an Everton pre-season game in Bilbao in 1988, with about twelve of the lads singing 'Liza Radley' on the train across France – then an eight-year-old B-side! Everyone knew every word. That summed up The Jam.

AFTERWORD

It would've been on John Peel's show (who else?!) where I first heard The Jam. April '77. His late-night show was a must listen for me and my music lovin' pals, and the band were in session that night.

My anticipation was high and boy, they didn't disappoint. Delivering high octane versions of 'In The City', 'Art School', 'I've Changed My Address' and 'The Modern World'. The first three songs I would devour a month later on their debut album, whilst 'The Modern World' would be a single later that year and the song we named our school punk fanzine after.

The first time I actually became aware of The Jam was through reading about them via the music papers. Me and my school mates had started buying the *New Musical Express*, *Melody Maker* and *Sounds* in 1976, and would regularly pass them around. All of us were galvanised by this exciting new scene that the papers were beginning to call punk and new wave. I first started noticing gig reviews, then interviews. They certainly stood out from the rest of the safety pin brigade. Looking resplendent in their black suits, white shirts, black ties and playing their Rickenbacker guitars, just like my other favourites, The Beatles.

For Gary Crowley, 'Their songs held up a mirror to our lives'

Through these articles I discovered they were only a couple of years older than me, which was important as most other groups until then seemed so much older. I instantly liked the cut of their jib. What they were saying about their hopes for punk and their obvious Mod influences. Mod, you see, was something that particularly fascinated me, as my cool uncle and auntie had been Mods and would often regale me with their memories.

Immediately after hearing that session, then seeing them not long after on *Top Of The Pops* with an electrifying performance of debut single 'In The City', we wasted no time in finding out where the band were playing next time in London. We decided their show at Battersea Town Hall on Monday 27th June was going to be the one, counting down the days excitedly.

Talk about a Road to Damascus moment. That night changed my life. Fired by their passion and performance (you could not take your eyes off them), their songs captured the angst of not only being a teenager at that time but held up a mirror to the world we were living in. They very quickly became my favourite band.

SOLID BOND IN YOUR HEART

Over the next five years, of all the bands that resonated with me (and there were many), The Jam stood tall. Never ones to let the grass grown beneath their collective feet, over the course of six albums and a raft of classic singles, they became one of the most consistent, successful and well-loved bands. With each release becoming a little more adventurous and incorporating influences from sixties pop through to soul and post-punk.

They really were a lifestyle to me and my friends. Paul Weller was once asked who his favourite teachers were at school and famously answered, 'There were four of 'em. Their names were John, Paul, George and Ringo!' For us, it was him, Joe Strummer and Terry Hall who gave us a bonus education.

Their relationship with their audience was also a special one. I know because I was that soldier. They were so incredibly supportive to me and my endeavours. Paul was famous for personally answering fan mail, whilst the band were known and loved for allowing ticketless fans into venues to watch them soundcheck.

Though it sat uneasily for them, the band were spokesman for our generation. The underdogs. Their songs held up a mirror to our lives. Little vignettes of the everyday, starring characters we could all relate to, pierced with tinges of youthful idealism, disappointment and alienation never far away.

I could wax lyrical all day about The Jam and what they personally meant to me, what my favourite songs and albums are (they change every day, of course) and how the concerts stay cherished in my memory forever. But all I know is I am so grateful they came and brightened up my life.

Thanks for the memories, lads.

Gary Crowley, November 2024

ACKNOWLEDGEMENTS

Thank you to the many loyal fans who supplied stories. Your help and support is much appreciated. The same goes for those who provided added insight and answered queries. I felt I knew a lot about The Jam, but some of you know far more. Many of you were lucky enough to see the band, others – like me – missed out but proved passionate about that amazing body of work.

I must personally thank Bruce and Rick for their past interviews with me that I drew upon in this book. The same goes for other interviewees included whose conversations with me pre-dated this project, not least Steve Brookes, Mick Talbot and Nicky Weller. As for Steve Carver, Den Davis, Russell Hastings and Guy Helliker, you were a great help. I need to pay homage to Jo Bartlett, part of her contribution included on her https://indiethroughthelookingglass.com/ pages, Tony Fletcher for his excerpt from *Boy About Town* (William Heinemann, 2013) and Paolo Hewitt for excerpts from *Paul Weller: The Changing Man* (Bantam Press, 2007). Then there's Brett 'Buddy' Ascott, Mickey Bradley, Gary Crowley, Ray Gange, Dave Hemingway, Graham Jones, Don Powell, Mathew Priest, Ian Prowse, John Robb and Debsey Wykes. Thanks all.

Thank you also to Beth Arzy, Mark Baxter, Tony Beesley, Paul Cookson, Stuart Deabill, Derek D'Souza (www.derekdsouzaphotography.com), Dom De Vivo, Daryl Easlea, Vic Falsetta, Elaine McGinty, Gered Mankowitz, Dennis Munday, Alan 'Fred' Pipes, John Reed, Neil Sheasby and Steve Smith.

Under the flag of research, I've listened to so many great Jam recordings, from early demos to compositions that ended up as Style Council numbers. And I'll never tire of that wonderful catalogue, so thank you Paul, Bruce and Rick. The latter's https://www.thejamfan.net/ online presence was useful, as were Kevin Lock's https://thejam.org.uk/ pages, and the 1976/82 dates in the splendid *Thick As Thieves: Personal Situations With The Jam* by Ian Snowball and Stuart Deabill (Marshall Cavendish, 2012), and the knowledge of fellow Woking FC fan Mark Doyle.

I credit Nicky Horne and John Peel for early championing of The Jam, my transistor radio under the pillow in the late seventies, but there's an additional debt to my brother Mark and mates Alan Hill and Steve Miles, their impeccable music taste putting me on the right path. And without Richard Houghton, this book would not have happened, so thanks for all his support and generosity, and a nod to those who supported this venture from the start, including Kevin Acott, Alan Burrows, Prentice James, Mark Railston, and John Winstanley. Thanks also to Karl Kathuria for the proofreading.

SOLID BOND IN YOUR HEART

On the home front, my better half, Jayne, again played a blinder as I spent countless hours in front of a computer screen or talking Weller, Buckler and Foxton on the phone, putting up with my 'exclusive' anecdotes, the same going for our girls, Molly and Lottie. Once this book is out, we can properly explore our new Cornish patch, and I promise to turn the computer off more often.

Everything I do also requires credit to my dear departed mum and dad, bringing me up proper, that support now largely provided by sisters Sue, Jackie and Tracy, and their families. And talking of that, there's the Jam family. We hear a lot within about the generosity of Ann and John Weller, and others who served behind the scenes in this proper family business, another great reason to love The Jam.

Malcom Wyatt
January 2025

ABOUT THE AUTHOR

Guildford-born music writer and editor Malcolm Wyatt recently relocated to Cornwall with his better half, Jayne. A foster carer and former journalist for whom geography rules out too many Woking FC visits these days, he previously wrote *Wild! Wild! Wild! A People's History of Slade* (Spenwood Books, 2023) and *This Day In Music's Guide to The Clash* (This Day In Music Books, 2018). Once this book is out, Malc and Jayne will no doubt be enquiring about taking on another rescue dog to help them explore their new patch.

You can find examples of his feature-interviews at www.writewyattuk.com and contact him about The Jam, Slade and much more at thedayiwasthere@gmail.com.

The author with his copy of Sound Affects

Photo by Lottie Wyatt

ALSO PUBLISHED BY SPENWOOD BOOKS

Cream – A People's History

Queen – A People's History

Thin Lizzy – A People's History

Goin' Down De Mont – A People's History of Rock & Pop Concerts at Leicester's De Montfort Hall

The Rolling Stones in the Sixties – A People's History

All Down The Line – A People's History of the Rolling Stones 1972 North American tour

Gonna See All My Friends – A People's History of Fairport Convention

All The Songs Sound The Same – The Wedding Present

Tell Everyone – A People's History of the Faces

Wild! Wild! Wild! A People's History of Slade

All Our Loving – A People's History of The Beatles

Wish You Were Here – A People's History of Pink Floyd

This Guitar Has Seconds To Live – A People's History of The Who

Cropredy Capers – Another People's History of Fairport Convention

Just Backdated – Melody Maker: Seven Years in the Seventies

The Ukrainians – From Kyiv to the Kosmos

All The Young Punks – A People's History of The Clash

Magical Highs – Alvin Lee & Me

Jimi Hendrix – The Day I Was There

Prince – The Day I Was There

The Stranglers – Live (Excerpts)

Sometimes These Words Just Don't Have To Be Said – The Wedding Present

Simple Minds: Heart of the Crowd – A Fan History

Led Zeppelin: Whole Lotta Love – A People's History

SPECIAL THANKS

GRIFF & MICHELE WITH ONE 'L' • STUART STEELES • ANDY MILLER
ANDY & CAROL FARMER • KEITH DITCH-BURN • PAUL EDWARDS • JONATHAN ABNETT
TONY METCALF • TOM O'BRIEN • GRAHAM FIRTH • LES GLOVER
PETER FIRMO (GHOSTS: THE SPIRIT OF THE JAM) • LLOYD GREY • JOHN TIDESWELL
TONY COWDRILL • JOHN TOMSETT • VINCENT MAGANZINI
DYLAN WHITE • IVAR HAMILTON • JOHN WINSTANLEY • MAT BERRY
JULIE GOODYEAR • JANIE MARKHAM • SHAUN BAKER & ROCCO
RICHARD MURPHY (& PAUL MURPHY 17/3/65 - 7/8/86, RIP) • GORDON WARING
KEVIN CAWLEY • NICK YOUNG • KARL FRENCH • PAUL DREDGE • JACQUELINE KEMP
SUSAN KIRK • PAUL GAMMON • MICHAEL PORTER • IAN BURBEDGE
ANDREW CLARKE • AMER ATHAR • TIM EATON & DAVE NUTSEY • MICHAEL DOWNES
PHILIP BRIGHAM • DEAN STANDERWICK • ANDREW SCREEN
GRAHAM BOWDEN • BRIAN YOUNG • SCOTT NEWSON • KEVIN SMITH
PAUL CRINNION • AIDAN KEHOE • SEAN WASTELL • ALAN WHITE
CHRISTINE HARRISON • PAUL WILLIAMS • JOHN SUTHERAN • GARY COULSON
ANDREW MULLANEY • LUKE PEPPARD • CHRISTOPHER M AVIS • ANDREW COOPER
NICK BUTLER • PAUL THOMPSON • SHARON HOLMES • STEVE AYLEN
ANDY LINTOTT • JAMES BULL • PAUL HADLEY • PAUL HODGKINSON
CHRIS PRITCHETT • PAUL JOHNSTON • MALCOLM GOODE • GAVIN BICKERTON-JONES
DOMINIC ALLEN • GARETH GORDON-WILKIN • CHRIS BRISBOURNE
SUE & STEVE WHITE • RICHARD NOBLE • MARCUS MARSDEN • GORDON TOAL
WILLOW WOYCKE • MARK RAILSTON • PETER BOWERS • JON FLYNN
PHILIP ANDREW • IAN TRAYNOR • JOHN WINSTANLEY • PAUL ROBINSON
CHRIS BITHELL • RICHARD HERRING • ANDY MAYS • BRENDAN FINNEGAN
ED SILVESTER & JOHN SILVESTER • BILL ROCKETT • SHAUN WATKINS
MENZIES CLARK • LYNNE OGLESBY • NEIL SHIDE • GRAEME DAWSON
DAVIE QUINN • PRENTICE JAMES • GRAHAM DELASALLE • LUCY A LEVASON
SANDY MCLEAN • LAURENCE WEIGHT • IAN CRABB • STEVEN O'DRISCOLL
LEE & SHARON BRUCE • ANTHONY MILLER & WAYNE HOLMES